THE MIND'S ARROW
ARCHER COE

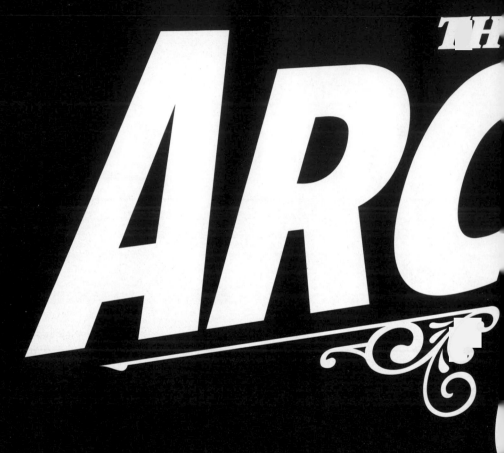

Written By:
JAMIE S. RICH

Illustrated By:
DAN CHRISTENSEN

TH
ARC

Edited By:
JILL BEATON

Designed By:
JASON STOREY

MIND'S ARROW

HER

COE

THE THOUSAND NATURAL SHOCKS

Oni Press, Inc.
Publisher, Joe Nozemack
Editor in Chief, James Lucas Jones
Director of Sales, Cheyenne Allott
Director of Publicity, John Schork
Production Manager, Troy Look
Senior Designer, Jason Storey
Editor, Charlie Chu
Associate Editor, Robin Herrera
Inventory Coordinator, Brad Rooks
Administrative Assistant, Ari Yarwood
Office Assistant, Jung Lee
Production Assistant, Jared Jones

Oni Press
1305 SE Martin Luther King Jr. Blvd.,
Suite A
Portland, OR 97214

onipress.com
facebook.com/onipress • twitter.com/onipress • onipress.tumblr.com

confessions123.com
dcdrawings.blogspot.com

First Edition: June 2014

ISBN 978-1-62010-121-6 • eISBN 978-1-62010-126-1

Library of Congress Control Number: 2013923278

1 3 5 7 9 10 8 6 4 2

Printed in China.

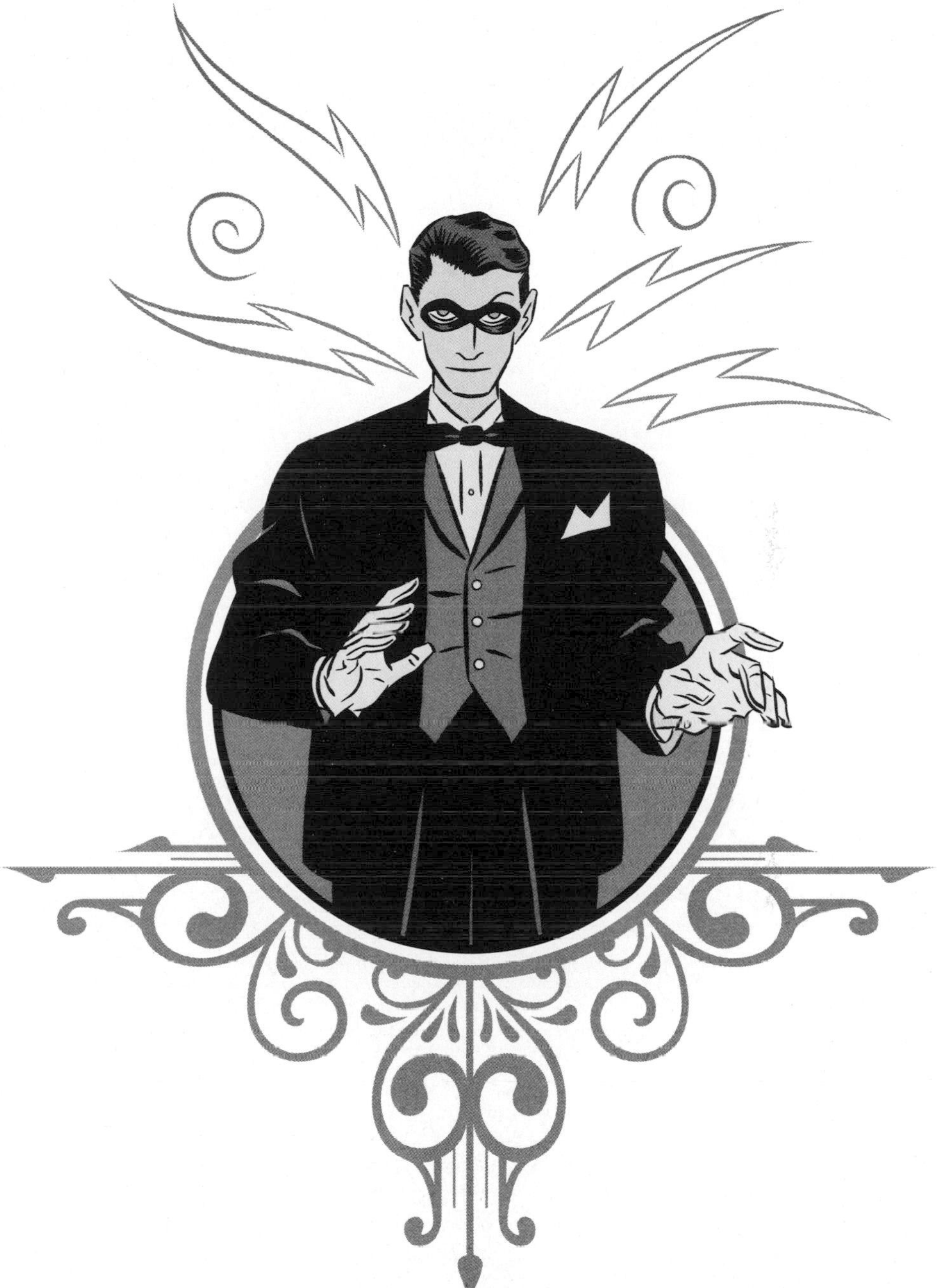

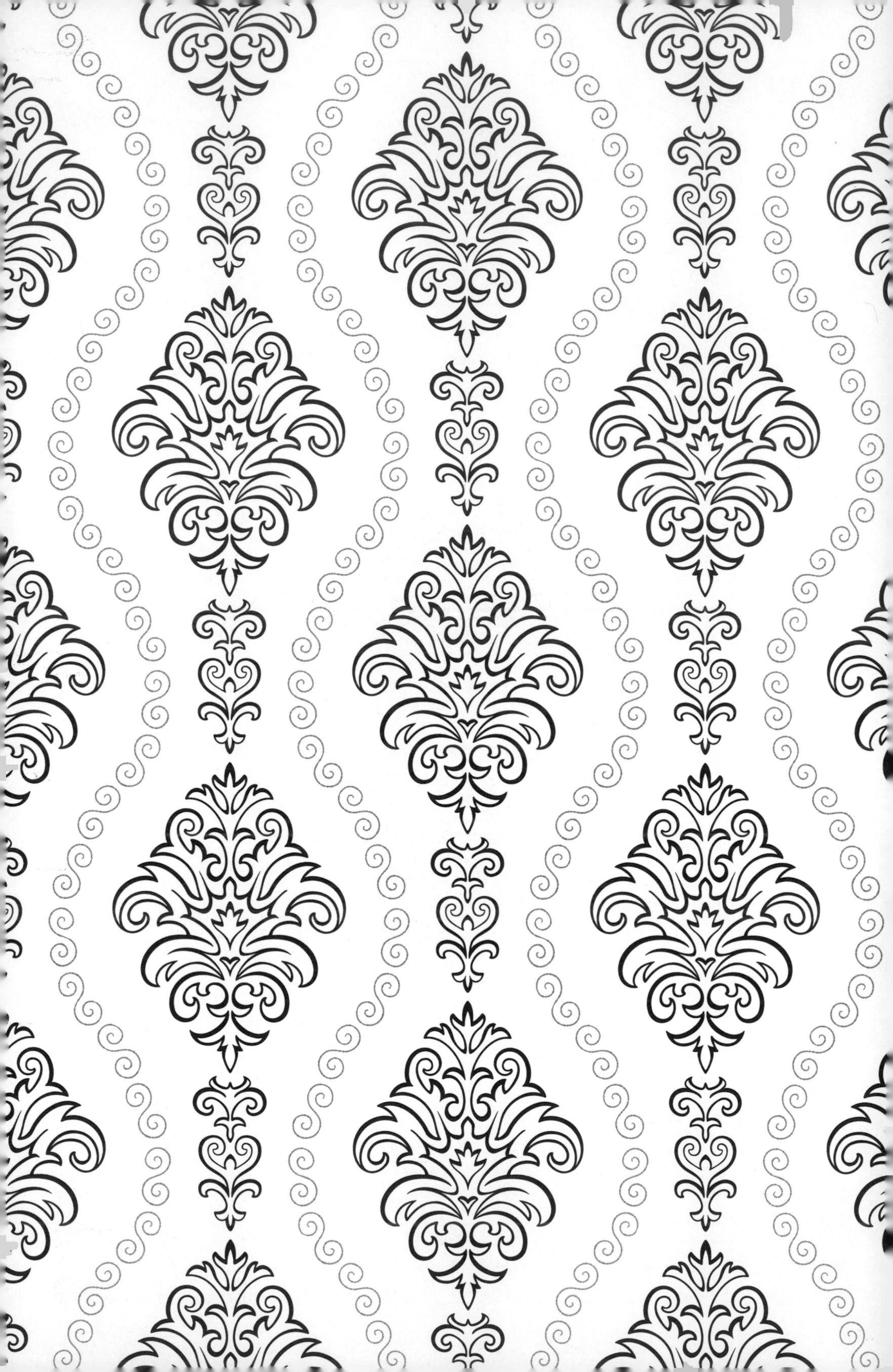

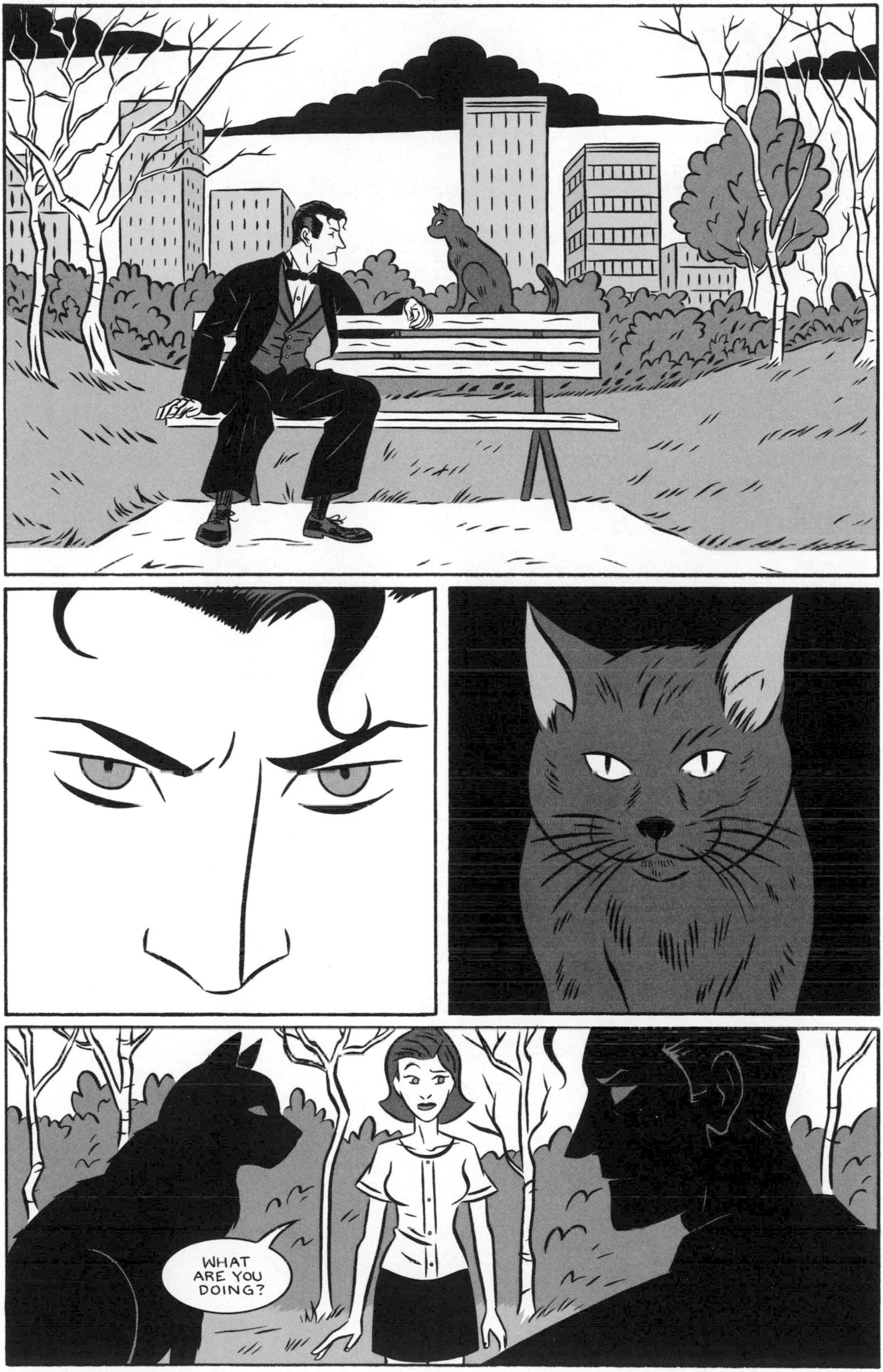
WHAT ARE YOU DOING?

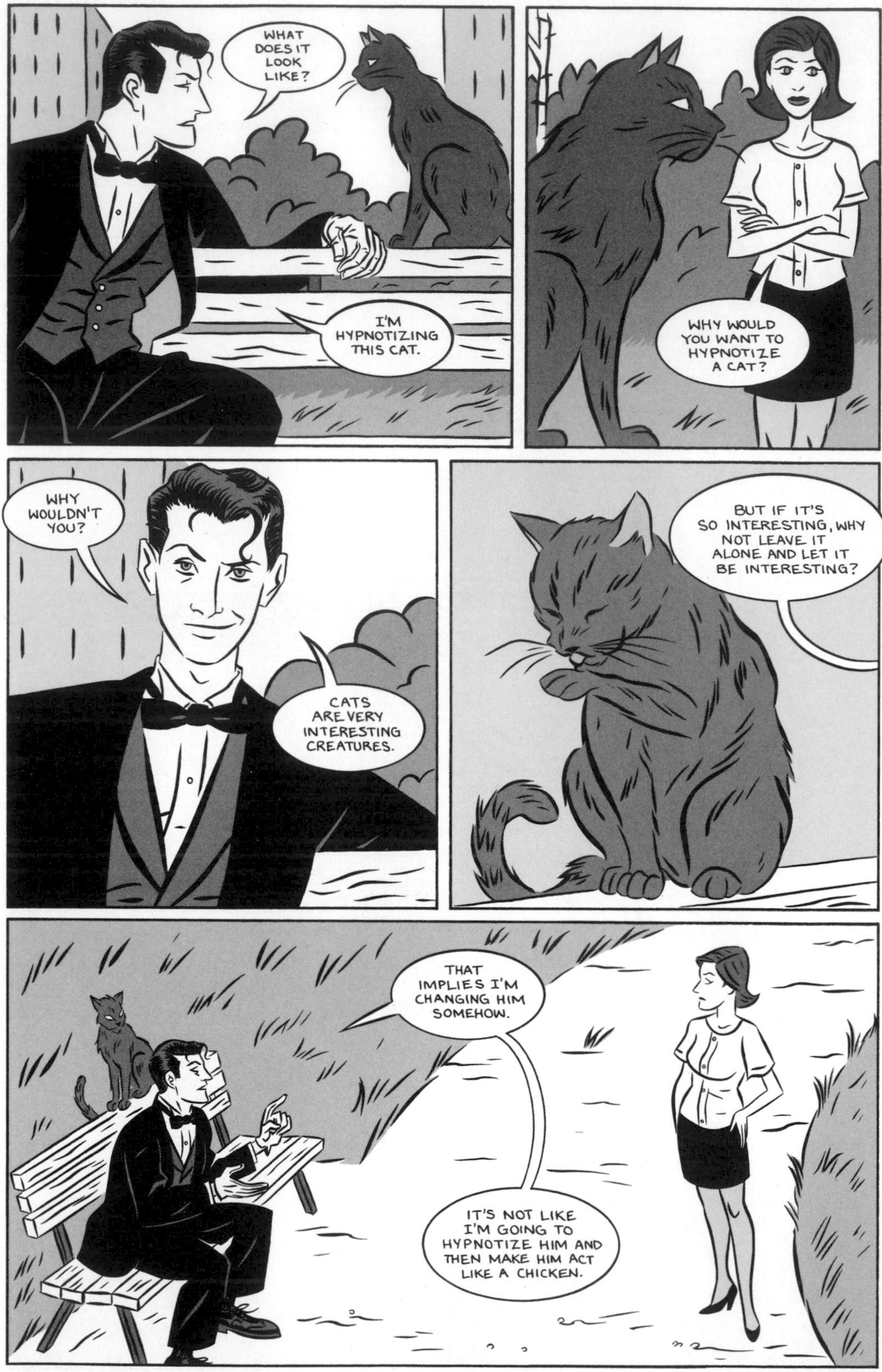
WHAT DOES IT LOOK LIKE?
I'M HYPNOTIZING THIS CAT.
WHY WOULD YOU WANT TO HYPNOTIZE A CAT?
WHY WOULDN'T YOU?
CATS ARE VERY INTERESTING CREATURES.
BUT IF IT'S SO INTERESTING, WHY NOT LEAVE IT ALONE AND LET IT BE INTERESTING?
THAT IMPLIES I'M CHANGING HIM SOMEHOW.
IT'S NOT LIKE I'M GOING TO HYPNOTIZE HIM AND THEN MAKE HIM ACT LIKE A CHICKEN.

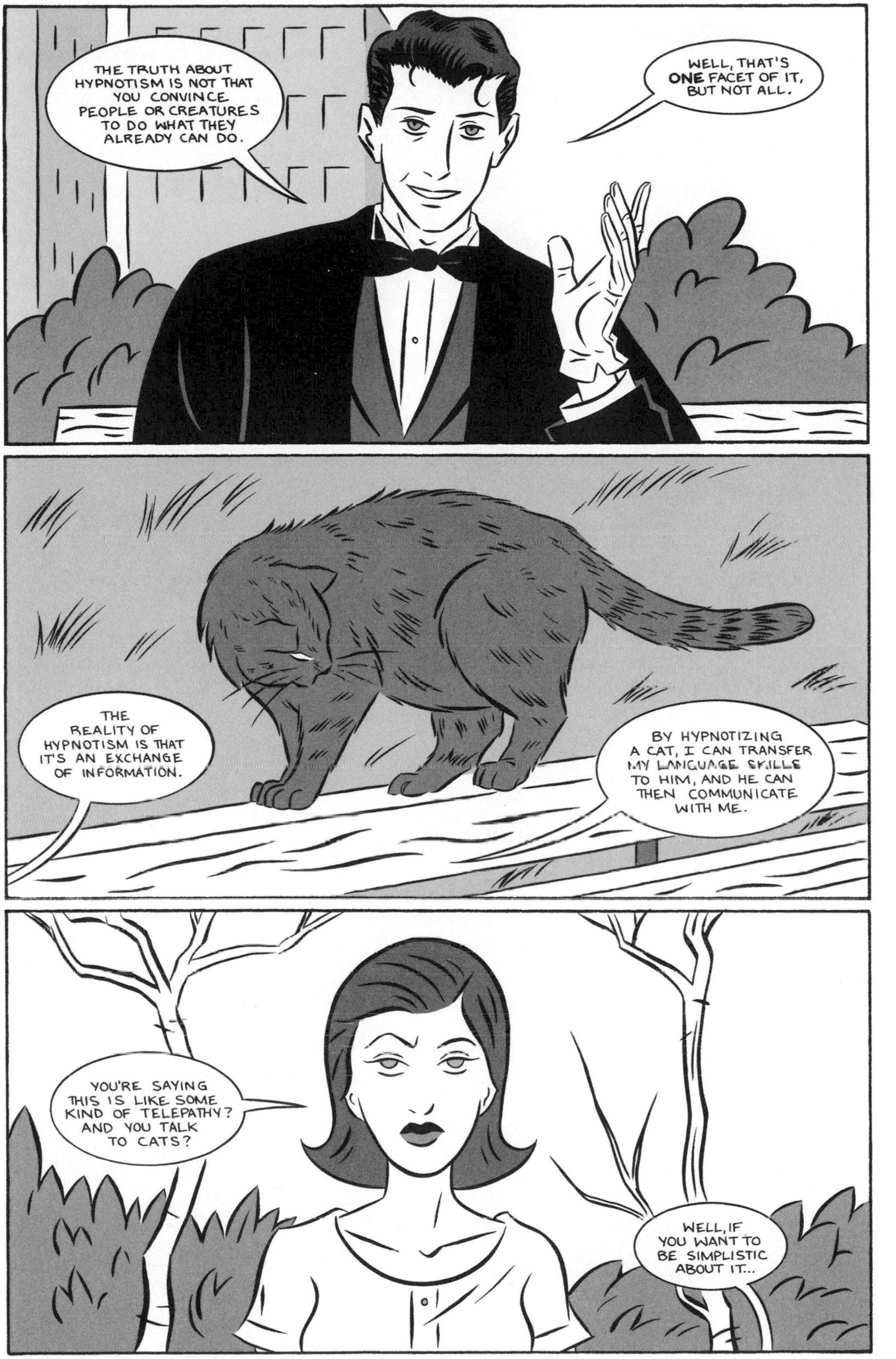
THE TRUTH ABOUT HYPNOTISM IS NOT THAT YOU CONVINCE PEOPLE OR CREATURES TO DO WHAT THEY ALREADY CAN DO.
WELL, THAT'S ONE FACET OF IT, BUT NOT ALL.
THE REALITY OF HYPNOTISM IS THAT IT'S AN EXCHANGE OF INFORMATION.
BY HYPNOTIZING A CAT, I CAN TRANSFER MY LANGUAGE SKILLS TO HIM, AND HE CAN THEN COMMUNICATE WITH ME.
YOU'RE SAYING THIS IS LIKE SOME KIND OF TELEPATHY? AND YOU TALK TO CATS?
WELL, IF YOU WANT TO BE SIMPLISTIC ABOUT IT...

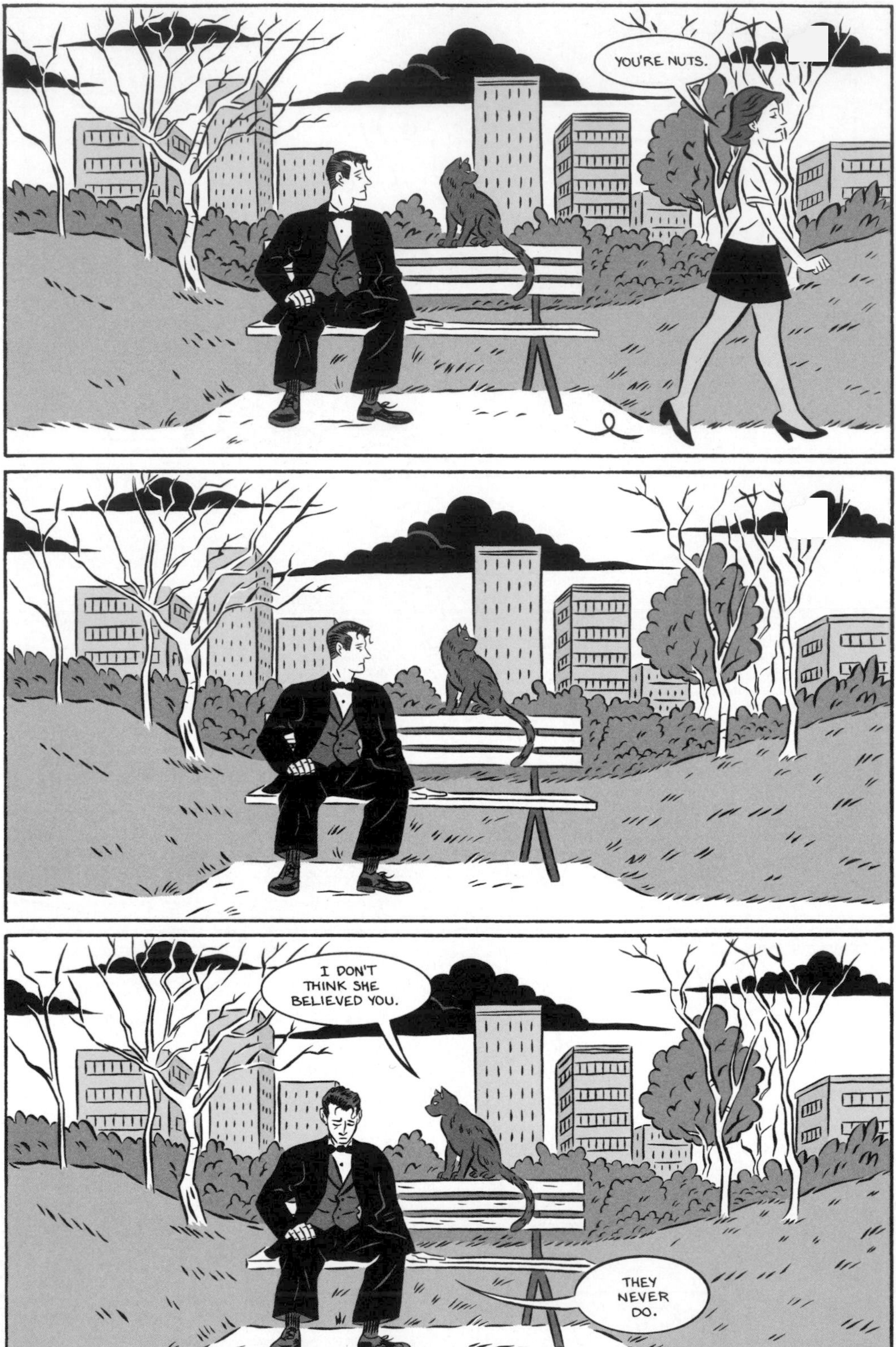
YOU'RE NUTS.
I DON'T THINK SHE BELIEVED YOU.
THEY NEVER DO.

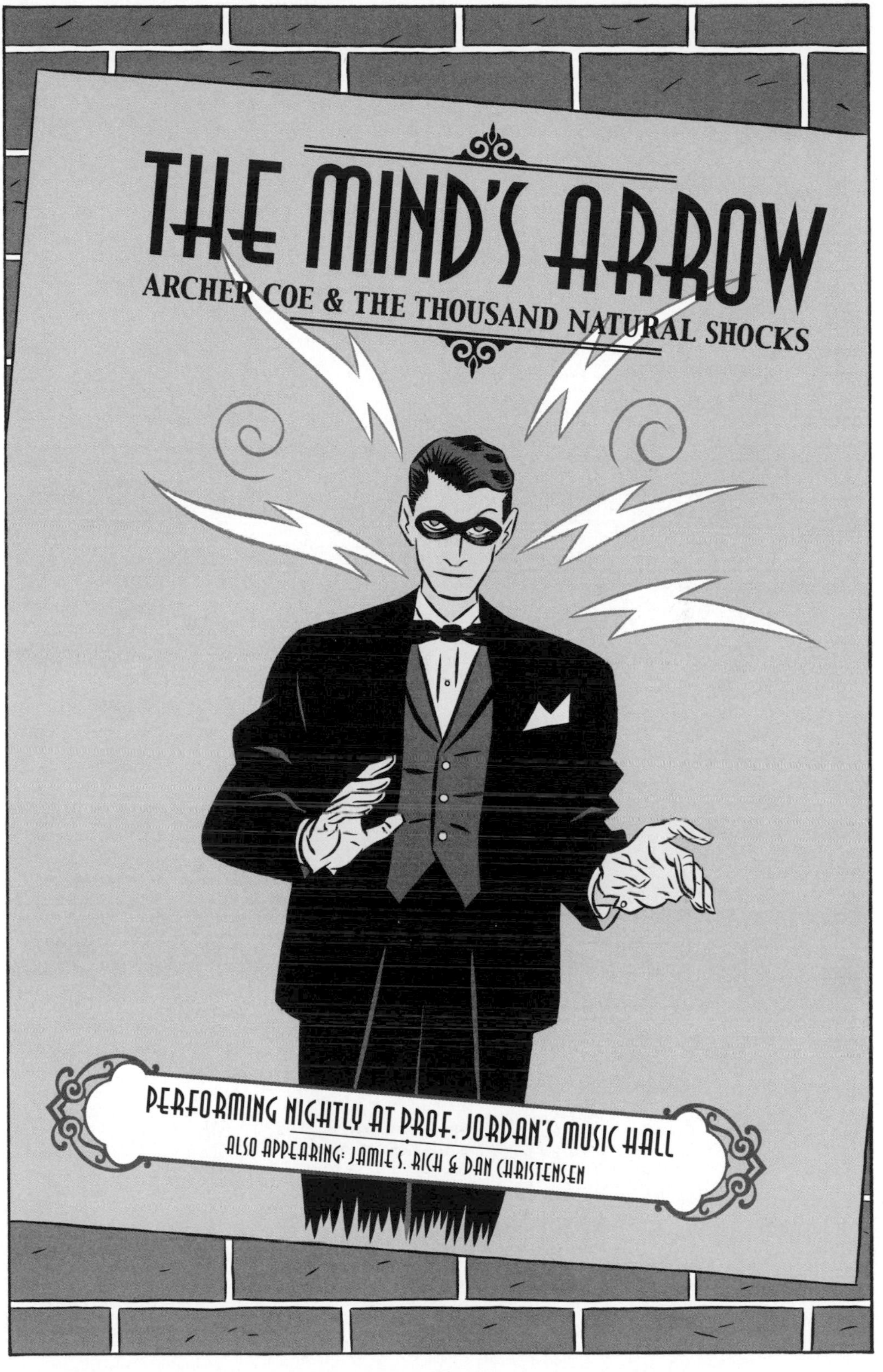
THE MIND'S ARROW
ARCHER COE & THE THOUSAND NATURAL SHOCKS
PERFORMING NIGHTLY AT PROF. JORDAN'S MUSIC HALL
ALSO APPEARING: JAMIE S. RICH & DAN CHRISTENSEN

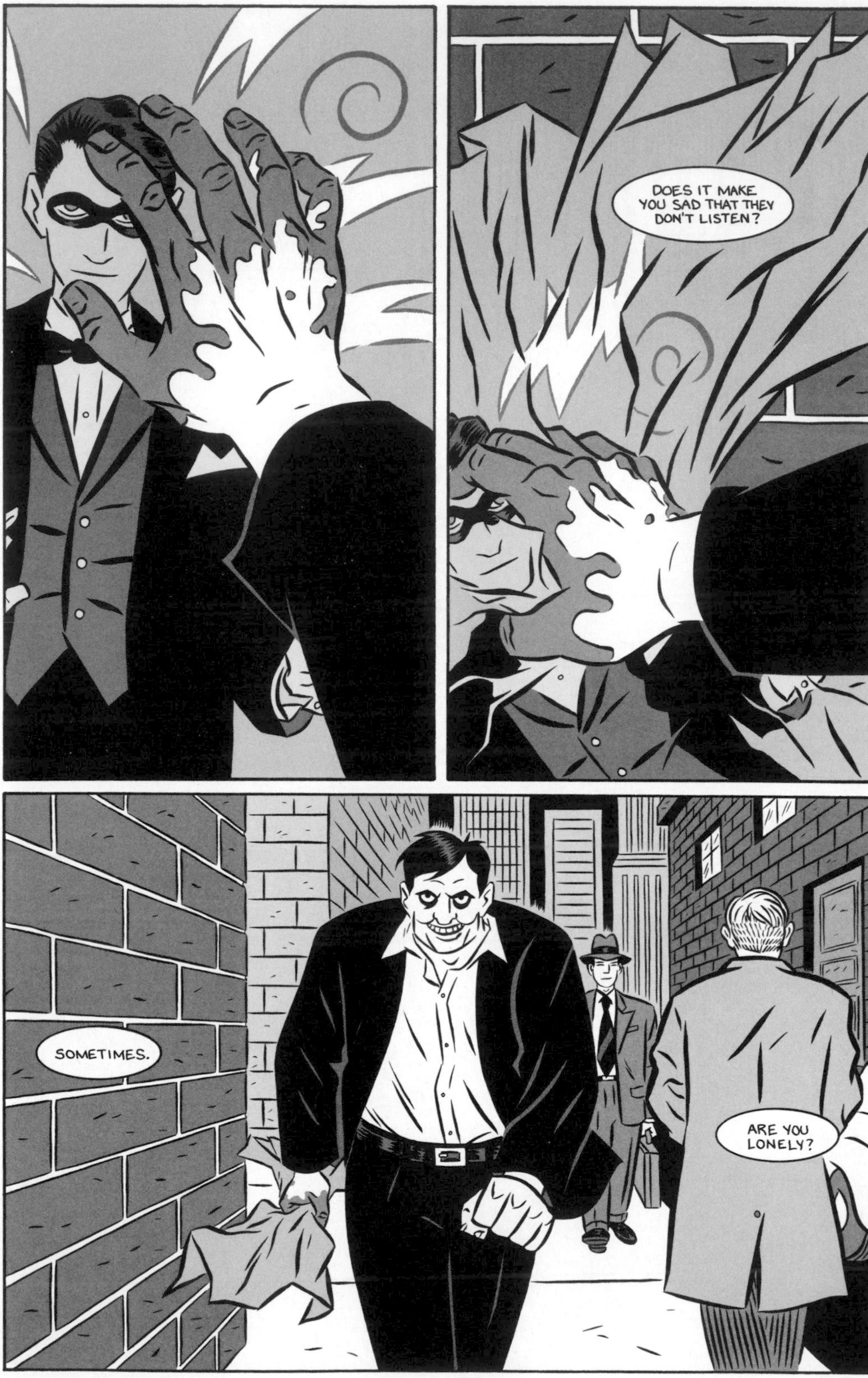
DOES IT MAKE YOU SAD THAT THEY DON'T LISTEN?
SOMETIMES.
ARE YOU LONELY?

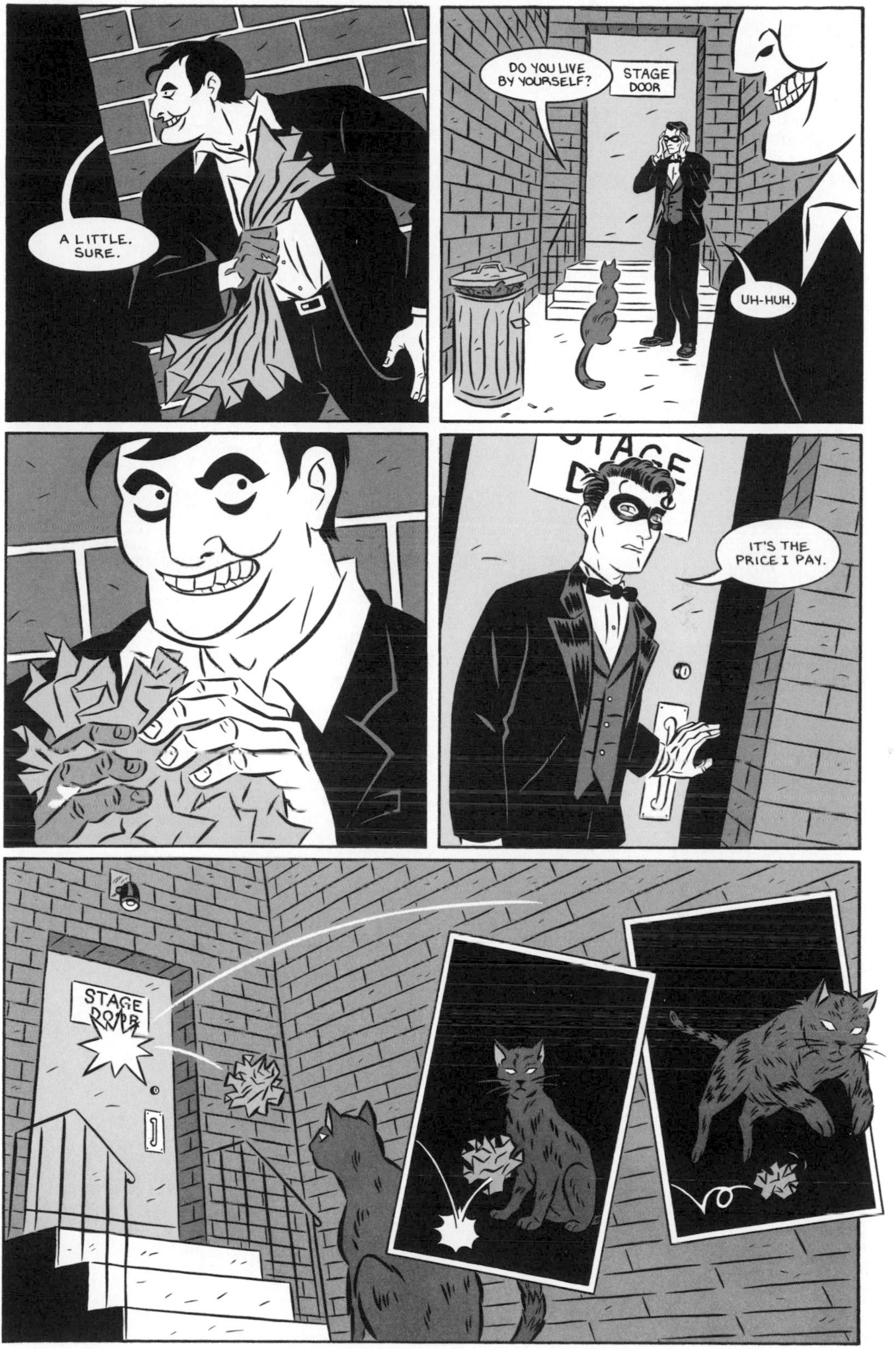
A LITTLE. SURE.
DO YOU LIVE BY YOURSELF?
STAGE DOOR
UH-HUH.
IT'S THE PRICE I PAY.
STAGE DOOR

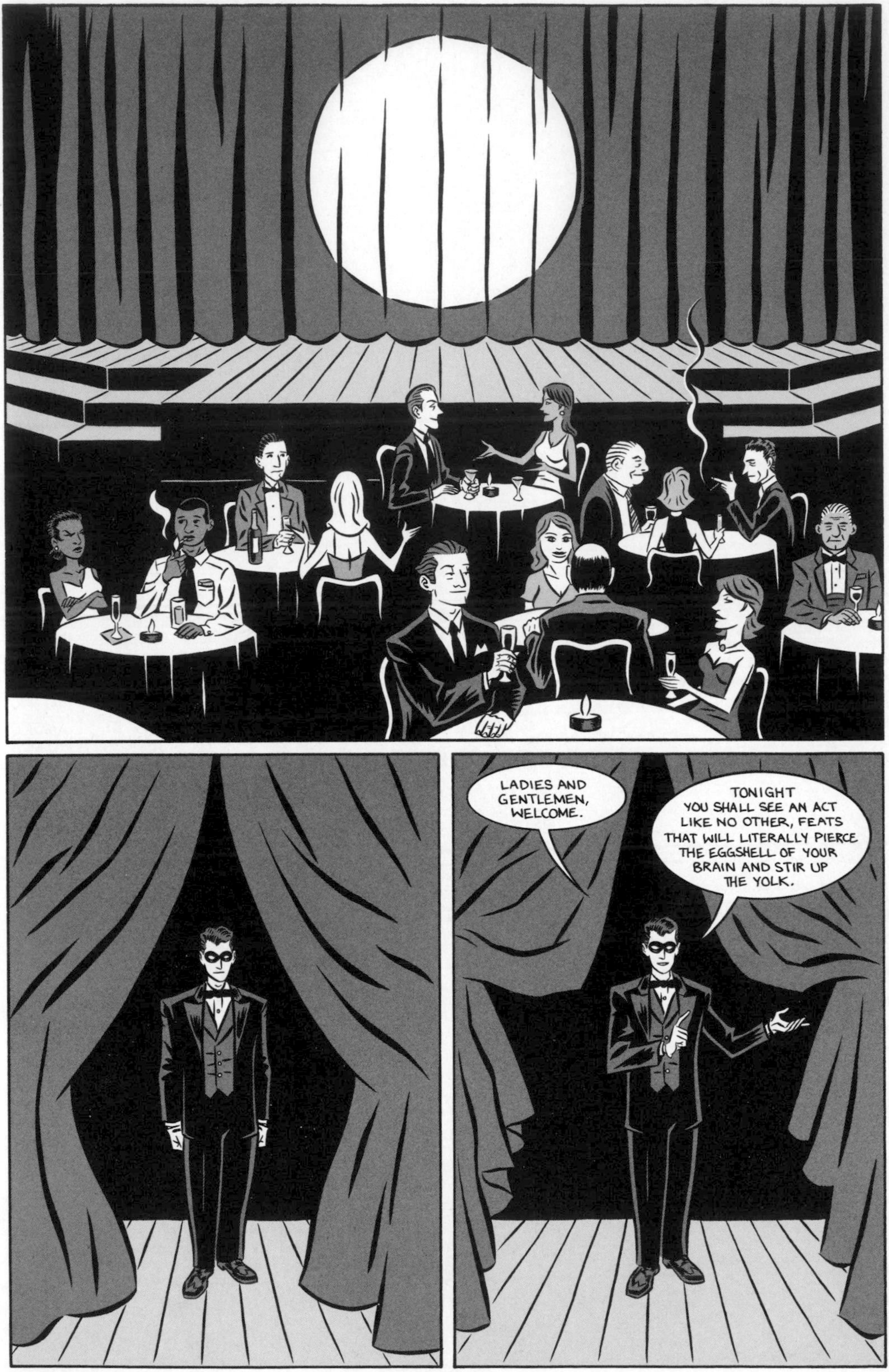
LADIES AND GENTLEMEN, WELCOME.
TONIGHT YOU SHALL SEE AN ACT LIKE NO OTHER, FEATS THAT WILL LITERALLY PIERCE THE EGGSHELL OF YOUR BRAIN AND STIR UP THE YOLK.

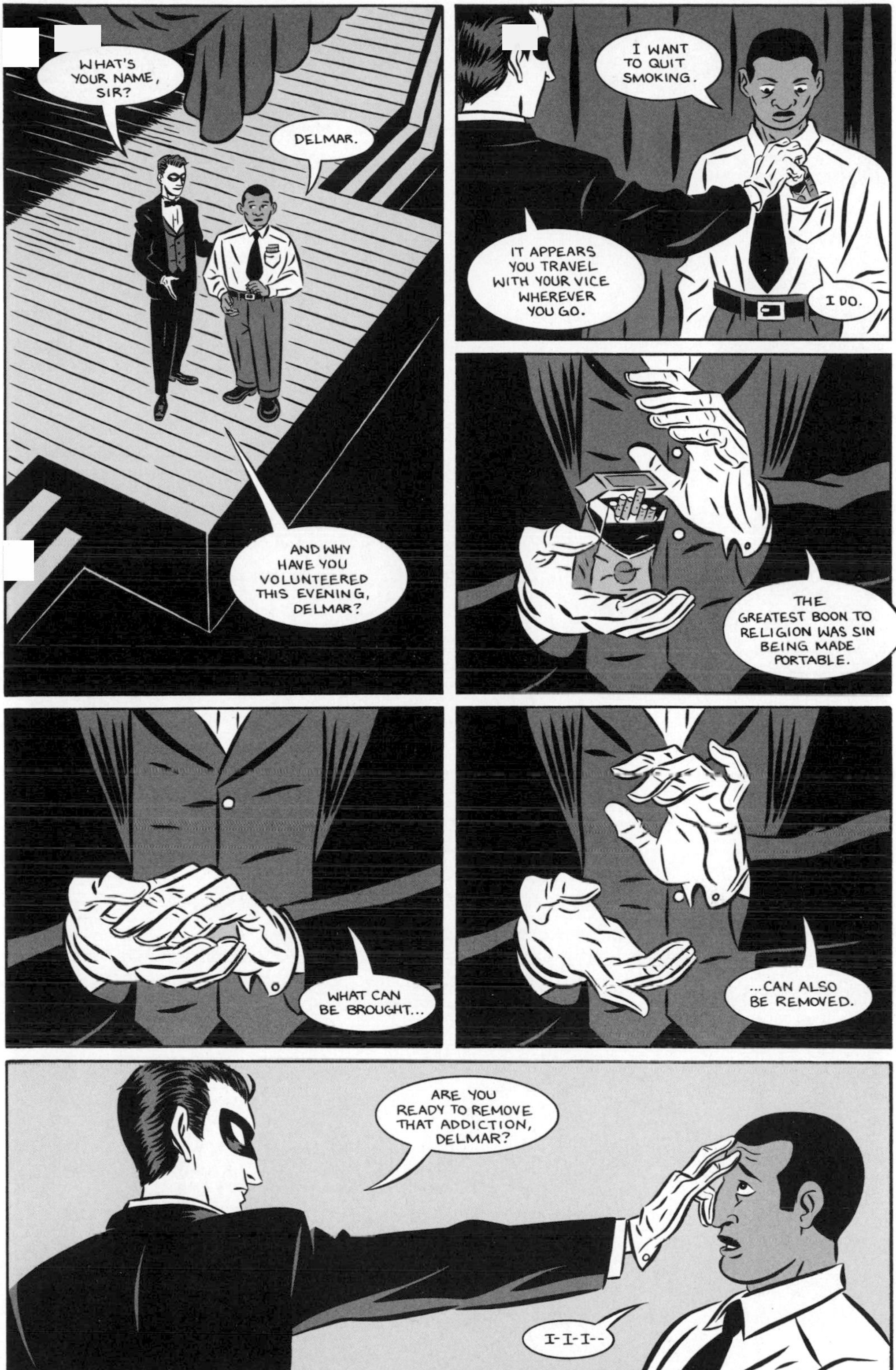
WHAT'S YOUR NAME, SIR?
DELMAR.
AND WHY HAVE YOU VOLUNTEERED THIS EVENING, DELMAR?
I WANT TO QUIT SMOKING.
IT APPEARS YOU TRAVEL WITH YOUR VICE WHEREVER YOU GO.
I DO.
THE GREATEST BOON TO RELIGION WAS SIN BEING MADE PORTABLE.
WHAT CAN BE BROUGHT...
...CAN ALSO BE REMOVED.
ARE YOU READY TO REMOVE THAT ADDICTION, DELMAR?
I-I-I--

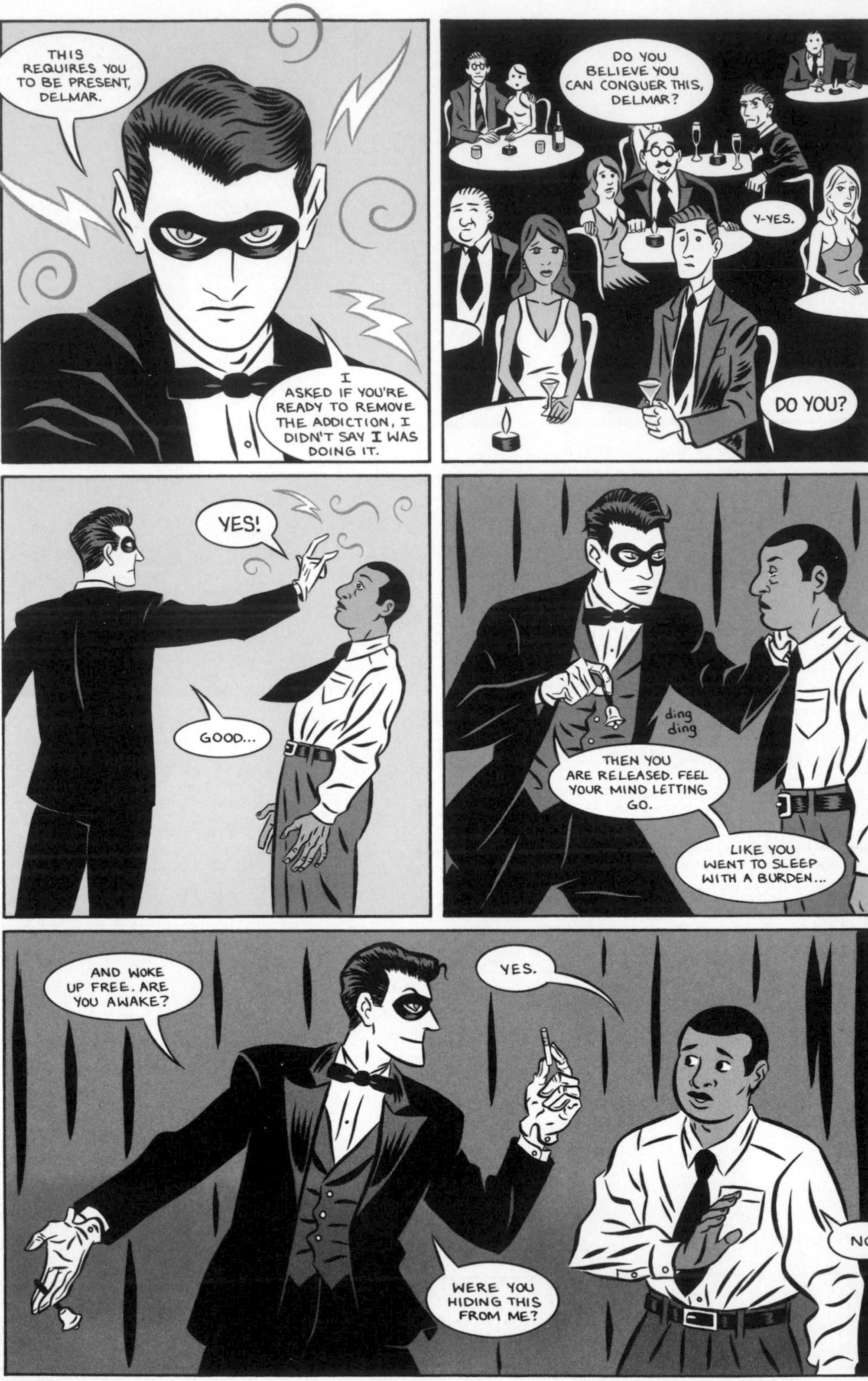
THIS REQUIRES YOU TO BE PRESENT, DELMAR.
I ASKED IF YOU'RE READY TO REMOVE THE ADDICTION, I DIDN'T SAY I WAS DOING IT.
DO YOU BELIEVE YOU CAN CONQUER THIS, DELMAR?
Y-YES.
DO YOU?
YES!
GOOD...
ding ding
THEN YOU ARE RELEASED. FEEL YOUR MIND LETTING GO.
LIKE YOU WENT TO SLEEP WITH A BURDEN...
AND WOKE UP FREE. ARE YOU AWAKE?
YES.
WERE YOU HIDING THIS FROM ME?
NO!

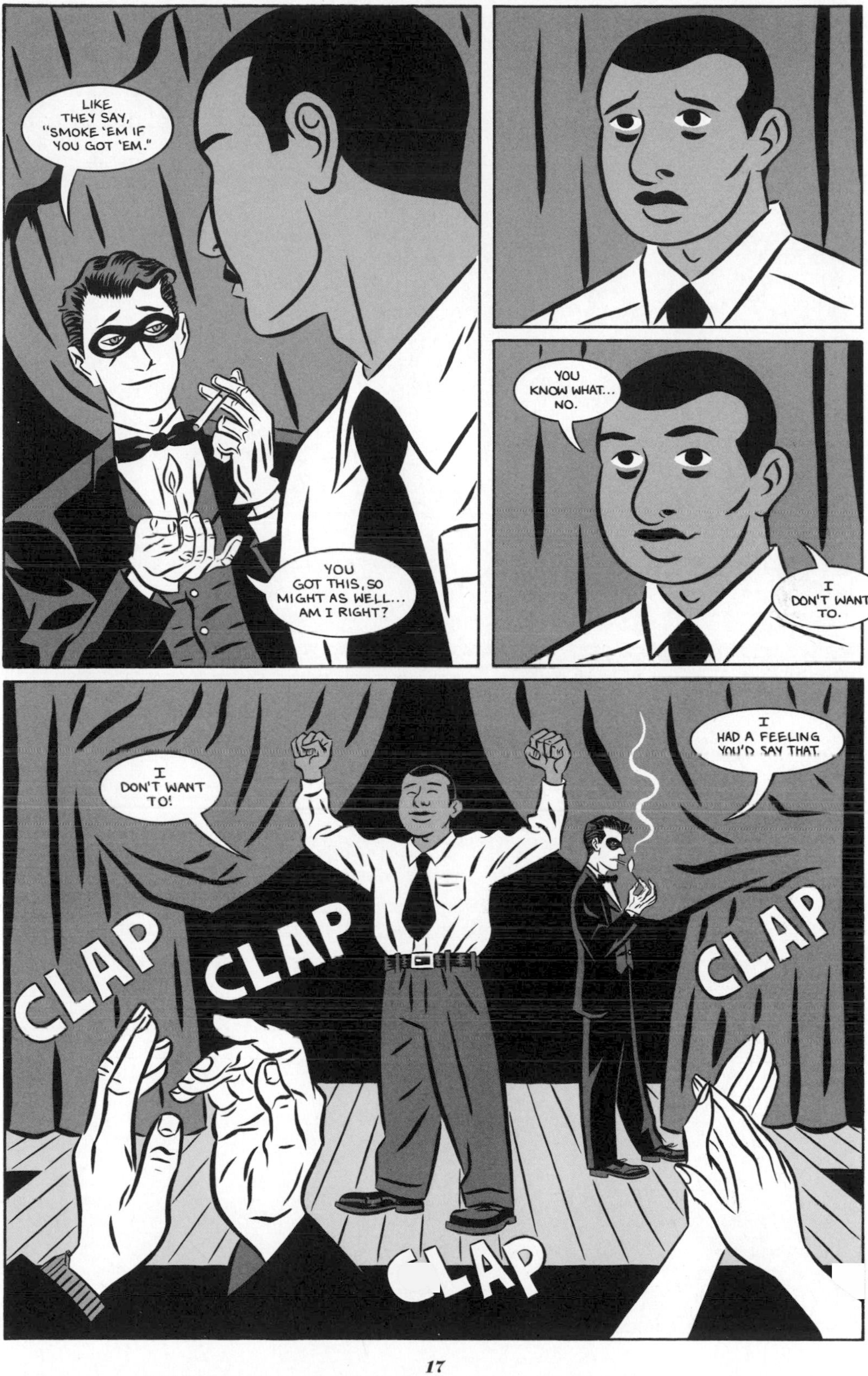
LIKE THEY SAY, "SMOKE 'EM IF YOU GOT 'EM."
YOU GOT THIS, SO MIGHT AS WELL... AM I RIGHT?
YOU KNOW WHAT... NO.
I DON'T WANT TO.
I DON'T WANT TO!
I HAD A FEELING YOU'D SAY THAT.
CLAP
CLAP
CLAP
CLAP

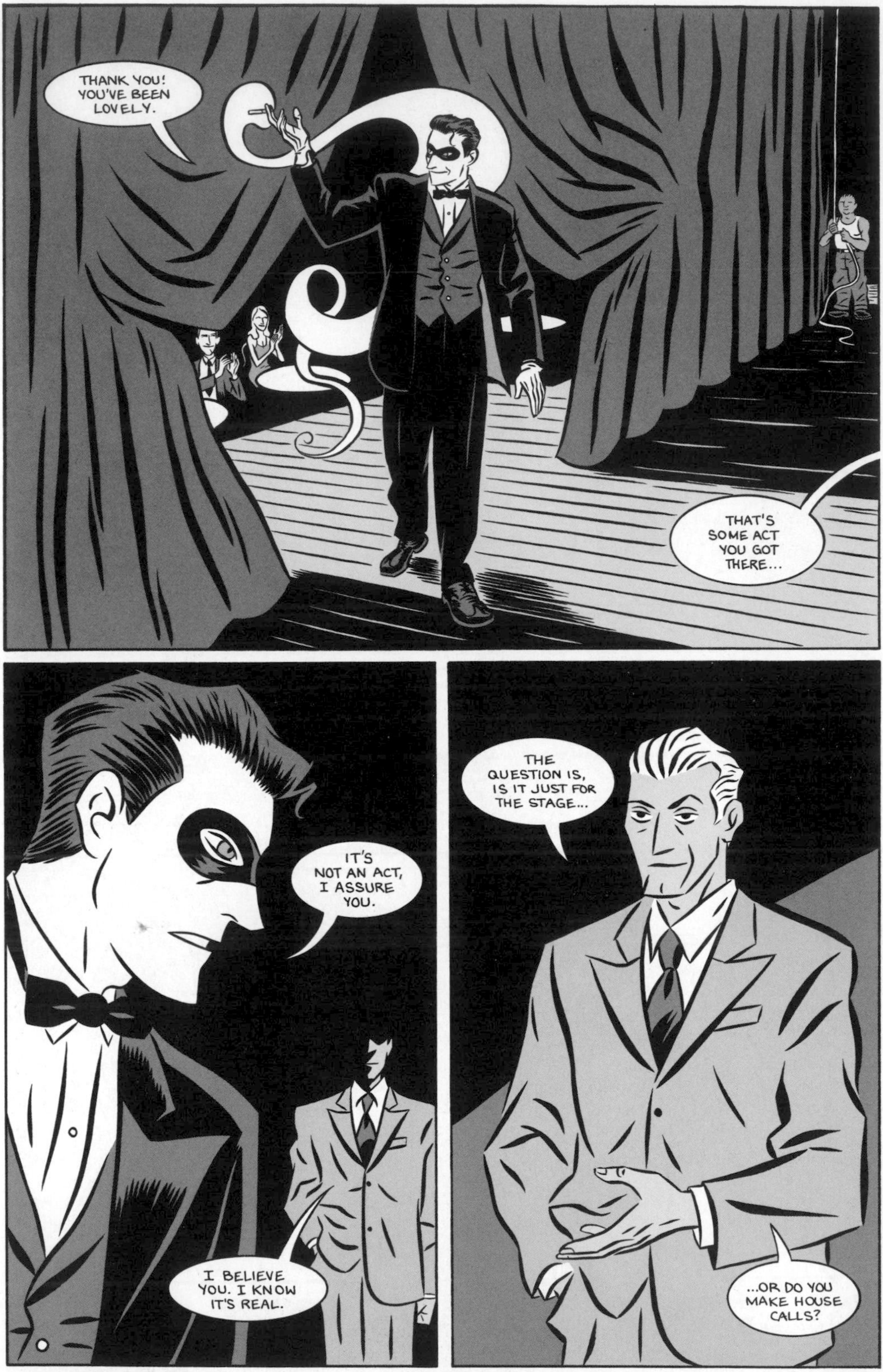
THANK YOU! YOU'VE BEEN LOVELY.
THAT'S SOME ACT YOU GOT THERE...
IT'S NOT AN ACT, I ASSURE YOU.
I BELIEVE YOU. I KNOW IT'S REAL.
THE QUESTION IS, IS IT JUST FOR THE STAGE...
...OR DO YOU MAKE HOUSE CALLS?

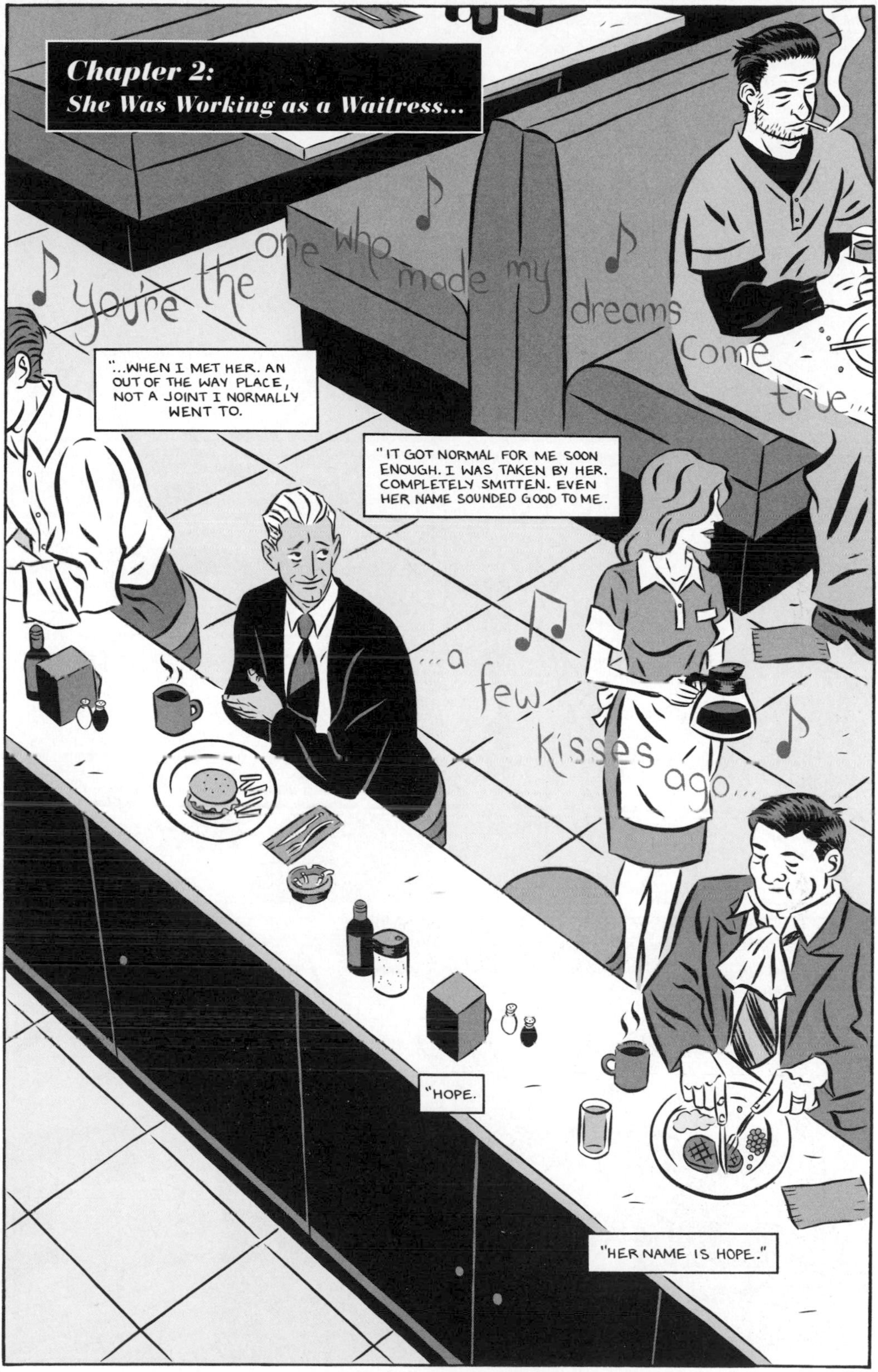
Chapter 2:
She Was Working as a Waitress...
you're the one who made my dreams come true...
"...WHEN I MET HER. AN OUT OF THE WAY PLACE, NOT A JOINT I NORMALLY WENT TO.
"IT GOT NORMAL FOR ME SOON ENOUGH. I WAS TAKEN BY HER. COMPLETELY SMITTEN. EVEN HER NAME SOUNDED GOOD TO ME.
...a few kisses ago...
"HOPE.
"HER NAME IS HOPE."

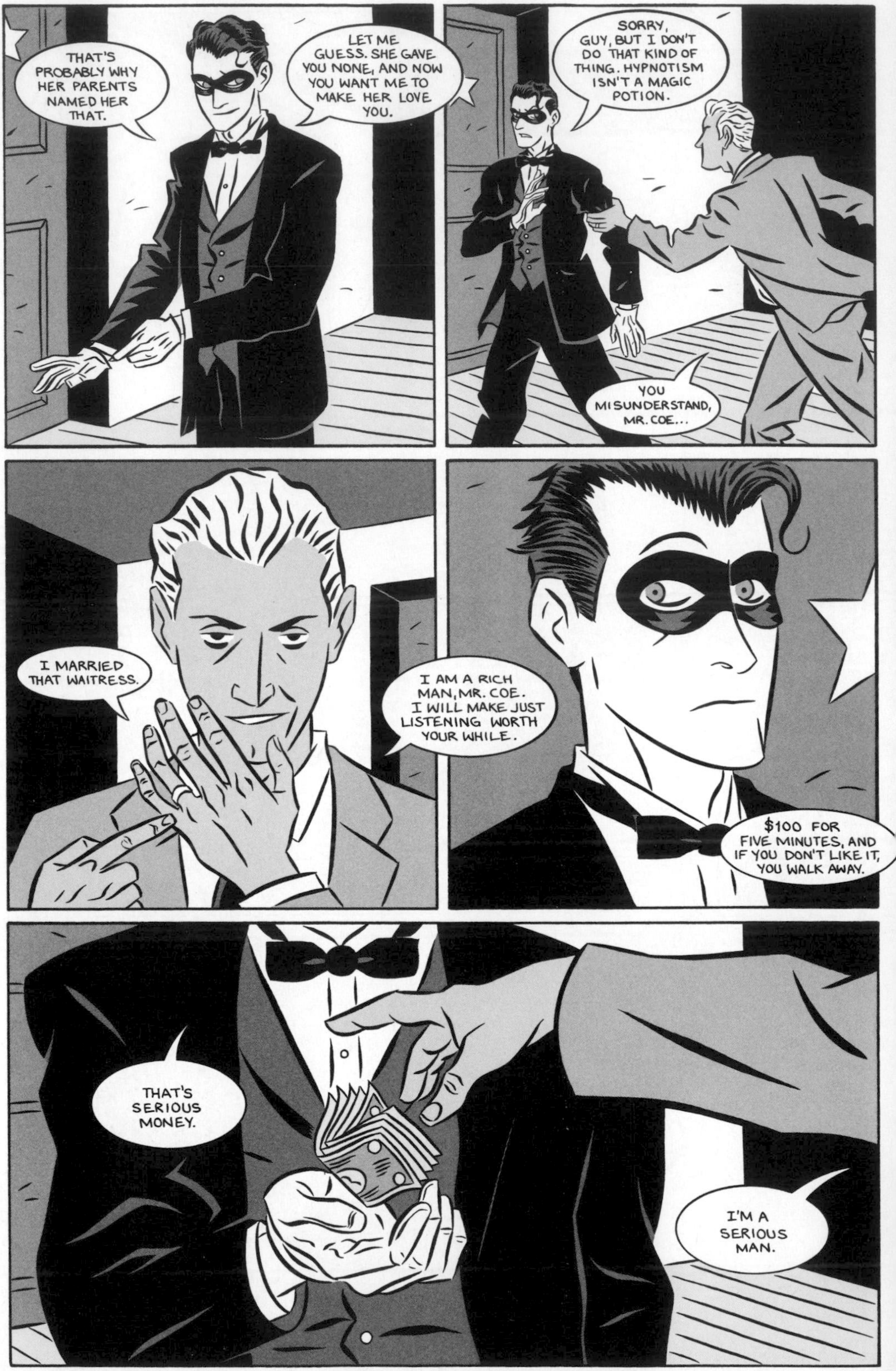
THAT'S PROBABLY WHY HER PARENTS NAMED HER THAT.
LET ME GUESS. SHE GAVE YOU NONE, AND NOW YOU WANT ME TO MAKE HER LOVE YOU.
SORRY, GUY, BUT I DON'T DO THAT KIND OF THING. HYPNOTISM ISN'T A MAGIC POTION.
YOU MISUNDERSTAND, MR. COE...
I MARRIED THAT WAITRESS.
I AM A RICH MAN, MR. COE. I WILL MAKE JUST LISTENING WORTH YOUR WHILE.
$100 FOR FIVE MINUTES, AND IF YOU DON'T LIKE IT, YOU WALK AWAY.
THAT'S SERIOUS MONEY.
I'M A SERIOUS MAN.

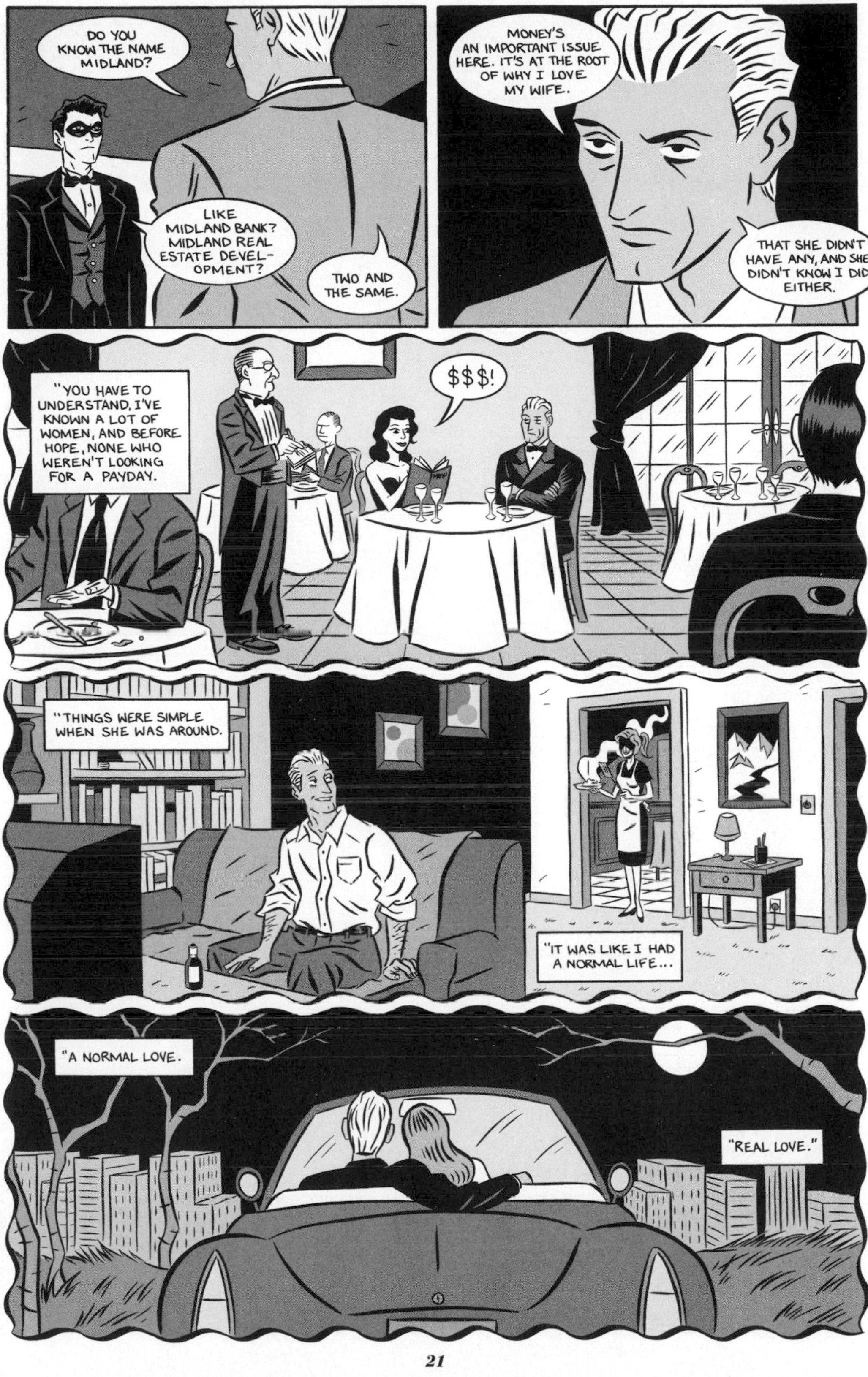
DO YOU KNOW THE NAME MIDLAND?
LIKE MIDLAND BANK? MIDLAND REAL ESTATE DEVEL-OPMENT?
TWO AND THE SAME.
MONEY'S AN IMPORTANT ISSUE HERE. IT'S AT THE ROOT OF WHY I LOVE MY WIFE.
THAT SHE DIDN'T HAVE ANY, AND SHE DIDN'T KNOW I DID EITHER.
"YOU HAVE TO UNDERSTAND, I'VE KNOWN A LOT OF WOMEN, AND BEFORE HOPE, NONE WHO WEREN'T LOOKING FOR A PAYDAY.
$$$!
"THINGS WERE SIMPLE WHEN SHE WAS AROUND.
"IT WAS LIKE I HAD A NORMAL LIFE...
"A NORMAL LOVE.
"REAL LOVE."

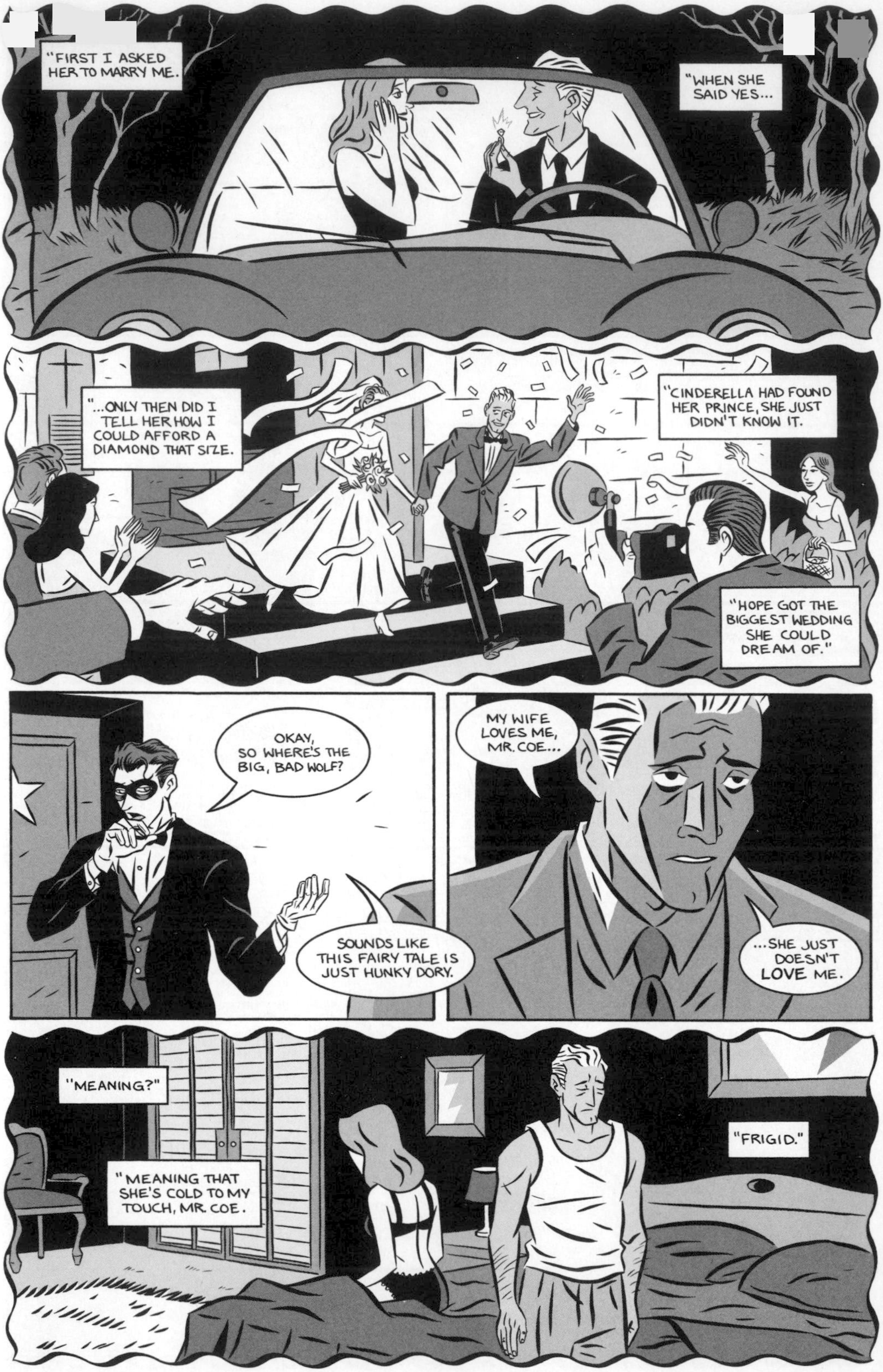
"FIRST I ASKED HER TO MARRY ME.
"WHEN SHE SAID YES...
"...ONLY THEN DID I TELL HER HOW I COULD AFFORD A DIAMOND THAT SIZE.
"CINDERELLA HAD FOUND HER PRINCE, SHE JUST DIDN'T KNOW IT.
"HOPE GOT THE BIGGEST WEDDING SHE COULD DREAM OF."
OKAY, SO WHERE'S THE BIG, BAD WOLF?
SOUNDS LIKE THIS FAIRY TALE IS JUST HUNKY DORY.
MY WIFE LOVES ME, MR. COE...
...SHE JUST DOESN'T LOVE ME.
"MEANING?"
"MEANING THAT SHE'S COLD TO MY TOUCH, MR. COE.
"FRIGID."

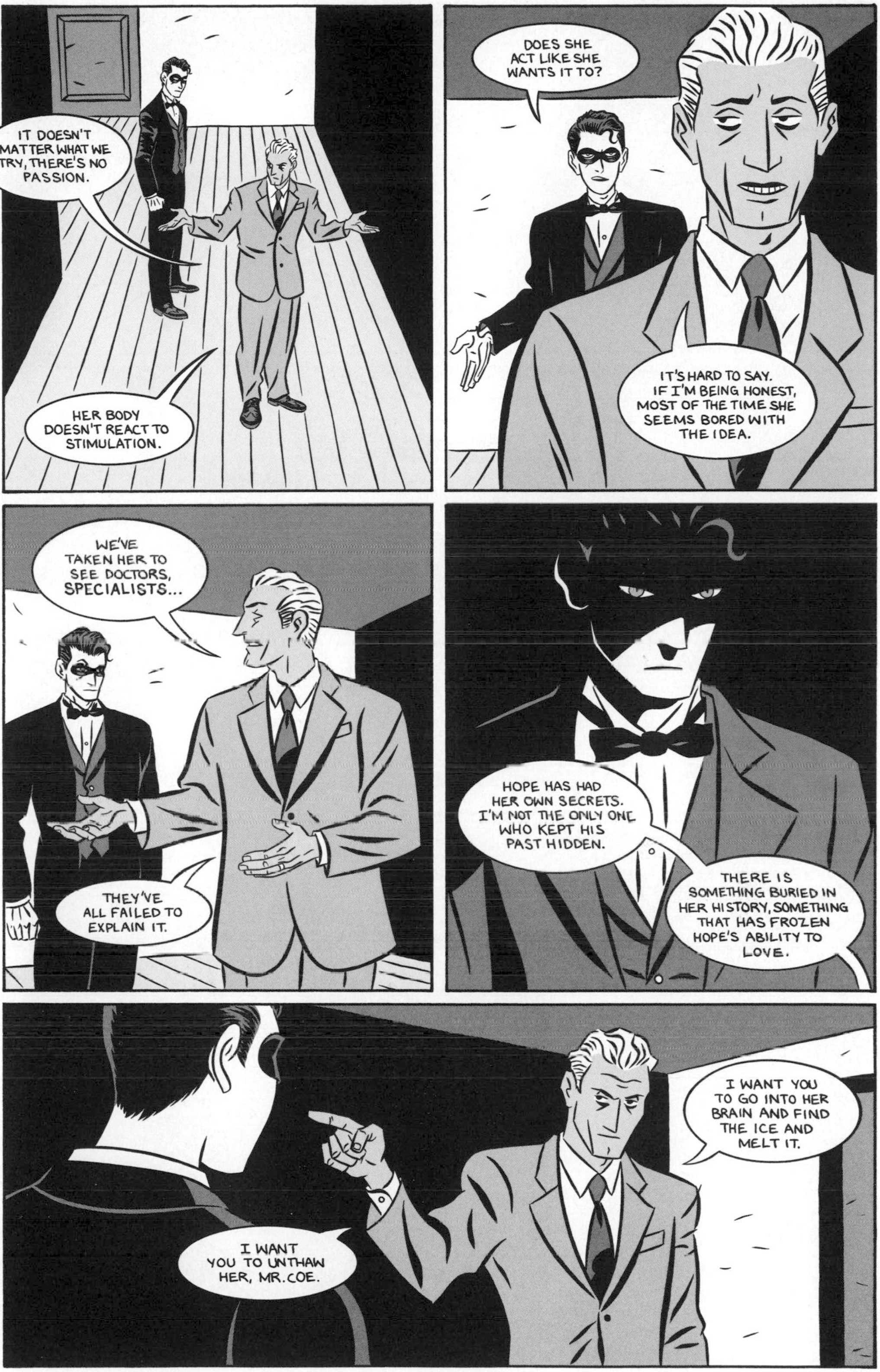
IT DOESN'T MATTER WHAT WE TRY, THERE'S NO PASSION.
HER BODY DOESN'T REACT TO STIMULATION.
DOES SHE ACT LIKE SHE WANTS IT TO?
IT'S HARD TO SAY. IF I'M BEING HONEST, MOST OF THE TIME SHE SEEMS BORED WITH THE IDEA.
WE'VE TAKEN HER TO SEE DOCTORS, SPECIALISTS...
THEY'VE ALL FAILED TO EXPLAIN IT.
HOPE HAS HAD HER OWN SECRETS. I'M NOT THE ONLY ONE WHO KEPT HIS PAST HIDDEN.
THERE IS SOMETHING BURIED IN HER HISTORY, SOMETHING THAT HAS FROZEN HOPE'S ABILITY TO LOVE.
I WANT YOU TO GO INTO HER BRAIN AND FIND THE ICE AND MELT IT.
I WANT YOU TO UNTHAW HER, MR. COE.

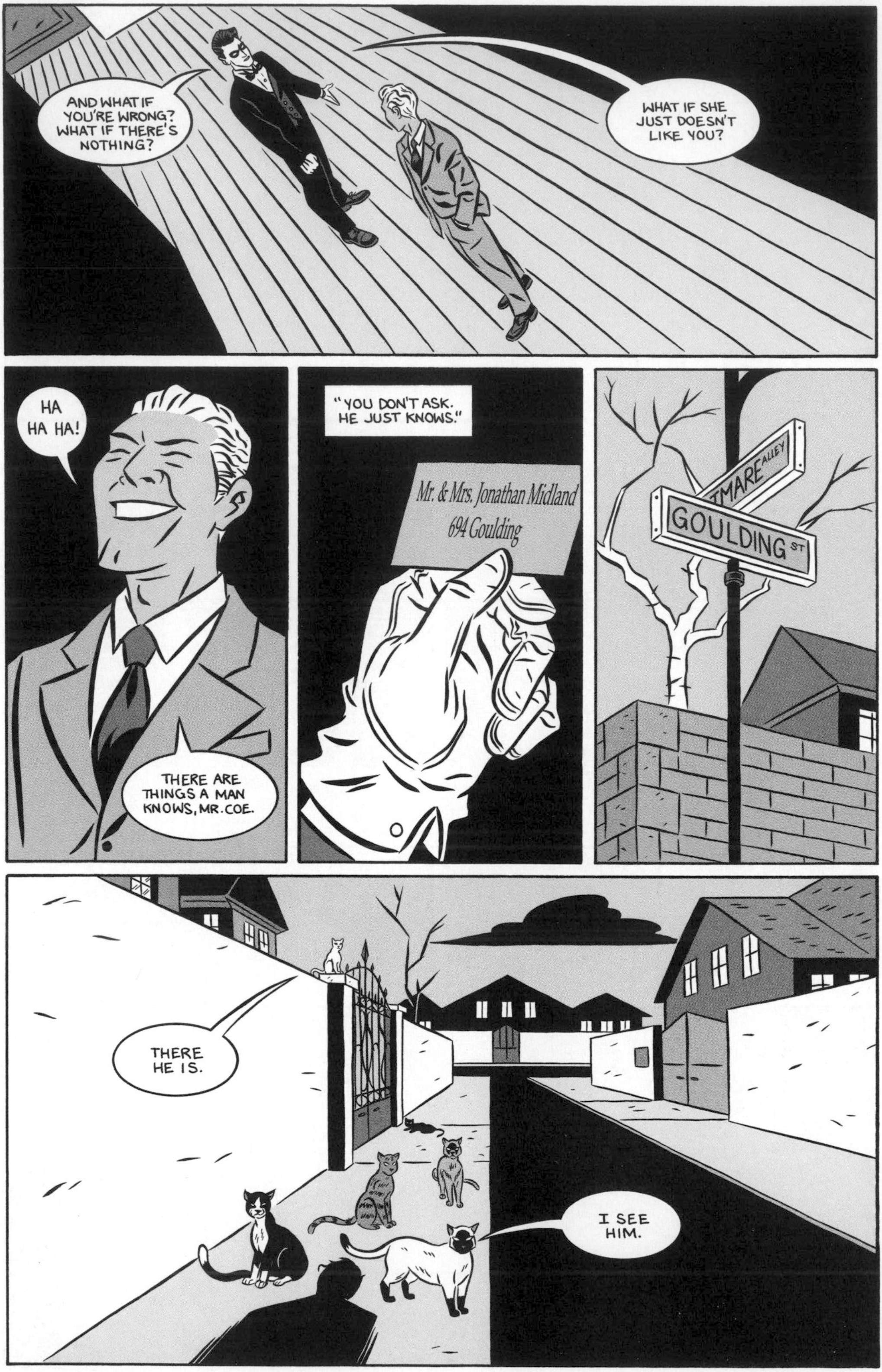
AND WHAT IF YOU'RE WRONG? WHAT IF THERE'S NOTHING?
WHAT IF SHE JUST DOESN'T LIKE YOU?
HA HA HA!
THERE ARE THINGS A MAN KNOWS, MR. COE.
"YOU DON'T ASK. HE JUST KNOWS."
Mr. & Mrs. Jonathan Midland
694 Goulding
TMARE ALLEY
GOULDING ST
THERE HE IS.
I SEE HIM.

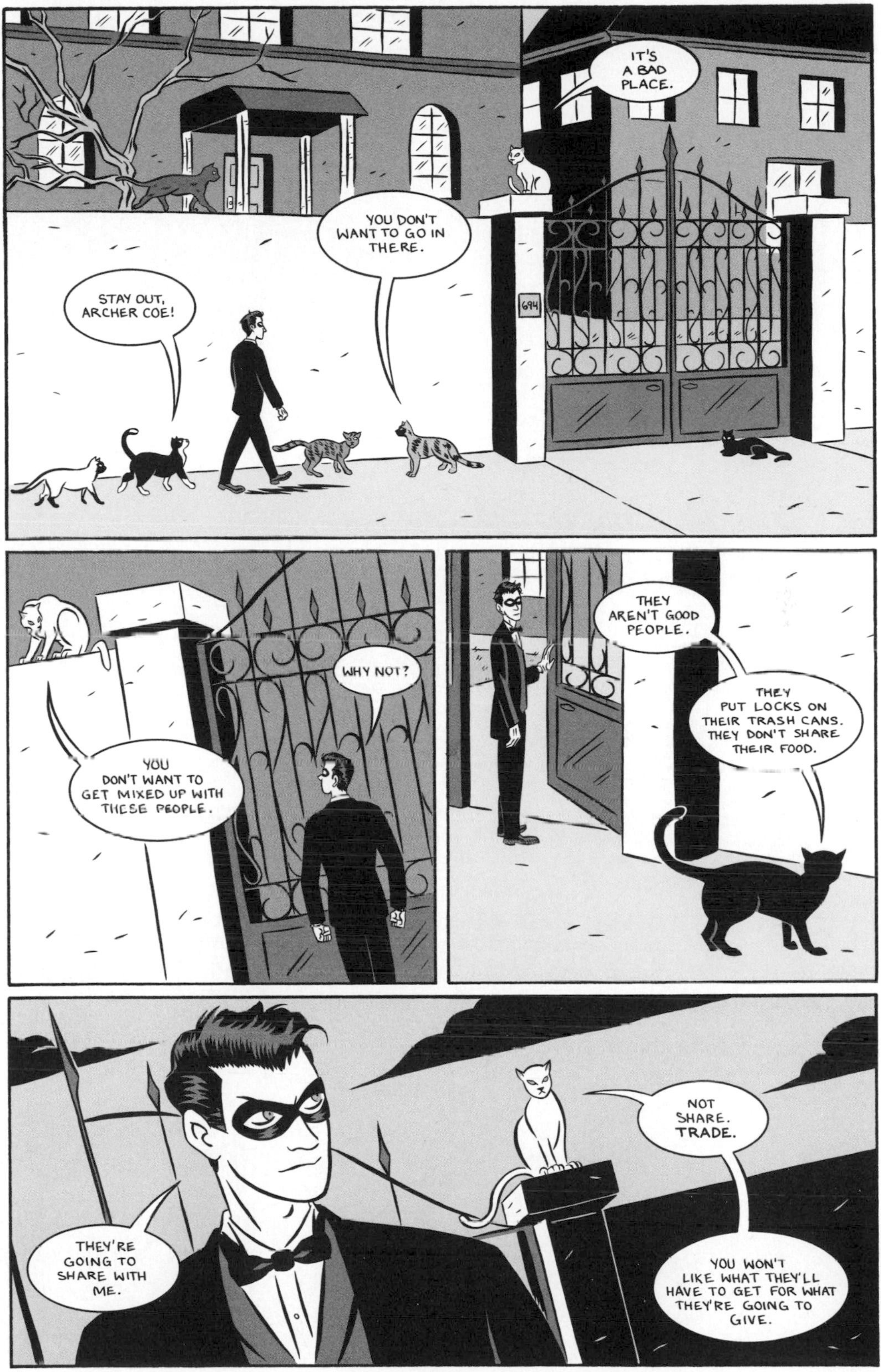
IT'S A BAD PLACE.
YOU DON'T WANT TO GO IN THERE.
STAY OUT, ARCHER COE!
694
WHY NOT?
YOU DON'T WANT TO GET MIXED UP WITH THESE PEOPLE.
THEY AREN'T GOOD PEOPLE.
THEY PUT LOCKS ON THEIR TRASH CANS. THEY DON'T SHARE THEIR FOOD.
THEY'RE GOING TO SHARE WITH ME.
NOT SHARE. TRADE.
YOU WON'T LIKE WHAT THEY'LL HAVE TO GET FOR WHAT THEY'RE GOING TO GIVE.

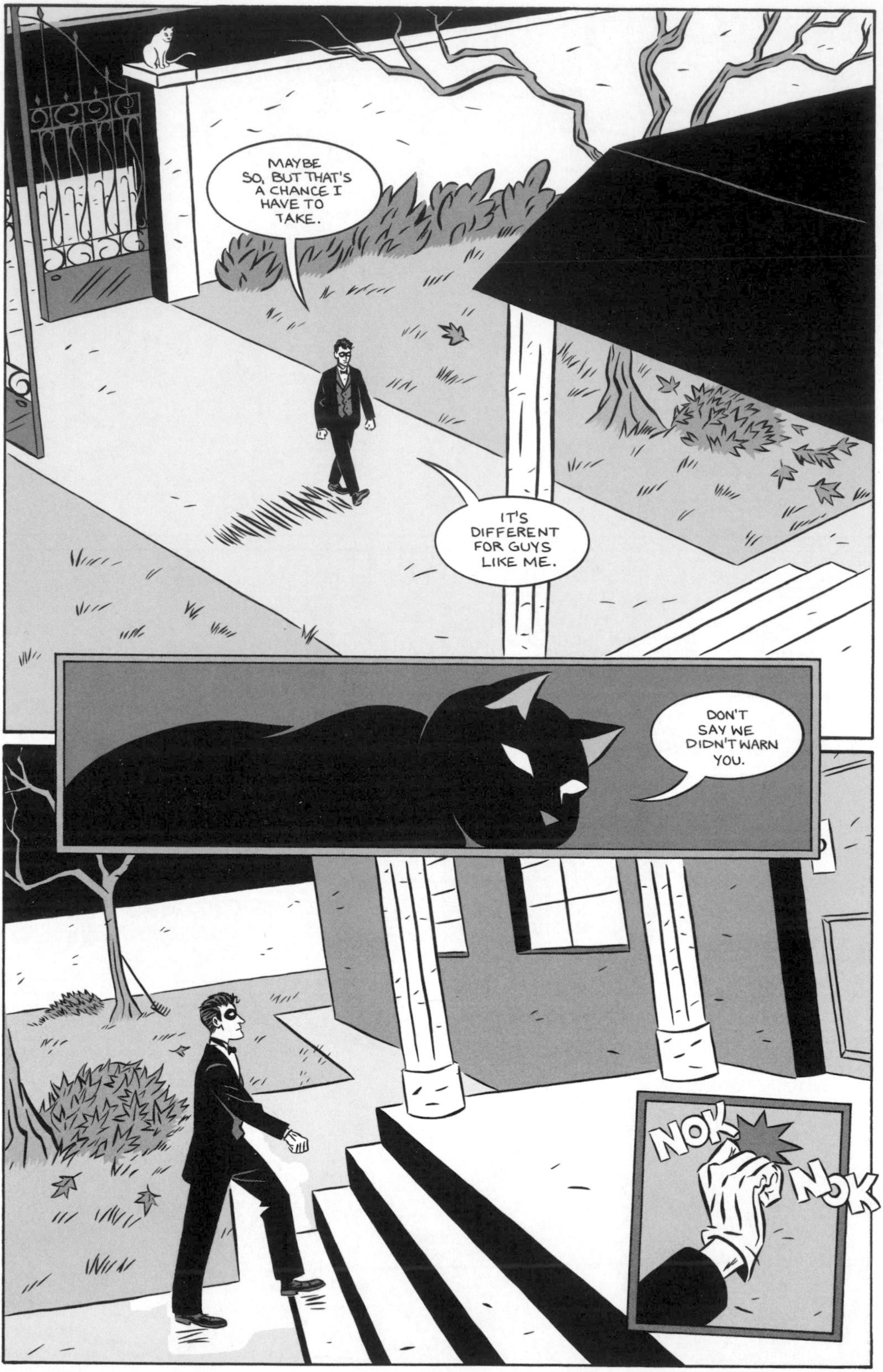
MAYBE SO, BUT THAT'S A CHANCE I HAVE TO TAKE.
IT'S DIFFERENT FOR GUYS LIKE ME.
DON'T SAY WE DIDN'T WARN YOU.
NOK NOK

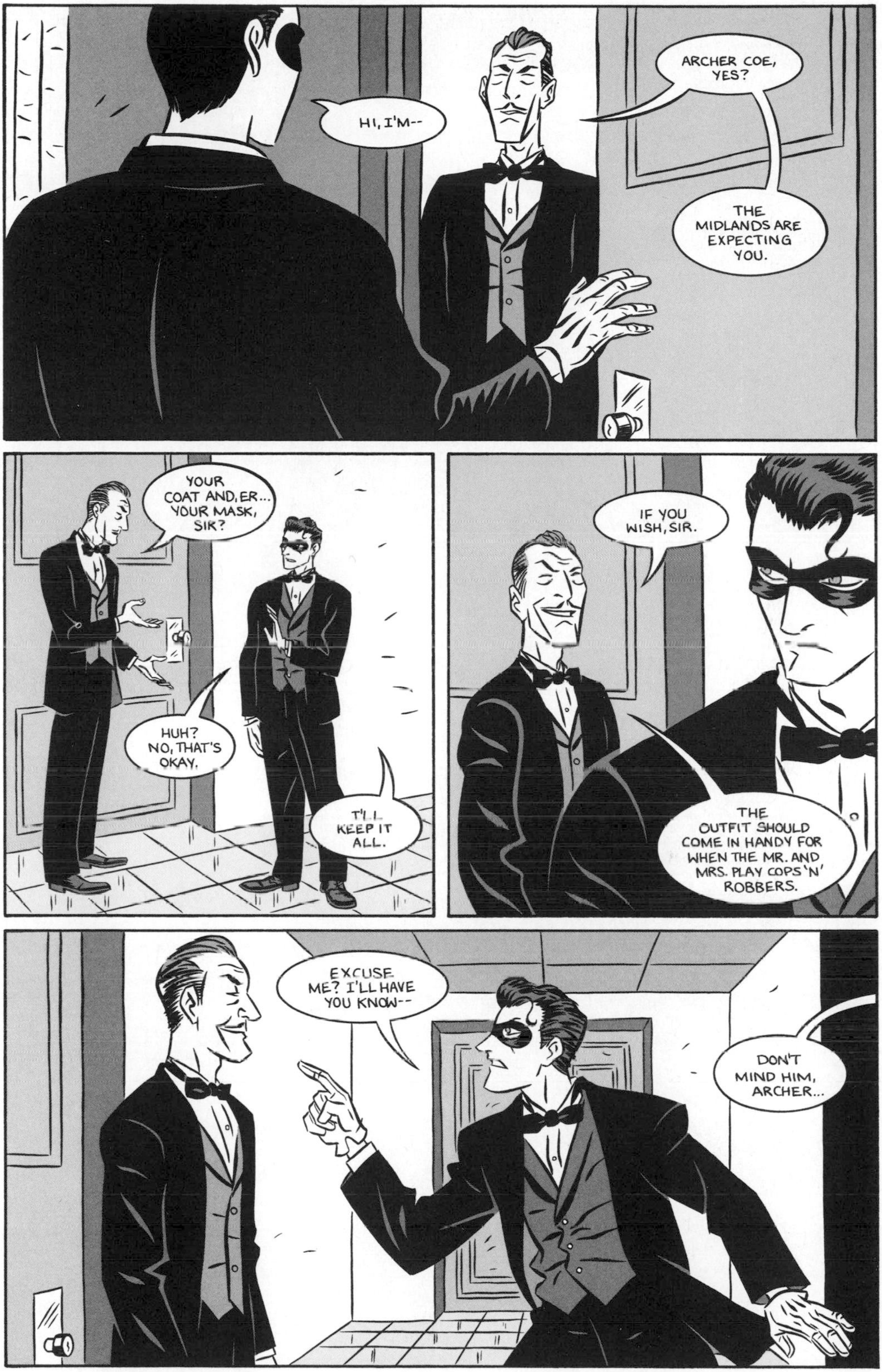
HI, I'M--
ARCHER COE, YES?
THE MIDLANDS ARE EXPECTING YOU.
YOUR COAT AND, ER... YOUR MASK, SIR?
HUH? NO, THAT'S OKAY.
I'LL KEEP IT ALL.
IF YOU WISH, SIR.
THE OUTFIT SHOULD COME IN HANDY FOR WHEN THE MR. AND MRS. PLAY COPS 'N' ROBBERS.
EXCUSE ME? I'LL HAVE YOU KNOW--
DON'T MIND HIM, ARCHER...

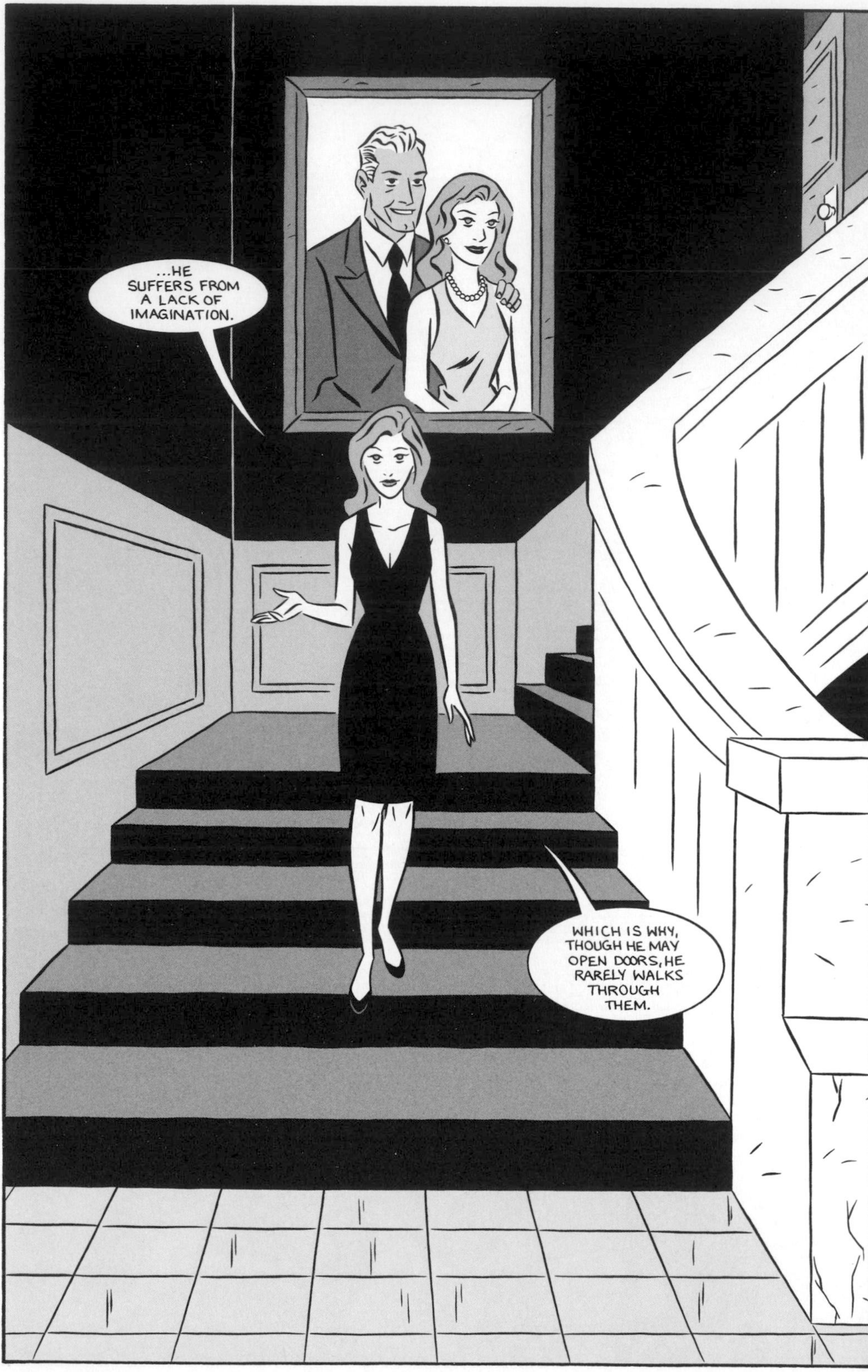
...HE SUFFERS FROM A LACK OF IMAGINATION.
WHICH IS WHY, THOUGH HE MAY OPEN DOORS, HE RARELY WALKS THROUGH THEM.

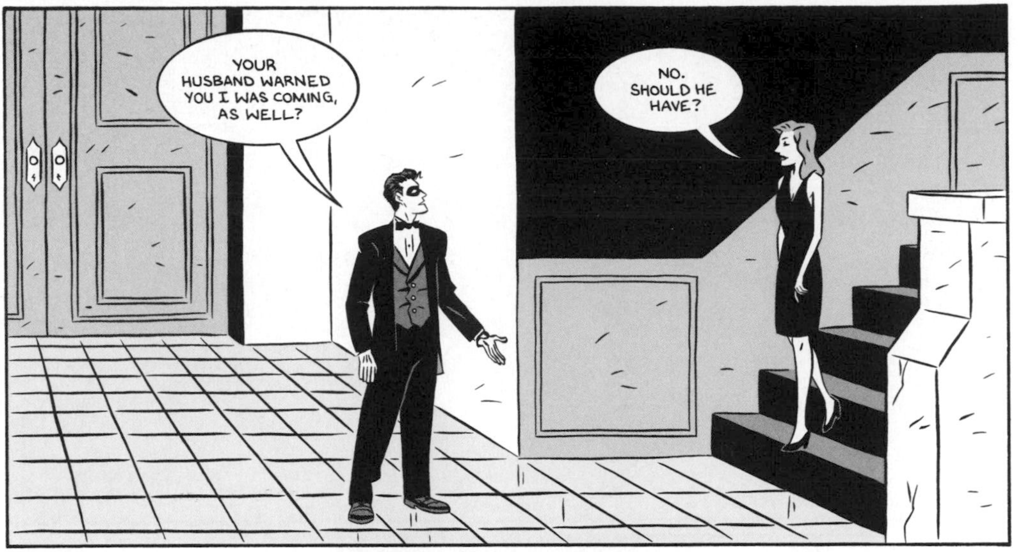
YOUR HUSBAND WARNED YOU I WAS COMING, AS WELL?
NO. SHOULD HE HAVE?

Chapter 3: Mrs. Lonely

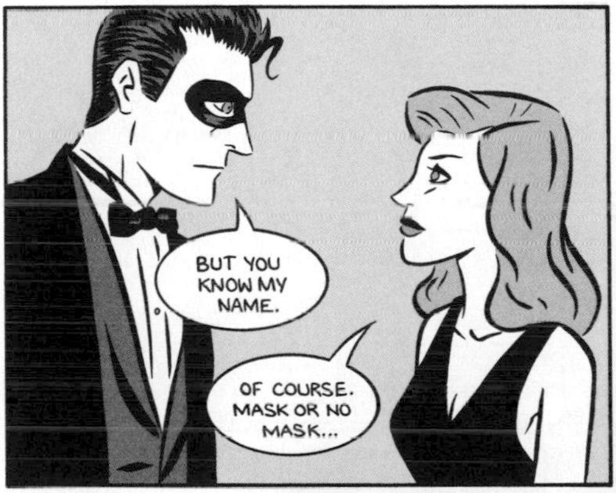
BUT YOU KNOW MY NAME.
OF COURSE. MASK OR NO MASK...

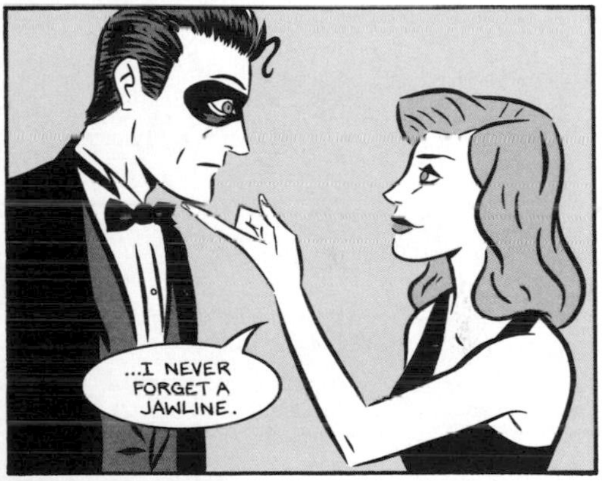
...I NEVER FORGET A JAWLINE.

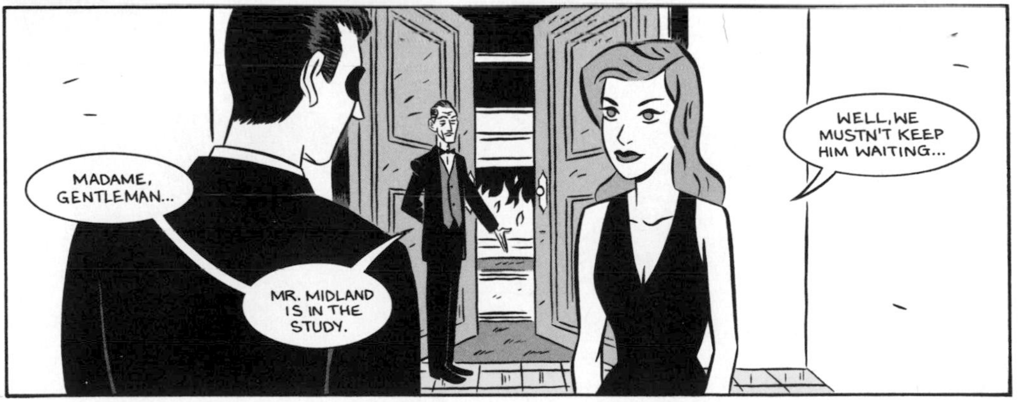
MADAME, GENTLEMAN...
MR. MIDLAND IS IN THE STUDY.
WELL, WE MUSTN'T KEEP HIM WAITING...

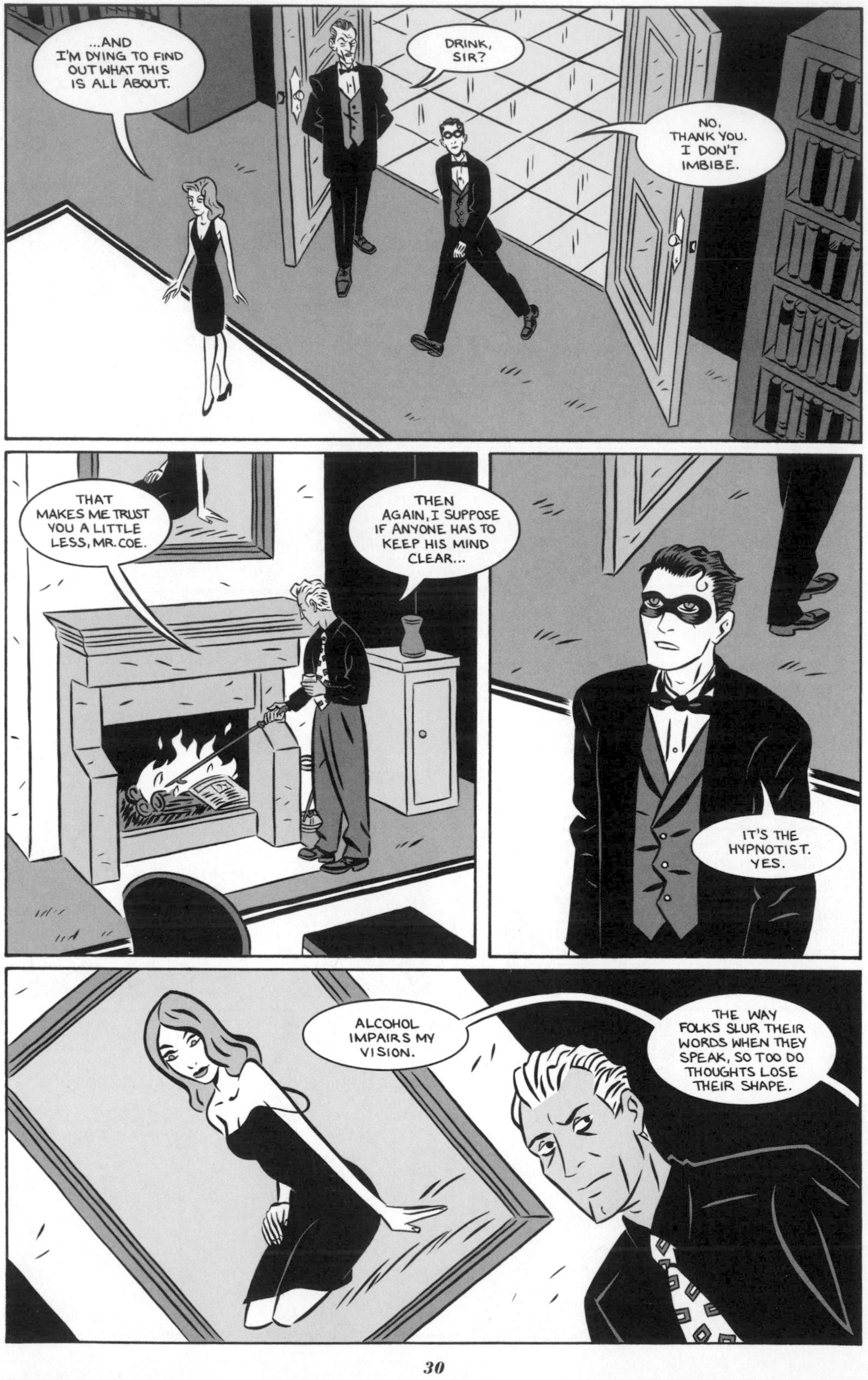
...AND I'M DYING TO FIND OUT WHAT THIS IS ALL ABOUT.
DRINK, SIR?
NO, THANK YOU. I DON'T IMBIBE.
THAT MAKES ME TRUST YOU A LITTLE LESS, MR. COE.
THEN AGAIN, I SUPPOSE IF ANYONE HAS TO KEEP HIS MIND CLEAR...
IT'S THE HYPNOTIST. YES.
ALCOHOL IMPAIRS MY VISION.
THE WAY FOLKS SLUR THEIR WORDS WHEN THEY SPEAK, SO TOO DO THOUGHTS LOSE THEIR SHAPE.

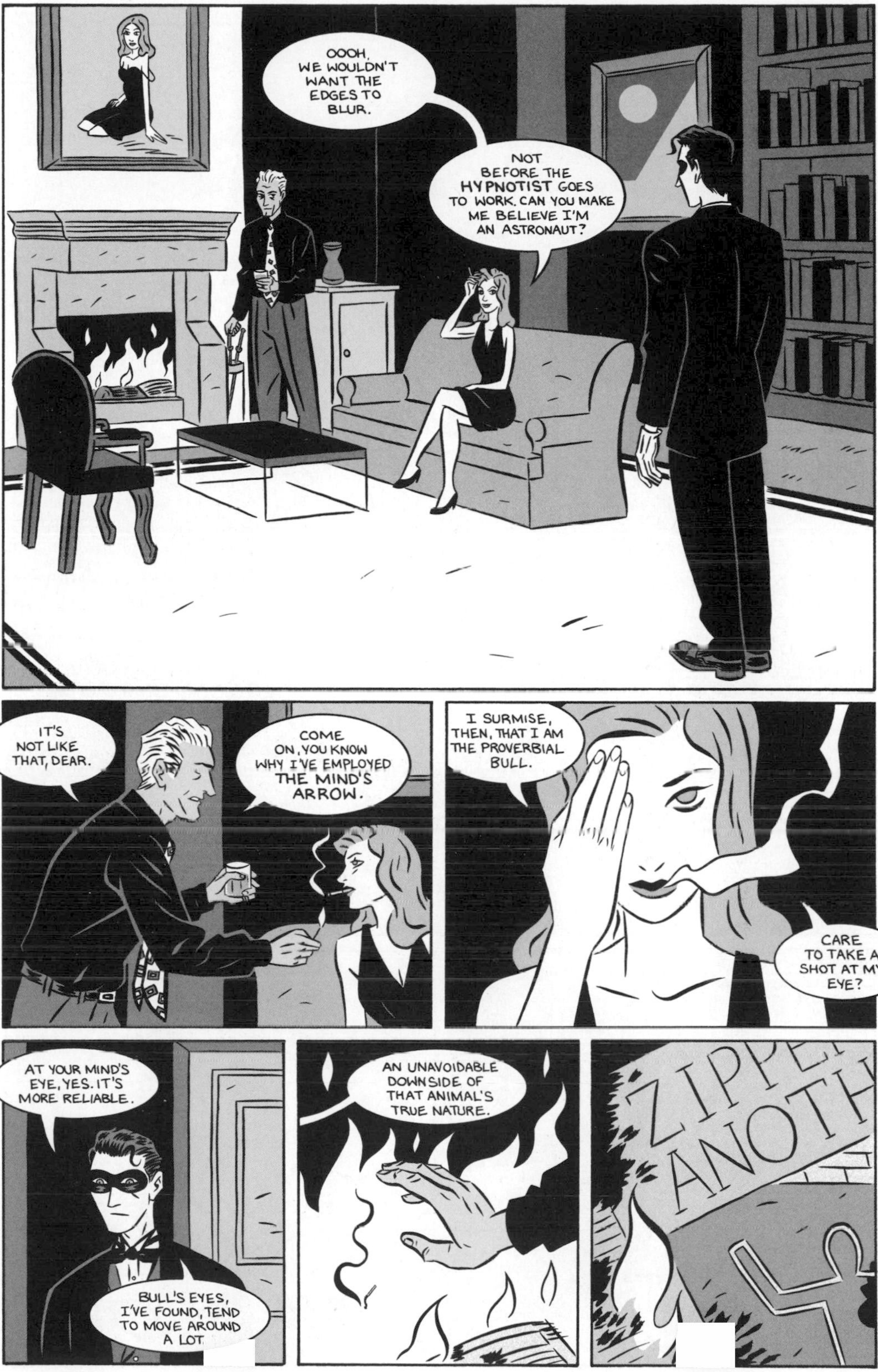
OOOH, WE WOULDN'T WANT THE EDGES TO BLUR.
NOT BEFORE THE HYPNOTIST GOES TO WORK. CAN YOU MAKE ME BELIEVE I'M AN ASTRONAUT?
IT'S NOT LIKE THAT, DEAR.
COME ON, YOU KNOW WHY I'VE EMPLOYED THE MIND'S ARROW.
I SURMISE, THEN, THAT I AM THE PROVERBIAL BULL.
CARE TO TAKE A SHOT AT MY EYE?
AT YOUR MIND'S EYE, YES. IT'S MORE RELIABLE.
BULL'S EYES, I'VE FOUND, TEND TO MOVE AROUND A LOT.
AN UNAVOIDABLE DOWNSIDE OF THAT ANIMAL'S TRUE NATURE.
ZIPPE
ANOTH

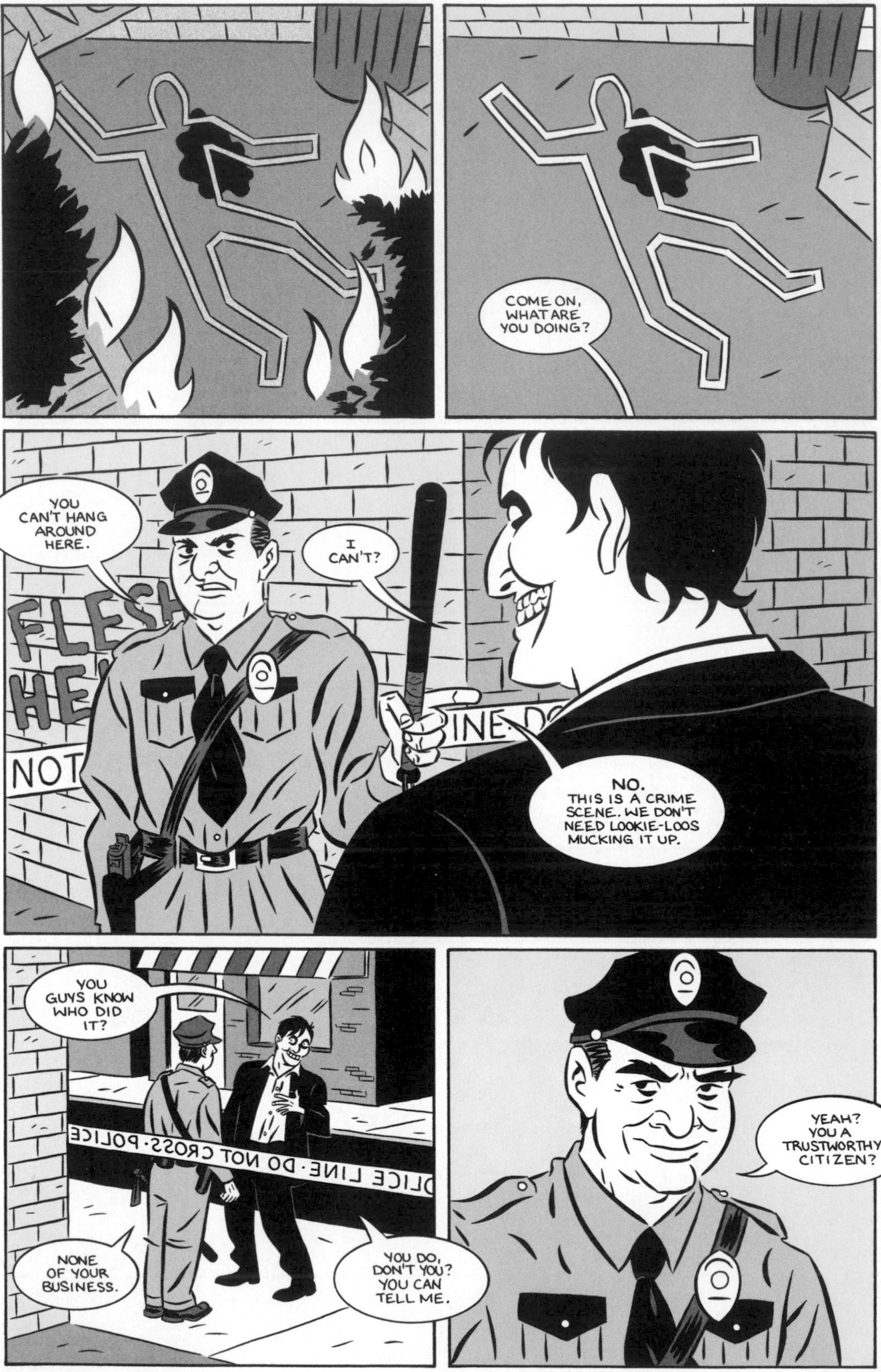
COME ON, WHAT ARE YOU DOING?
YOU CAN'T HANG AROUND HERE.
I CAN'T?
FLESH HE
NOT
INE·DO
NO. THIS IS A CRIME SCENE. WE DON'T NEED LOOKIE-LOOS MUCKING IT UP.
YOU GUYS KNOW WHO DID IT?
POLICE LINE · DO NOT CROSS · POLICE
NONE OF YOUR BUSINESS.
YOU DO, DON'T YOU? YOU CAN TELL ME.
YEAH? YOU A TRUSTWORTHY CITIZEN?

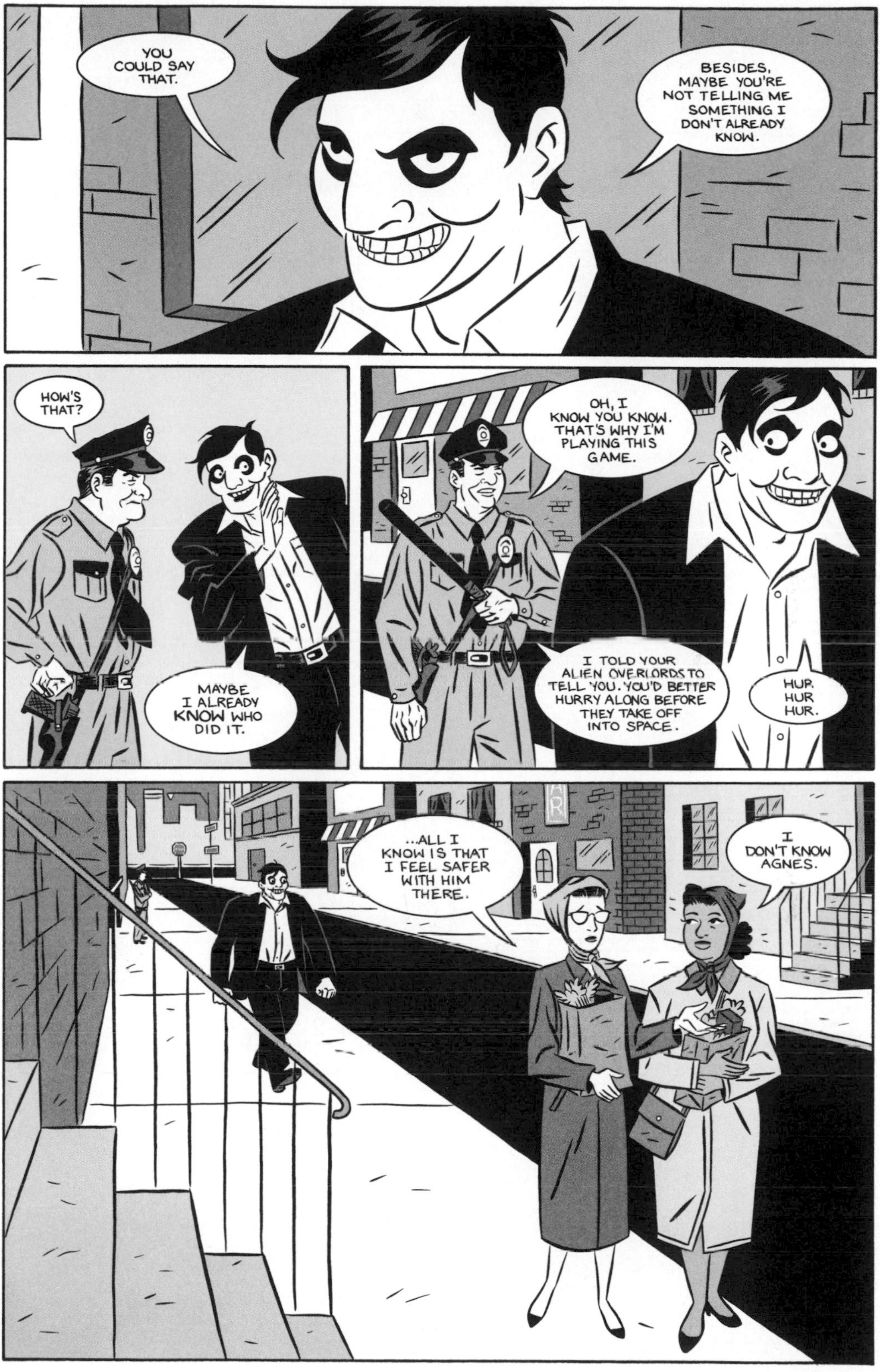
YOU COULD SAY THAT.
BESIDES, MAYBE YOU'RE NOT TELLING ME SOMETHING I DON'T ALREADY KNOW.
HOW'S THAT?
MAYBE I ALREADY KNOW WHO DID IT.
OH, I KNOW YOU KNOW. THAT'S WHY I'M PLAYING THIS GAME.
I TOLD YOUR ALIEN OVERLORDS TO TELL YOU. YOU'D BETTER HURRY ALONG BEFORE THEY TAKE OFF INTO SPACE.
HUR. HUR HUR.
...ALL I KNOW IS THAT I FEEL SAFER WITH HIM THERE.
I DON'T KNOW AGNES.

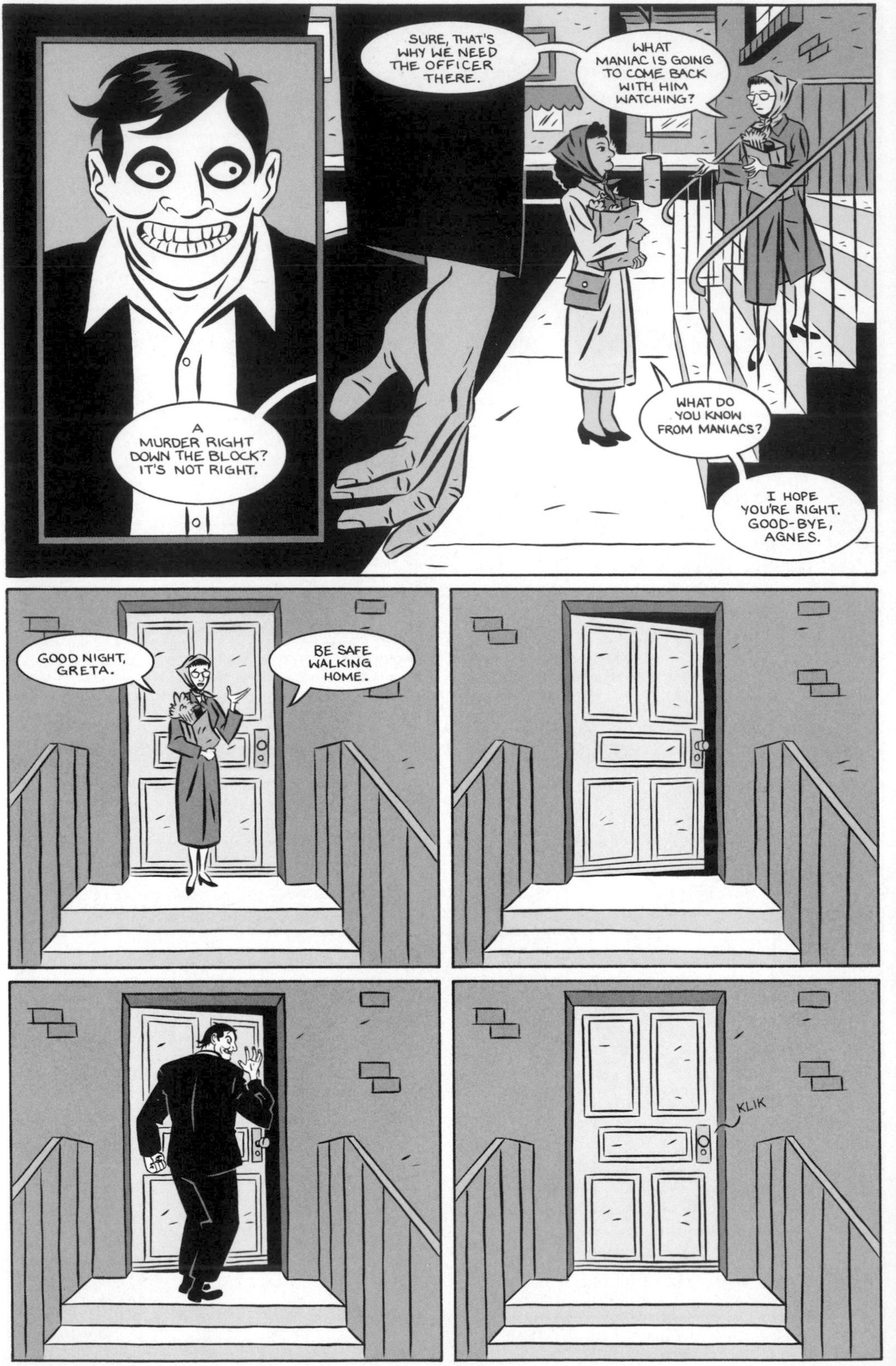
SURE, THAT'S WHY WE NEED THE OFFICER THERE.
WHAT MANIAC IS GOING TO COME BACK WITH HIM WATCHING?
A MURDER RIGHT DOWN THE BLOCK? IT'S NOT RIGHT.
WHAT DO YOU KNOW FROM MANIACS?
I HOPE YOU'RE RIGHT. GOOD-BYE, AGNES.
GOOD NIGHT, GRETA.
BE SAFE WALKING HOME.
KLIK

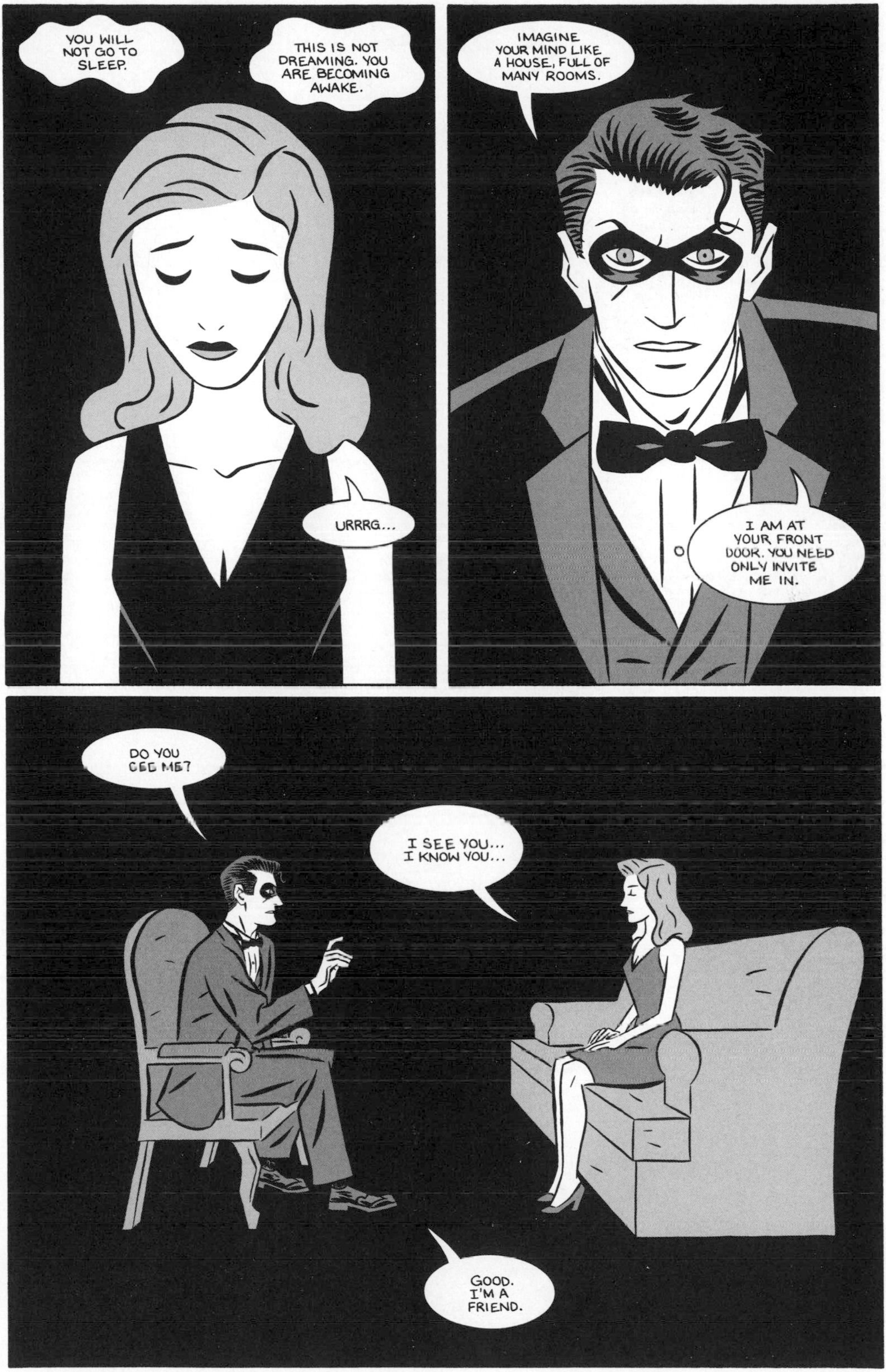
YOU WILL NOT GO TO SLEEP.
THIS IS NOT DREAMING. YOU ARE BECOMING AWAKE.
URRRG...
IMAGINE YOUR MIND LIKE A HOUSE, FULL OF MANY ROOMS.
I AM AT YOUR FRONT DOOR. YOU NEED ONLY INVITE ME IN.
DO YOU SEE ME?
I SEE YOU... I KNOW YOU...
GOOD. I'M A FRIEND.

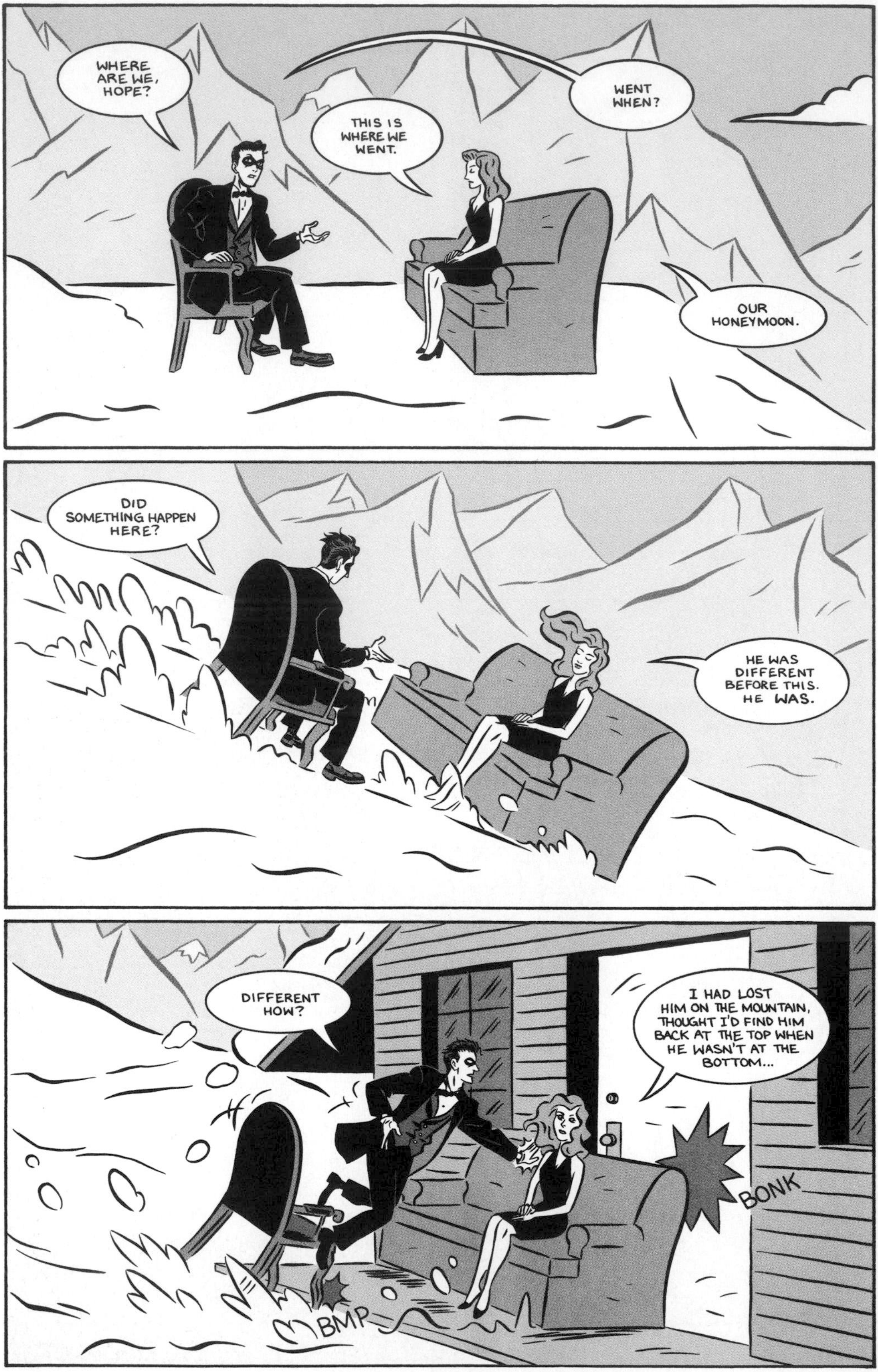
WHERE ARE WE, HOPE?
THIS IS WHERE WE WENT.
WENT WHEN?
OUR HONEYMOON.
DID SOMETHING HAPPEN HERE?
HE WAS DIFFERENT BEFORE THIS. HE WAS.
DIFFERENT HOW?
I HAD LOST HIM ON THE MOUNTAIN, THOUGHT I'D FIND HIM BACK AT THE TOP WHEN HE WASN'T AT THE BOTTOM...
BONK
BMP

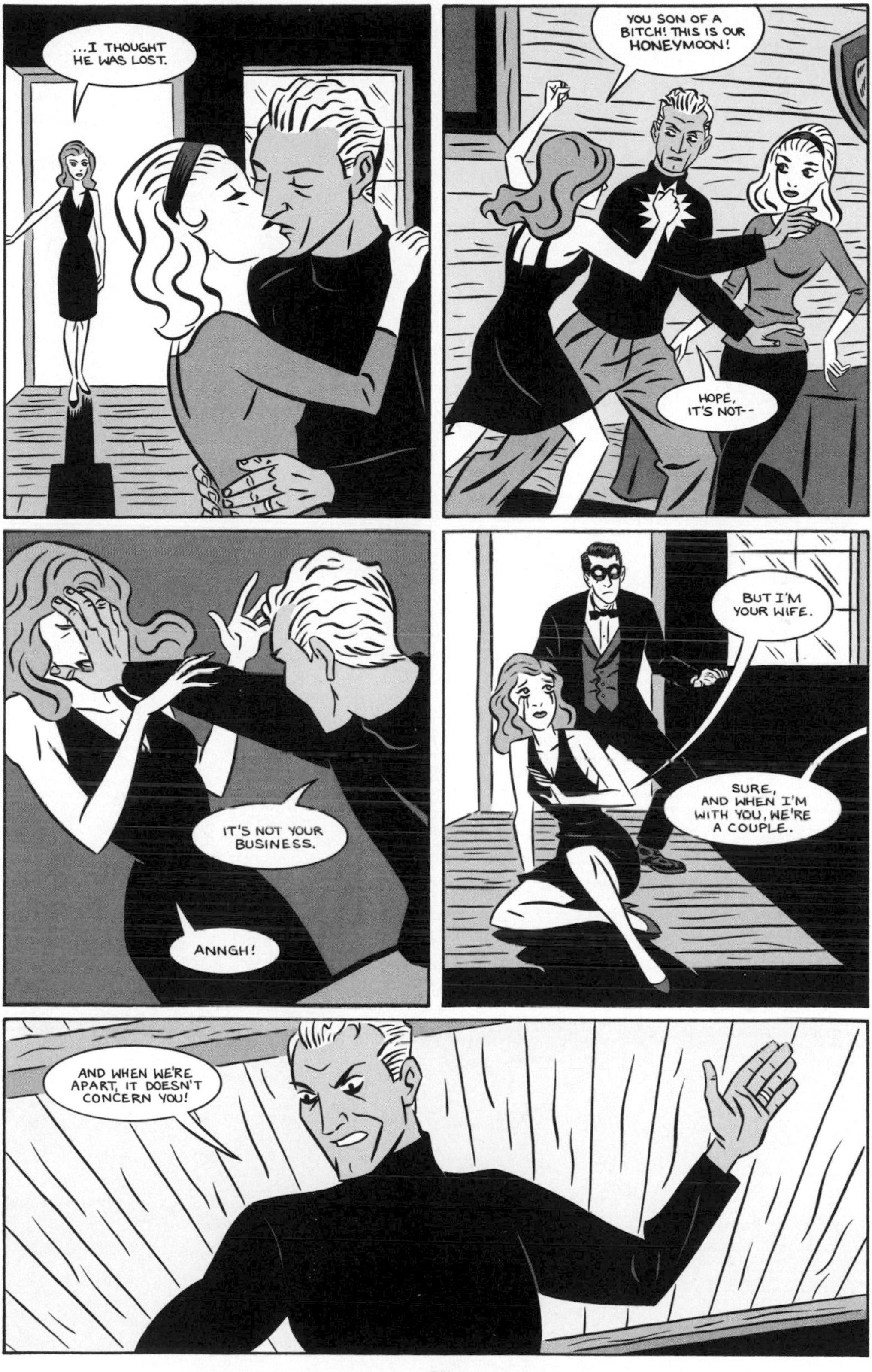
...I THOUGHT HE WAS LOST.
YOU SON OF A BITCH! THIS IS OUR HONEYMOON!
HOPE, IT'S NOT--
IT'S NOT YOUR BUSINESS.
ANNGH!
BUT I'M YOUR WIFE.
SURE, AND WHEN I'M WITH YOU, WE'RE A COUPLE.
AND WHEN WE'RE APART, IT DOESN'T CONCERN YOU!

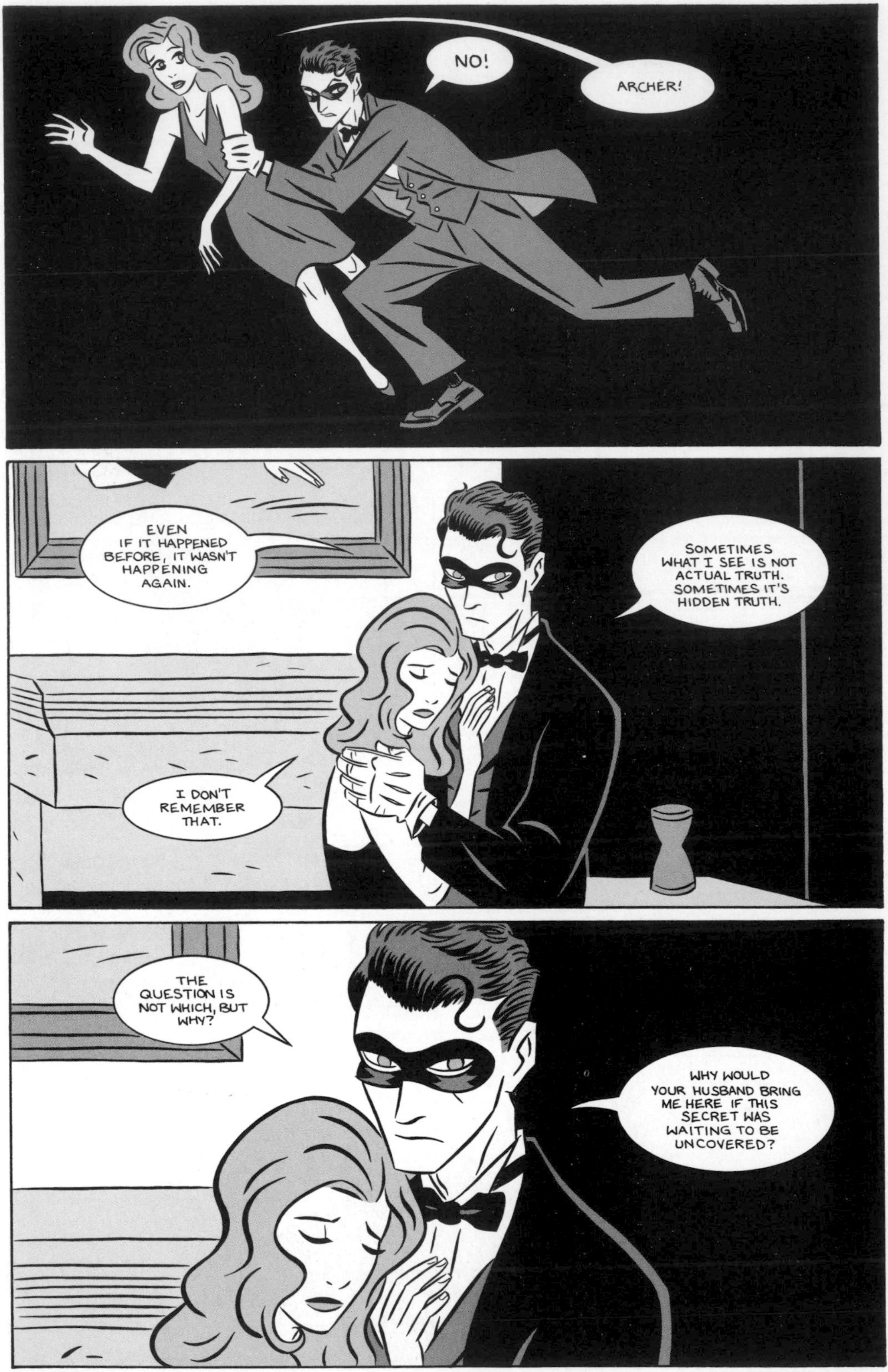
ARCHER!
NO!
EVEN IF IT HAPPENED BEFORE, IT WASN'T HAPPENING AGAIN.
SOMETIMES WHAT I SEE IS NOT ACTUAL TRUTH. SOMETIMES IT'S HIDDEN TRUTH.
I DON'T REMEMBER THAT.
THE QUESTION IS NOT WHICH, BUT WHY?
WHY WOULD YOUR HUSBAND BRING ME HERE IF THIS SECRET WAS WAITING TO BE UNCOVERED?

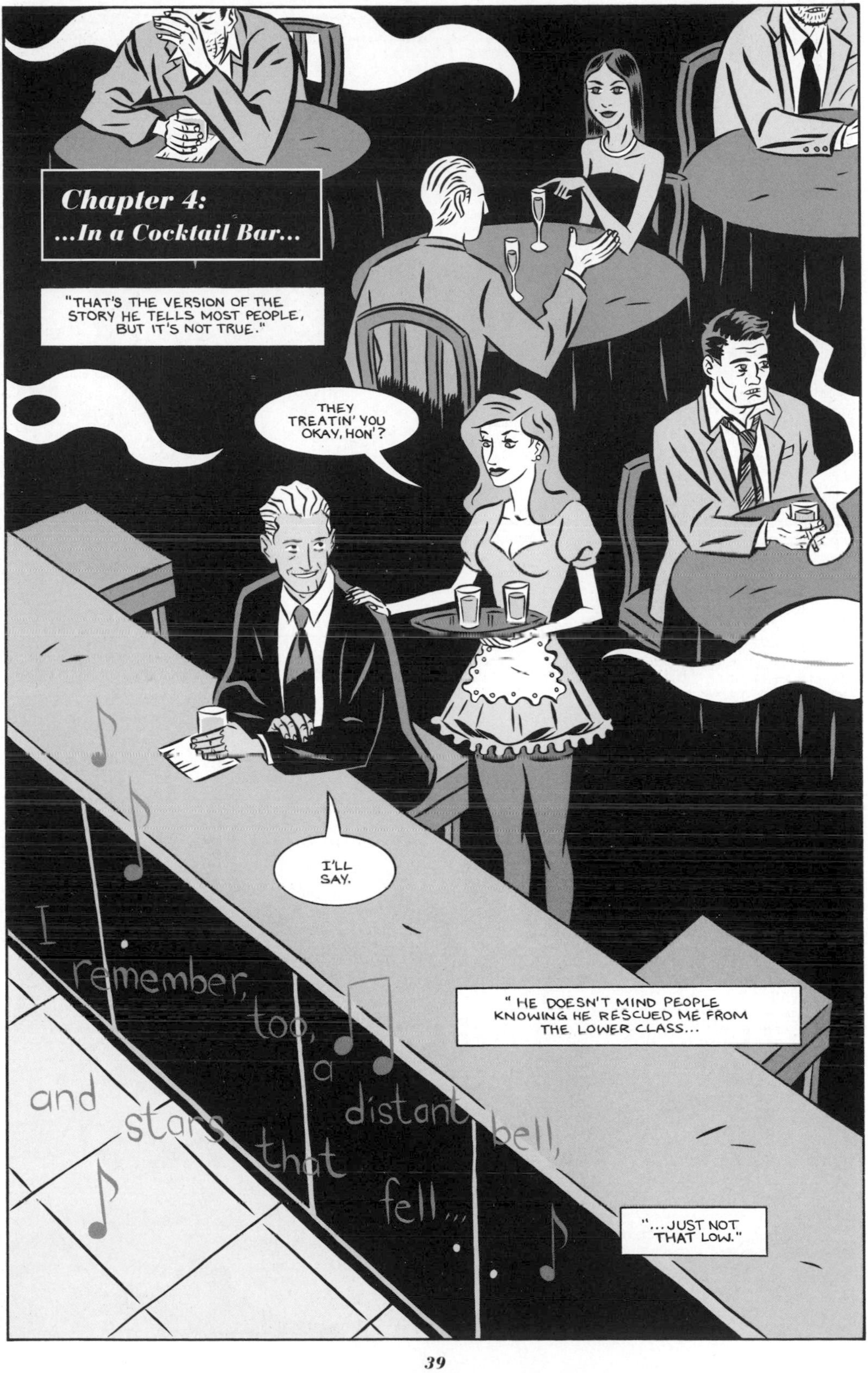
Chapter 4:
...In a Cocktail Bar...
"THAT'S THE VERSION OF THE STORY HE TELLS MOST PEOPLE, BUT IT'S NOT TRUE."
THEY TREATIN' YOU OKAY, HON'?
I'LL SAY.
I remember, too, a distant bell, and stars that fell...
"HE DOESN'T MIND PEOPLE KNOWING HE RESCUED ME FROM THE LOWER CLASS...
"...JUST NOT THAT LOW."

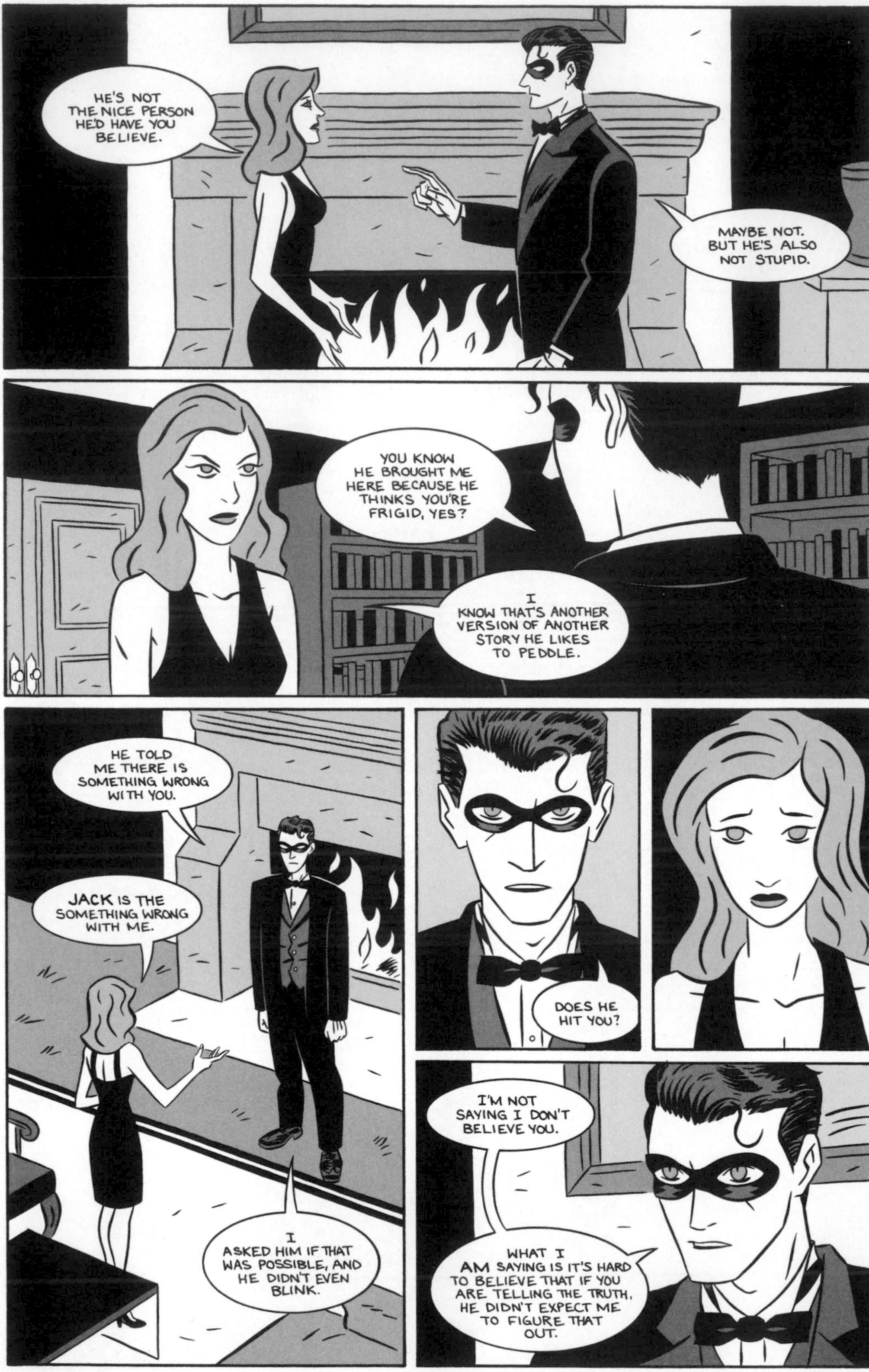
HE'S NOT THE NICE PERSON HE'D HAVE YOU BELIEVE.
MAYBE NOT. BUT HE'S ALSO NOT STUPID.
YOU KNOW HE BROUGHT ME HERE BECAUSE HE THINKS YOU'RE FRIGID, YES?
I KNOW THAT'S ANOTHER VERSION OF ANOTHER STORY HE LIKES TO PEDDLE.
HE TOLD ME THERE IS SOMETHING WRONG WITH YOU.
JACK IS THE SOMETHING WRONG WITH ME.
I ASKED HIM IF THAT WAS POSSIBLE, AND HE DIDN'T EVEN BLINK.
DOES HE HIT YOU?
I'M NOT SAYING I DON'T BELIEVE YOU.
WHAT I AM SAYING IS IT'S HARD TO BELIEVE THAT IF YOU ARE TELLING THE TRUTH, HE DIDN'T EXPECT ME TO FIGURE THAT OUT.

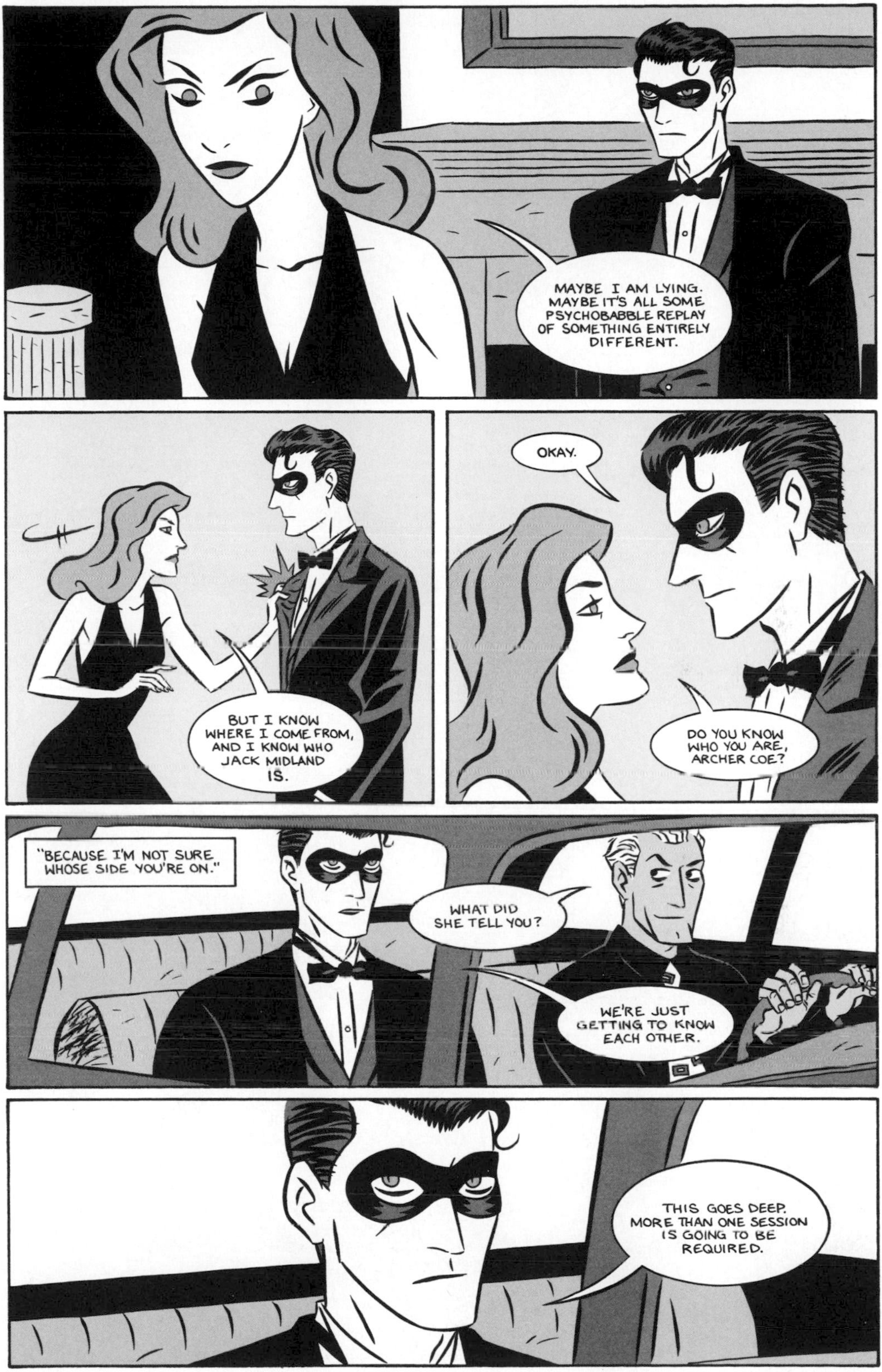
MAYBE I AM LYING. MAYBE IT'S ALL SOME PSYCHOBABBLE REPLAY OF SOMETHING ENTIRELY DIFFERENT.
BUT I KNOW WHERE I COME FROM, AND I KNOW WHO JACK MIDLAND IS.
OKAY.
DO YOU KNOW WHO YOU ARE, ARCHER COE?
"BECAUSE I'M NOT SURE WHOSE SIDE YOU'RE ON."
WHAT DID SHE TELL YOU?
WE'RE JUST GETTING TO KNOW EACH OTHER.
THIS GOES DEEP. MORE THAN ONE SESSION IS GOING TO BE REQUIRED.

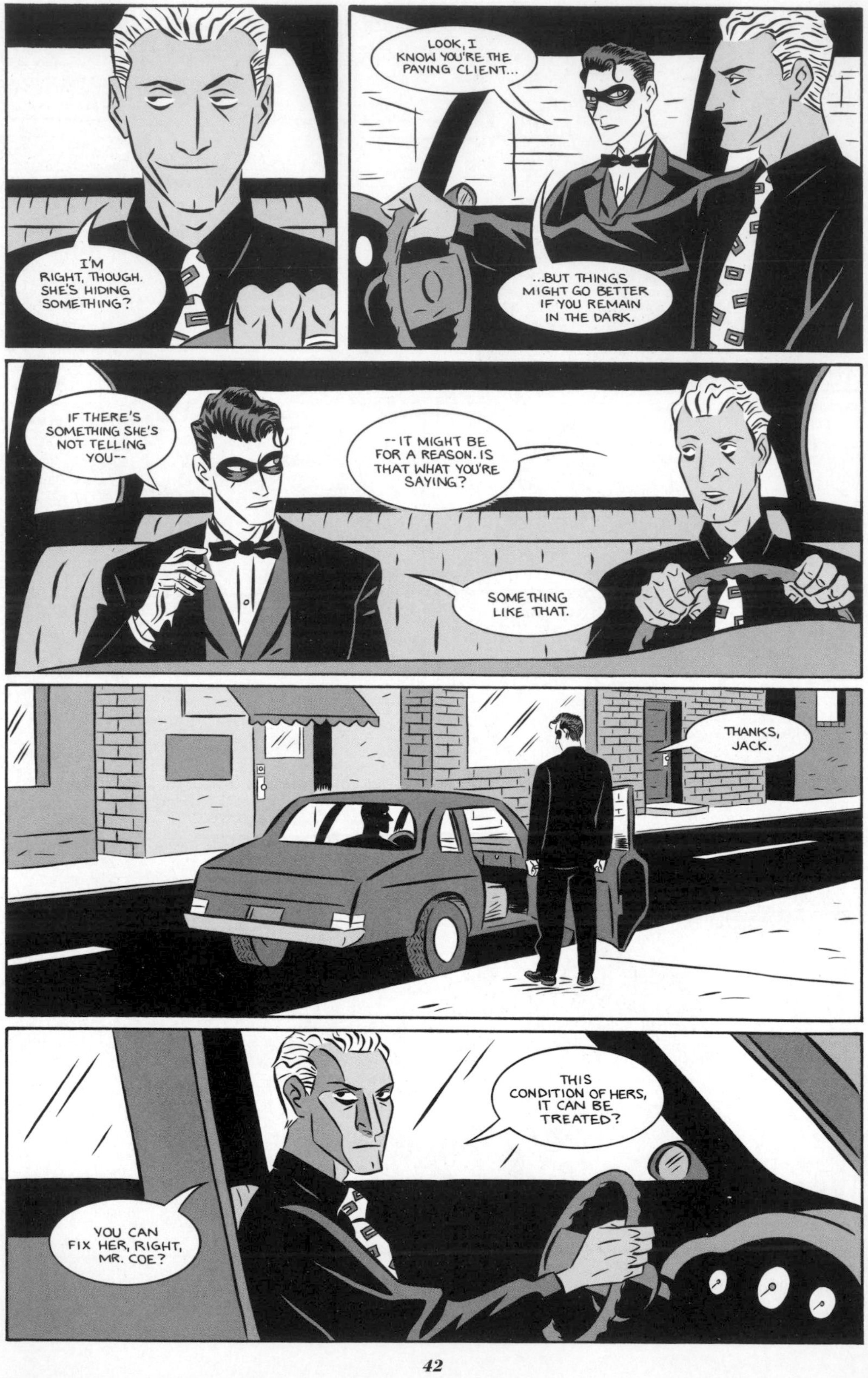
I'M RIGHT, THOUGH. SHE'S HIDING SOMETHING?
LOOK, I KNOW YOU'RE THE PAYING CLIENT...
...BUT THINGS MIGHT GO BETTER IF YOU REMAIN IN THE DARK.
IF THERE'S SOMETHING SHE'S NOT TELLING YOU--
--IT MIGHT BE FOR A REASON. IS THAT WHAT YOU'RE SAYING?
SOMETHING LIKE THAT.
THANKS, JACK.
THIS CONDITION OF HERS, IT CAN BE TREATED?
YOU CAN FIX HER, RIGHT, MR. COE?

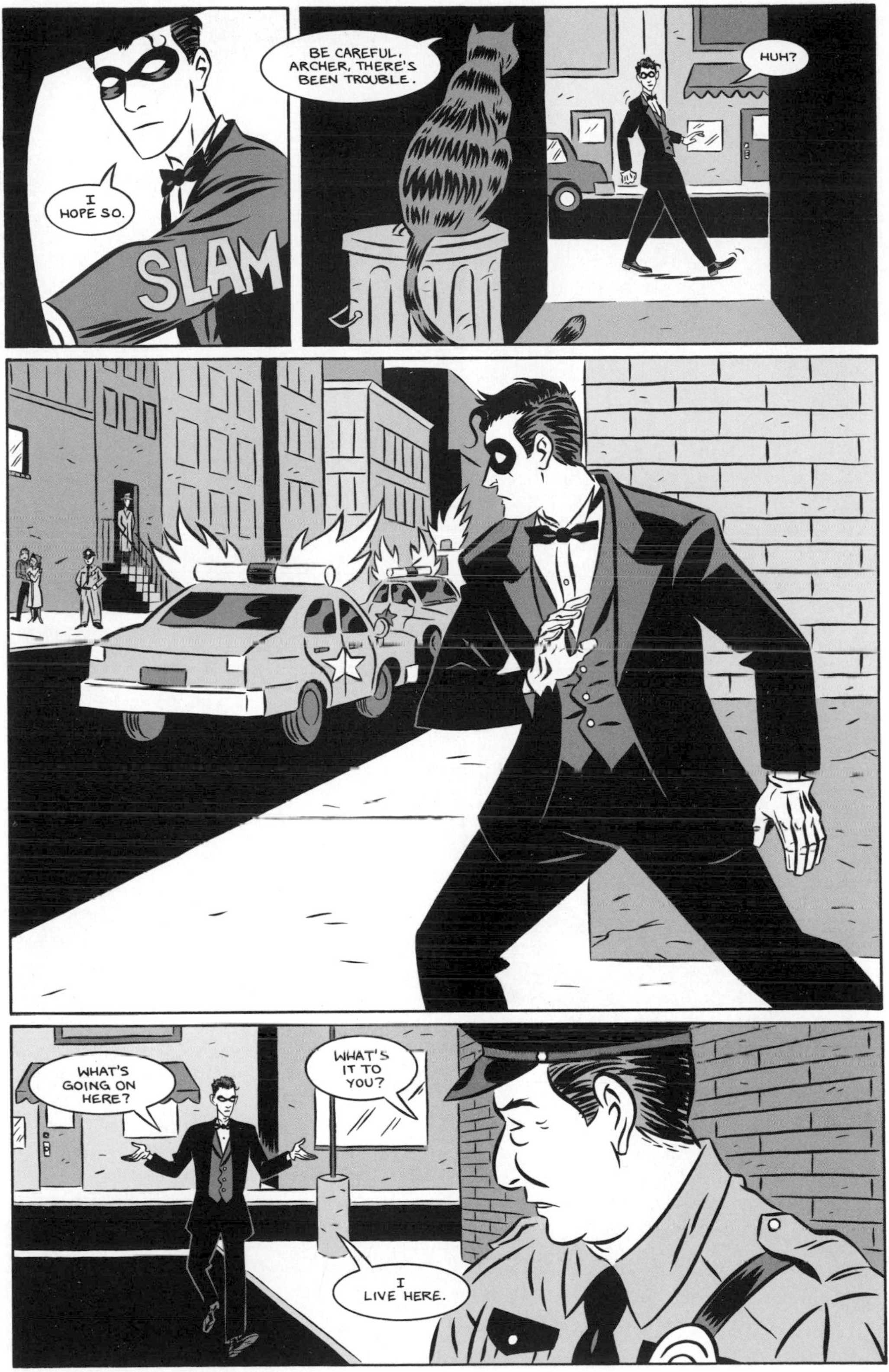
I HOPE SO.
SLAM
BE CAREFUL, ARCHER, THERE'S BEEN TROUBLE.
HUH?
WHAT'S GOING ON HERE?
WHAT'S IT TO YOU?
I LIVE HERE.

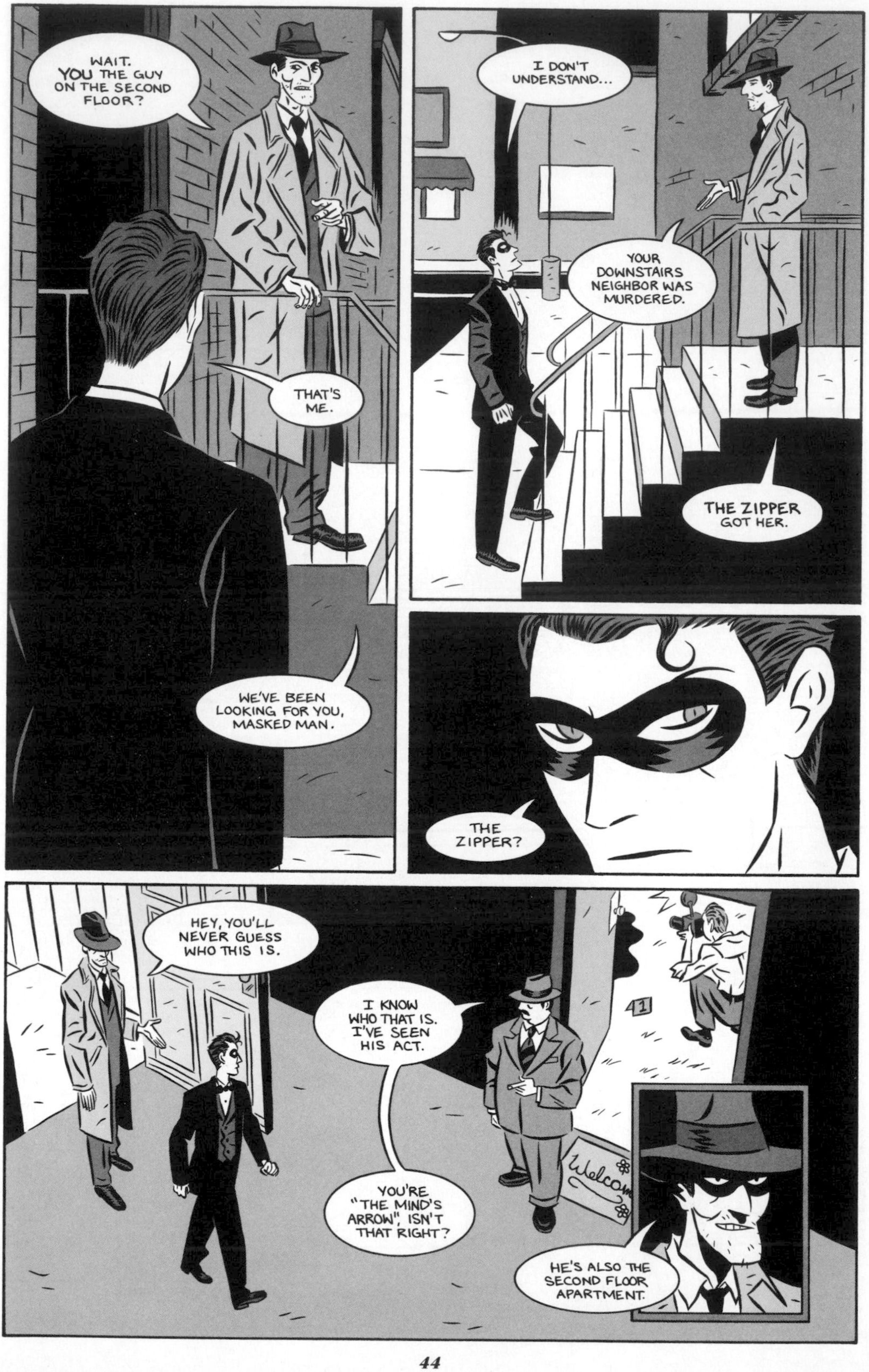

WAIT. YOU THE GUY ON THE SECOND FLOOR?
THAT'S ME.
WE'VE BEEN LOOKING FOR YOU, MASKED MAN.
I DON'T UNDERSTAND...
YOUR DOWNSTAIRS NEIGHBOR WAS MURDERED.
THE ZIPPER GOT HER.
THE ZIPPER?
HEY, YOU'LL NEVER GUESS WHO THIS IS.
I KNOW WHO THAT IS. I'VE SEEN HIS ACT.
YOU'RE "THE MIND'S ARROW", ISN'T THAT RIGHT?
HE'S ALSO THE SECOND FLOOR APARTMENT.

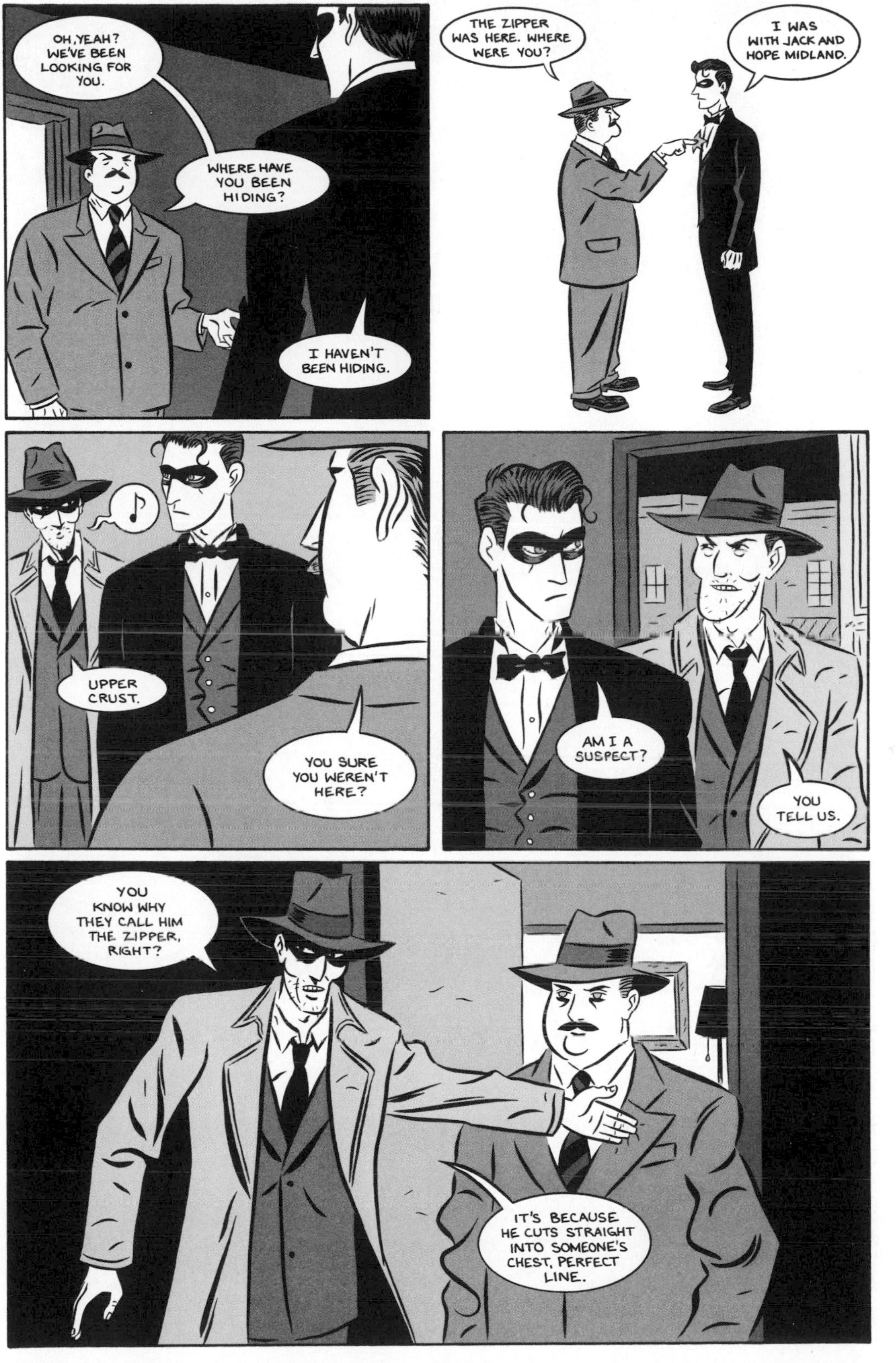
OH, YEAH? WE'VE BEEN LOOKING FOR YOU.
WHERE HAVE YOU BEEN HIDING?
I HAVEN'T BEEN HIDING.
THE ZIPPER WAS HERE. WHERE WERE YOU?
I WAS WITH JACK AND HOPE MIDLAND.
♪
UPPER CRUST.
YOU SURE YOU WEREN'T HERE?
AM I A SUSPECT?
YOU TELL US.
YOU KNOW WHY THEY CALL HIM THE ZIPPER, RIGHT?
IT'S BECAUSE HE CUTS STRAIGHT INTO SOMEONE'S CHEST, PERFECT LINE.

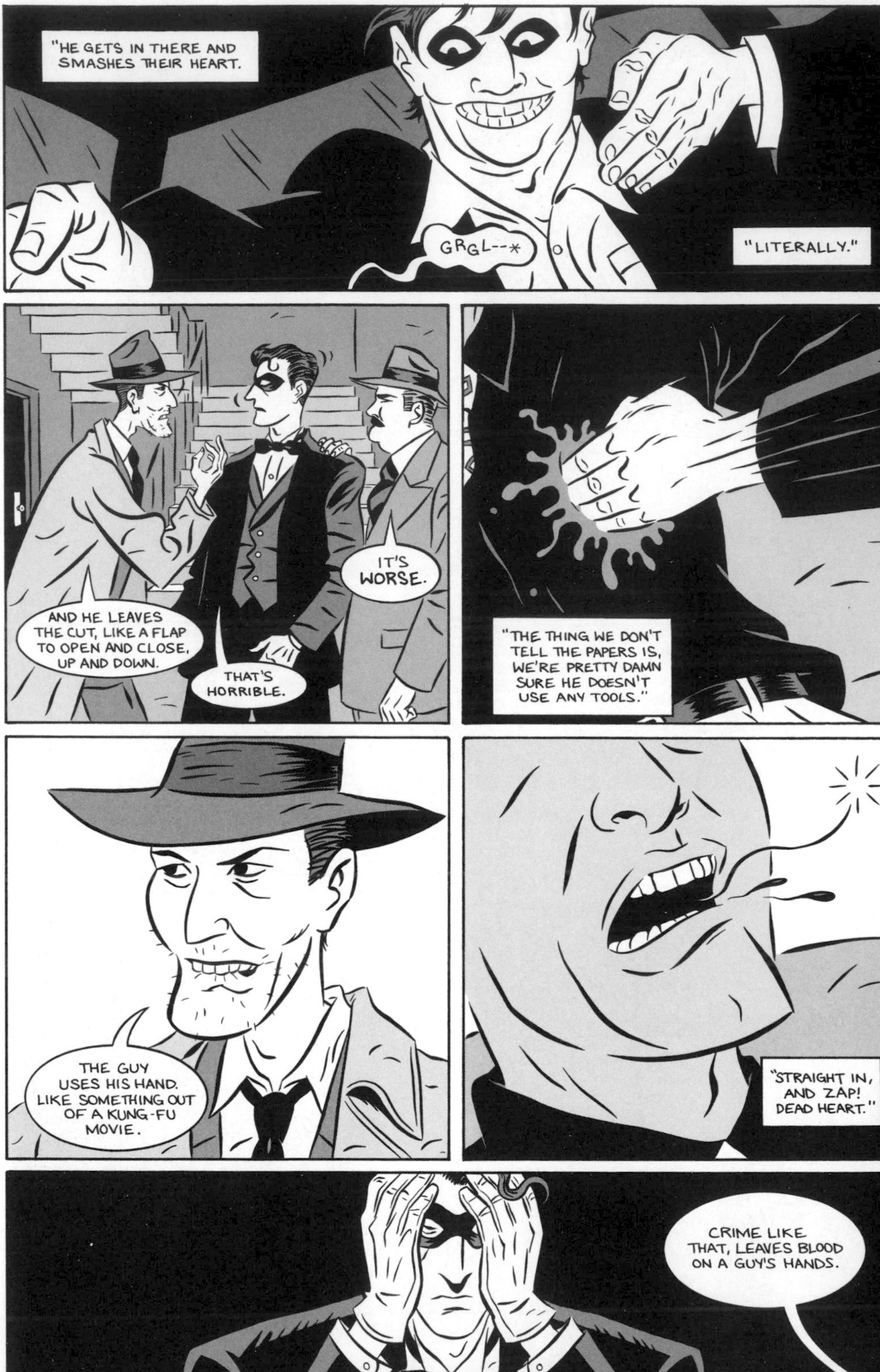
"HE GETS IN THERE AND SMASHES THEIR HEART.
GRGL--*
"LITERALLY."
AND HE LEAVES THE CUT, LIKE A FLAP TO OPEN AND CLOSE, UP AND DOWN.
THAT'S HORRIBLE.
IT'S WORSE.
"THE THING WE DON'T TELL THE PAPERS IS, WE'RE PRETTY DAMN SURE HE DOESN'T USE ANY TOOLS."
THE GUY USES HIS HAND. LIKE SOMETHING OUT OF A KUNG-FU MOVIE.
"STRAIGHT IN, AND ZAP! DEAD HEART."
CRIME LIKE THAT, LEAVES BLOOD ON A GUY'S HANDS.

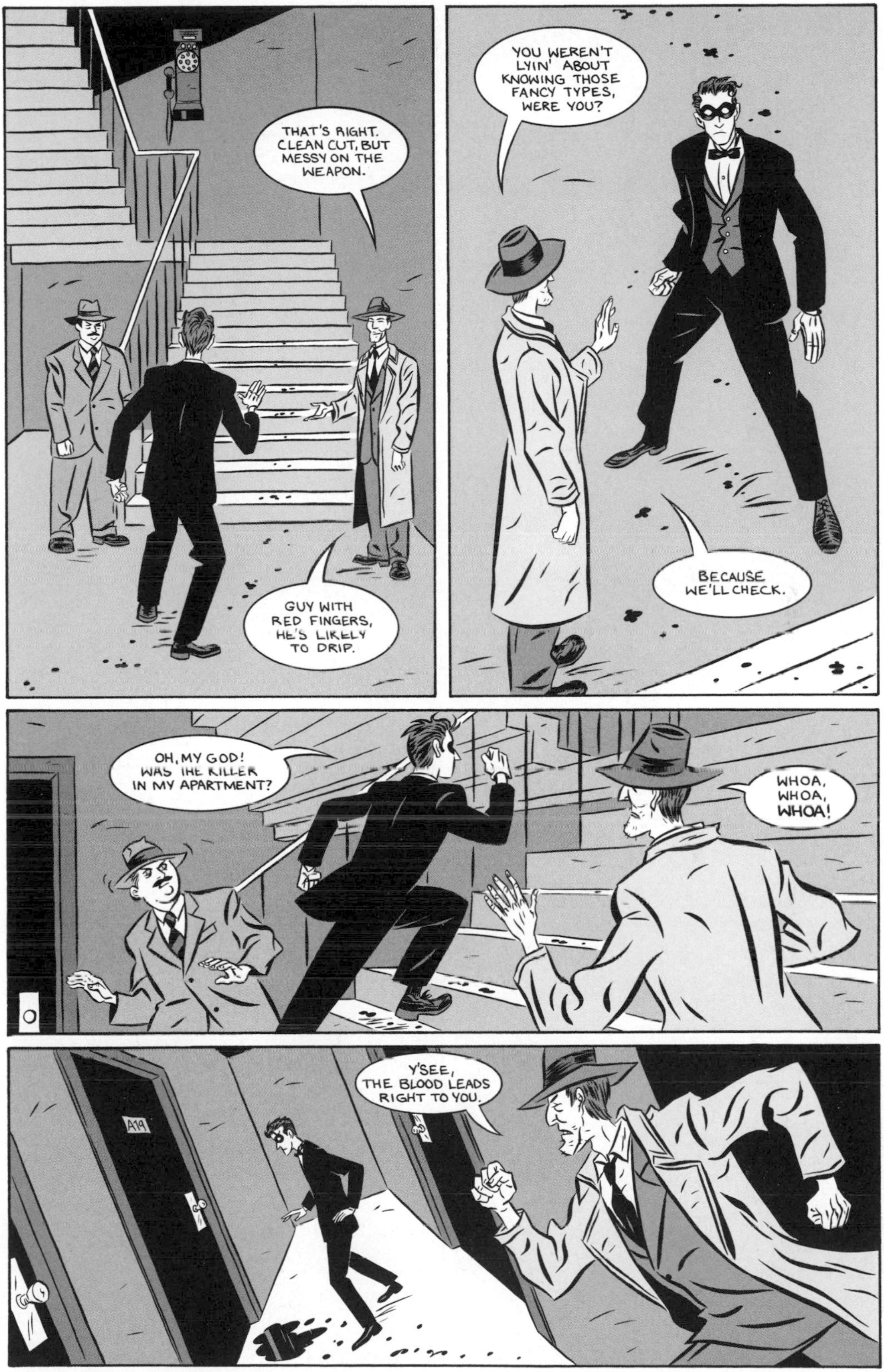
THAT'S RIGHT. CLEAN CUT, BUT MESSY ON THE WEAPON.
GUY WITH RED FINGERS, HE'S LIKELY TO DRIP.
YOU WEREN'T LYIN' ABOUT KNOWING THOSE FANCY TYPES, WERE YOU?
BECAUSE WE'LL CHECK.
OH, MY GOD! WAS THE KILLER IN MY APARTMENT?
WHOA, WHOA, WHOA!
Y'SEE, THE BLOOD LEADS RIGHT TO YOU.
A19

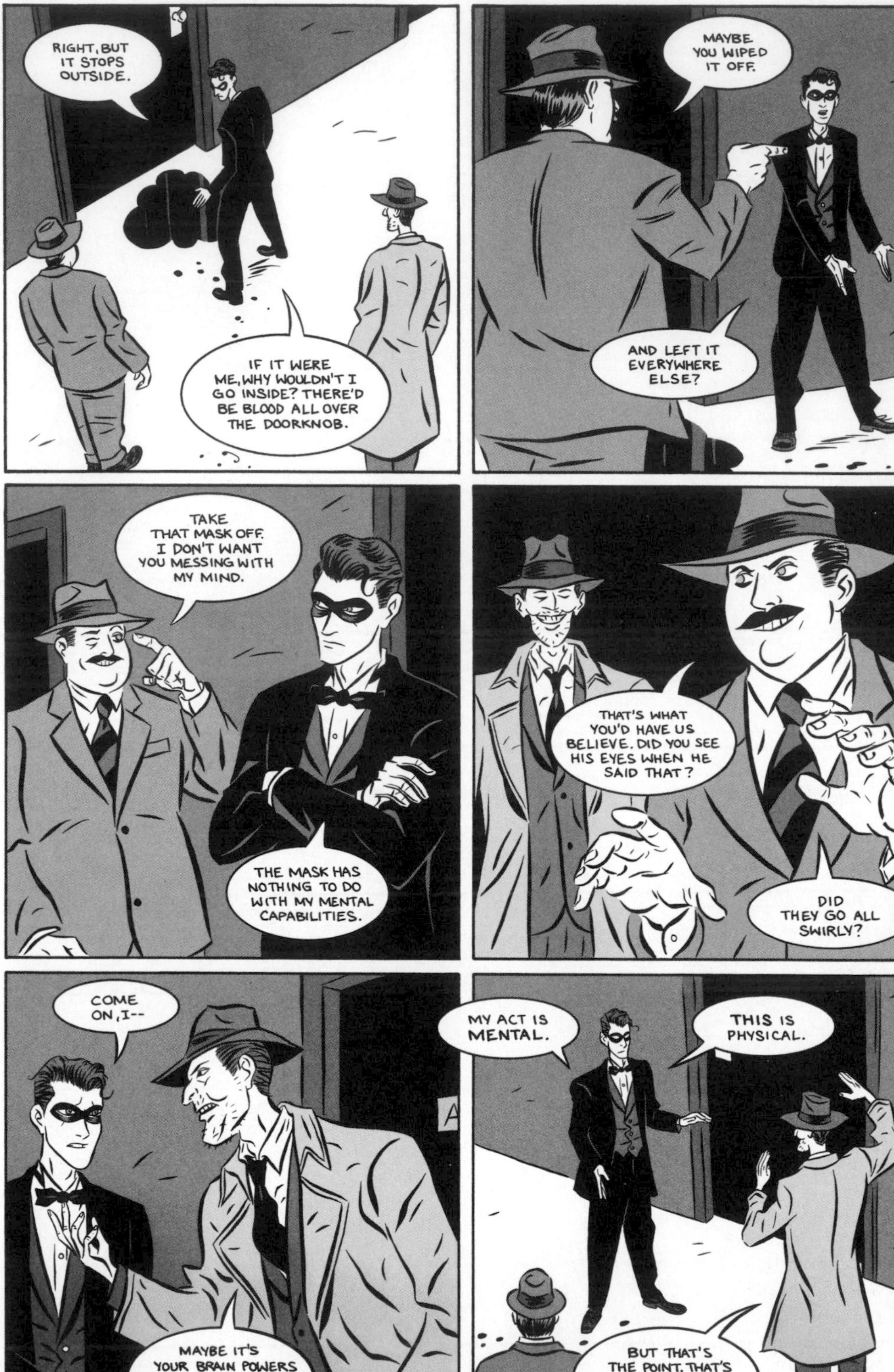
RIGHT, BUT IT STOPS OUTSIDE.
IF IT WERE ME, WHY WOULDN'T I GO INSIDE? THERE'D BE BLOOD ALL OVER THE DOORKNOB.
MAYBE YOU WIPED IT OFF.
AND LEFT IT EVERYWHERE ELSE?
TAKE THAT MASK OFF. I DON'T WANT YOU MESSING WITH MY MIND.
THE MASK HAS NOTHING TO DO WITH MY MENTAL CAPABILITIES.
THAT'S WHAT YOU'D HAVE US BELIEVE. DID YOU SEE HIS EYES WHEN HE SAID THAT?
DID THEY GO ALL SWIRLY?
COME ON, I--
MAYBE IT'S YOUR BRAIN POWERS THAT ALLOW YOU TO PIERCE THE CHESTS OF YOUR VICTIMS.
MY ACT IS MENTAL.
THIS IS PHYSICAL.
BUT THAT'S THE POINT. THAT'S HOW THE KARATE GUYS BREAK BOARDS AND STUFF.

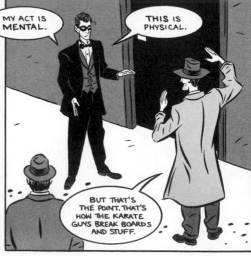

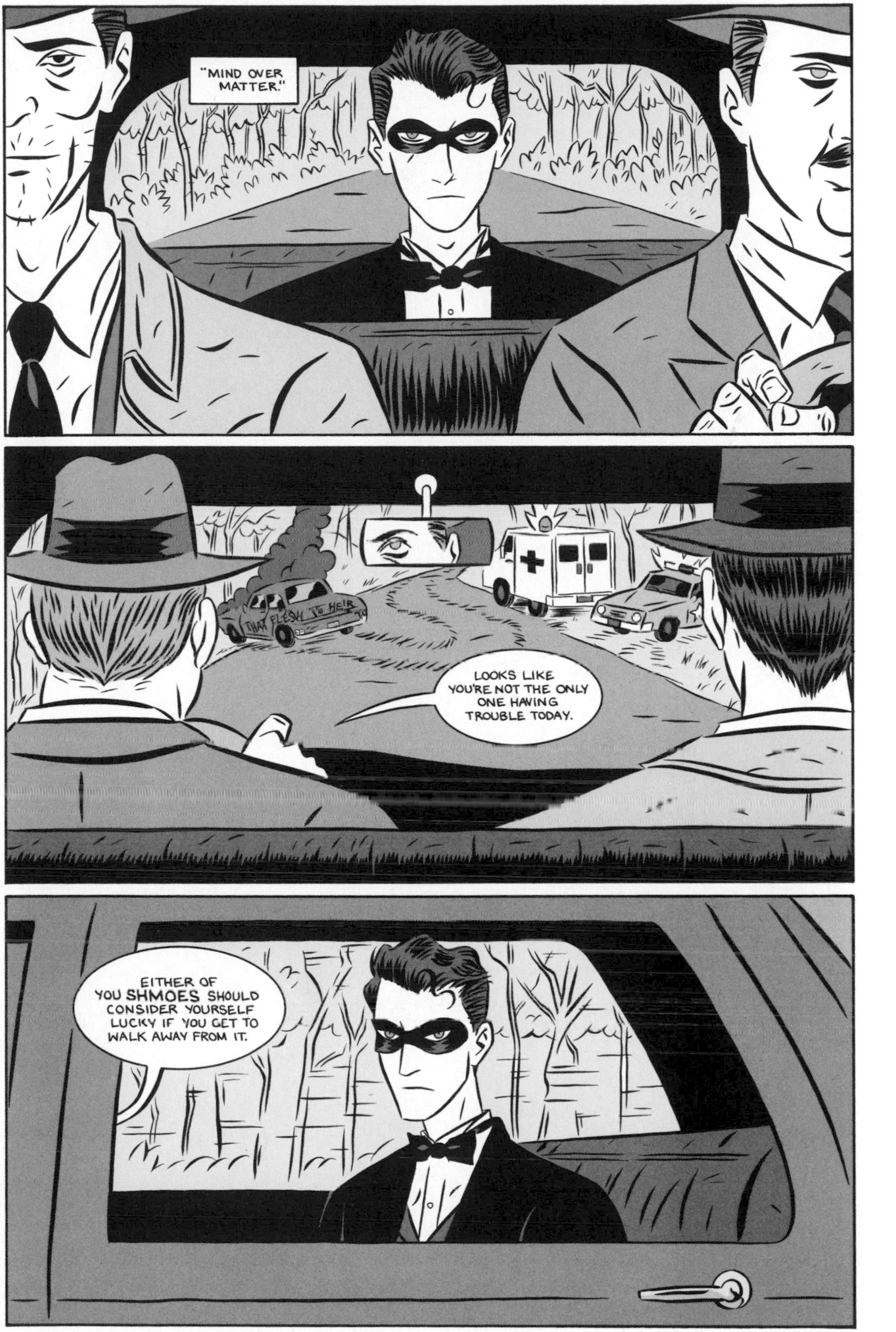
"MIND OVER MATTER."
LOOKS LIKE YOU'RE NOT THE ONLY ONE HAVING TROUBLE TODAY.
EITHER OF YOU SHMOES SHOULD CONSIDER YOURSELF LUCKY IF YOU GET TO WALK AWAY FROM IT.

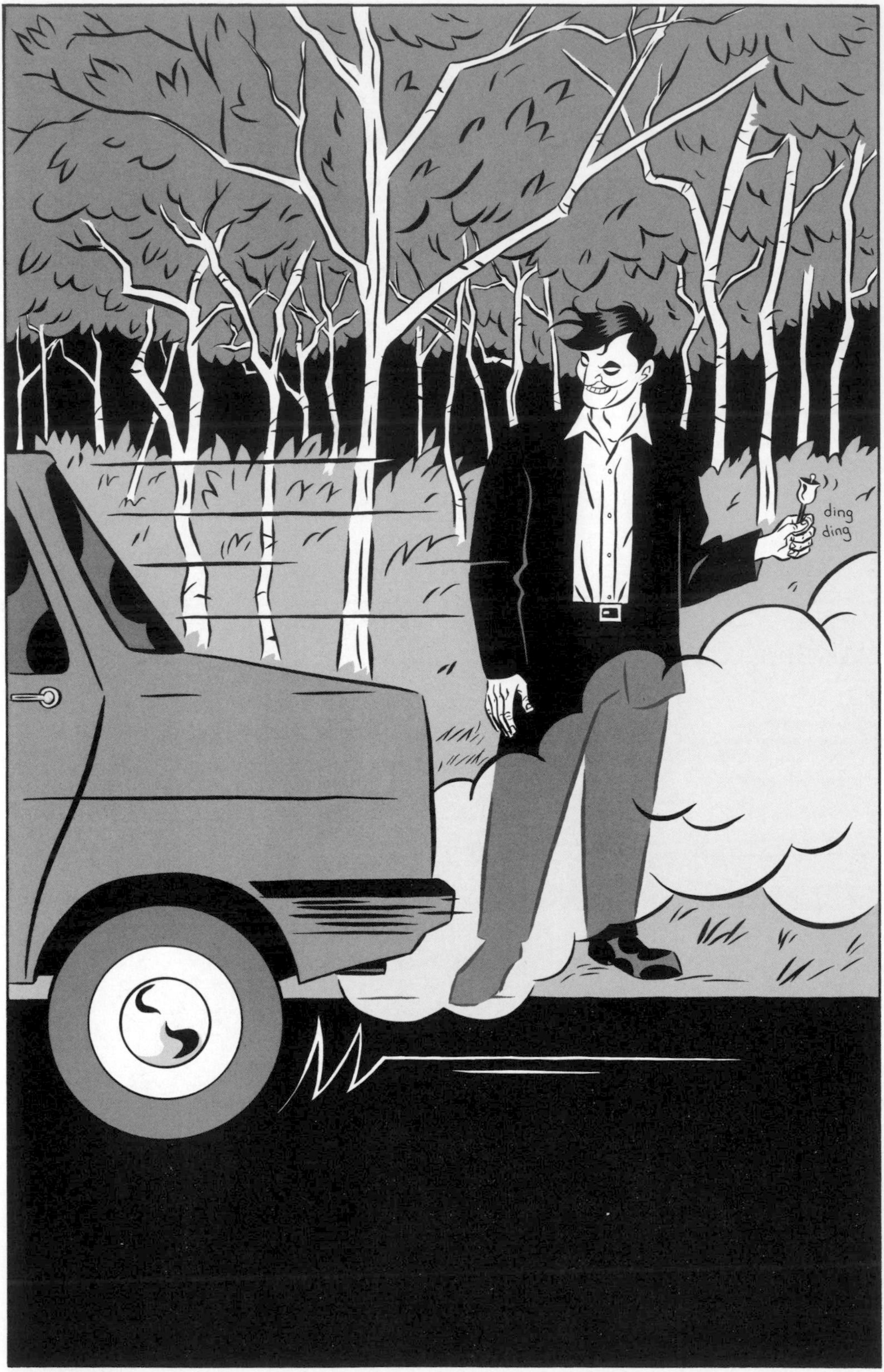
ding
ding

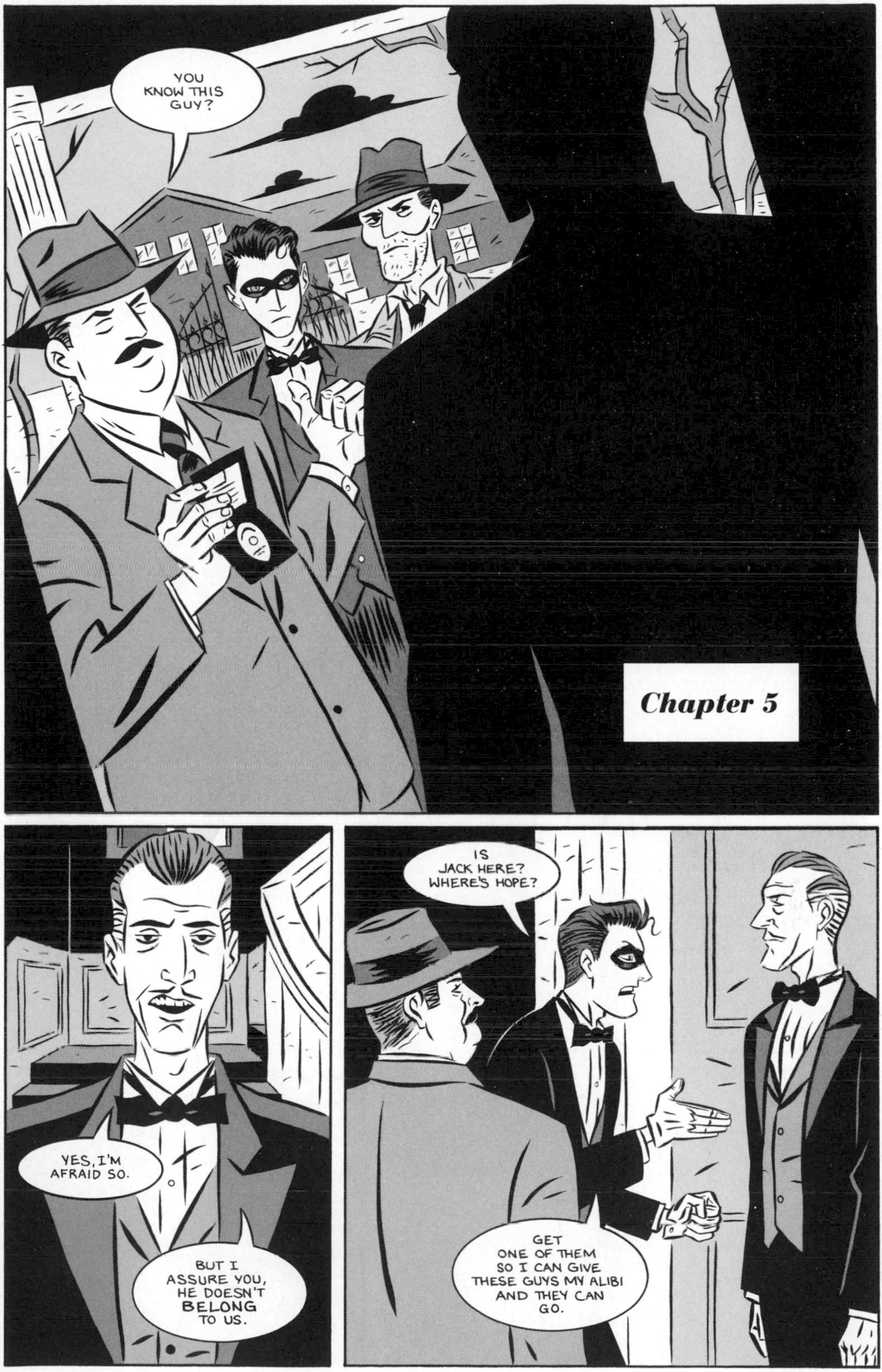
YOU KNOW THIS GUY?
Chapter 5
YES, I'M AFRAID SO.
BUT I ASSURE YOU, HE DOESN'T BELONG TO US.
IS JACK HERE? WHERE'S HOPE?
GET ONE OF THEM SO I CAN GIVE THESE GUYS MY ALIBI AND THEY CAN GO.

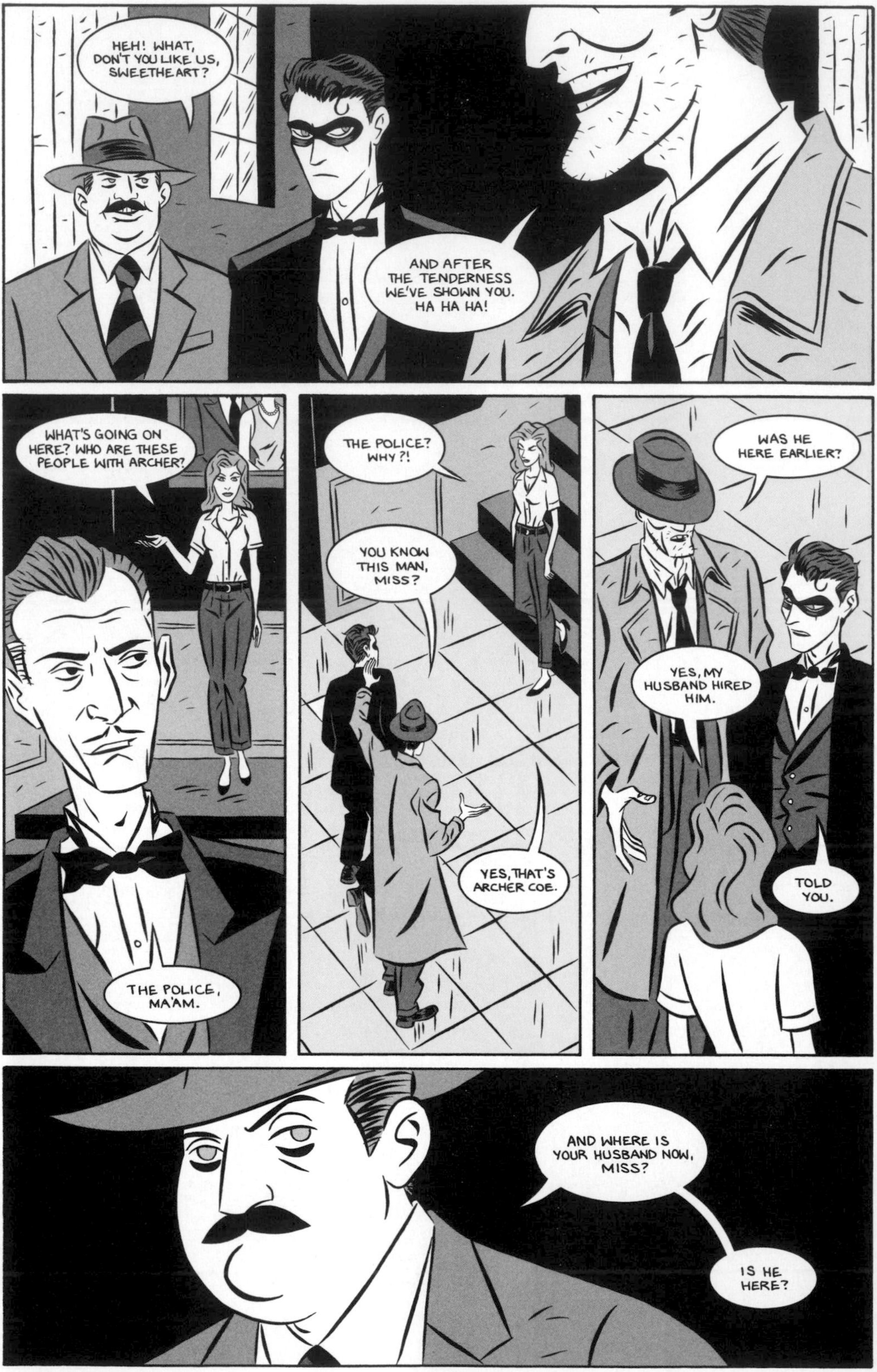
HEH! WHAT, DON'T YOU LIKE US, SWEETHEART?
AND AFTER THE TENDERNESS WE'VE SHOWN YOU. HA HA HA!
WHAT'S GOING ON HERE? WHO ARE THESE PEOPLE WITH ARCHER?
THE POLICE, MA'AM.
THE POLICE? WHY?!
YOU KNOW THIS MAN, MISS?
YES, THAT'S ARCHER COE.
WAS HE HERE EARLIER?
YES, MY HUSBAND HIRED HIM.
TOLD YOU.
AND WHERE IS YOUR HUSBAND NOW, MISS?
IS HE HERE?

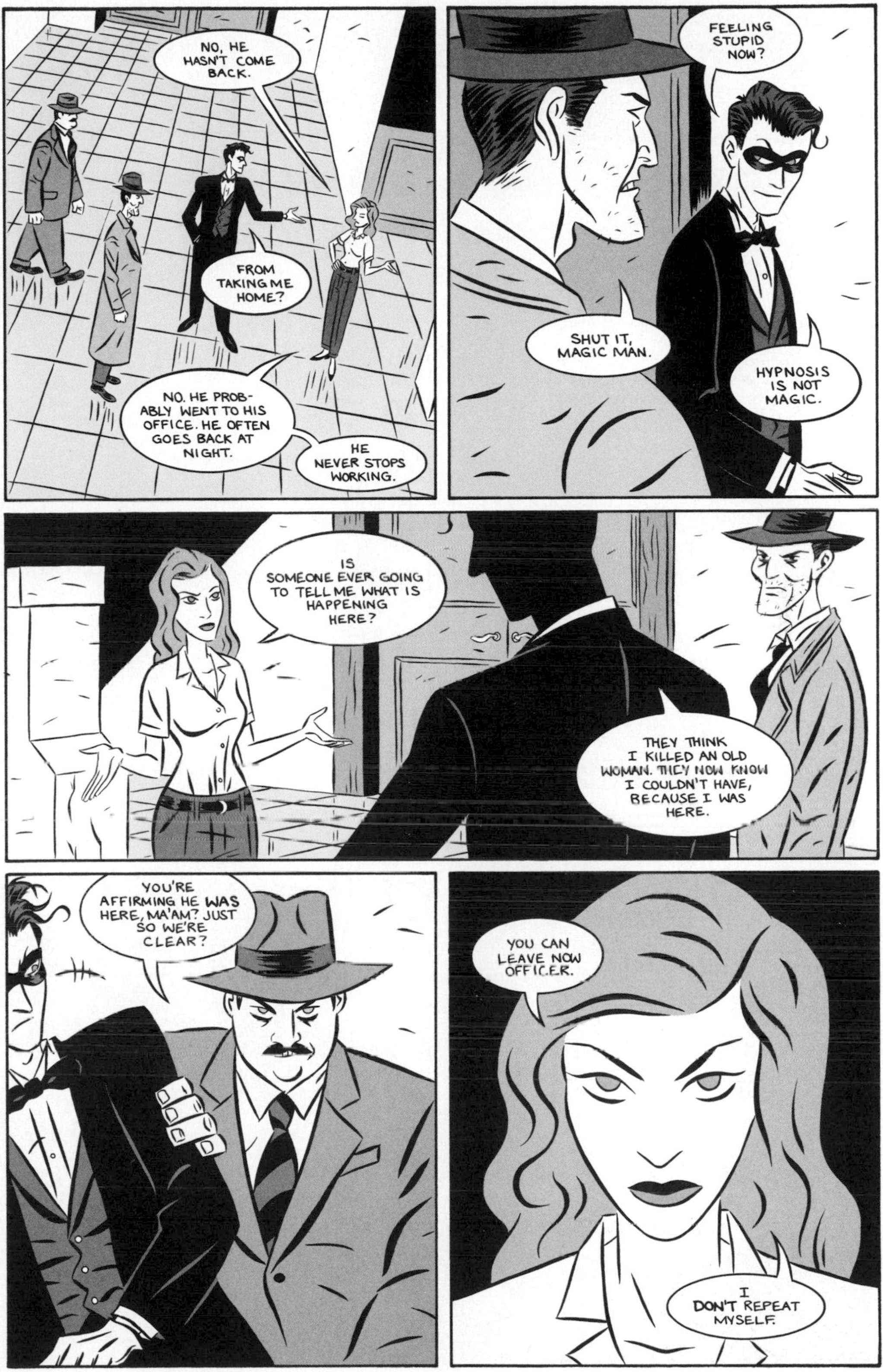
NO, HE HASN'T COME BACK.
FROM TAKING ME HOME?
NO. HE PROBABLY WENT TO HIS OFFICE. HE OFTEN GOES BACK AT NIGHT.
HE NEVER STOPS WORKING.
FEELING STUPID NOW?
SHUT IT, MAGIC MAN.
HYPNOSIS IS NOT MAGIC.
IS SOMEONE EVER GOING TO TELL ME WHAT IS HAPPENING HERE?
THEY THINK I KILLED AN OLD WOMAN. THEY NOW KNOW I COULDN'T HAVE, BECAUSE I WAS HERE.
YOU'RE AFFIRMING HE **WAS** HERE, MA'AM? JUST SO WE'RE CLEAR?
YOU CAN LEAVE NOW OFFICER.
I **DON'T** REPEAT MYSELF.

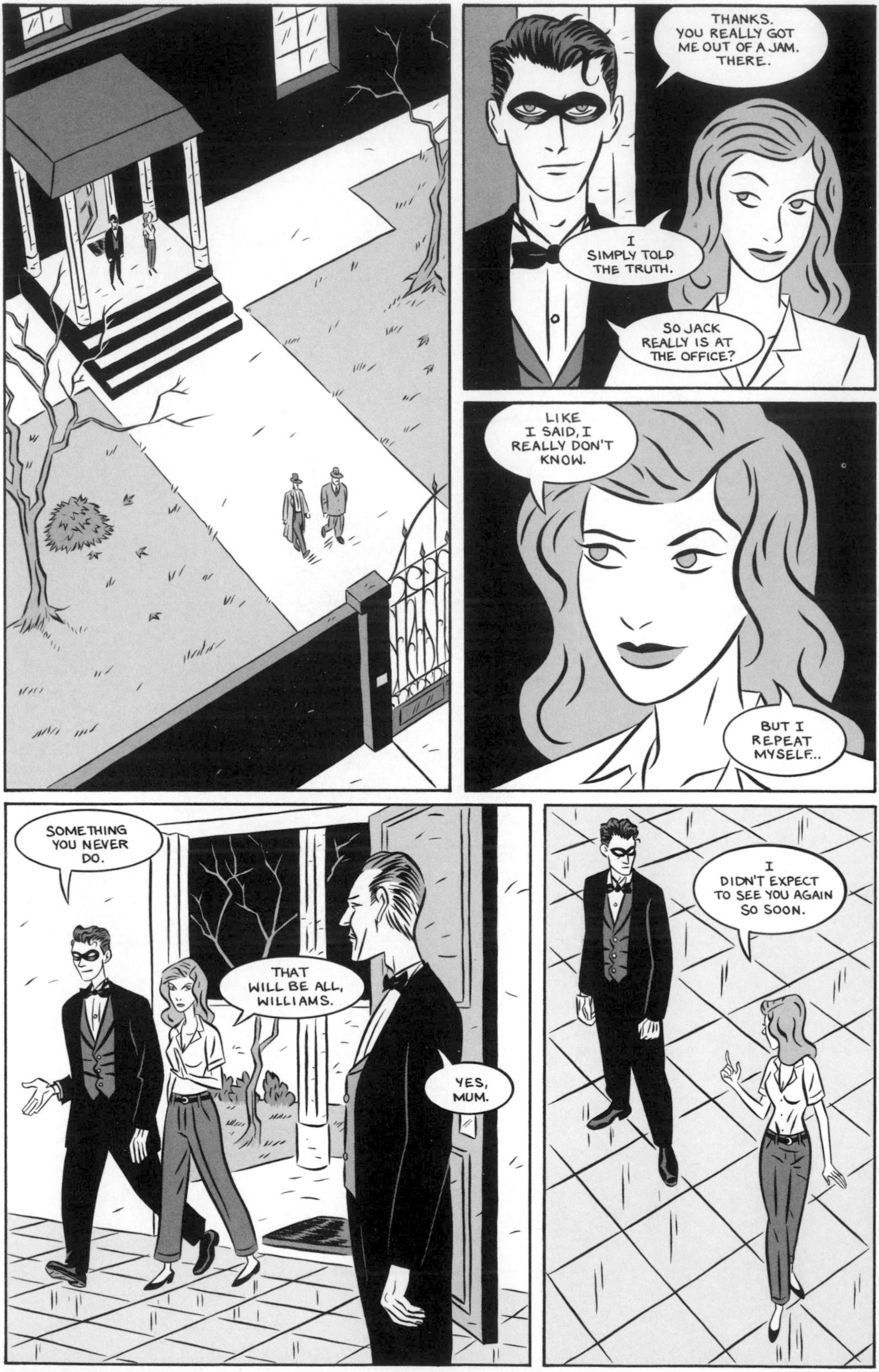
THANKS. YOU REALLY GOT ME OUT OF A JAM. THERE.
I SIMPLY TOLD THE TRUTH.
SO JACK REALLY IS AT THE OFFICE?
LIKE I SAID, I REALLY DON'T KNOW.
BUT I REPEAT MYSELF..
SOMETHING YOU NEVER DO.
THAT WILL BE ALL, WILLIAMS.
YES, MUM.
I DIDN'T EXPECT TO SEE YOU AGAIN SO SOON.

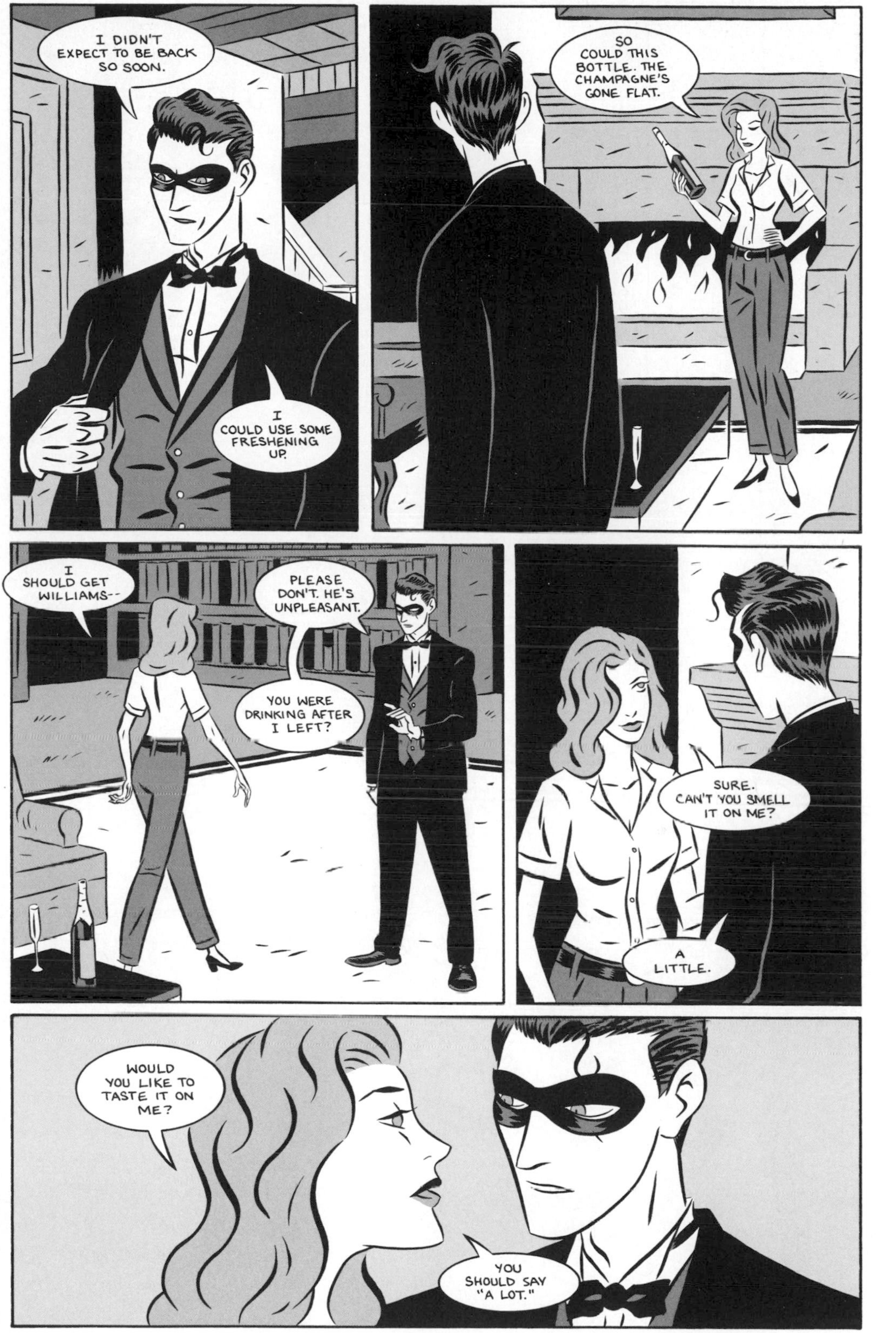

I DIDN'T EXPECT TO BE BACK SO SOON.
I COULD USE SOME FRESHENING UP.
SO COULD THIS BOTTLE. THE CHAMPAGNE'S GONE FLAT.
I SHOULD GET WILLIAMS--
PLEASE DON'T. HE'S UNPLEASANT.
YOU WERE DRINKING AFTER I LEFT?
SURE. CAN'T YOU SMELL IT ON ME?
A LITTLE.
WOULD YOU LIKE TO TASTE IT ON ME?
YOU SHOULD SAY "A LOT."

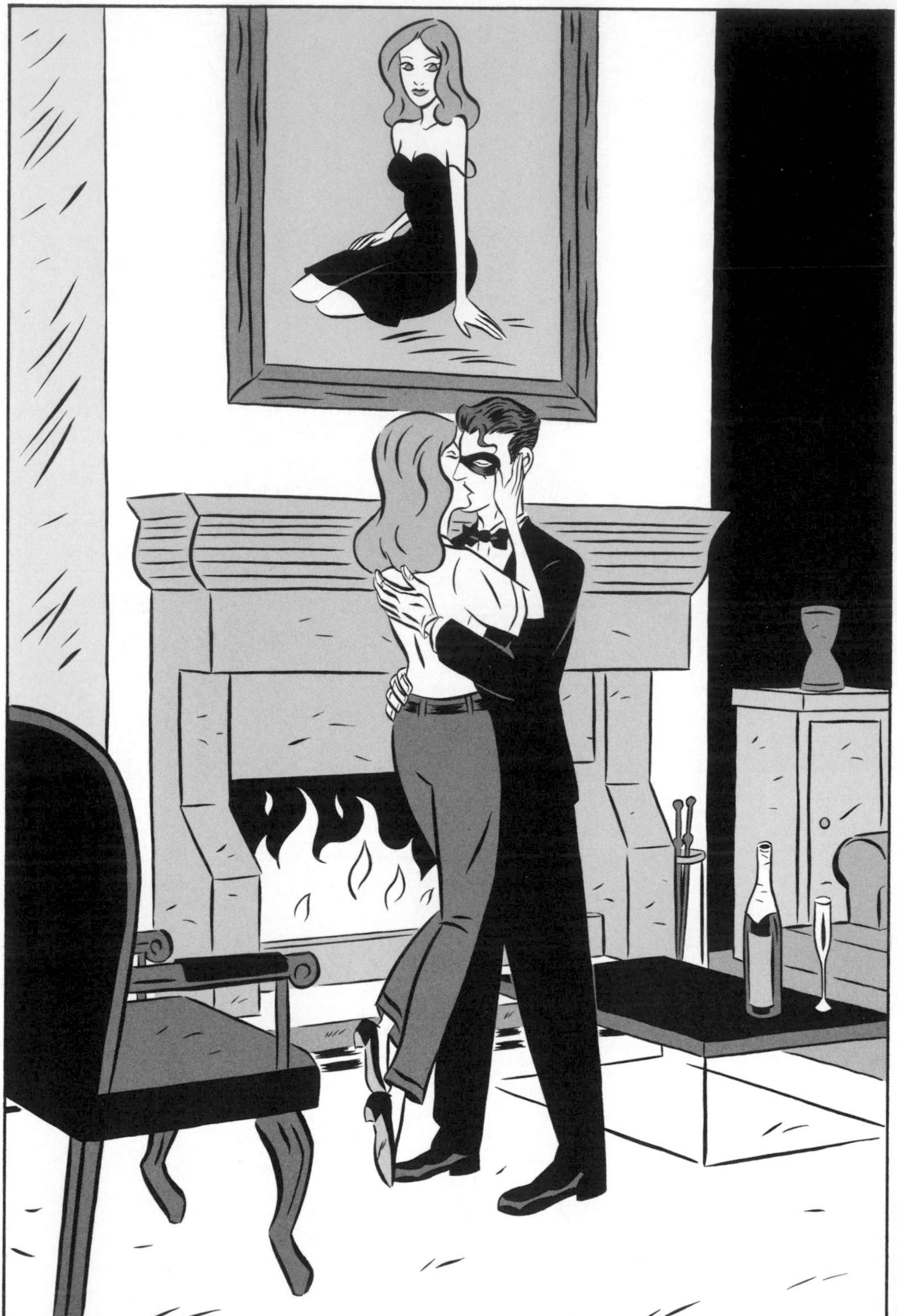

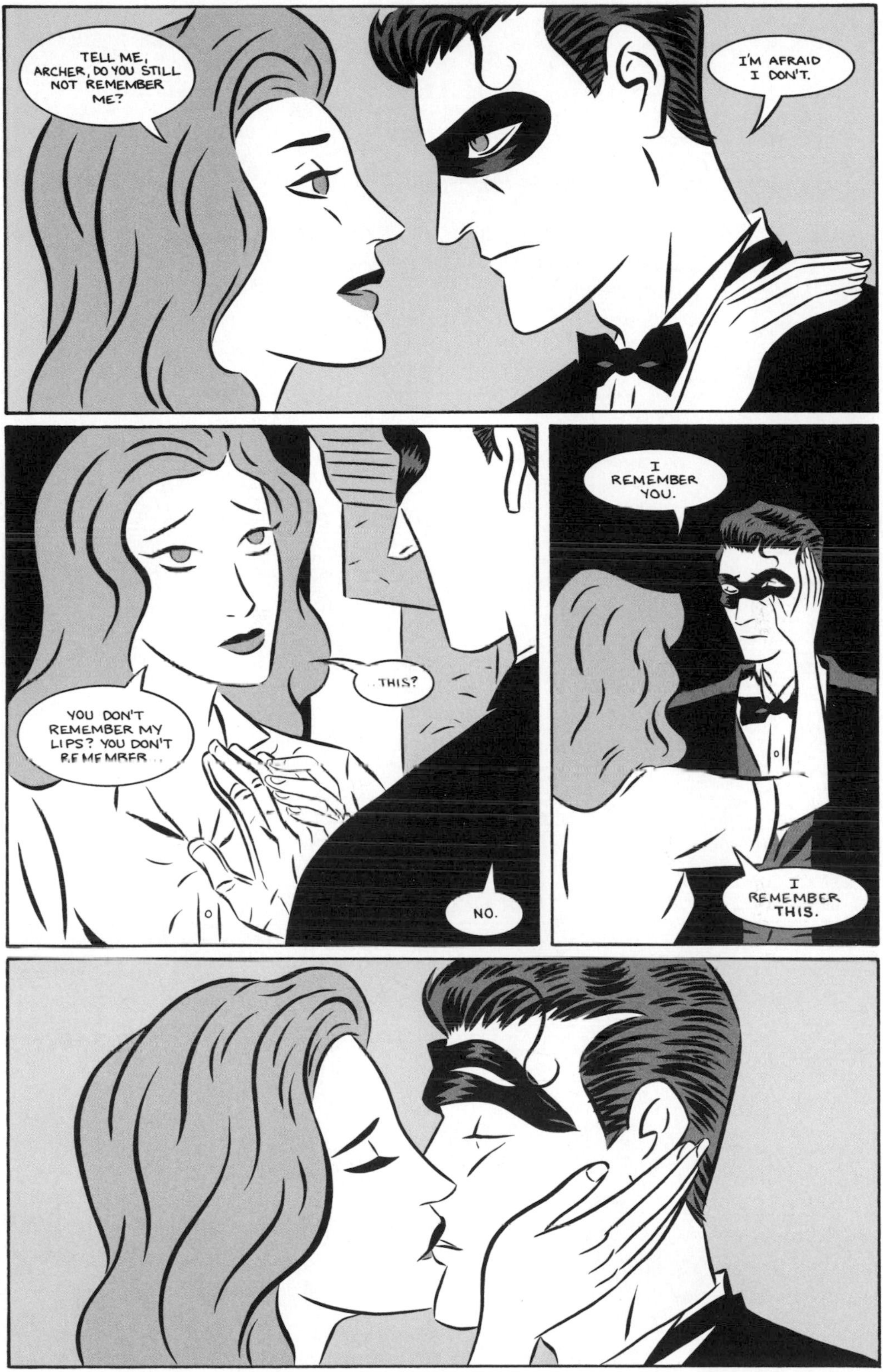
TELL ME, ARCHER, DO YOU STILL NOT REMEMBER ME?
I'M AFRAID I DON'T.
YOU DON'T REMEMBER MY LIPS? YOU DON'T REMEMBER...
...THIS?
NO.
I REMEMBER YOU.
I REMEMBER THIS.

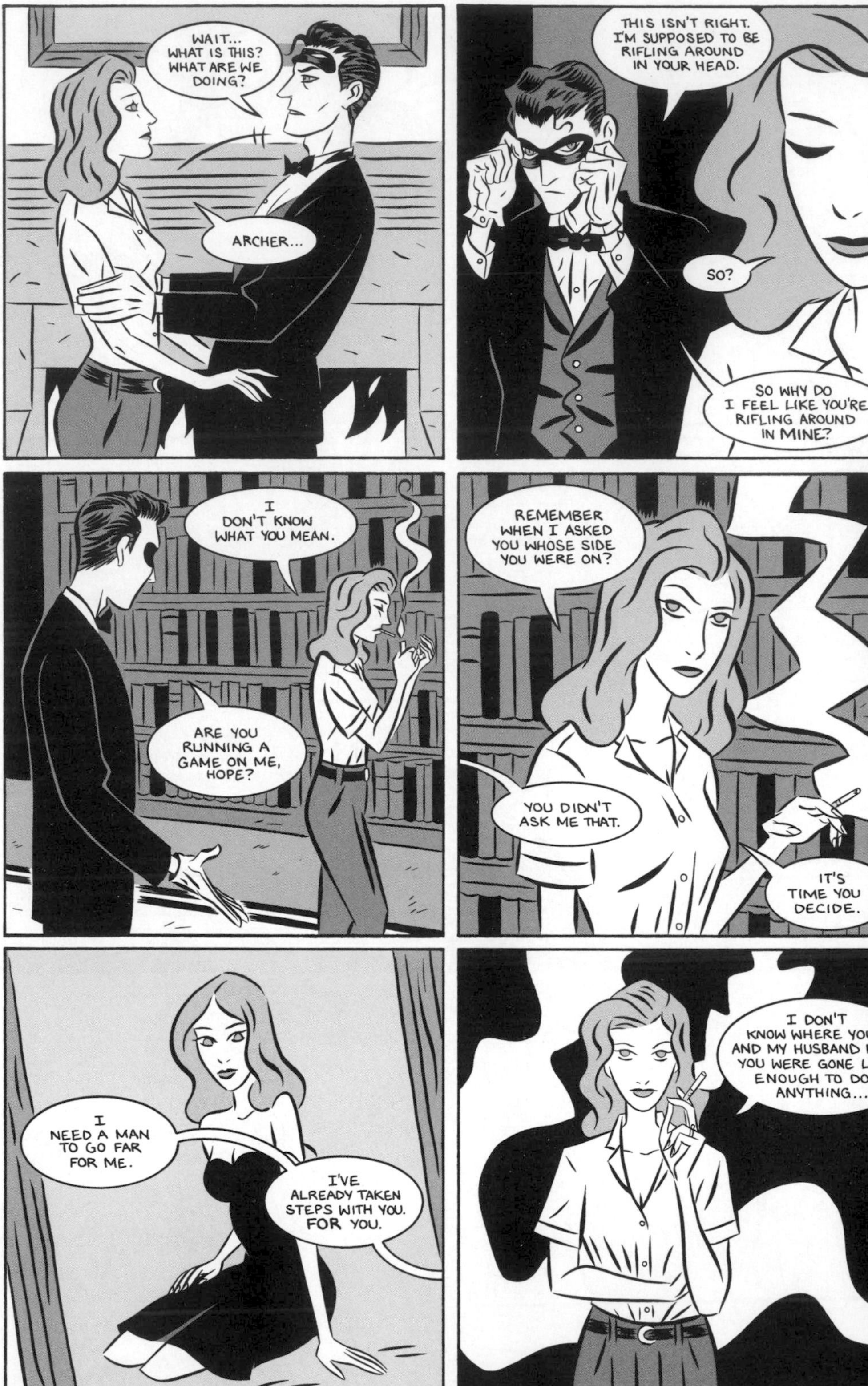
WAIT... WHAT IS THIS? WHAT ARE WE DOING?
ARCHER...
THIS ISN'T RIGHT. I'M SUPPOSED TO BE RIFLING AROUND IN YOUR HEAD.
SO?
SO WHY DO I FEEL LIKE YOU'RE RIFLING AROUND IN MINE?
I DON'T KNOW WHAT YOU MEAN.
ARE YOU RUNNING A GAME ON ME, HOPE?
REMEMBER WHEN I ASKED YOU WHOSE SIDE YOU WERE ON?
YOU DIDN'T ASK ME THAT.
IT'S TIME YOU DECIDE.
I NEED A MAN TO GO FAR FOR ME.
I'VE ALREADY TAKEN STEPS WITH YOU. FOR YOU.
I DON'T KNOW WHERE YOU AND MY HUSBAND WENT. YOU WERE GONE LONG ENOUGH TO DO ANYTHING...

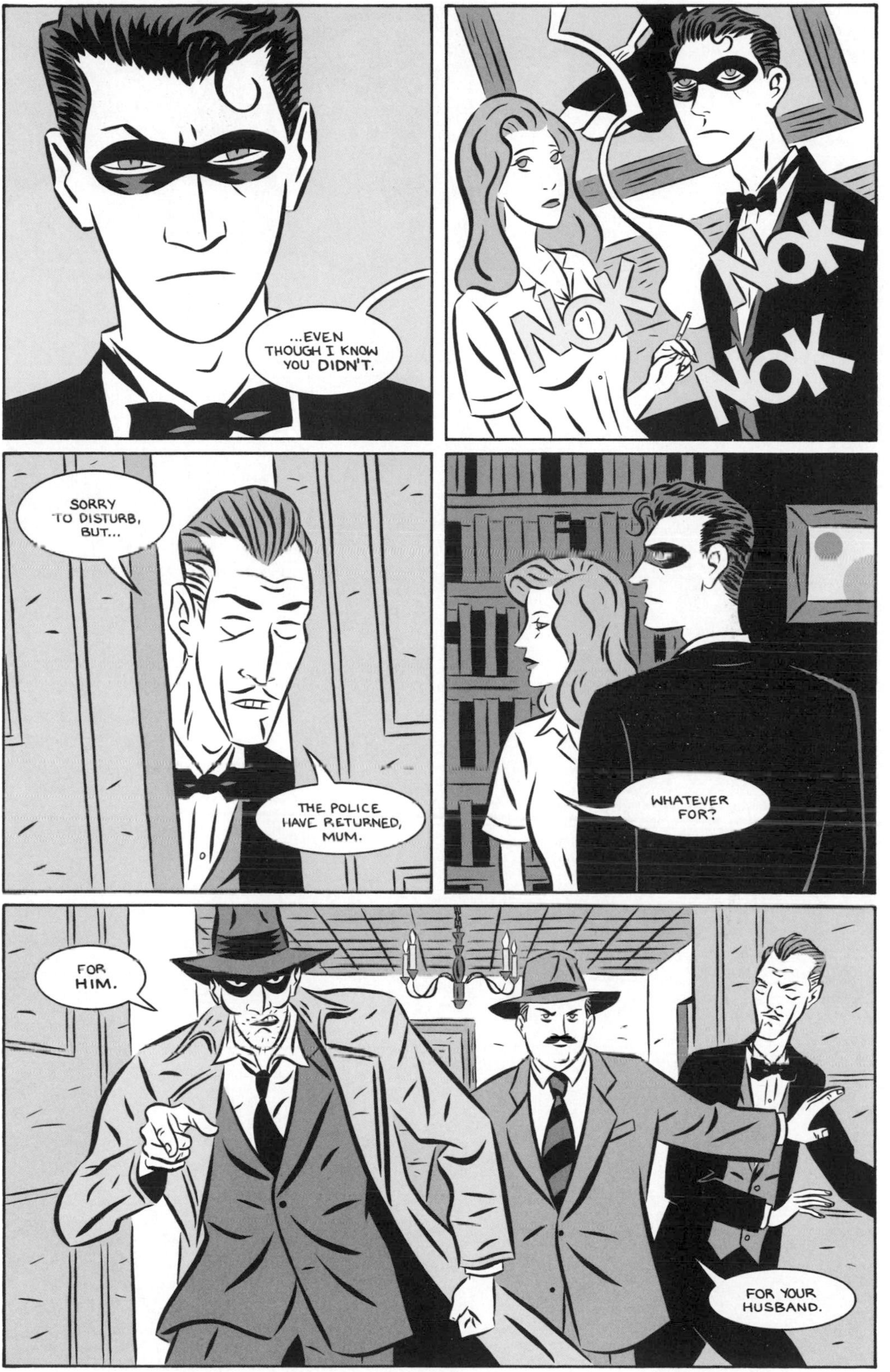
...EVEN THOUGH I KNOW YOU DIDN'T.
NOK
NOK
NOK
SORRY TO DISTURB, BUT...
THE POLICE HAVE RETURNED, MUM.
WHATEVER FOR?
FOR HIM.
FOR YOUR HUSBAND.

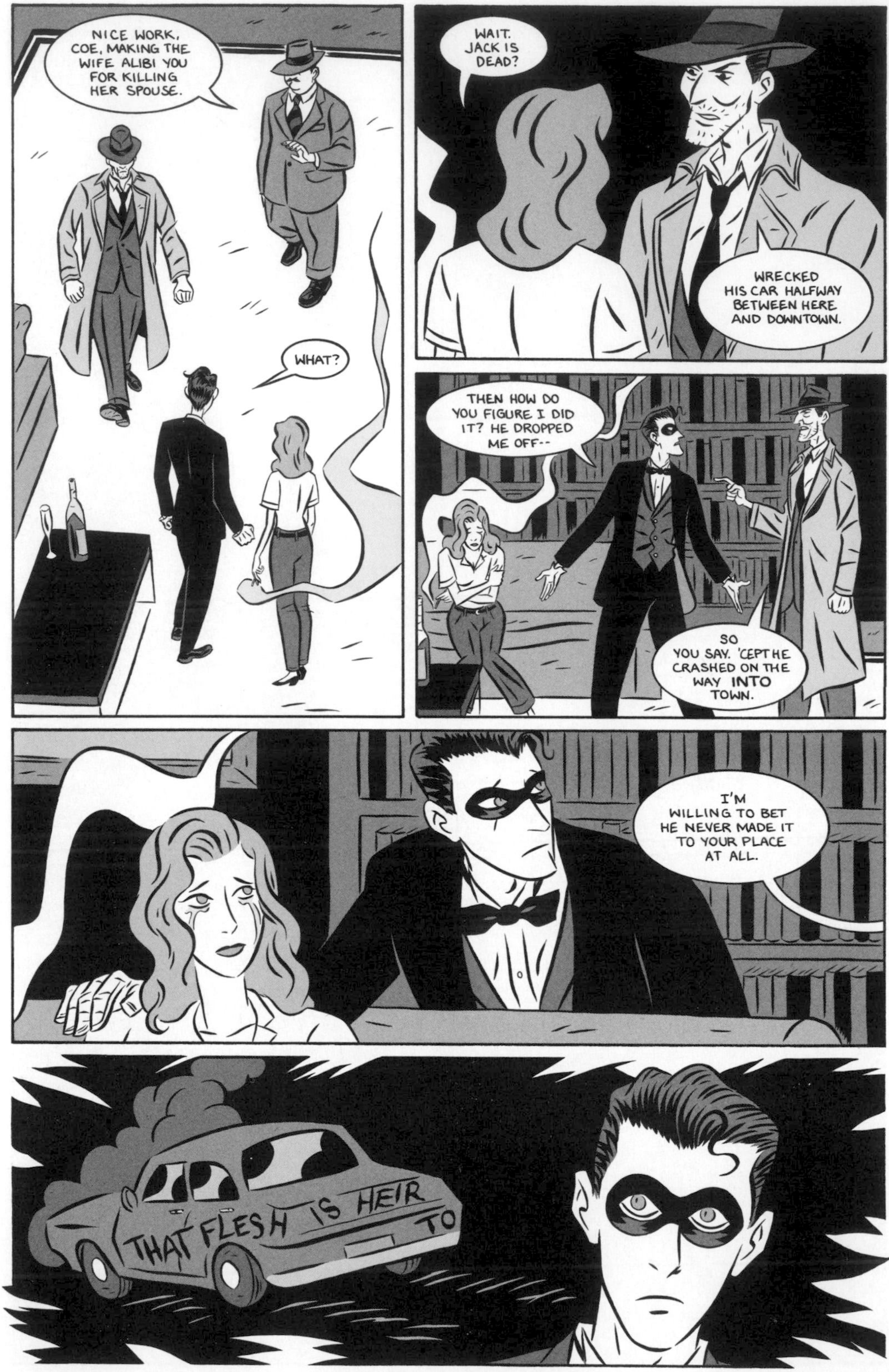
NICE WORK, COE, MAKING THE WIFE ALIBI YOU FOR KILLING HER SPOUSE.
WHAT?
WAIT. JACK IS DEAD?
WRECKED HIS CAR HALFWAY BETWEEN HERE AND DOWNTOWN.
THEN HOW DO YOU FIGURE I DID IT? HE DROPPED ME OFF--
SO YOU SAY. 'CEPT HE CRASHED ON THE WAY INTO TOWN.
I'M WILLING TO BET HE NEVER MADE IT TO YOUR PLACE AT ALL.
THAT FLESH IS HEIR TO

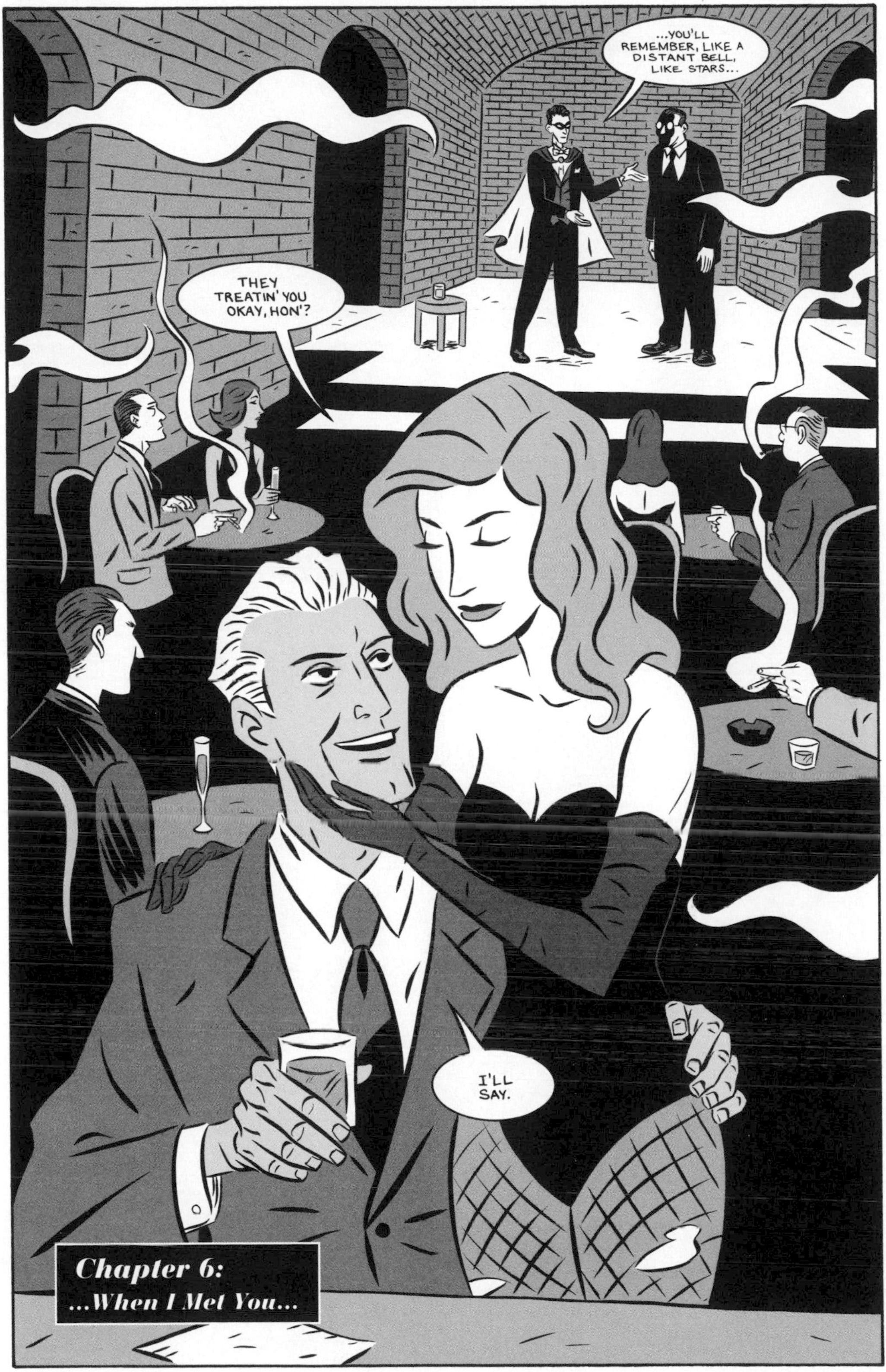
...YOU'LL REMEMBER, LIKE A DISTANT BELL, LIKE STARS...
THEY TREATIN' YOU OKAY, HON'?
I'LL SAY.
Chapter 6:
...When I Met You...

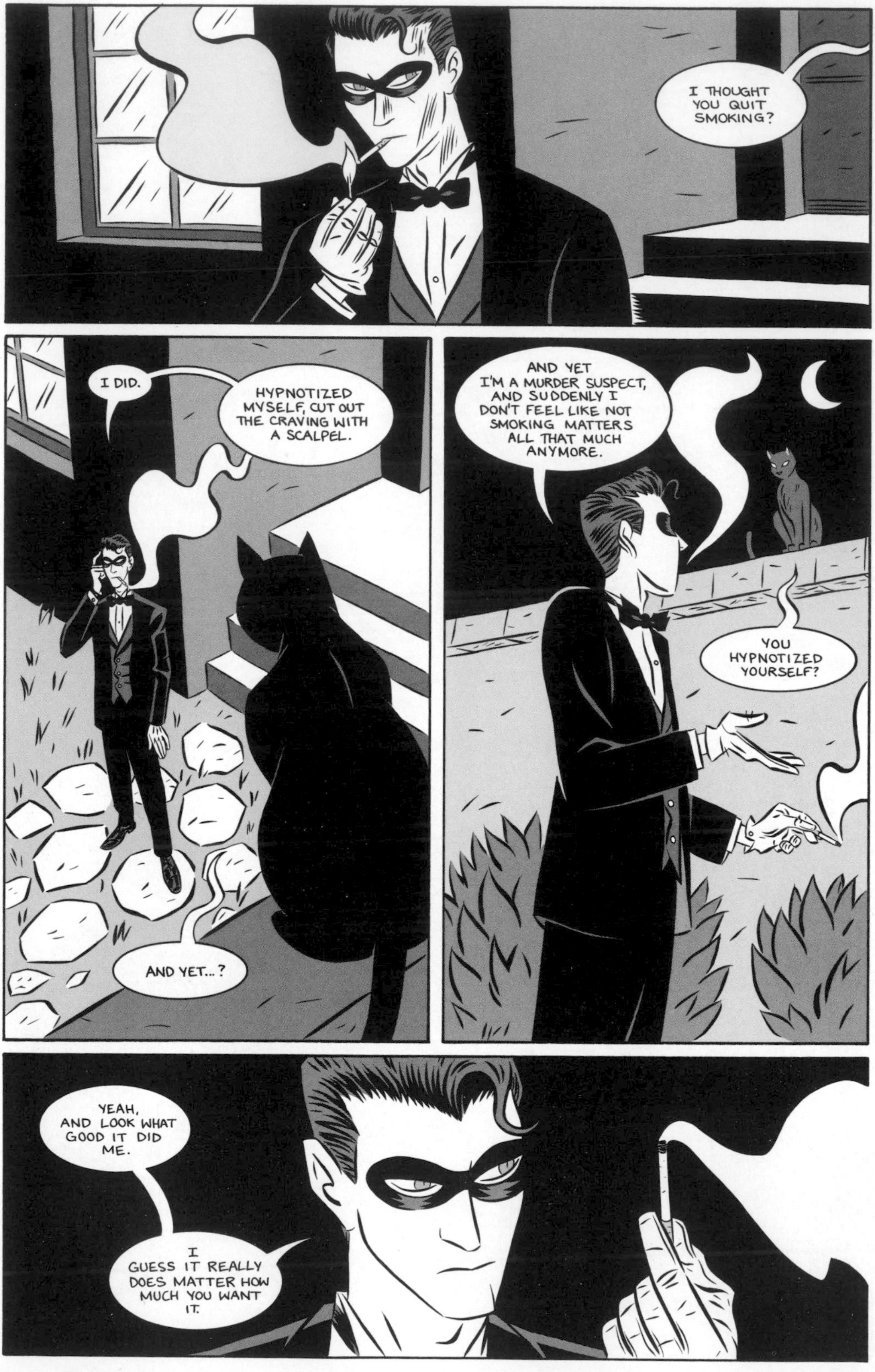
I THOUGHT YOU QUIT SMOKING?
I DID.
HYPNOTIZED MYSELF, CUT OUT THE CRAVING WITH A SCALPEL.
AND YET...?
AND YET I'M A MURDER SUSPECT, AND SUDDENLY I DON'T FEEL LIKE NOT SMOKING MATTERS ALL THAT MUCH ANYMORE.
YOU HYPNOTIZED YOURSELF?
YEAH, AND LOOK WHAT GOOD IT DID ME.
I GUESS IT REALLY DOES MATTER HOW MUCH YOU WANT IT.

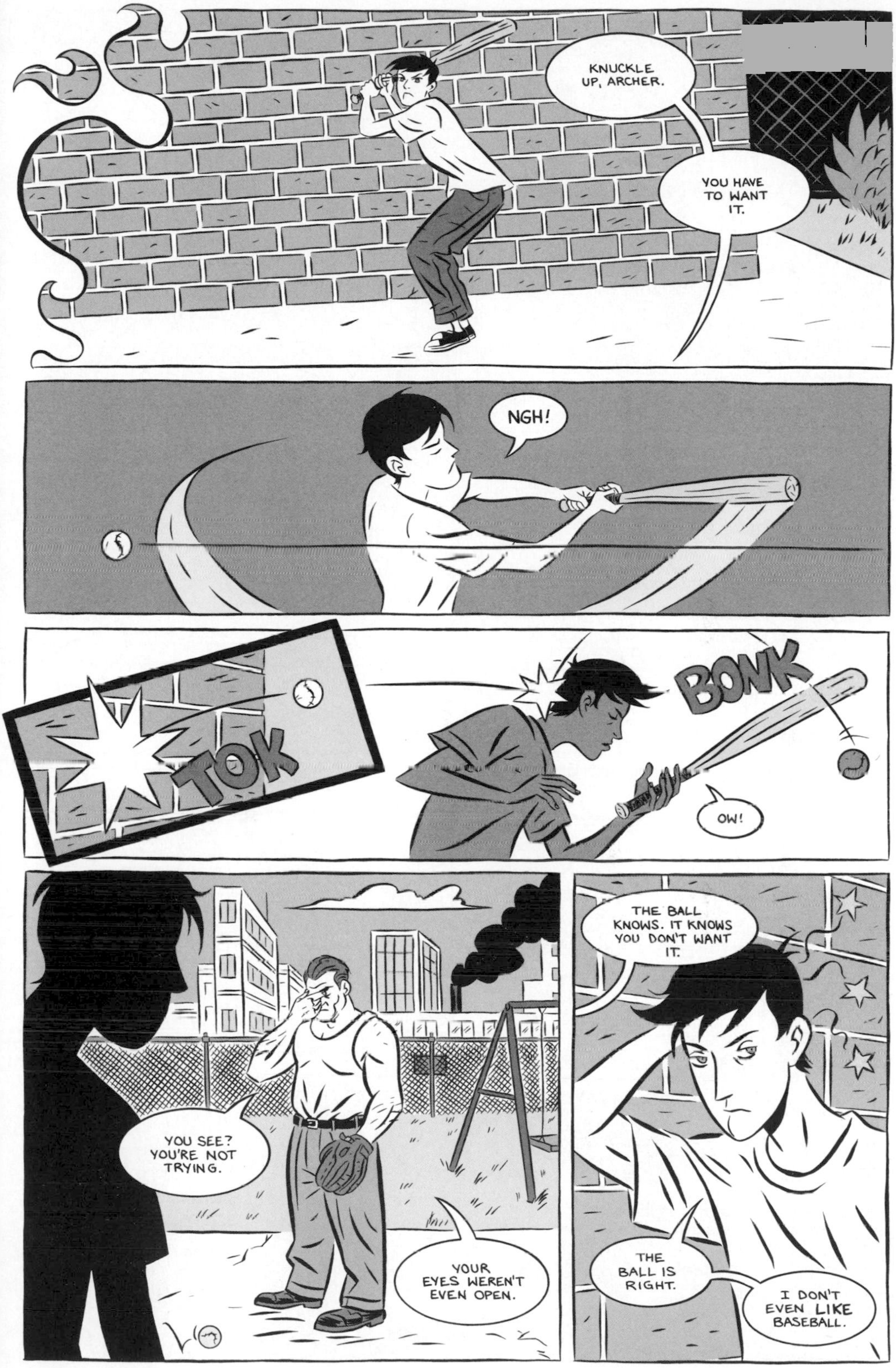
KNUCKLE UP, ARCHER.
YOU HAVE TO WANT IT.
NGH!
TOK
BONK
OW!
YOU SEE? YOU'RE NOT TRYING.
YOUR EYES WEREN'T EVEN OPEN.
THE BALL KNOWS. IT KNOWS YOU DON'T WANT IT.
THE BALL IS RIGHT.
I DON'T EVEN LIKE BASEBALL.

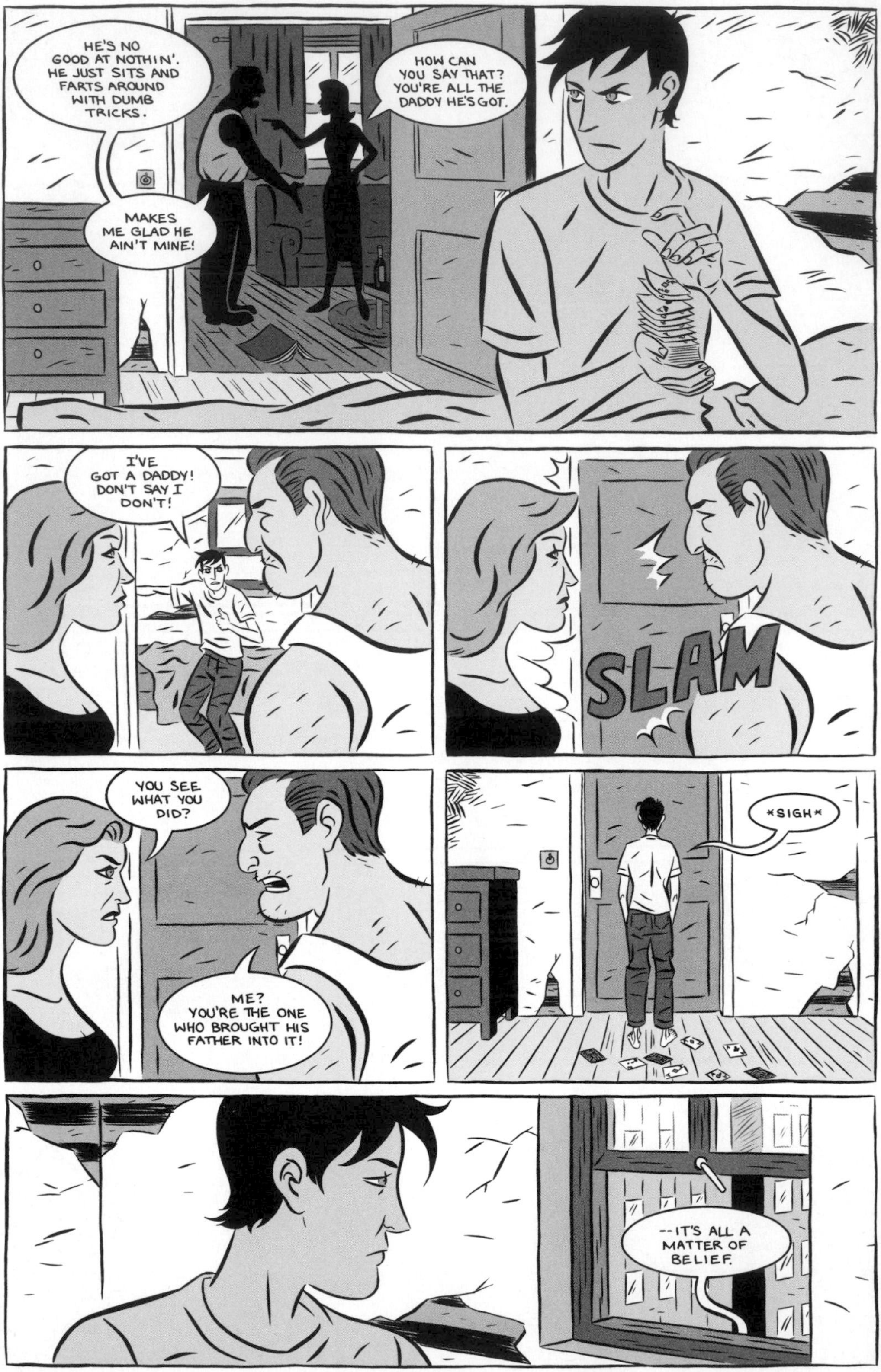

HE'S NO GOOD AT NOTHIN'. HE JUST SITS AND FARTS AROUND WITH DUMB TRICKS.
MAKES ME GLAD HE AIN'T MINE!
HOW CAN YOU SAY THAT? YOU'RE ALL THE DADDY HE'S GOT.
I'VE GOT A DADDY! DON'T SAY I DON'T!
SLAM
YOU SEE WHAT YOU DID?
ME? YOU'RE THE ONE WHO BROUGHT HIS FATHER INTO IT!
SIGH
--IT'S ALL A MATTER OF BELIEF.

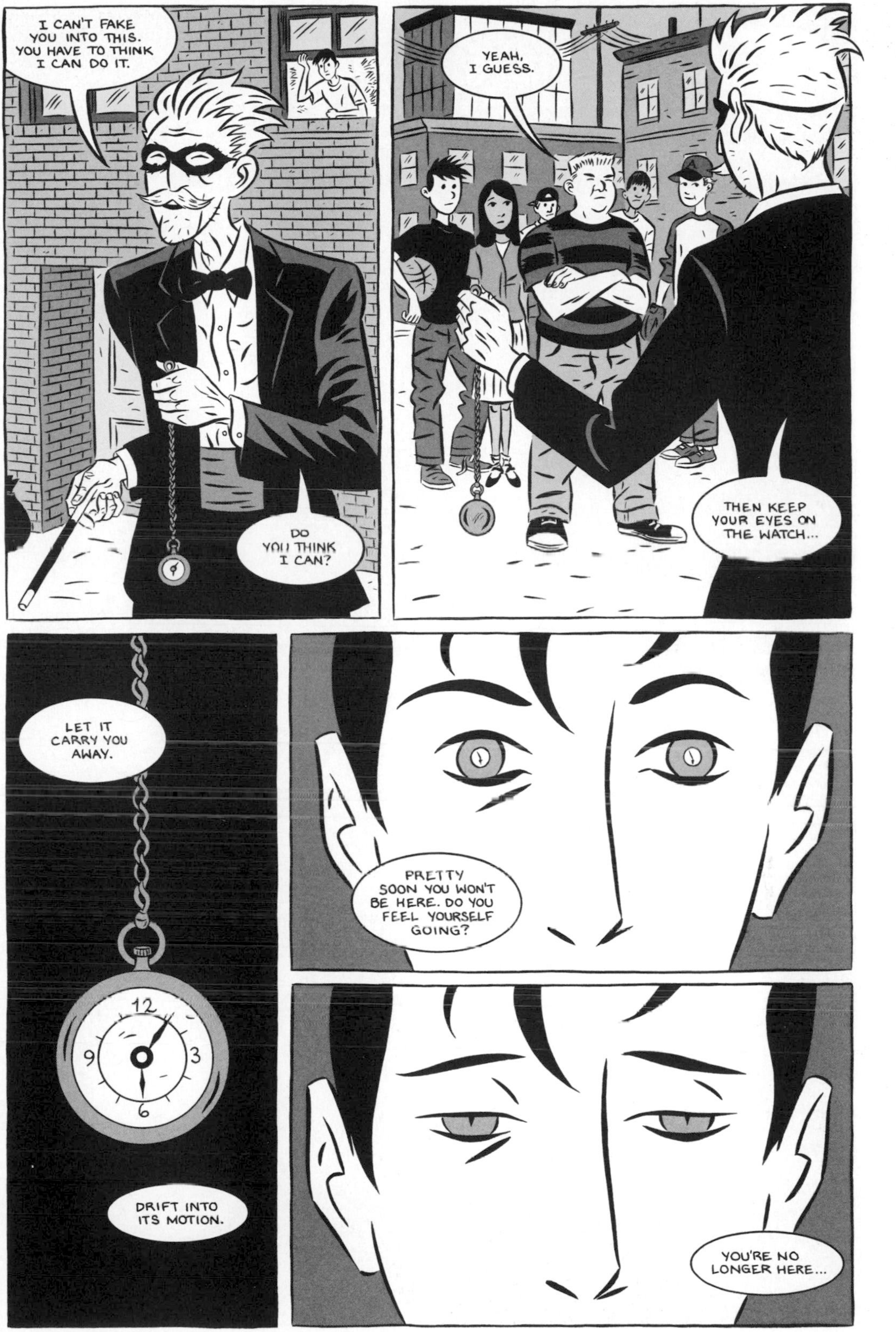
I CAN'T FAKE YOU INTO THIS. YOU HAVE TO THINK I CAN DO IT.
DO YOU THINK I CAN?
YEAH, I GUESS.
THEN KEEP YOUR EYES ON THE WATCH...
LET IT CARRY YOU AWAY.
DRIFT INTO ITS MOTION.
PRETTY SOON YOU WON'T BE HERE. DO YOU FEEL YOURSELF GOING?
YOU'RE NO LONGER HERE...

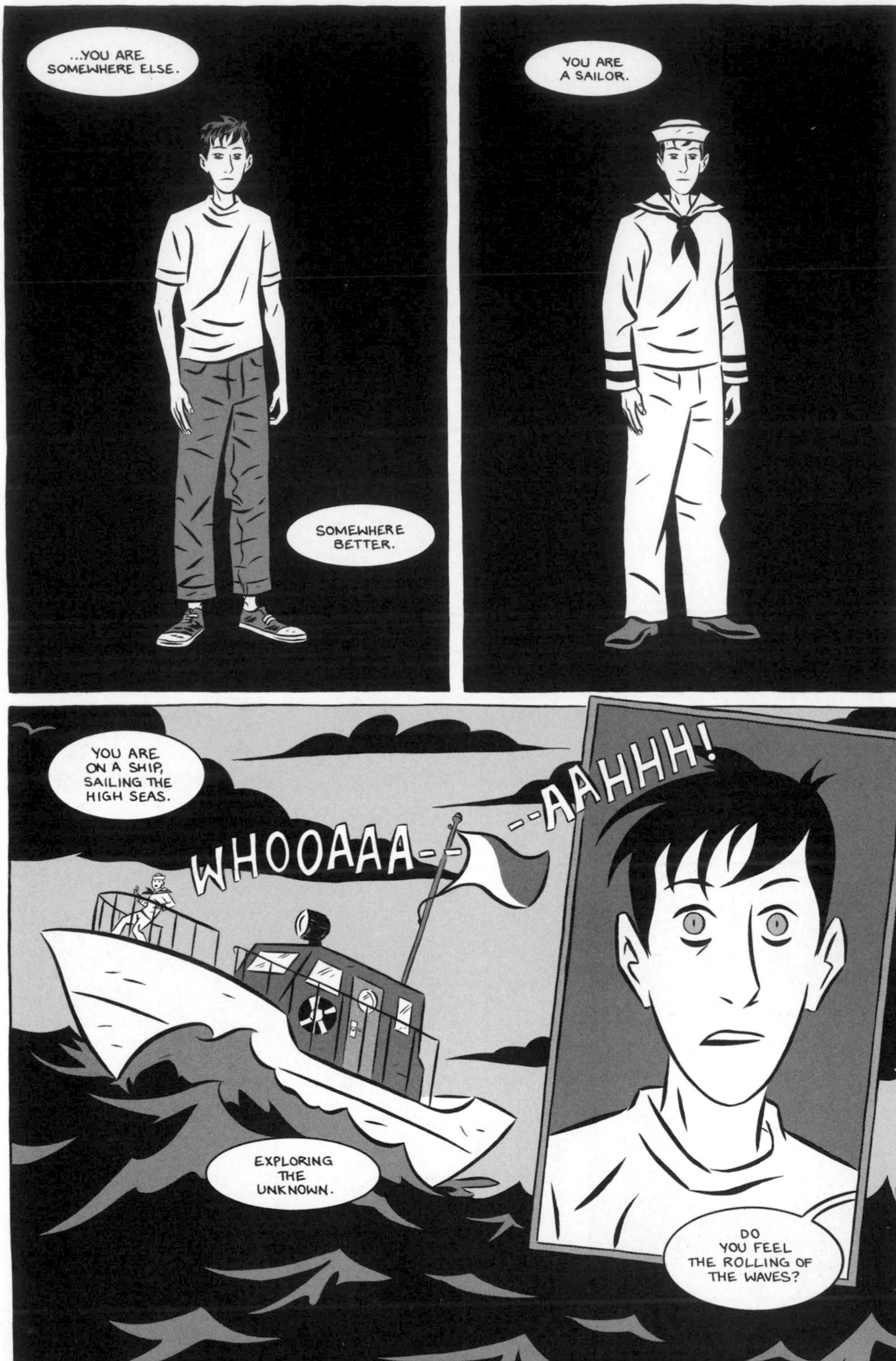
...YOU ARE SOMEWHERE ELSE.
SOMEWHERE BETTER.
YOU ARE A SAILOR.
YOU ARE ON A SHIP, SAILING THE HIGH SEAS.
WHOOAAA--
--AAHHHH!
EXPLORING THE UNKNOWN.
DO YOU FEEL THE ROLLING OF THE WAVES?

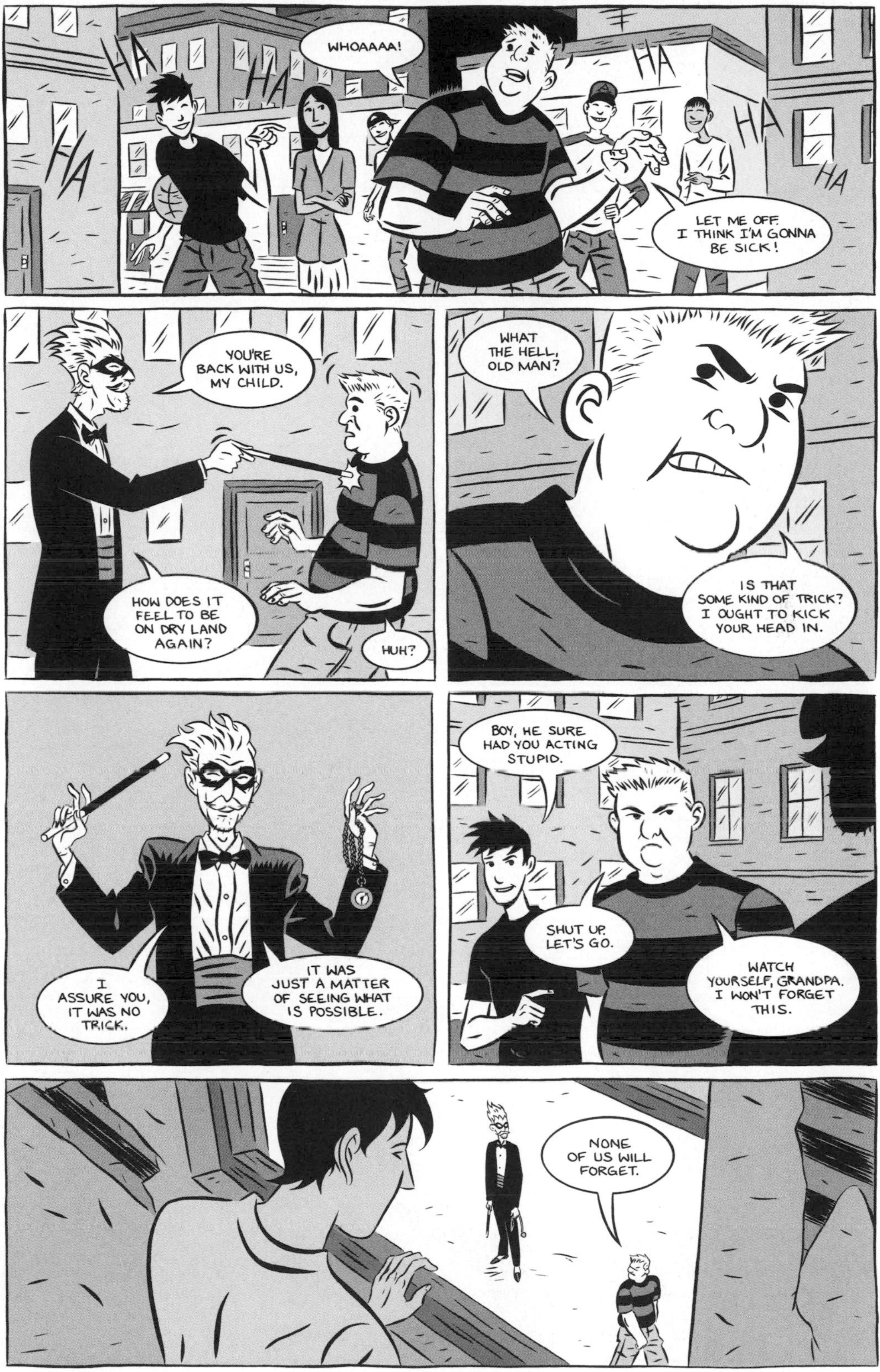

HA
HA
HA
WHOAAAA!
HA
HA
HA
LET ME OFF. I THINK I'M GONNA BE SICK!
YOU'RE BACK WITH US, MY CHILD.
HOW DOES IT FEEL TO BE ON DRY LAND AGAIN?
HUH?
WHAT THE HELL, OLD MAN?
IS THAT SOME KIND OF TRICK? I OUGHT TO KICK YOUR HEAD IN.
I ASSURE YOU, IT WAS NO TRICK.
IT WAS JUST A MATTER OF SEEING WHAT IS POSSIBLE.
BOY, HE SURE HAD YOU ACTING STUPID.
SHUT UP. LET'S GO.
WATCH YOURSELF, GRANDPA. I WON'T FORGET THIS.
NONE OF US WILL FORGET.

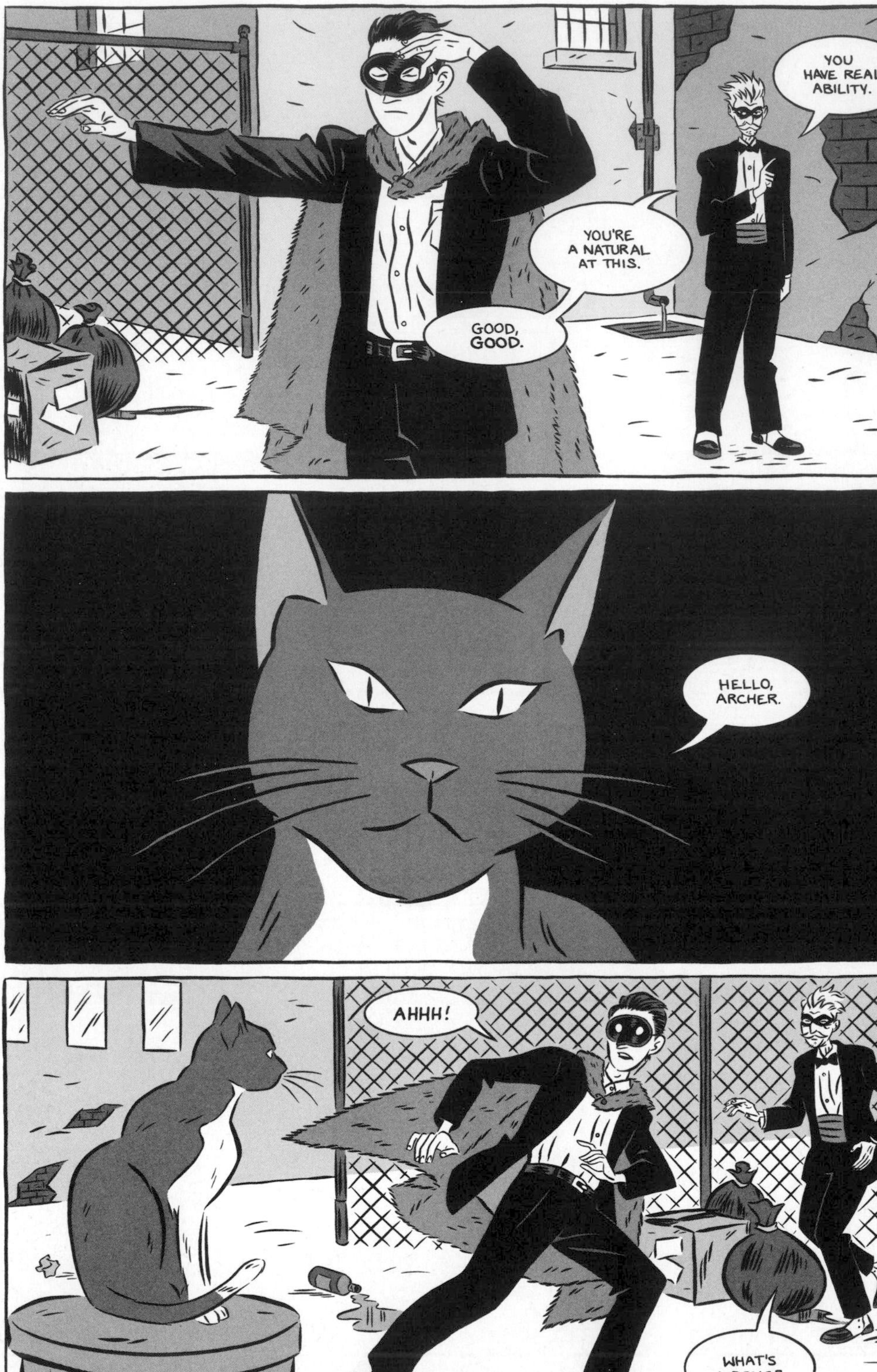
YOU HAVE REAL ABILITY.
YOU'RE A NATURAL AT THIS.
GOOD, GOOD.
HELLO, ARCHER.
AHHH!
WHAT'S WRONG?

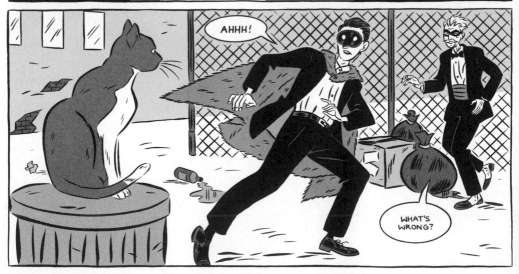

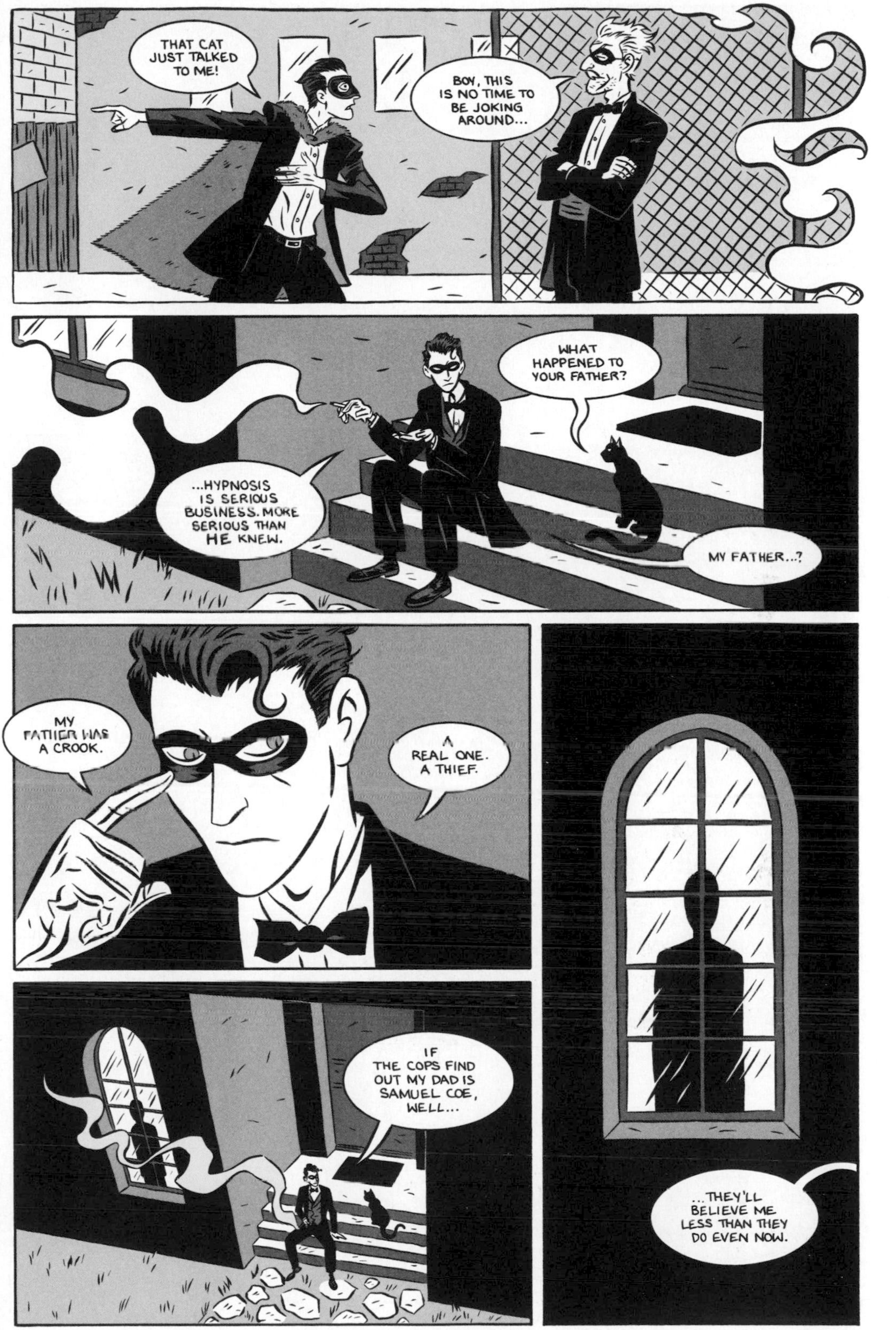
THAT CAT JUST TALKED TO ME!
BOY, THIS IS NO TIME TO BE JOKING AROUND...
WHAT HAPPENED TO YOUR FATHER?
...HYPNOSIS IS SERIOUS BUSINESS. MORE SERIOUS THAN HE KNEW.
MY FATHER...?
MY FATHER WAS A CROOK.
A REAL ONE. A THIEF.
IF THE COPS FIND OUT MY DAD IS SAMUEL COE, WELL...
...THEY'LL BELIEVE ME LESS THAN THEY DO EVEN NOW.

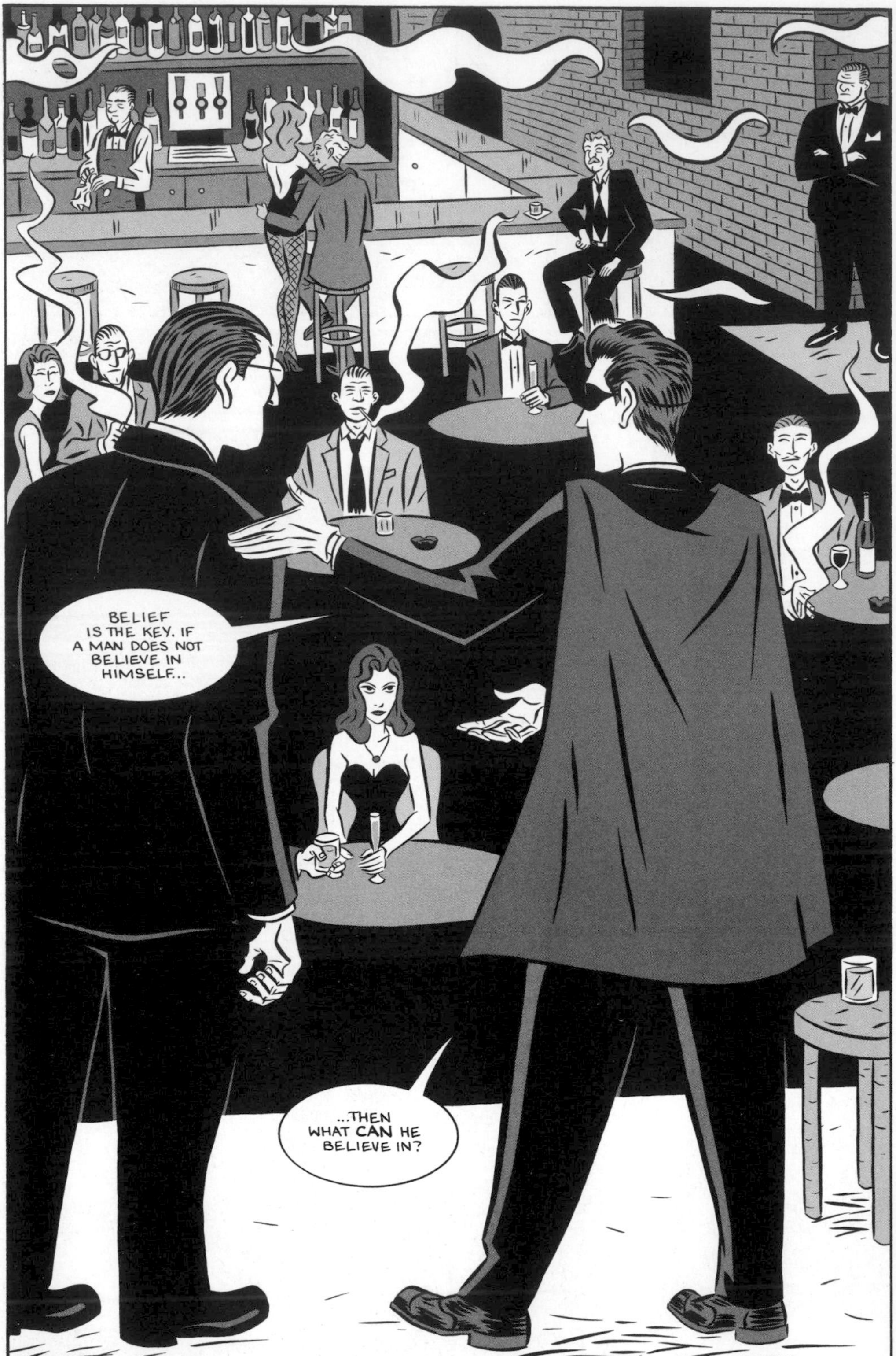
BELIEF IS THE KEY. IF A MAN DOES NOT BELIEVE IN HIMSELF...
...THEN WHAT CAN HE BELIEVE IN?

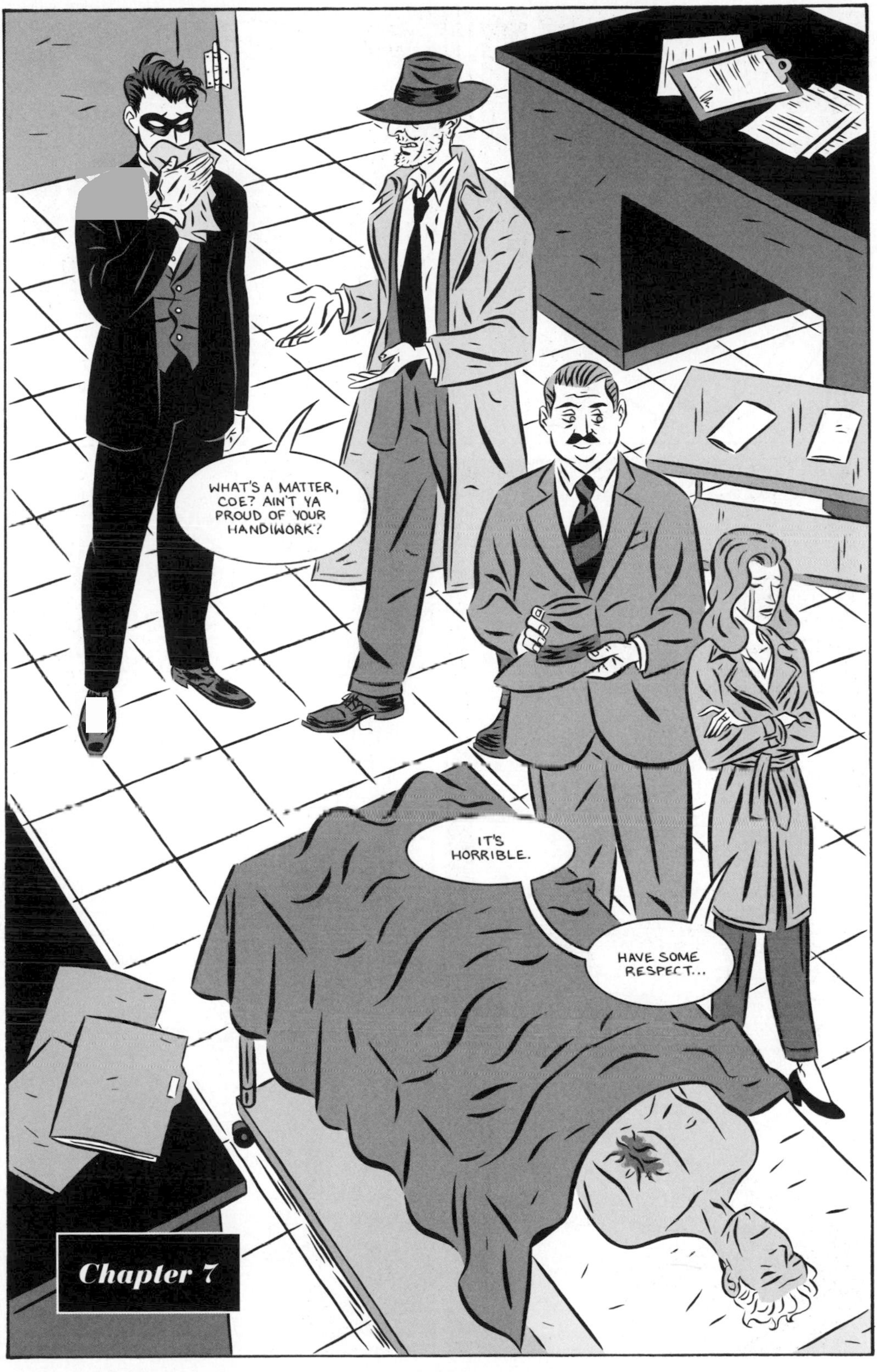
WHAT'S A MATTER, COE? AIN'T YA PROUD OF YOUR HANDIWORK?
IT'S HORRIBLE.
HAVE SOME RESPECT...
Chapter 7

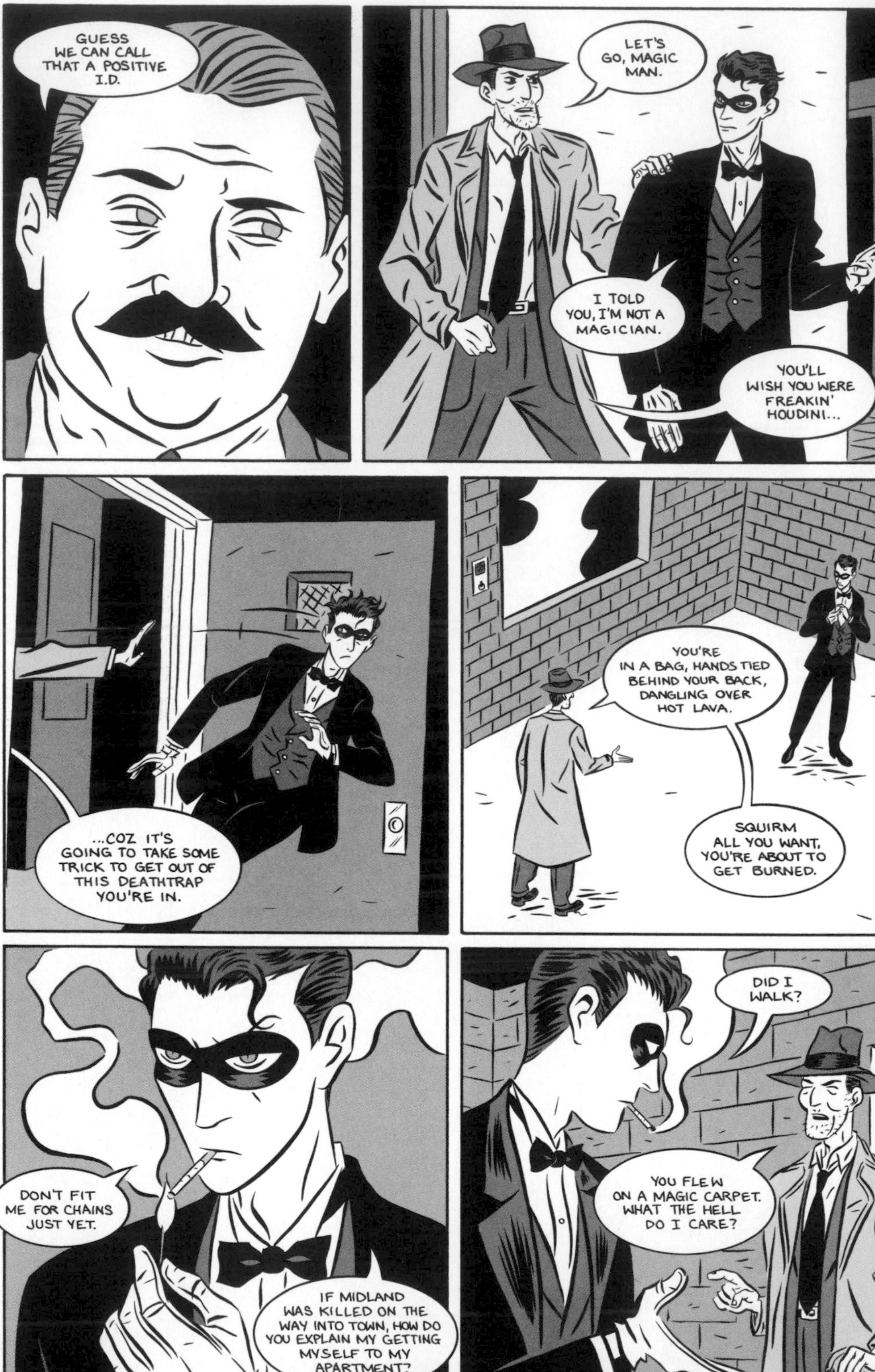

GUESS WE CAN CALL THAT A POSITIVE I.D.
LET'S GO, MAGIC MAN.
I TOLD YOU, I'M NOT A MAGICIAN.
YOU'LL WISH YOU WERE FREAKIN' HOUDINI...
...COZ IT'S GOING TO TAKE SOME TRICK TO GET OUT OF THIS DEATHTRAP YOU'RE IN.
YOU'RE IN A BAG, HANDS TIED BEHIND YOUR BACK, DANGLING OVER HOT LAVA.
SQUIRM ALL YOU WANT, YOU'RE ABOUT TO GET BURNED.
DON'T FIT ME FOR CHAINS JUST YET.
IF MIDLAND WAS KILLED ON THE WAY INTO TOWN, HOW DO YOU EXPLAIN MY GETTING MYSELF TO MY APARTMENT?
DID I WALK?
YOU FLEW ON A MAGIC CARPET. WHAT THE HELL DO I CARE?

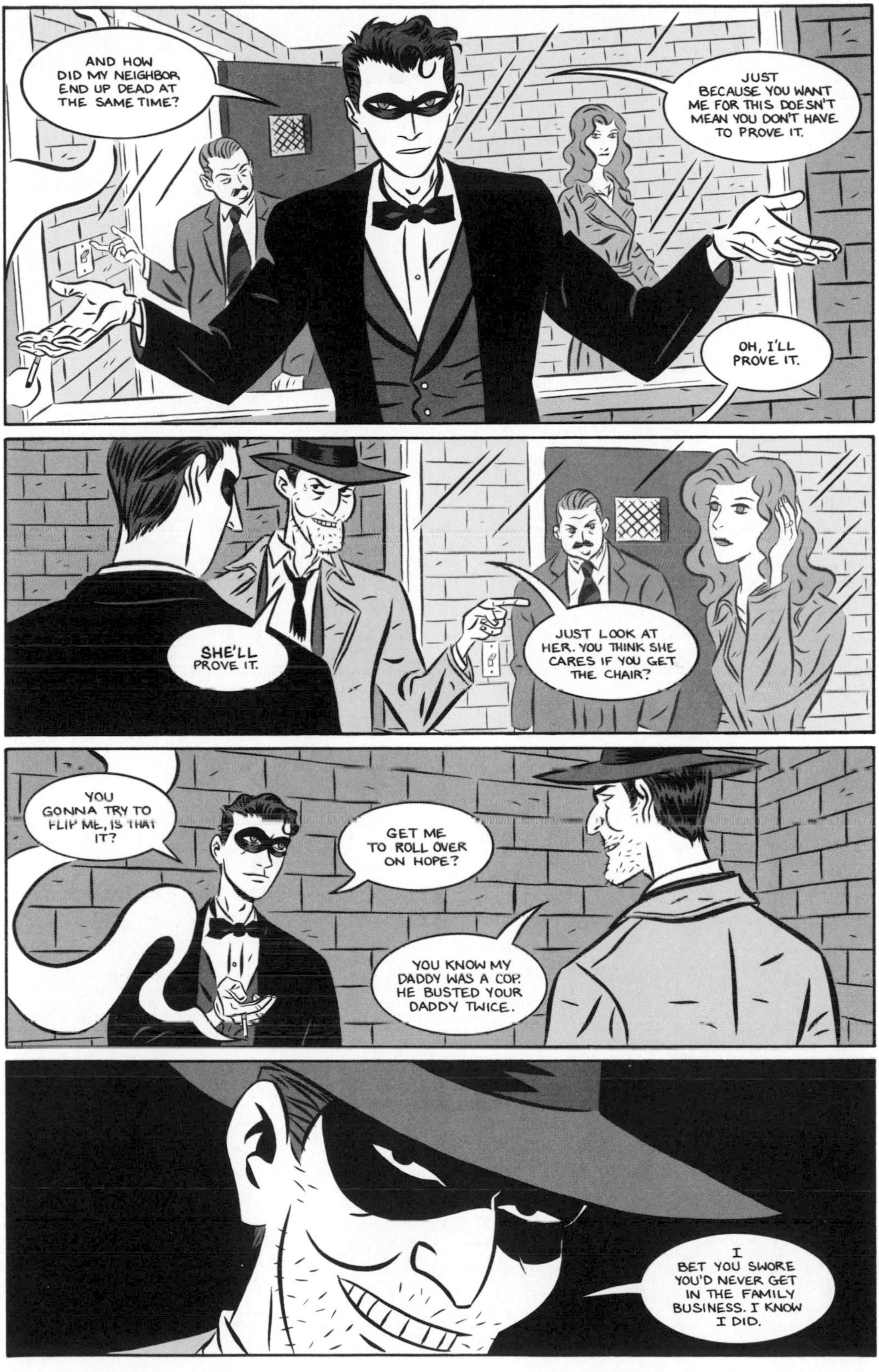
AND HOW DID MY NEIGHBOR END UP DEAD AT THE SAME TIME?
JUST BECAUSE YOU WANT ME FOR THIS DOESN'T MEAN YOU DON'T HAVE TO PROVE IT.
OH, I'LL PROVE IT.
SHE'LL PROVE IT.
JUST LOOK AT HER. YOU THINK SHE CARES IF YOU GET THE CHAIR?
YOU GONNA TRY TO FLIP ME, IS THAT IT?
GET ME TO ROLL OVER ON HOPE?
YOU KNOW MY DADDY WAS A COP. HE BUSTED YOUR DADDY TWICE.
I BET YOU SWORE YOU'D NEVER GET IN THE FAMILY BUSINESS. I KNOW I DID.

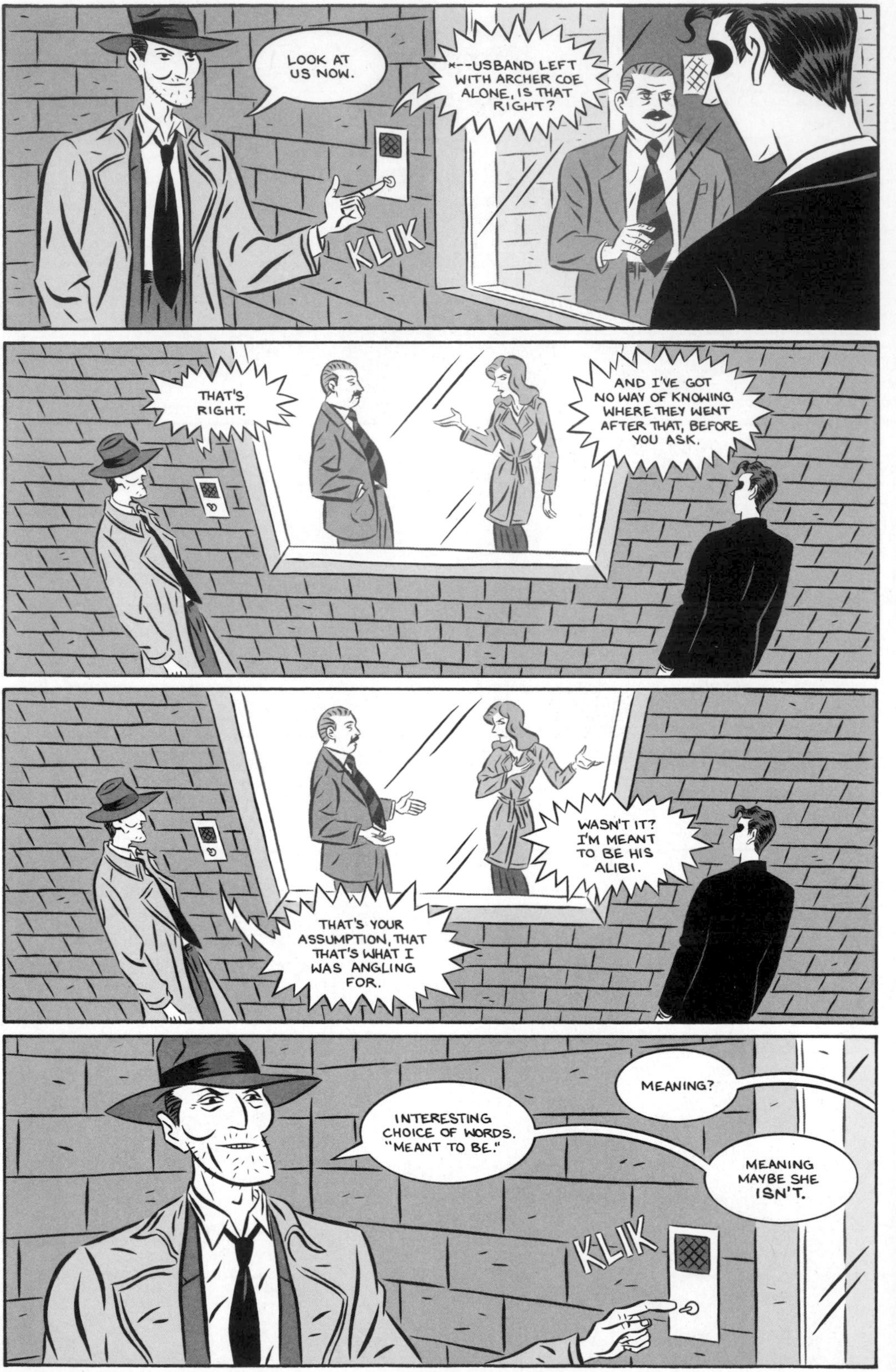

LOOK AT US NOW.
*--USBAND LEFT WITH ARCHER COE ALONE, IS THAT RIGHT?
KLIK
THAT'S RIGHT.
AND I'VE GOT NO WAY OF KNOWING WHERE THEY WENT AFTER THAT, BEFORE YOU ASK.
WASN'T IT? I'M MEANT TO BE HIS ALIBI.
THAT'S YOUR ASSUMPTION, THAT THAT'S WHAT I WAS ANGLING FOR.
MEANING?
INTERESTING CHOICE OF WORDS. "MEANT TO BE."
MEANING MAYBE SHE ISN'T.
KLIK

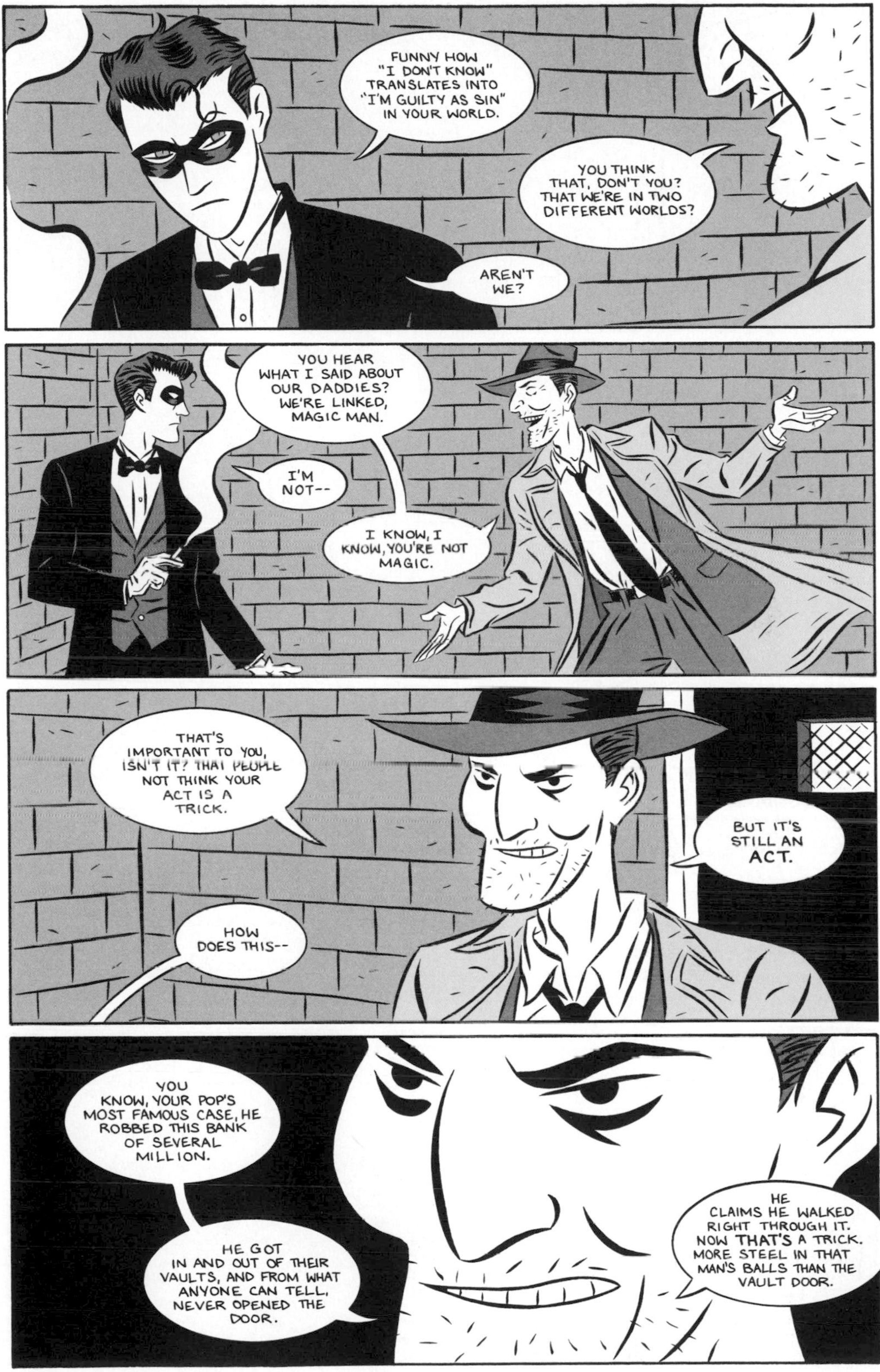
FUNNY HOW "I DON'T KNOW" TRANSLATES INTO "I'M GUILTY AS SIN" IN YOUR WORLD.
YOU THINK THAT, DON'T YOU? THAT WE'RE IN TWO DIFFERENT WORLDS?
AREN'T WE?
YOU HEAR WHAT I SAID ABOUT OUR DADDIES? WE'RE LINKED, MAGIC MAN.
I'M NOT--
I KNOW, I KNOW, YOU'RE NOT MAGIC.
THAT'S IMPORTANT TO YOU, ISN'T IT? THAT PEOPLE NOT THINK YOUR ACT IS A TRICK.
BUT IT'S STILL AN ACT.
HOW DOES THIS--
YOU KNOW, YOUR POP'S MOST FAMOUS CASE, HE ROBBED THIS BANK OF SEVERAL MILLION.
HE GOT IN AND OUT OF THEIR VAULTS, AND FROM WHAT ANYONE CAN TELL, NEVER OPENED THE DOOR.
HE CLAIMS HE WALKED RIGHT THROUGH IT. NOW THAT'S A TRICK. MORE STEEL IN THAT MAN'S BALLS THAN THE VAULT DOOR.

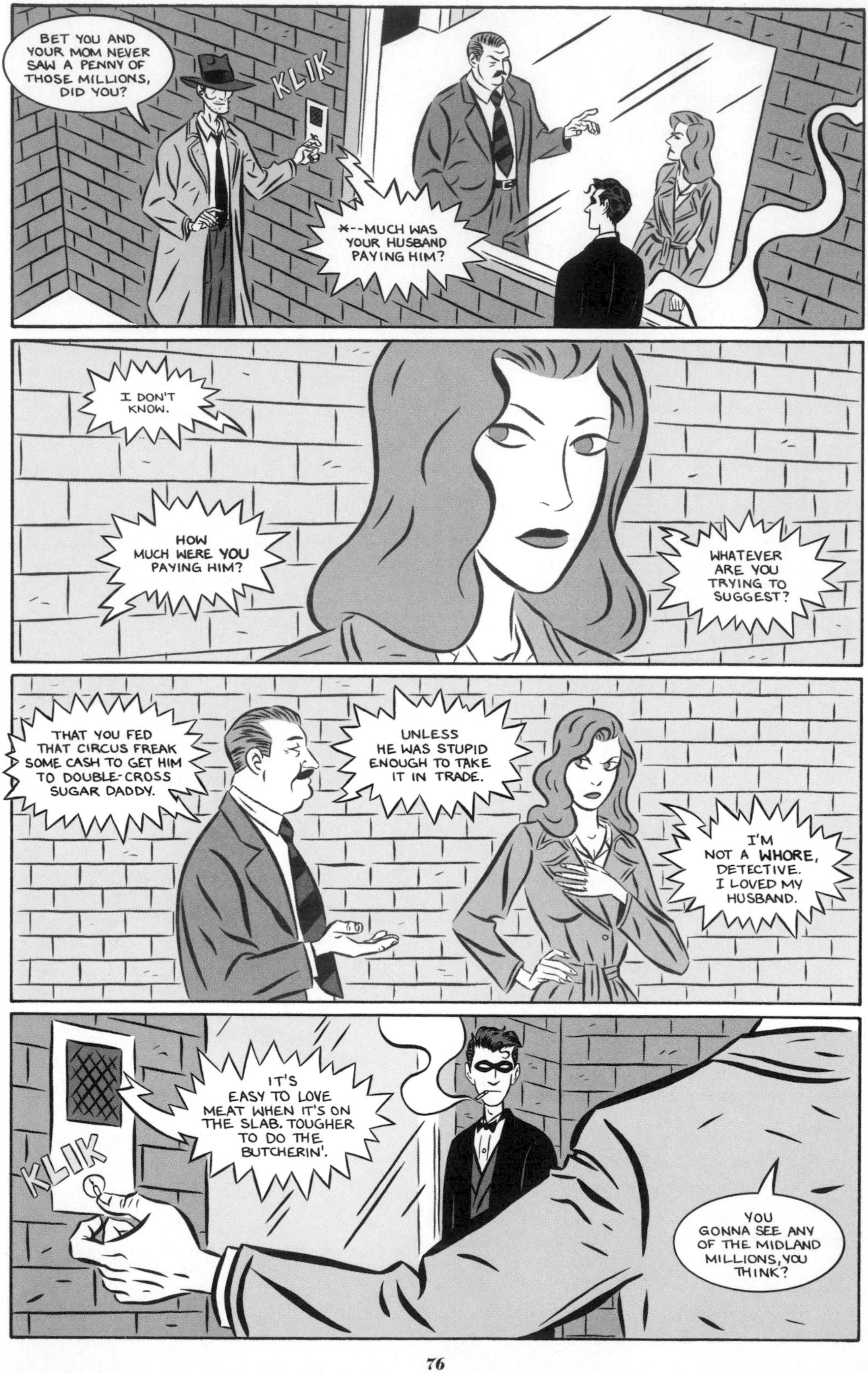
BET YOU AND YOUR MOM NEVER SAW A PENNY OF THOSE MILLIONS, DID YOU?
KLIK
*--MUCH WAS YOUR HUSBAND PAYING HIM?
I DON'T KNOW.
HOW MUCH WERE YOU PAYING HIM?
WHATEVER ARE YOU TRYING TO SUGGEST?
THAT YOU FED THAT CIRCUS FREAK SOME CASH TO GET HIM TO DOUBLE-CROSS SUGAR DADDY.
UNLESS HE WAS STUPID ENOUGH TO TAKE IT IN TRADE.
I'M NOT A WHORE, DETECTIVE. I LOVED MY HUSBAND.
IT'S EASY TO LOVE MEAT WHEN IT'S ON THE SLAB. TOUGHER TO DO THE BUTCHERIN'.
KLIK
YOU GONNA SEE ANY OF THE MIDLAND MILLIONS, YOU THINK?

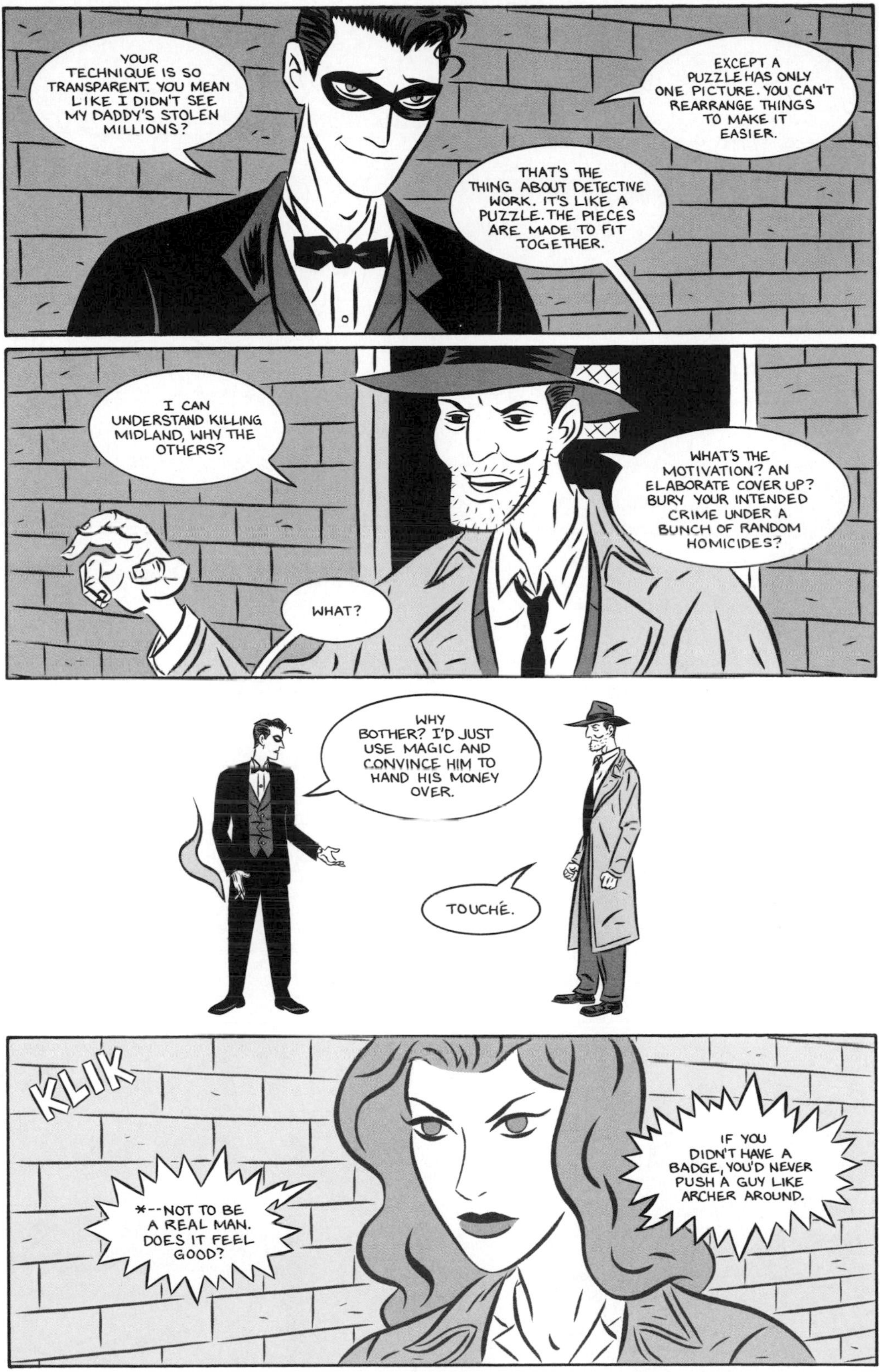
YOUR TECHNIQUE IS SO TRANSPARENT. YOU MEAN LIKE I DIDN'T SEE MY DADDY'S STOLEN MILLIONS?
THAT'S THE THING ABOUT DETECTIVE WORK. IT'S LIKE A PUZZLE. THE PIECES ARE MADE TO FIT TOGETHER.
EXCEPT A PUZZLE HAS ONLY ONE PICTURE. YOU CAN'T REARRANGE THINGS TO MAKE IT EASIER.
I CAN UNDERSTAND KILLING MIDLAND, WHY THE OTHERS?
WHAT'S THE MOTIVATION? AN ELABORATE COVER UP? BURY YOUR INTENDED CRIME UNDER A BUNCH OF RANDOM HOMICIDES?
WHAT?
WHY BOTHER? I'D JUST USE MAGIC AND CONVINCE HIM TO HAND HIS MONEY OVER.
TOUCHÉ.
KLIK
IF YOU DIDN'T HAVE A BADGE, YOU'D NEVER PUSH A GUY LIKE ARCHER AROUND.
*--NOT TO BE A REAL MAN. DOES IT FEEL GOOD?

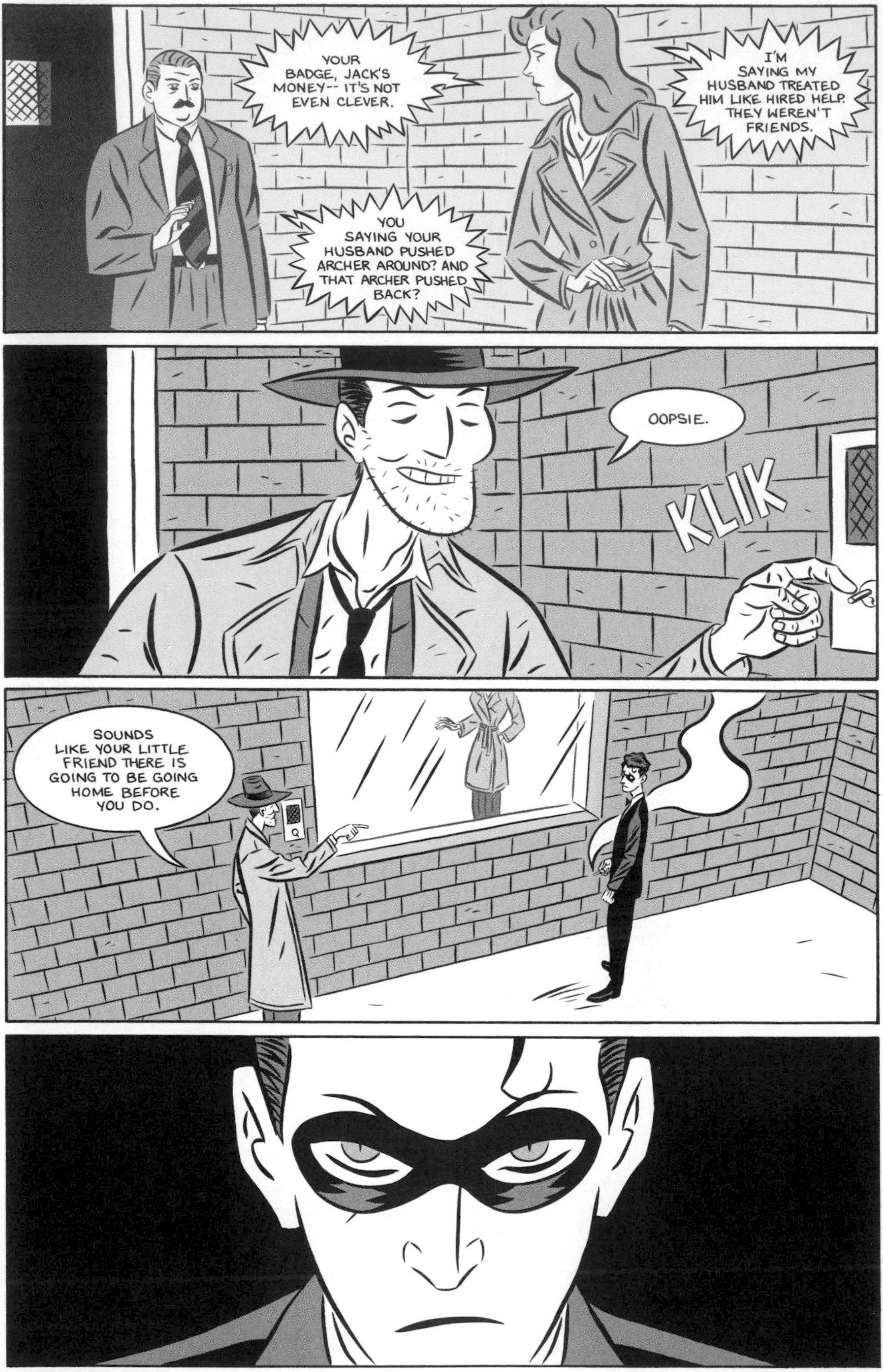
YOUR BADGE, JACK'S MONEY-- IT'S NOT EVEN CLEVER.
I'M SAYING MY HUSBAND TREATED HIM LIKE HIRED HELP. THEY WEREN'T FRIENDS.
YOU SAYING YOUR HUSBAND PUSHED ARCHER AROUND? AND THAT ARCHER PUSHED BACK?
OOPSIE.
KLIK
SOUNDS LIKE YOUR LITTLE FRIEND THERE IS GOING TO BE GOING HOME BEFORE YOU DO.
Q

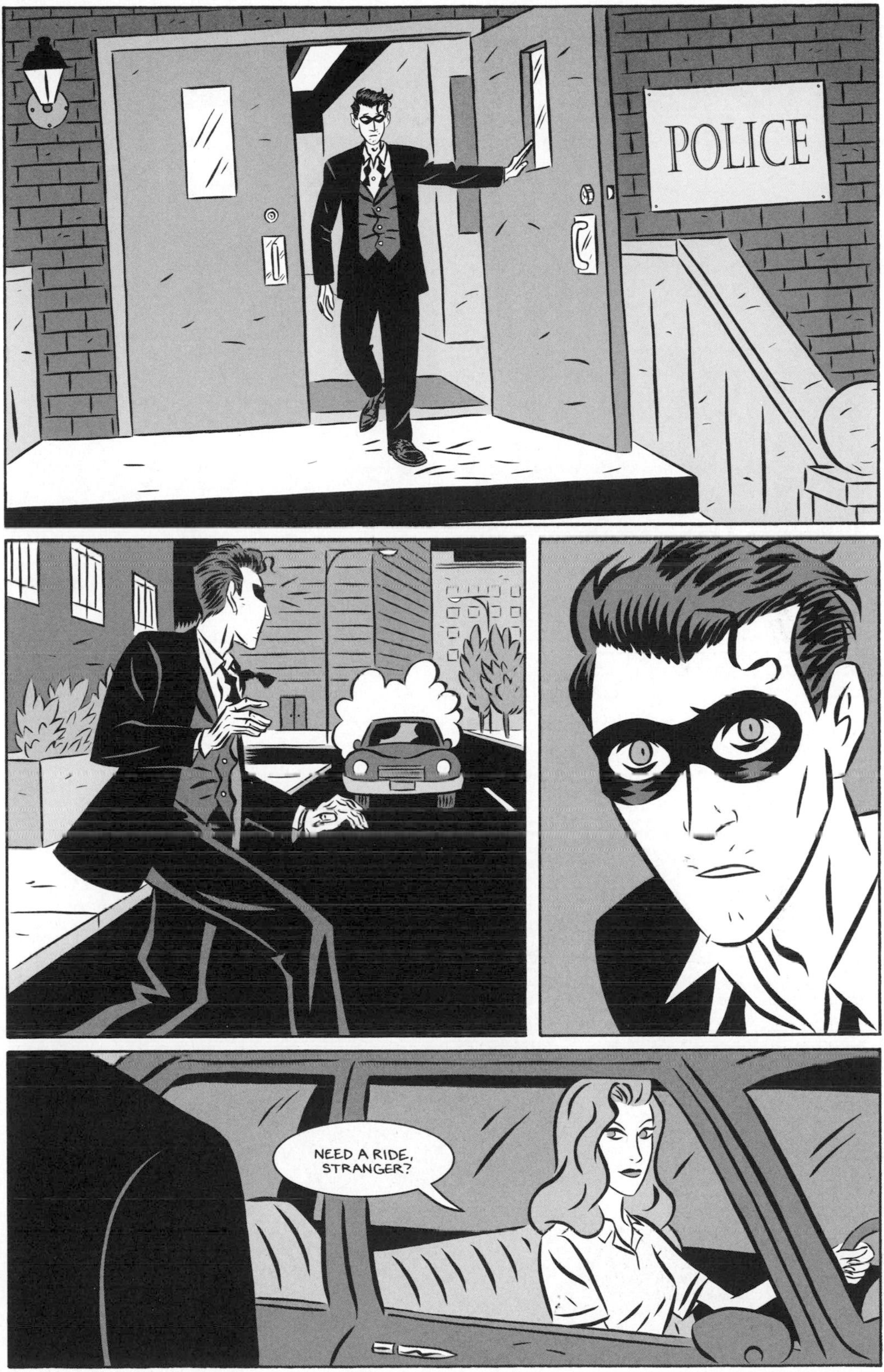
POLICE
NEED A RIDE, STRANGER?

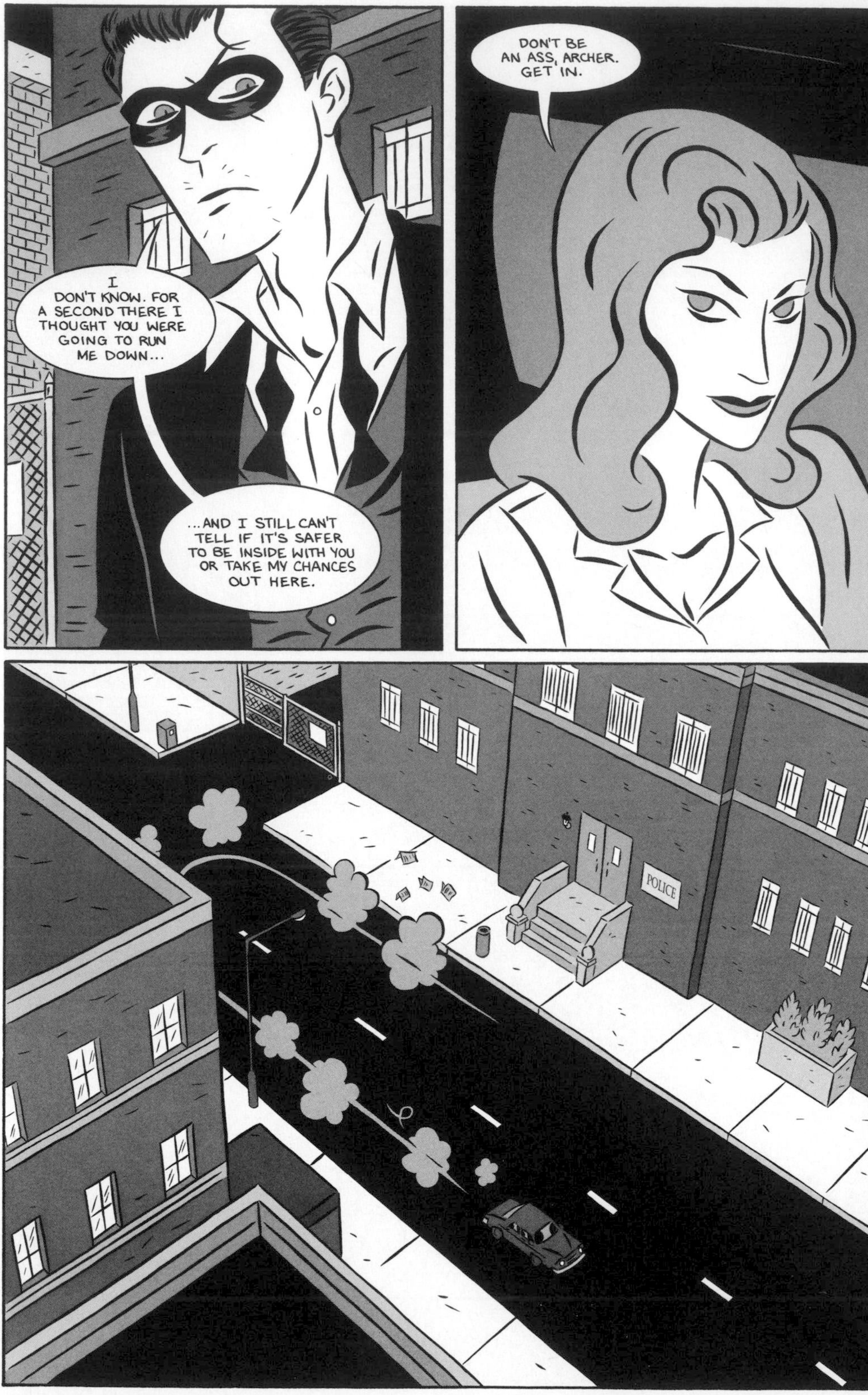
I DON'T KNOW. FOR A SECOND THERE I THOUGHT YOU WERE GOING TO RUN ME DOWN...
...AND I STILL CAN'T TELL IF IT'S SAFER TO BE INSIDE WITH YOU OR TAKE MY CHANCES OUT HERE.
DON'T BE AN ASS, ARCHER. GET IN.
POLICE

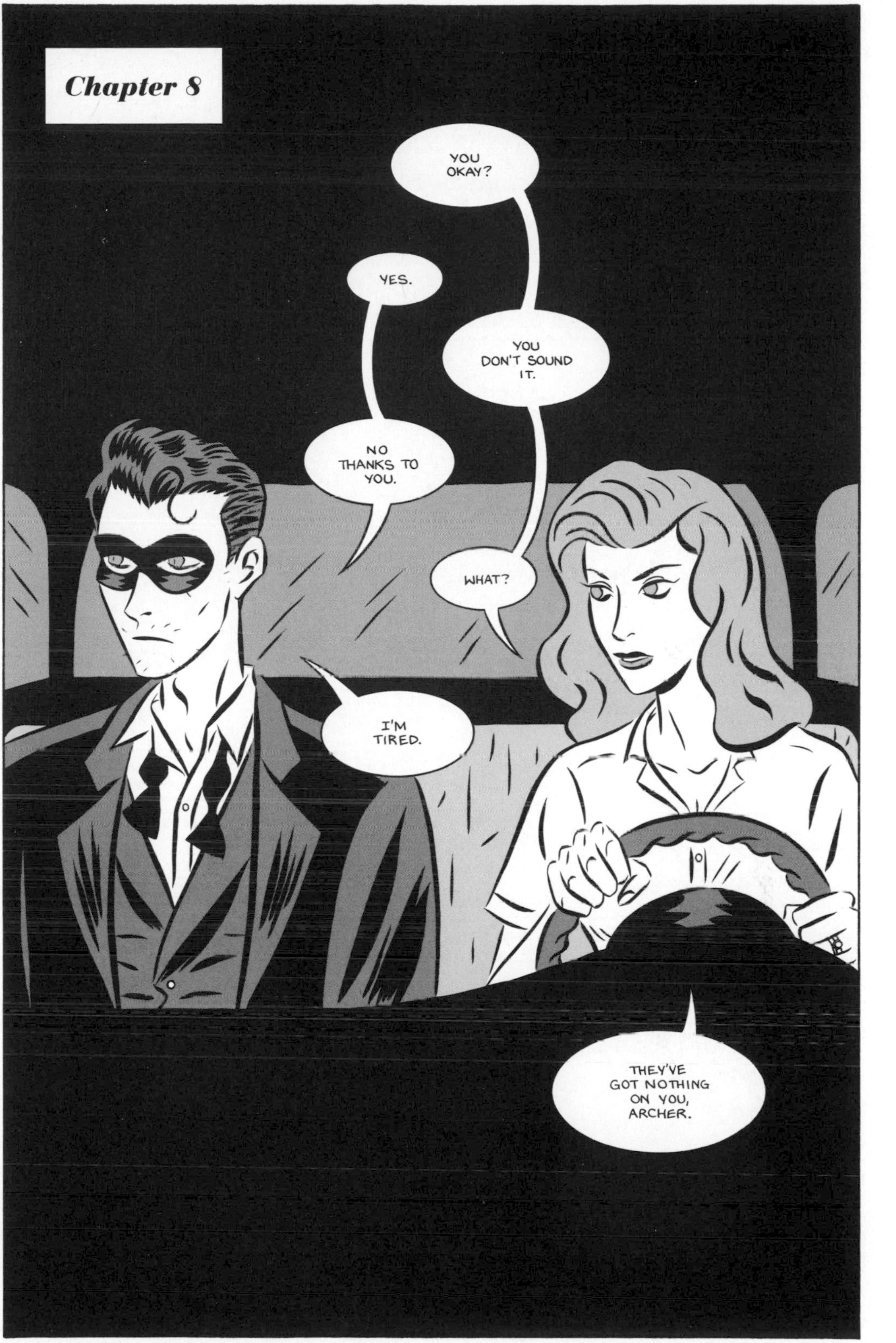
Chapter 8
YOU OKAY?
YES.
YOU DON'T SOUND IT.
NO THANKS TO YOU.
WHAT?
I'M TIRED.
THEY'VE GOT NOTHING ON YOU, ARCHER.

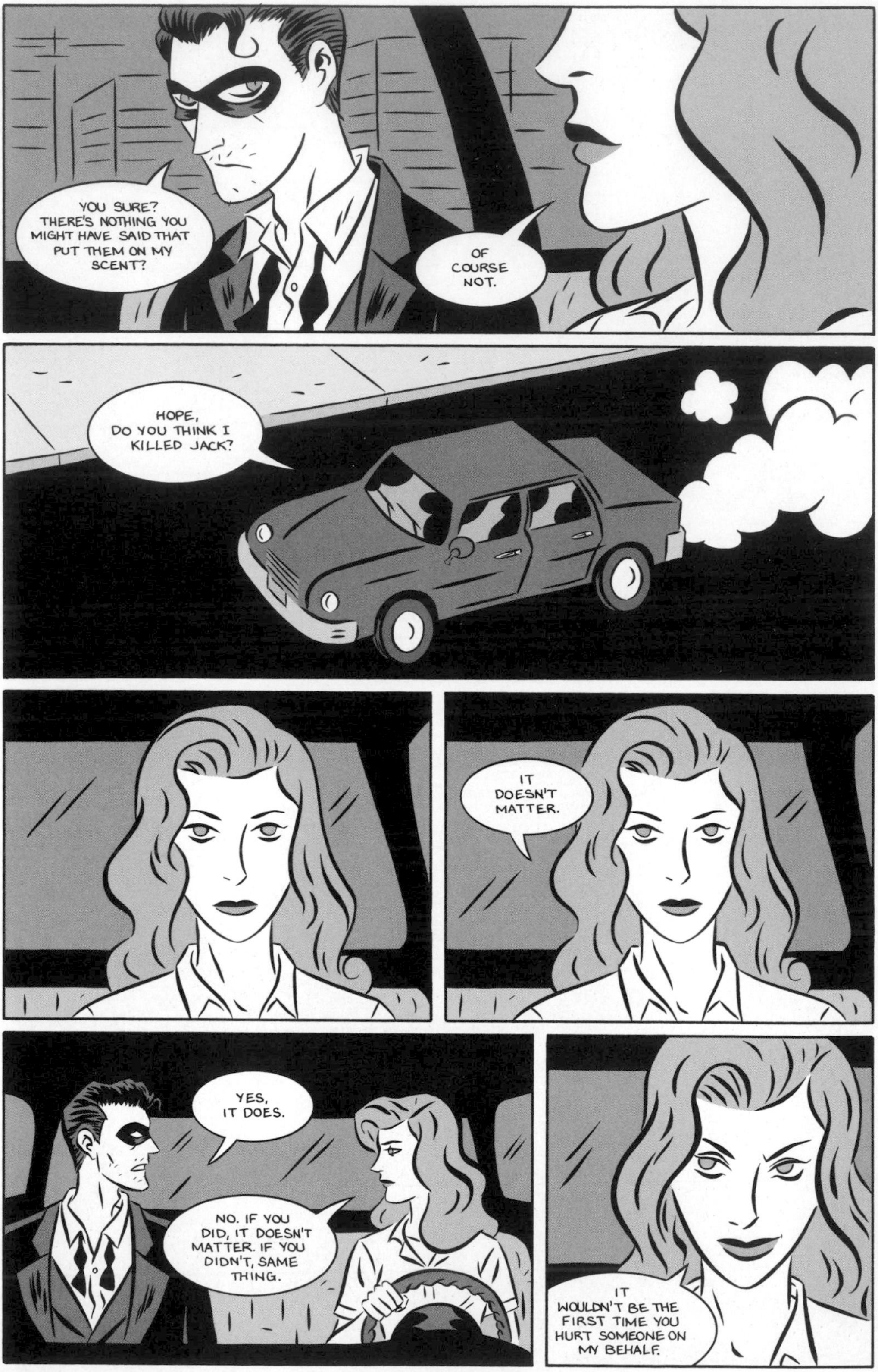
YOU SURE? THERE'S NOTHING YOU MIGHT HAVE SAID THAT PUT THEM ON MY SCENT?
OF COURSE NOT.
HOPE, DO YOU THINK I KILLED JACK?
IT DOESN'T MATTER.
YES, IT DOES.
NO. IF YOU DID, IT DOESN'T MATTER. IF YOU DIDN'T, SAME THING.
IT WOULDN'T BE THE FIRST TIME YOU HURT SOMEONE ON MY BEHALF.

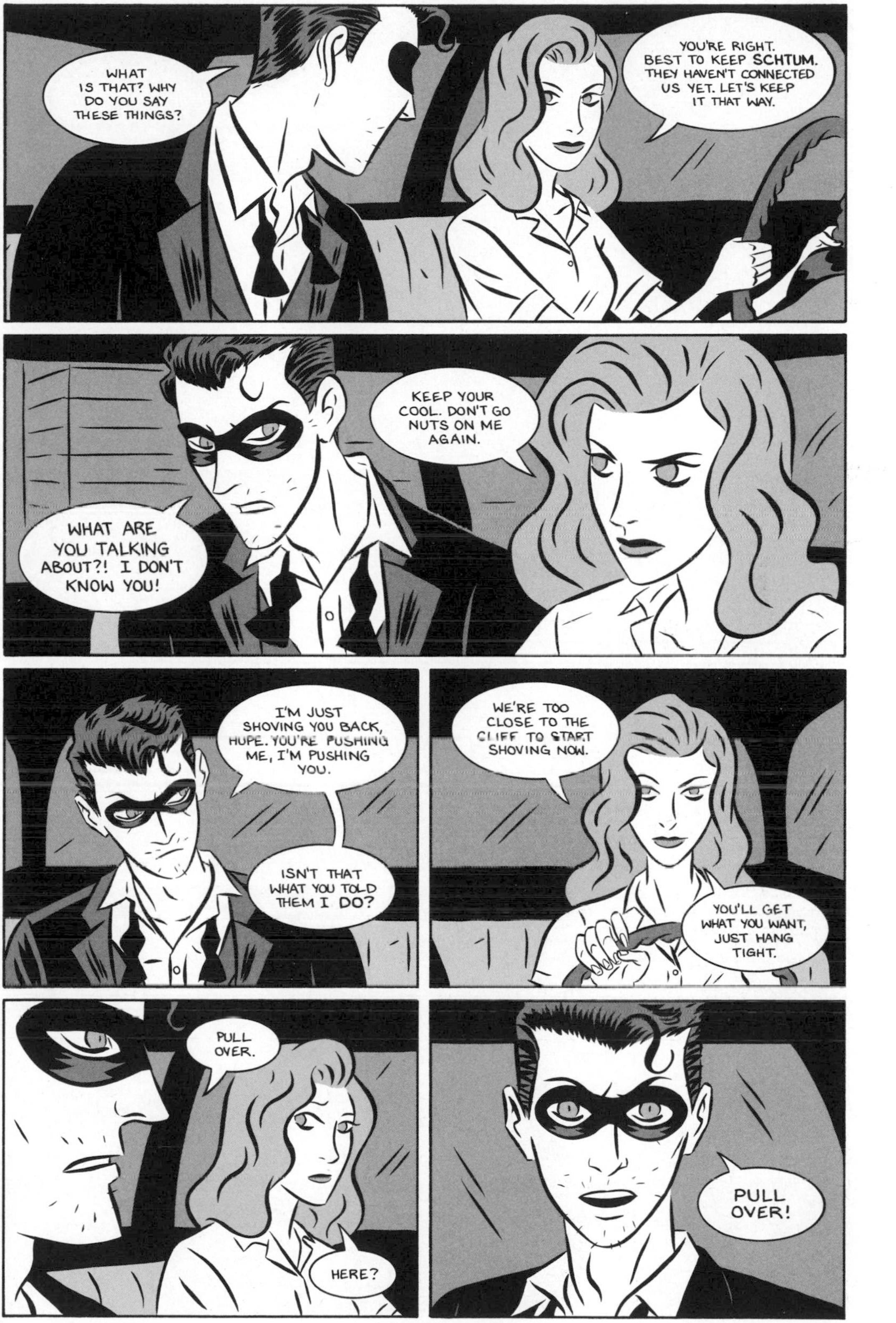
WHAT IS THAT? WHY DO YOU SAY THESE THINGS?
YOU'RE RIGHT. BEST TO KEEP SCHTUM. THEY HAVEN'T CONNECTED US YET. LET'S KEEP IT THAT WAY.
KEEP YOUR COOL. DON'T GO NUTS ON ME AGAIN.
WHAT ARE YOU TALKING ABOUT?! I DON'T KNOW YOU!
I'M JUST SHOVING YOU BACK, HOPE. YOU'RE PUSHING ME, I'M PUSHING YOU.
ISN'T THAT WHAT YOU TOLD THEM I DO?
WE'RE TOO CLOSE TO THE CLIFF TO START SHOVING NOW.
YOU'LL GET WHAT YOU WANT, JUST HANG TIGHT.
PULL OVER.
HERE?
PULL OVER!

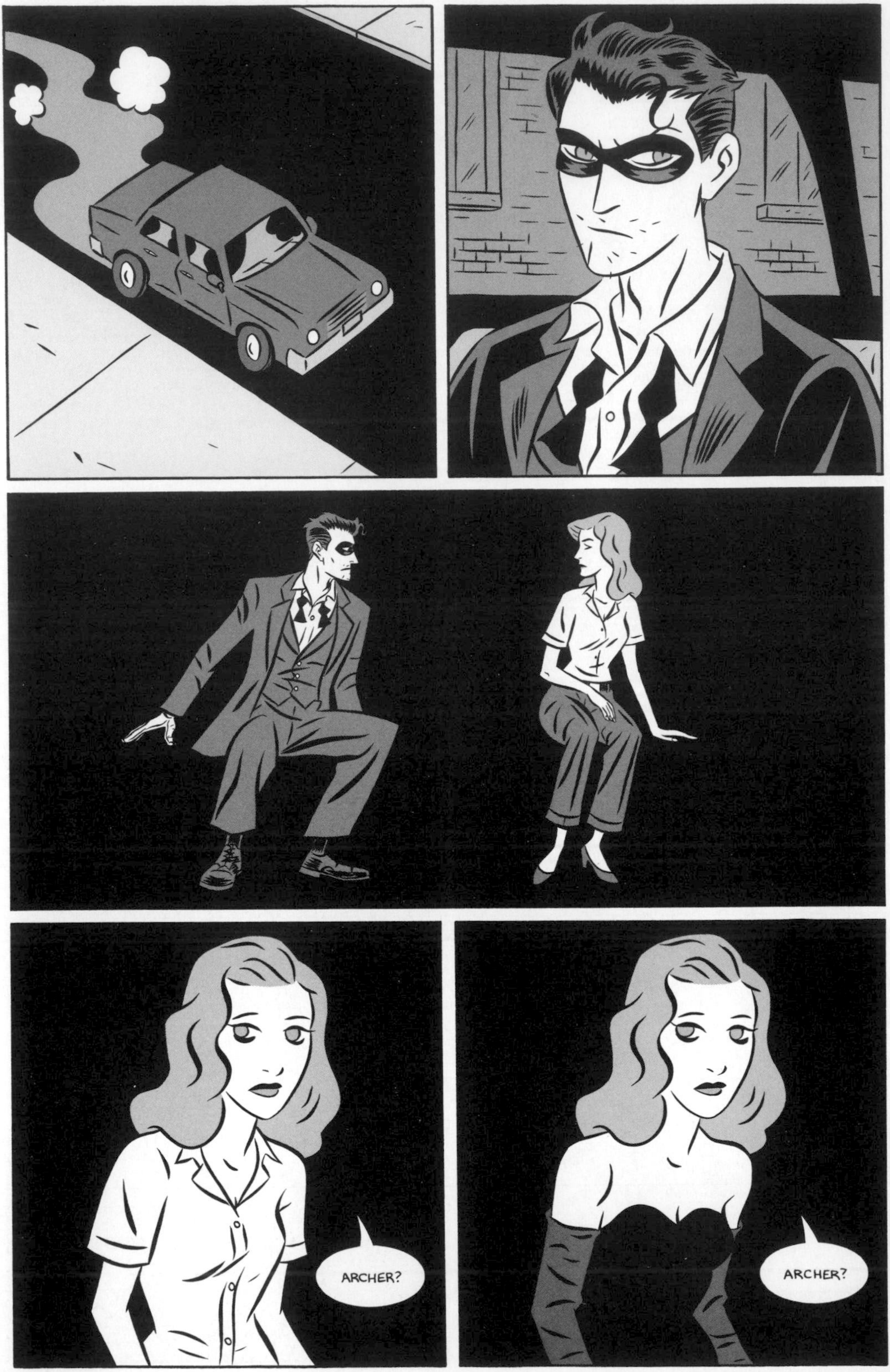
ARCHER?
ARCHER?

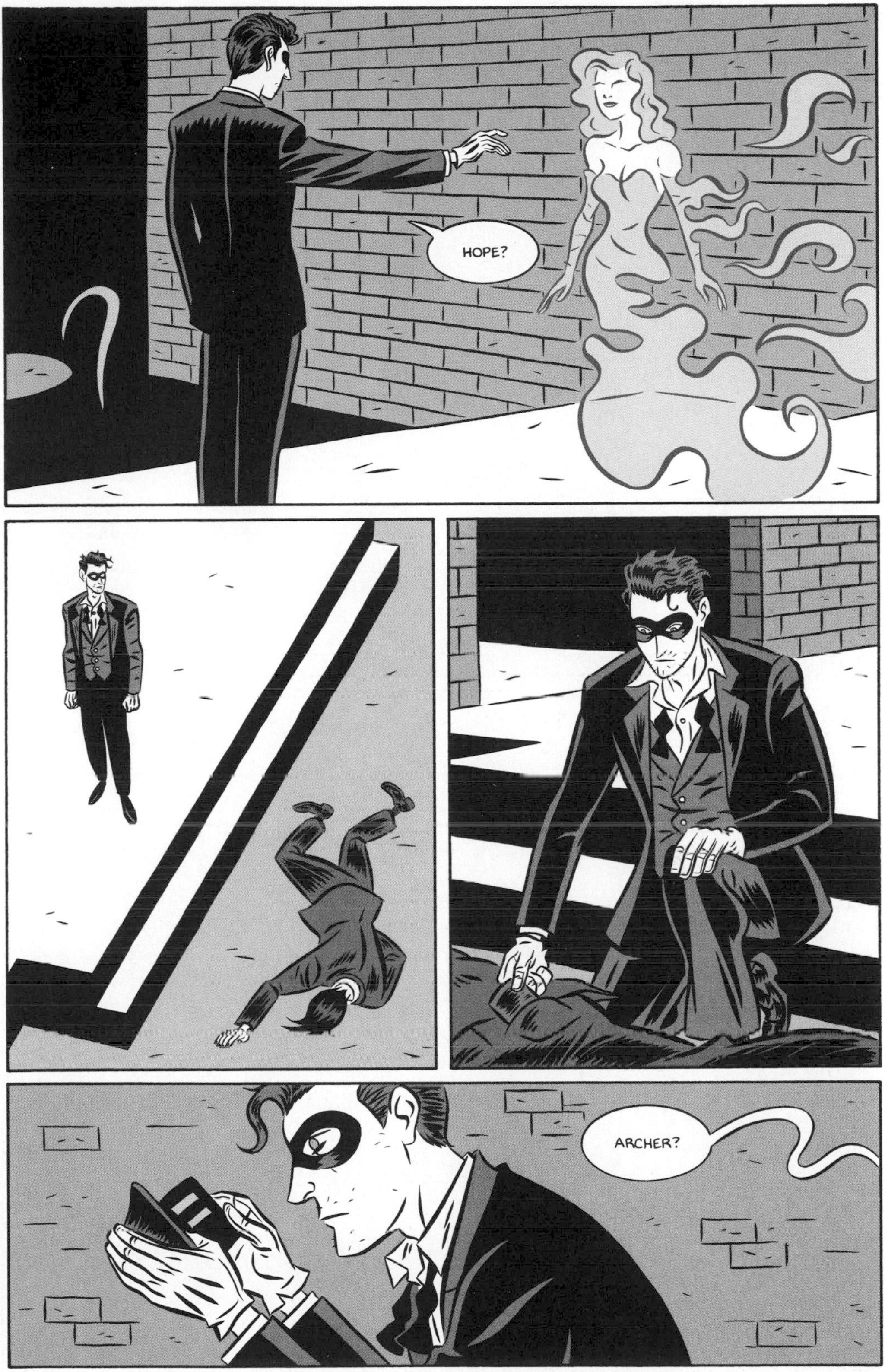
HOPE?
ARCHER?

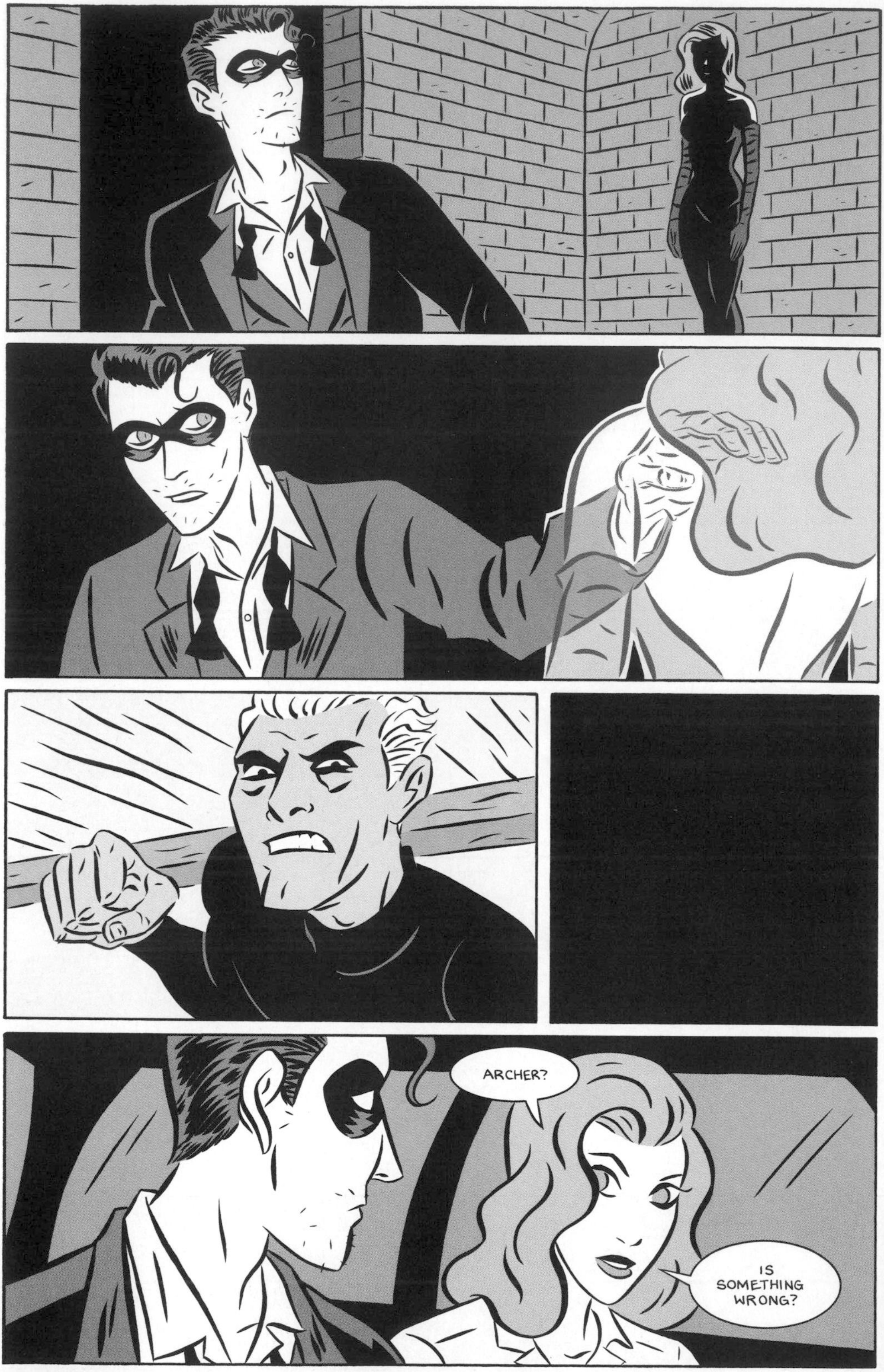
ARCHER?
IS SOMETHING WRONG?

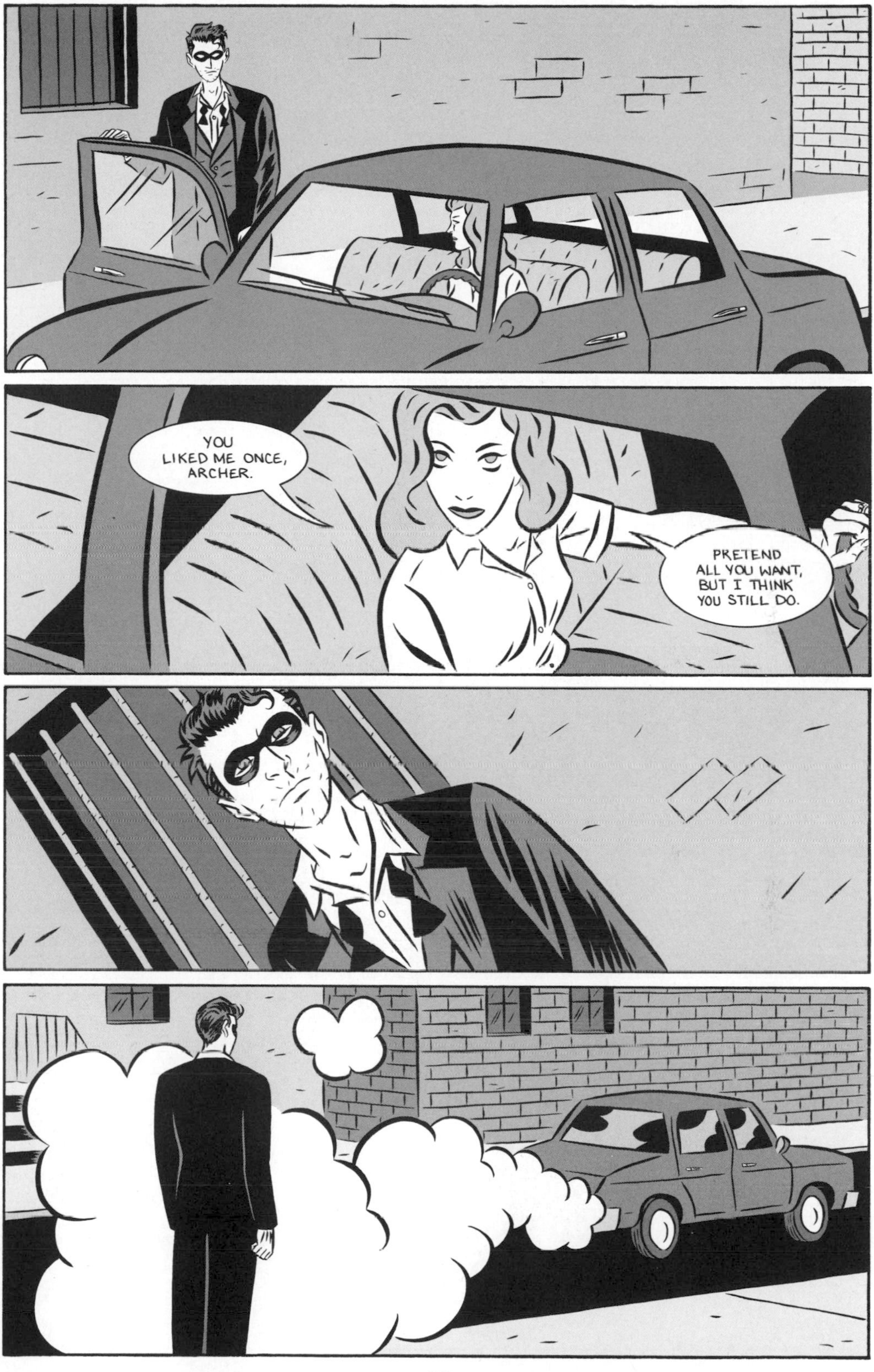
YOU LIKED ME ONCE, ARCHER.
PRETEND ALL YOU WANT, BUT I THINK YOU STILL DO.

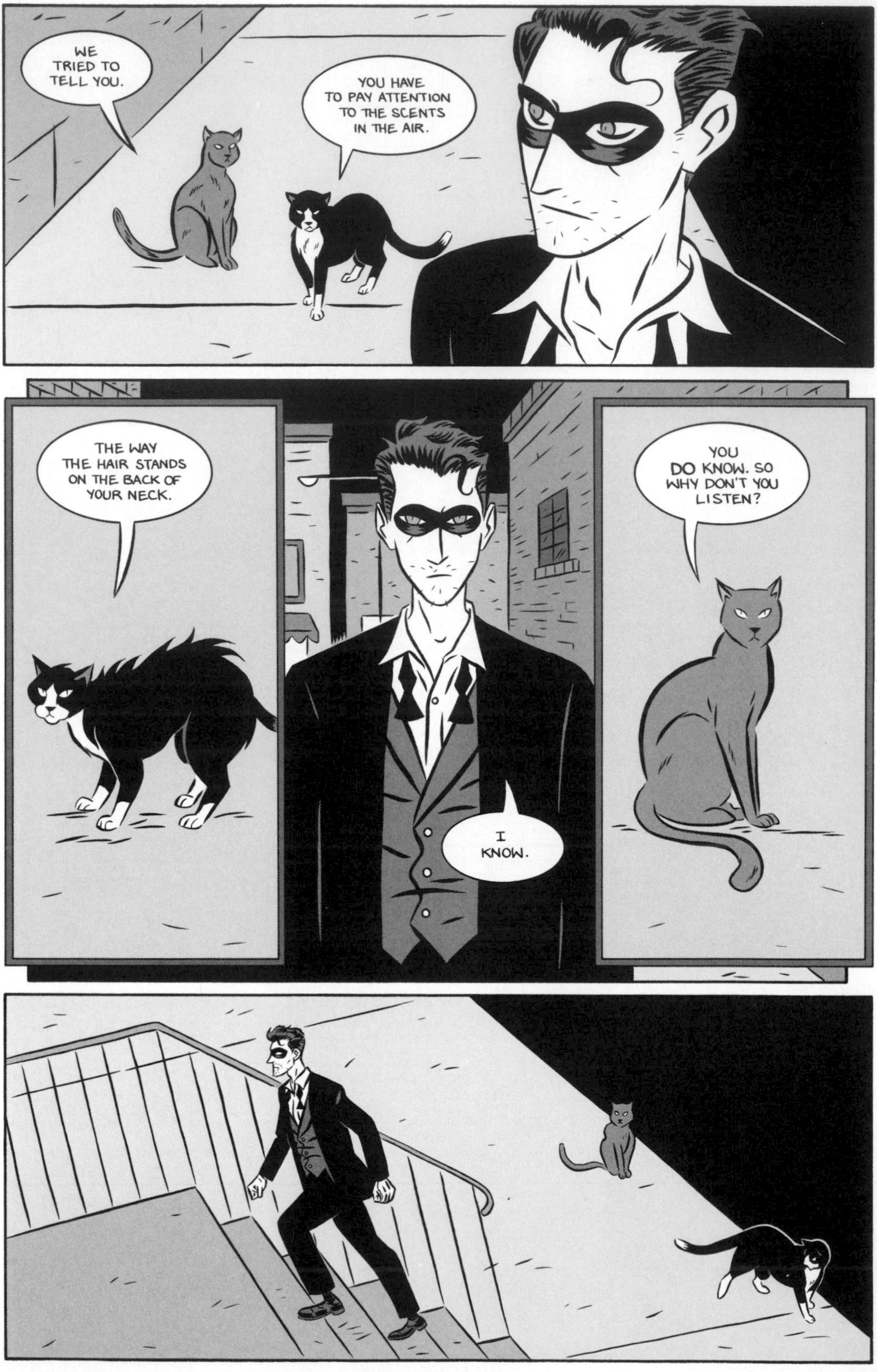
WE TRIED TO TELL YOU.
YOU HAVE TO PAY ATTENTION TO THE SCENTS IN THE AIR.
THE WAY THE HAIR STANDS ON THE BACK OF YOUR NECK.
YOU DO KNOW. SO WHY DON'T YOU LISTEN?
I KNOW.

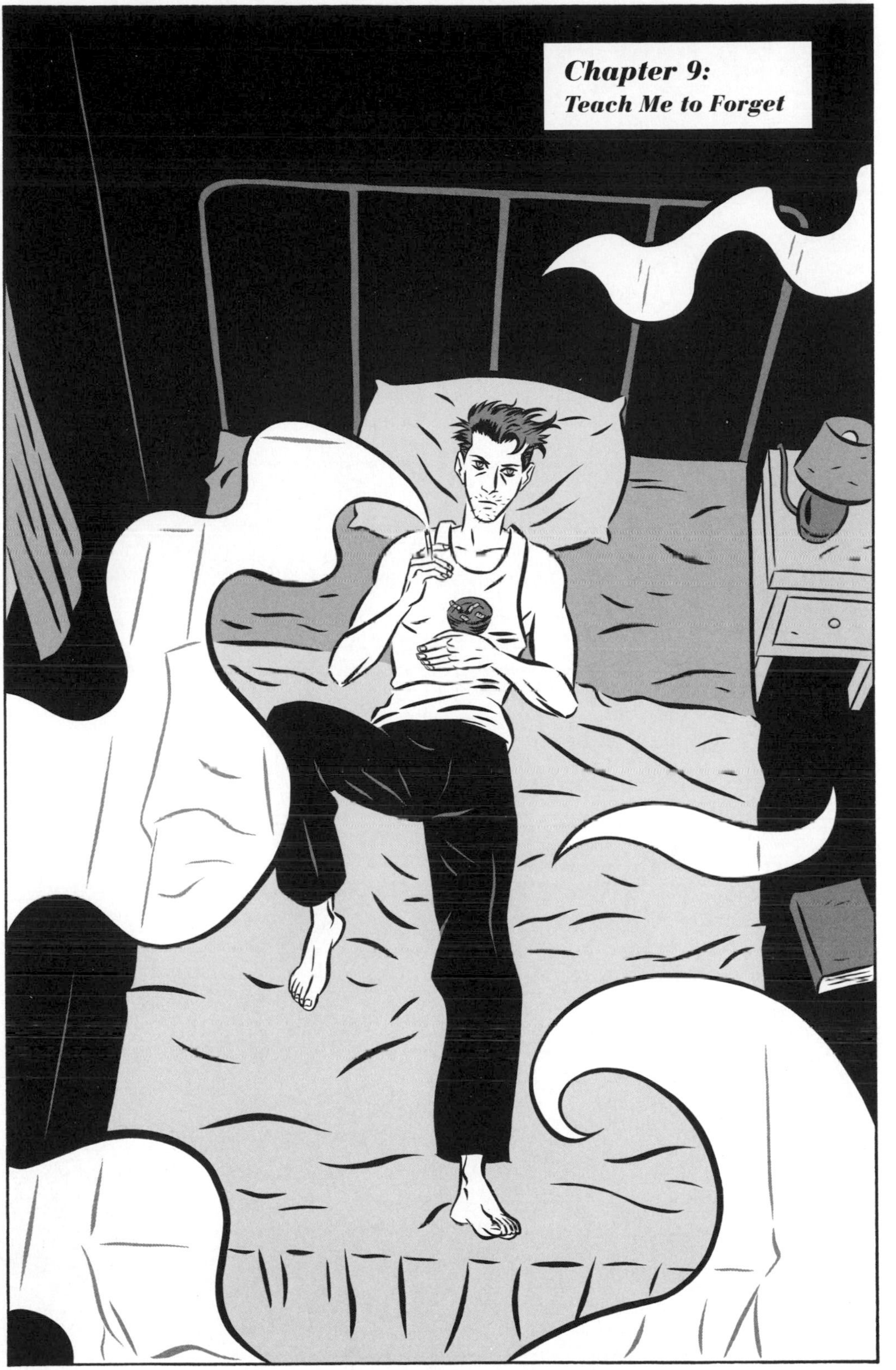
Chapter 9:
Teach Me to Forget

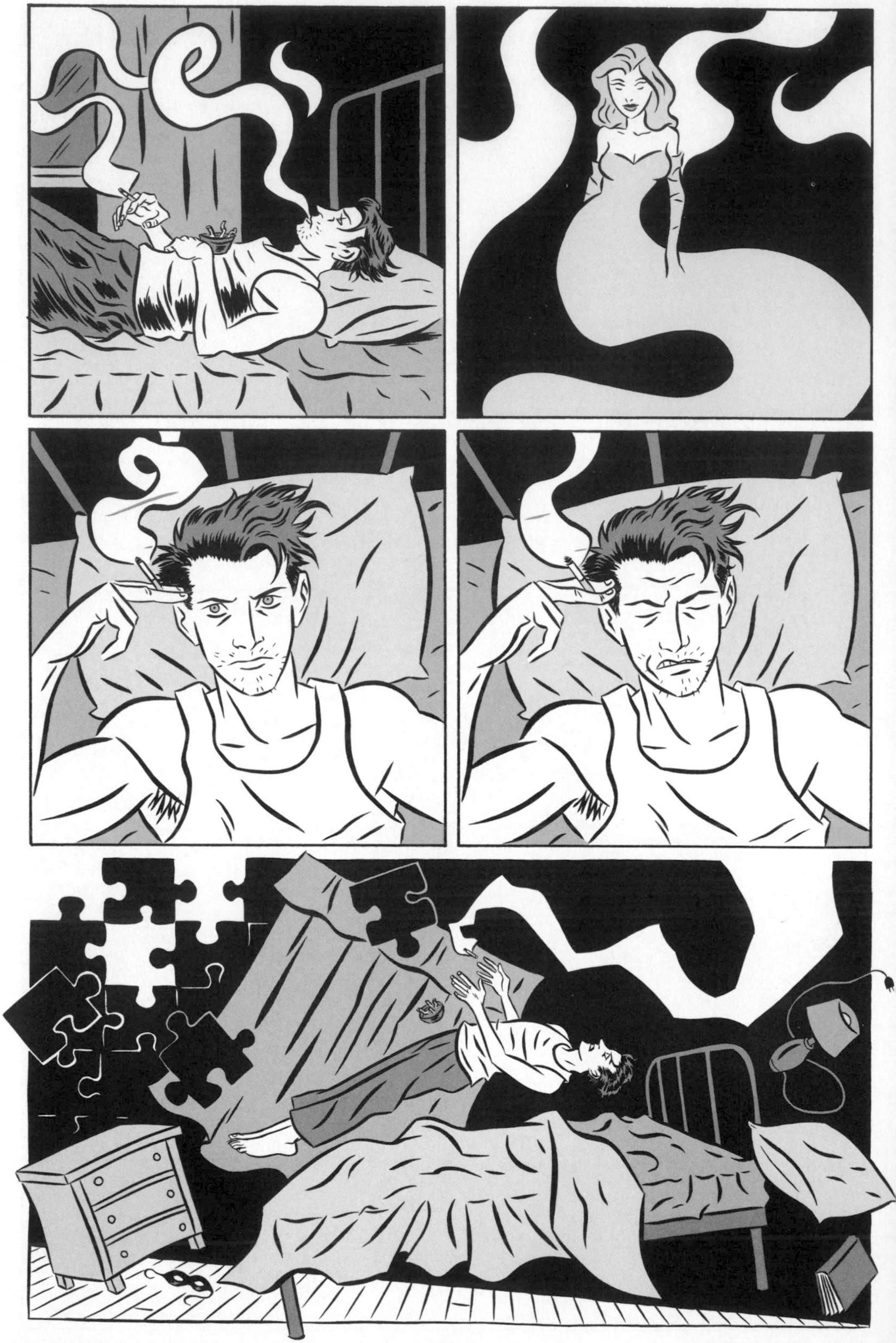

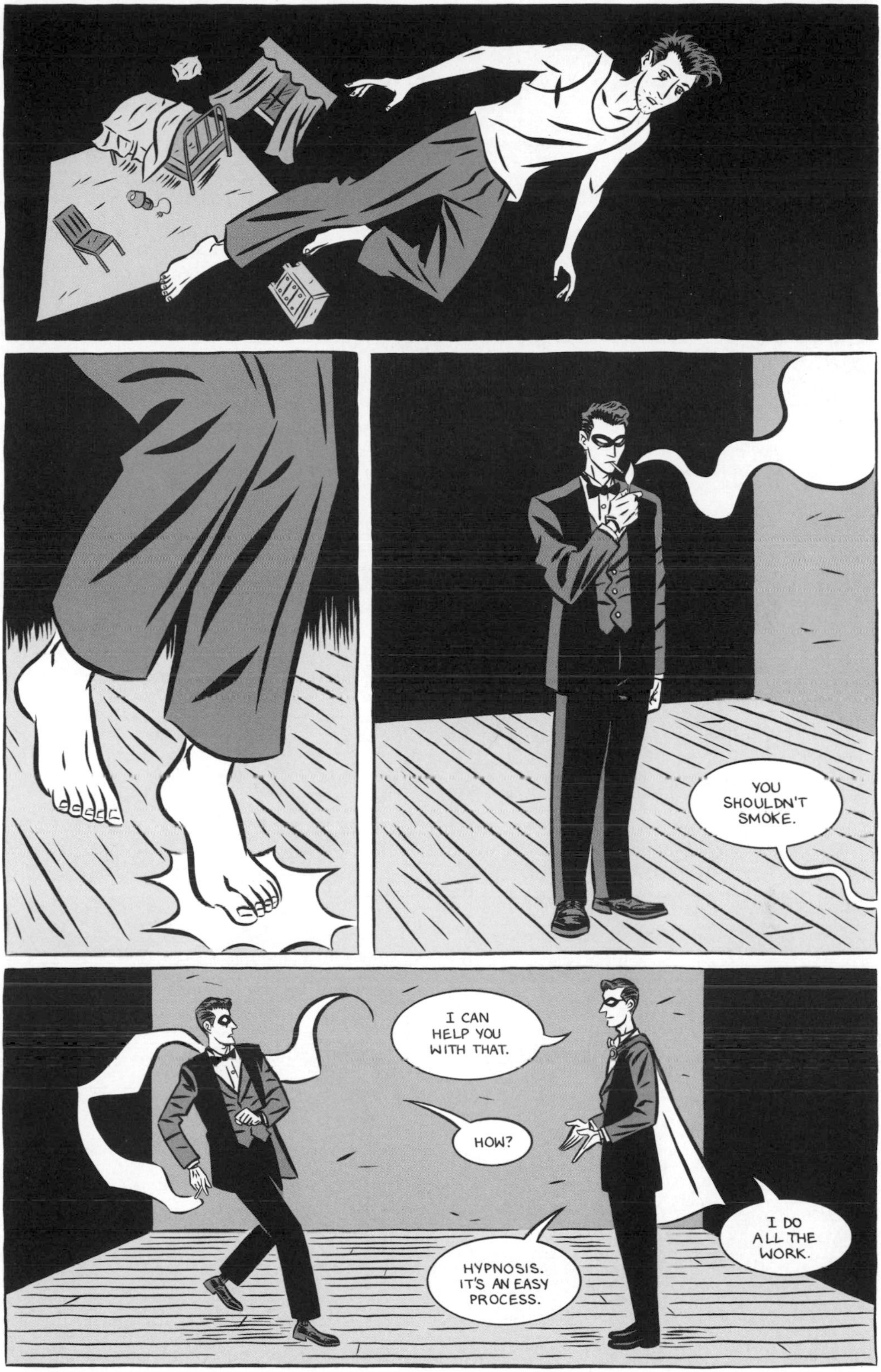
YOU SHOULDN'T SMOKE.
I CAN HELP YOU WITH THAT.
HOW?
HYPNOSIS. IT'S AN EASY PROCESS.
I DO ALL THE WORK.

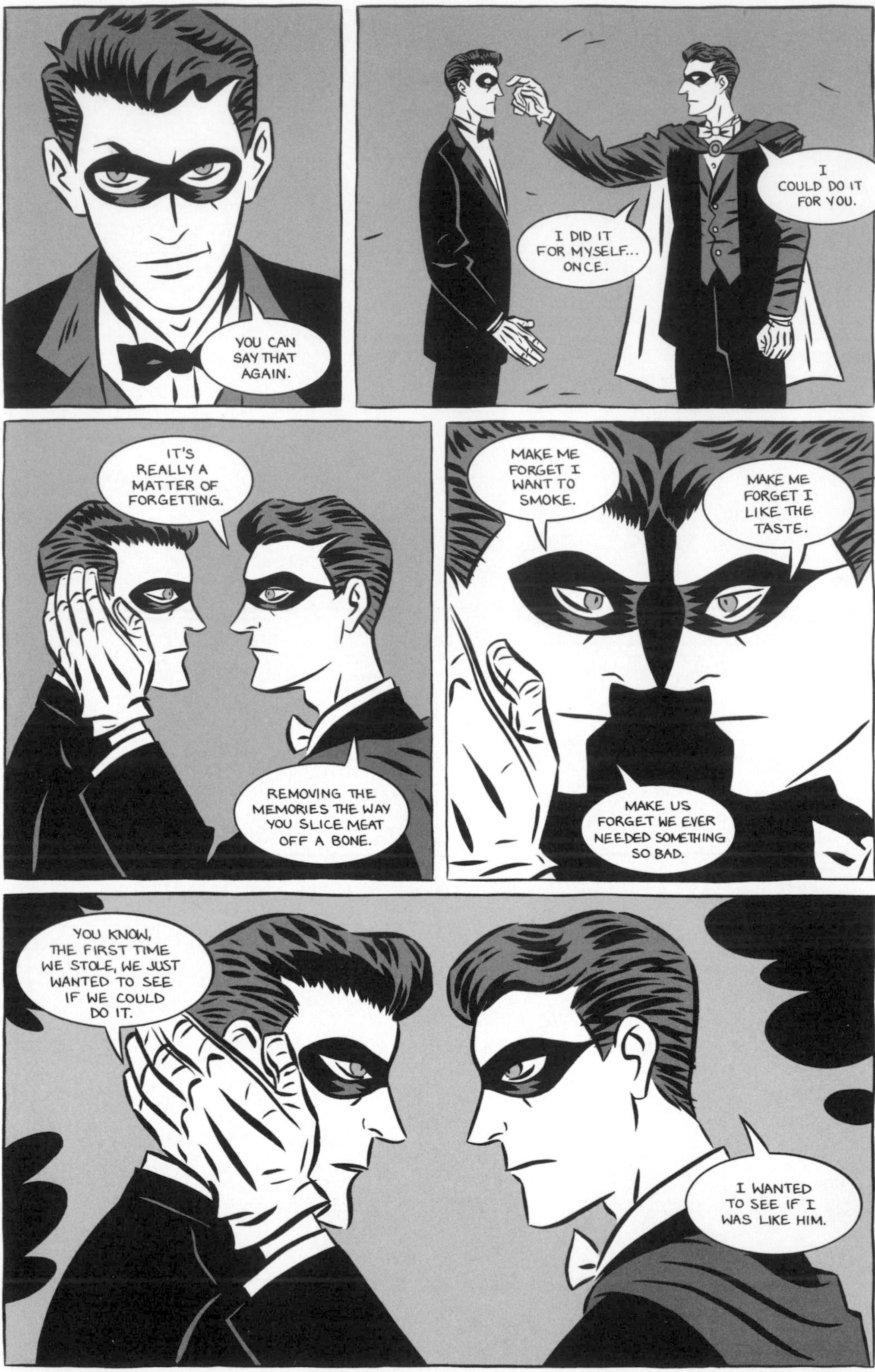
YOU CAN SAY THAT AGAIN.
I COULD DO IT FOR YOU.
I DID IT FOR MYSELF... ONCE.
IT'S REALLY A MATTER OF FORGETTING.
REMOVING THE MEMORIES THE WAY YOU SLICE MEAT OFF A BONE.
MAKE ME FORGET I WANT TO SMOKE.
MAKE ME FORGET I LIKE THE TASTE.
MAKE US FORGET WE EVER NEEDED SOMETHING SO BAD.
YOU KNOW, THE FIRST TIME WE STOLE, WE JUST WANTED TO SEE IF WE COULD DO IT.
I WANTED TO SEE IF I WAS LIKE HIM.

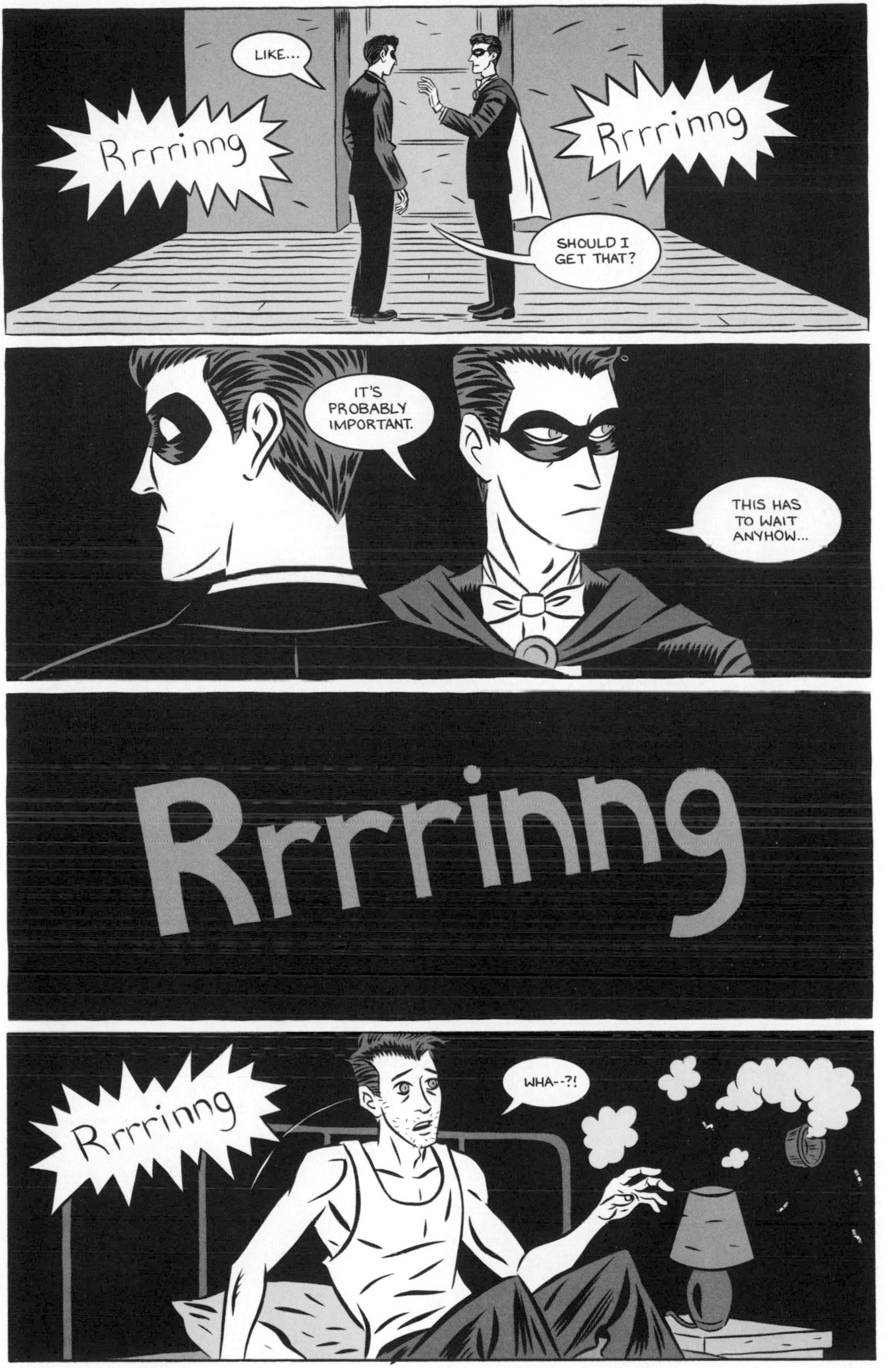
LIKE...
Rrrrinng
Rrrrinng
SHOULD I GET THAT?
IT'S PROBABLY IMPORTANT.
THIS HAS TO WAIT ANYHOW...
Rrrrinng
Rrrrinng
WHA--?!

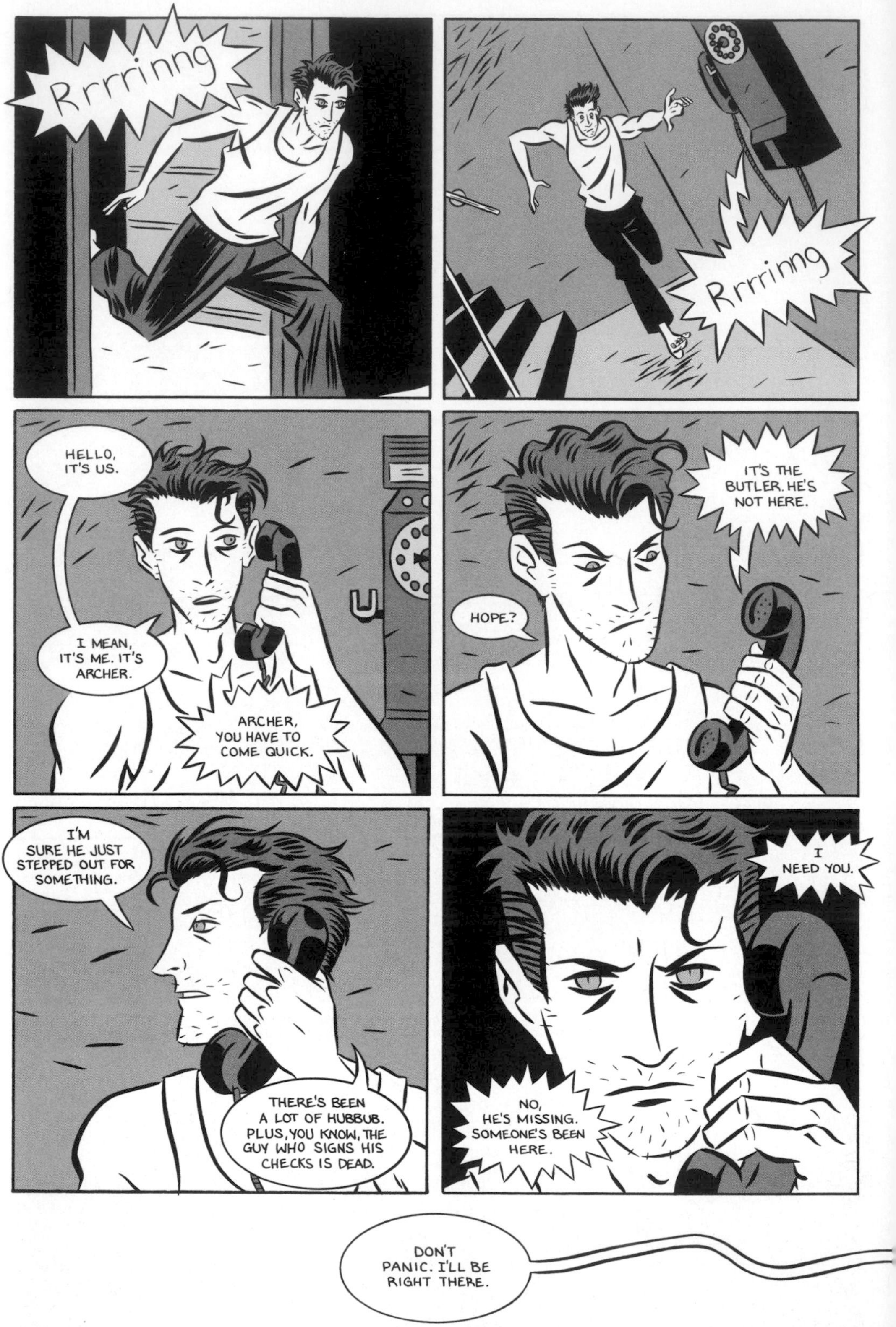
Rrrrinng
Rrrrinng
HELLO, IT'S US.
I MEAN, IT'S ME. IT'S ARCHER.
ARCHER, YOU HAVE TO COME QUICK.
HOPE?
IT'S THE BUTLER. HE'S NOT HERE.
I'M SURE HE JUST STEPPED OUT FOR SOMETHING.
THERE'S BEEN A LOT OF HUBBUB. PLUS, YOU KNOW, THE GUY WHO SIGNS HIS CHECKS IS DEAD.
NO, HE'S MISSING. SOMEONE'S BEEN HERE.
I NEED YOU.
DON'T PANIC. I'LL BE RIGHT THERE.

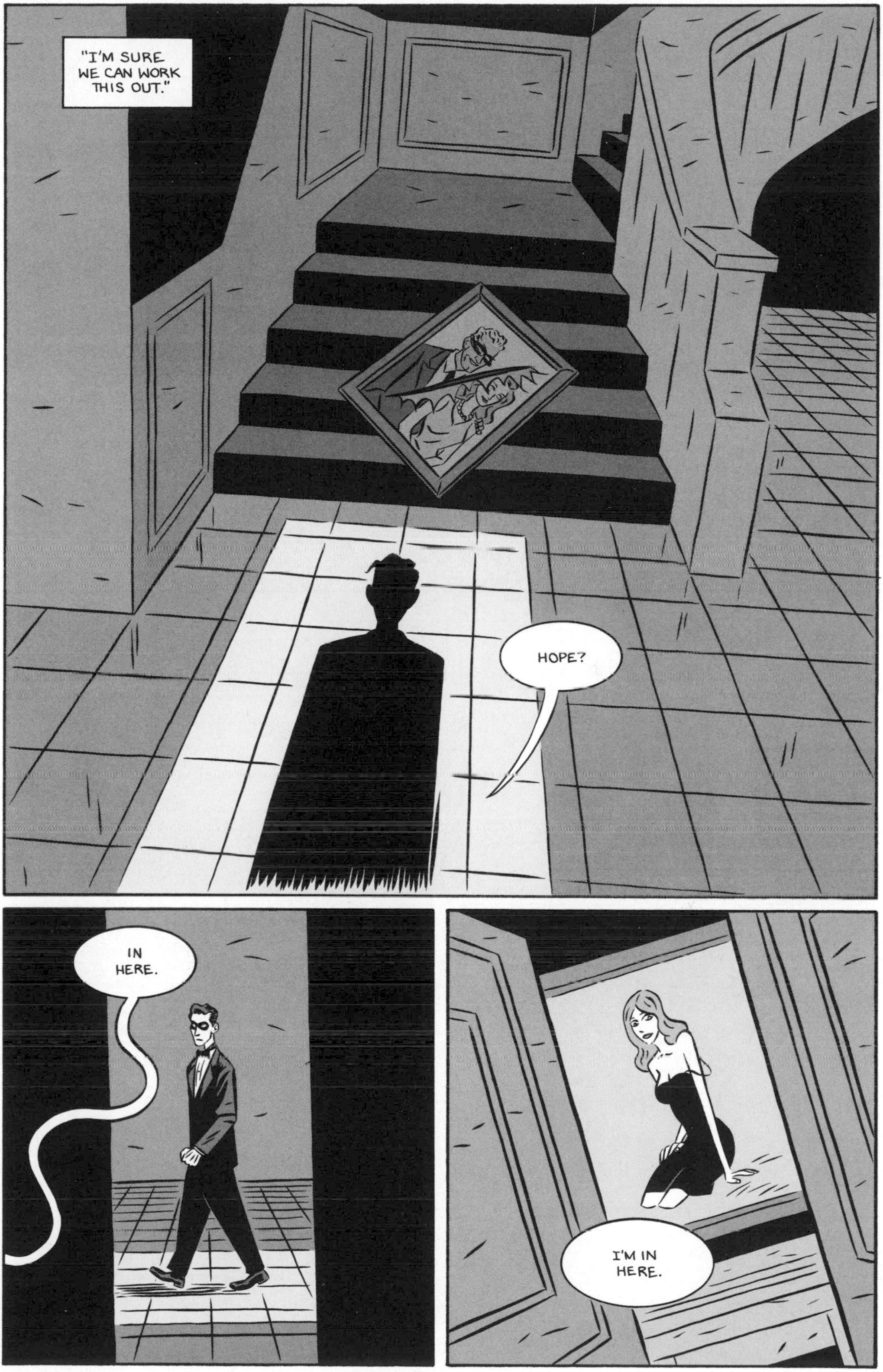
"I'M SURE WE CAN WORK THIS OUT."
HOPE?
IN HERE.
I'M IN HERE.

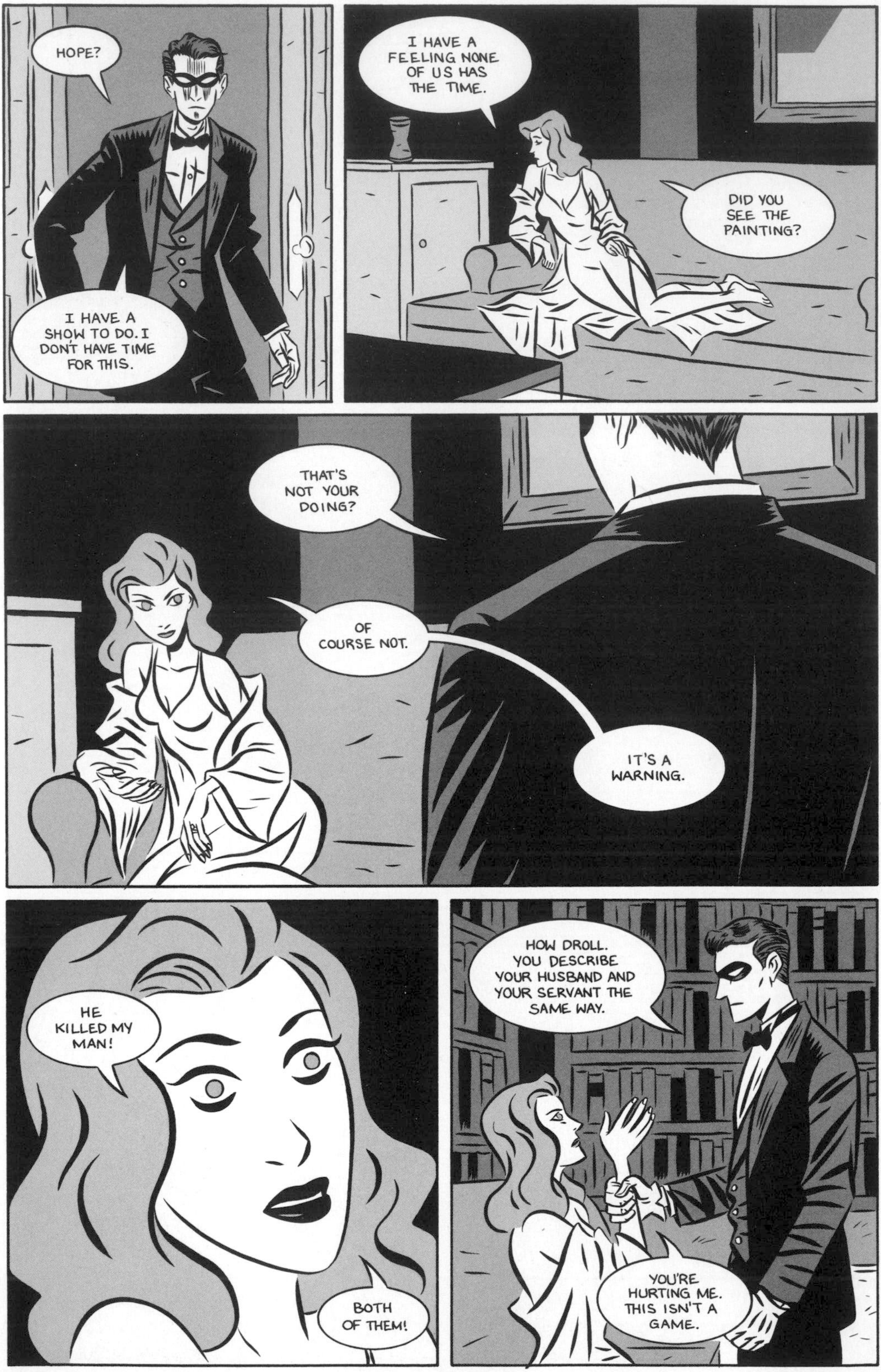
HOPE?
I HAVE A SHOW TO DO. I DON'T HAVE TIME FOR THIS.
I HAVE A FEELING NONE OF US HAS THE TIME.
DID YOU SEE THE PAINTING?
THAT'S NOT YOUR DOING?
OF COURSE NOT.
IT'S A WARNING.
HE KILLED MY MAN!
BOTH OF THEM!
HOW DROLL. YOU DESCRIBE YOUR HUSBAND AND YOUR SERVANT THE SAME WAY.
YOU'RE HURTING ME. THIS ISN'T A GAME.

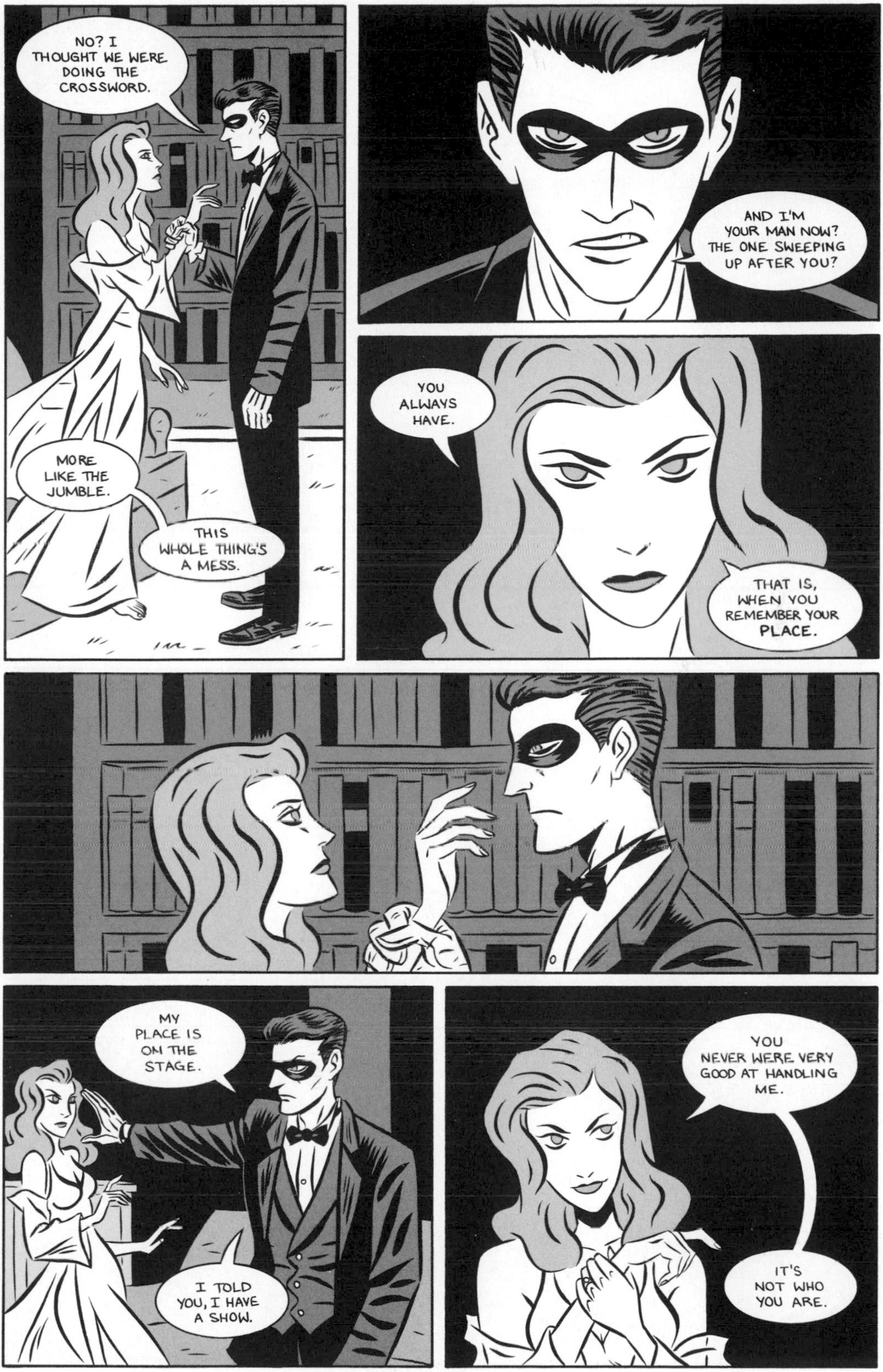
NO? I THOUGHT WE WERE DOING THE CROSSWORD.
MORE LIKE THE JUMBLE.
THIS WHOLE THING'S A MESS.
AND I'M YOUR MAN NOW? THE ONE SWEEPING UP AFTER YOU?
YOU ALWAYS HAVE.
THAT IS, WHEN YOU REMEMBER YOUR PLACE.
MY PLACE IS ON THE STAGE.
I TOLD YOU, I HAVE A SHOW.
YOU NEVER WERE VERY GOOD AT HANDLING ME.
IT'S NOT WHO YOU ARE.

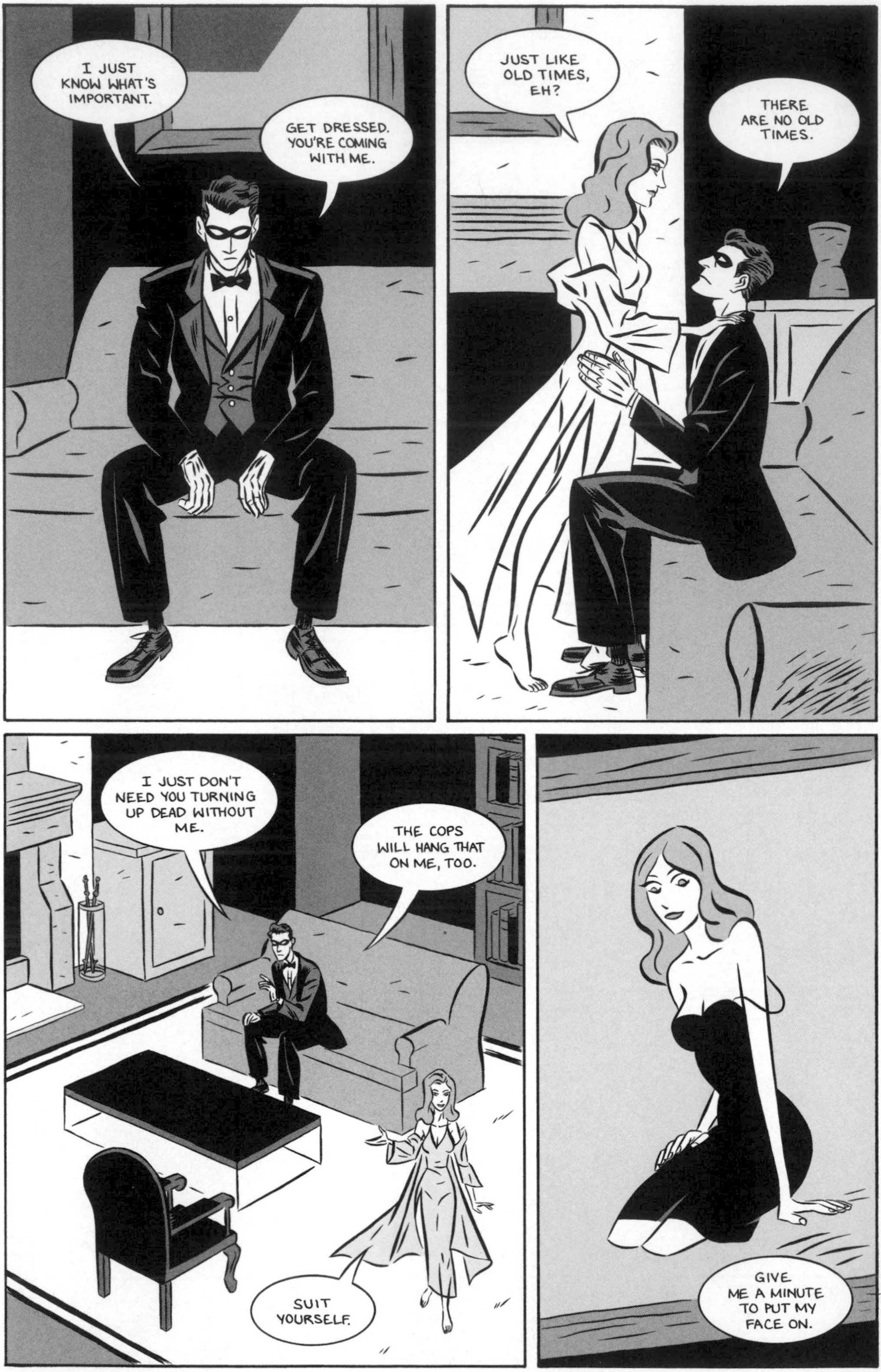
I JUST KNOW WHAT'S IMPORTANT.
GET DRESSED. YOU'RE COMING WITH ME.
JUST LIKE OLD TIMES, EH?
THERE ARE NO OLD TIMES.
I JUST DON'T NEED YOU TURNING UP DEAD WITHOUT ME.
THE COPS WILL HANG THAT ON ME, TOO.
SUIT YOURSELF.
GIVE ME A MINUTE TO PUT MY FACE ON.

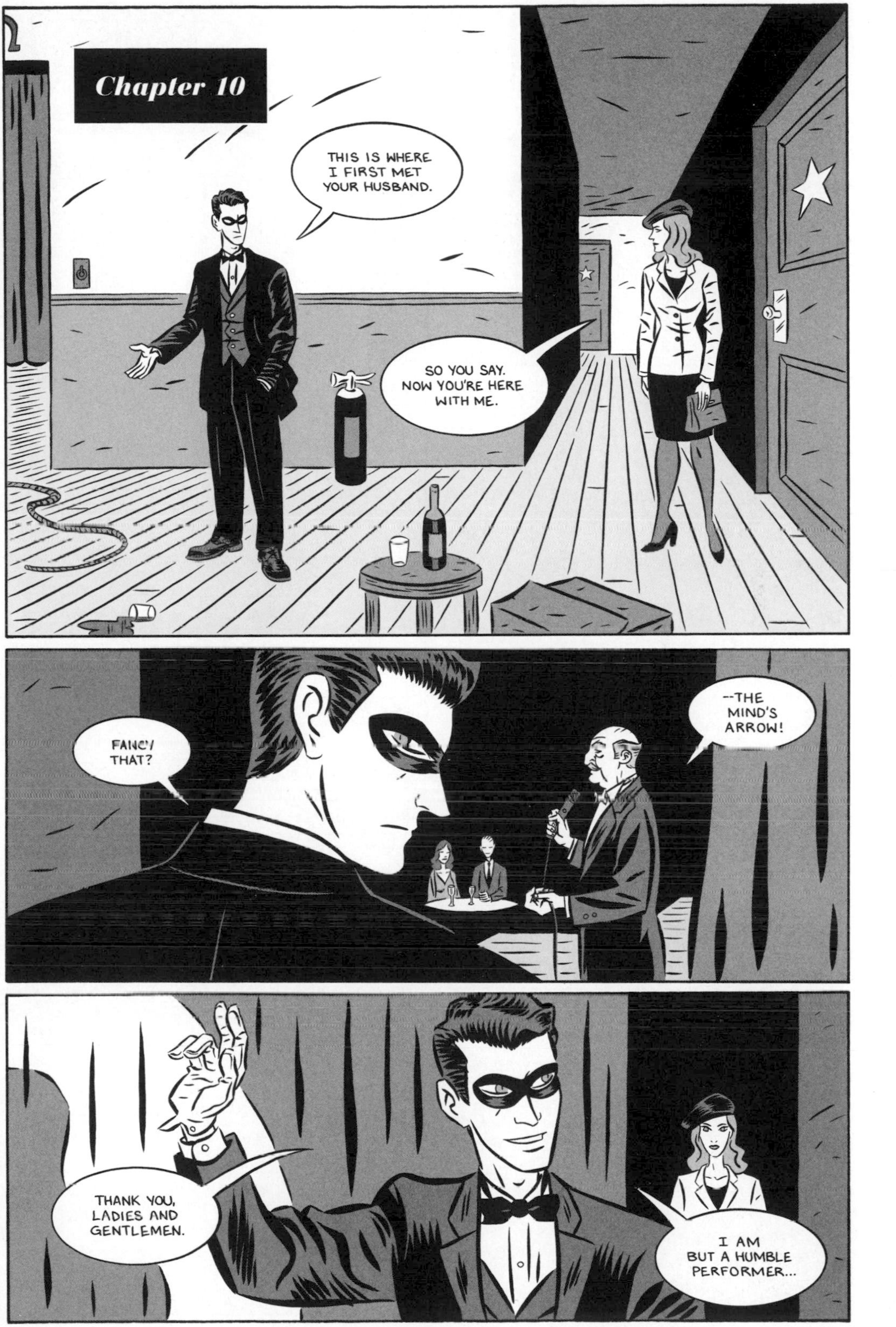
Chapter 10
THIS IS WHERE I FIRST MET YOUR HUSBAND.
SO YOU SAY. NOW YOU'RE HERE WITH ME.
FANCY THAT?
--THE MIND'S ARROW!
THANK YOU, LADIES AND GENTLEMEN.
I AM BUT A HUMBLE PERFORMER...

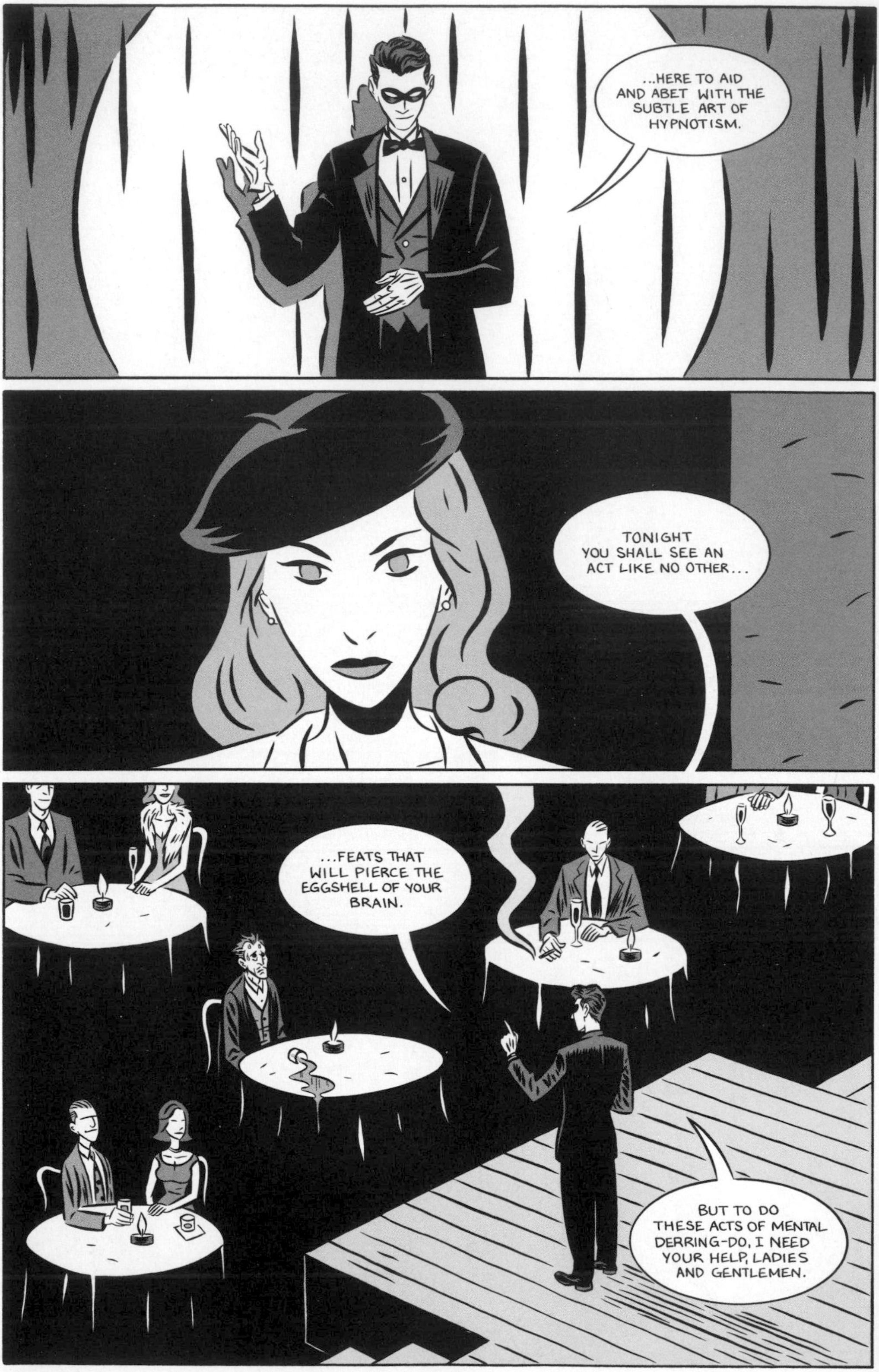
...HERE TO AID AND ABET WITH THE SUBTLE ART OF HYPNOTISM.
TONIGHT YOU SHALL SEE AN ACT LIKE NO OTHER...
...FEATS THAT WILL PIERCE THE EGGSHELL OF YOUR BRAIN.
BUT TO DO THESE ACTS OF MENTAL DERRING-DO, I NEED YOUR HELP, LADIES AND GENTLEMEN.

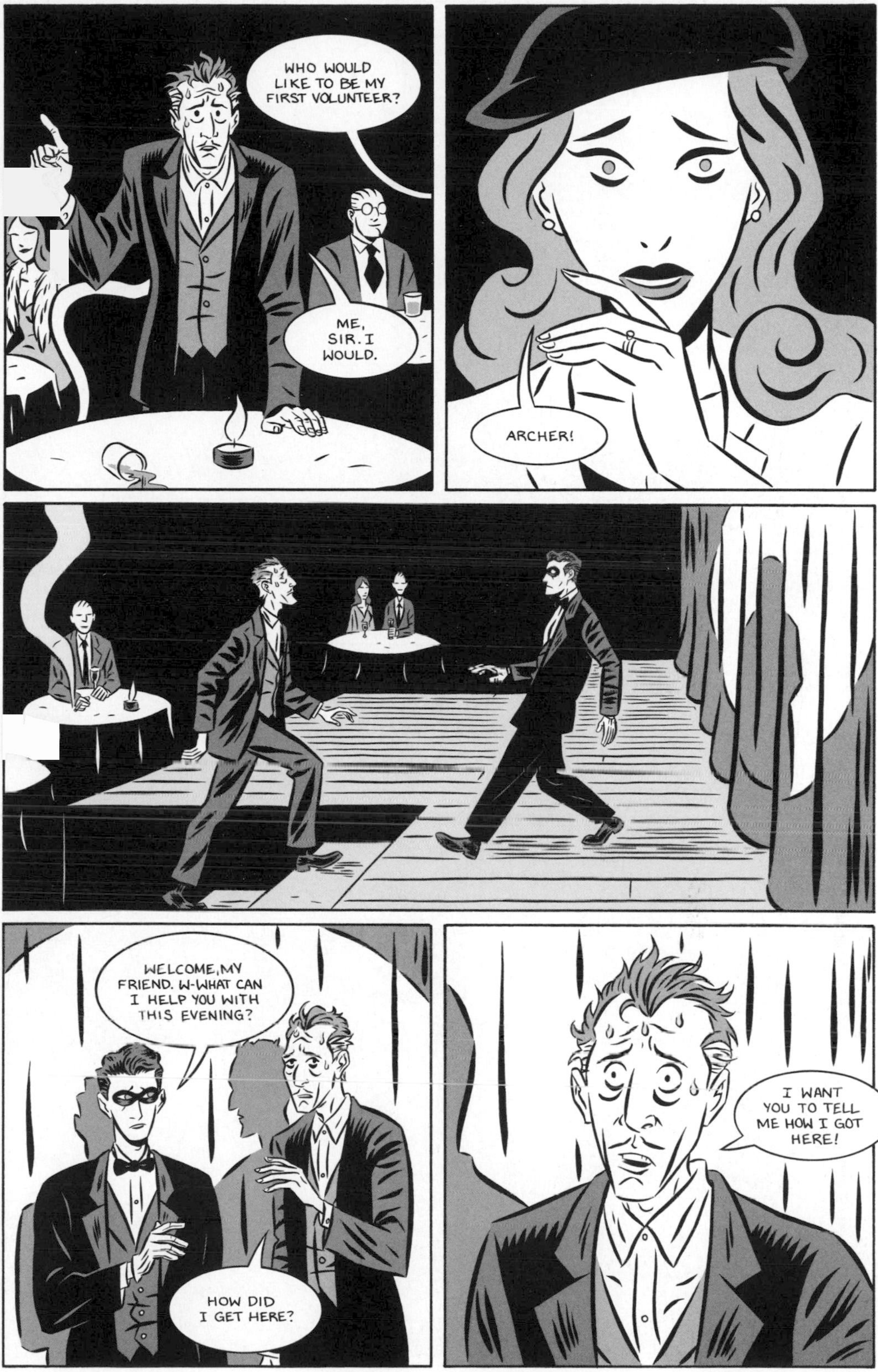
WHO WOULD LIKE TO BE MY FIRST VOLUNTEER?
ME, SIR. I WOULD.
ARCHER!
WELCOME, MY FRIEND. W-WHAT CAN I HELP YOU WITH THIS EVENING?
HOW DID I GET HERE?
I WANT YOU TO TELL ME HOW I GOT HERE!

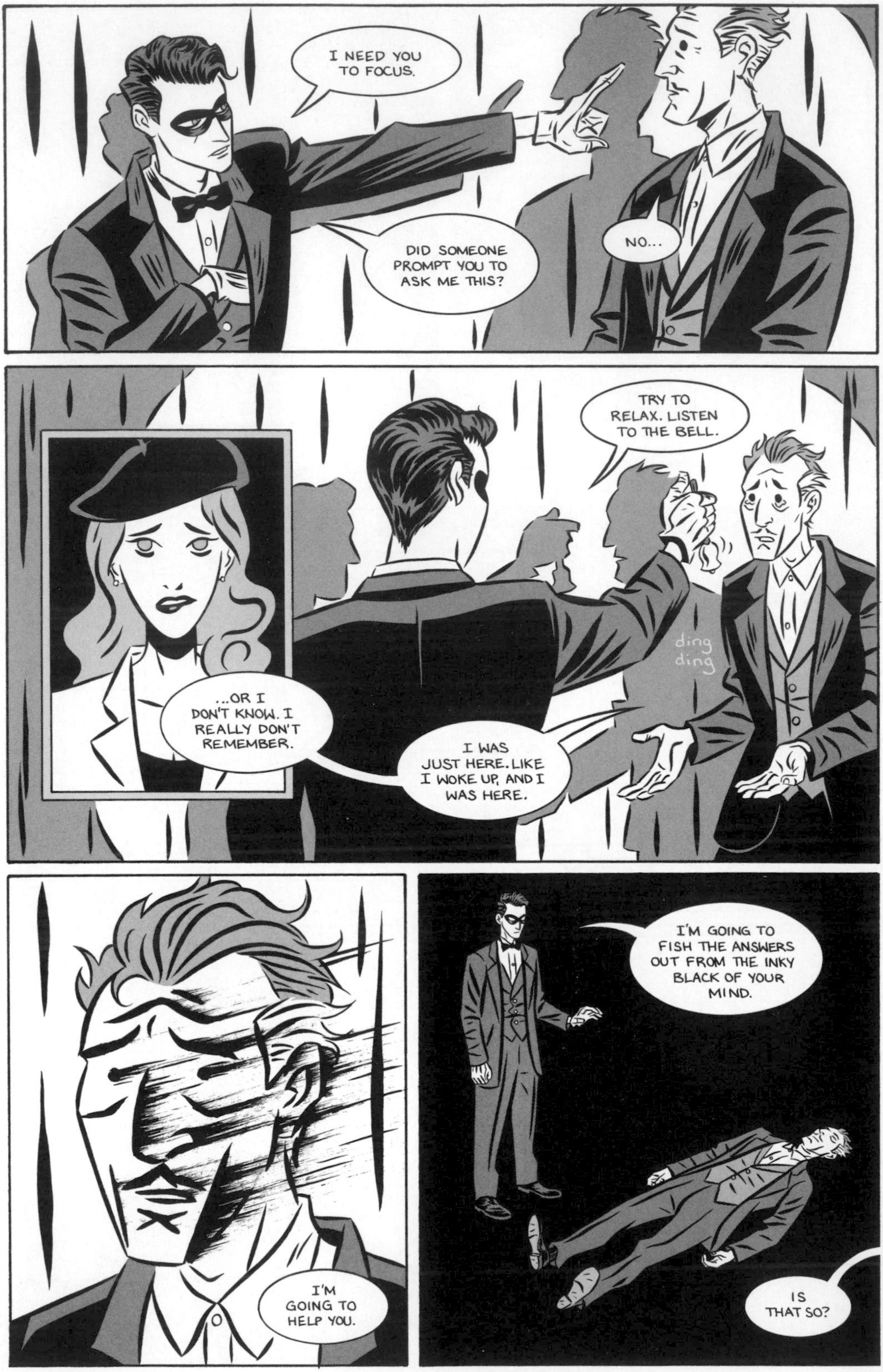
I NEED YOU TO FOCUS.
DID SOMEONE PROMPT YOU TO ASK ME THIS?
NO...
TRY TO RELAX. LISTEN TO THE BELL.
ding ding
I WAS JUST HERE. LIKE I WOKE UP, AND I WAS HERE.
...OR I DON'T KNOW. I REALLY DON'T REMEMBER.
I'M GOING TO HELP YOU.
I'M GOING TO FISH THE ANSWERS OUT FROM THE INKY BLACK OF YOUR MIND.
IS THAT SO?

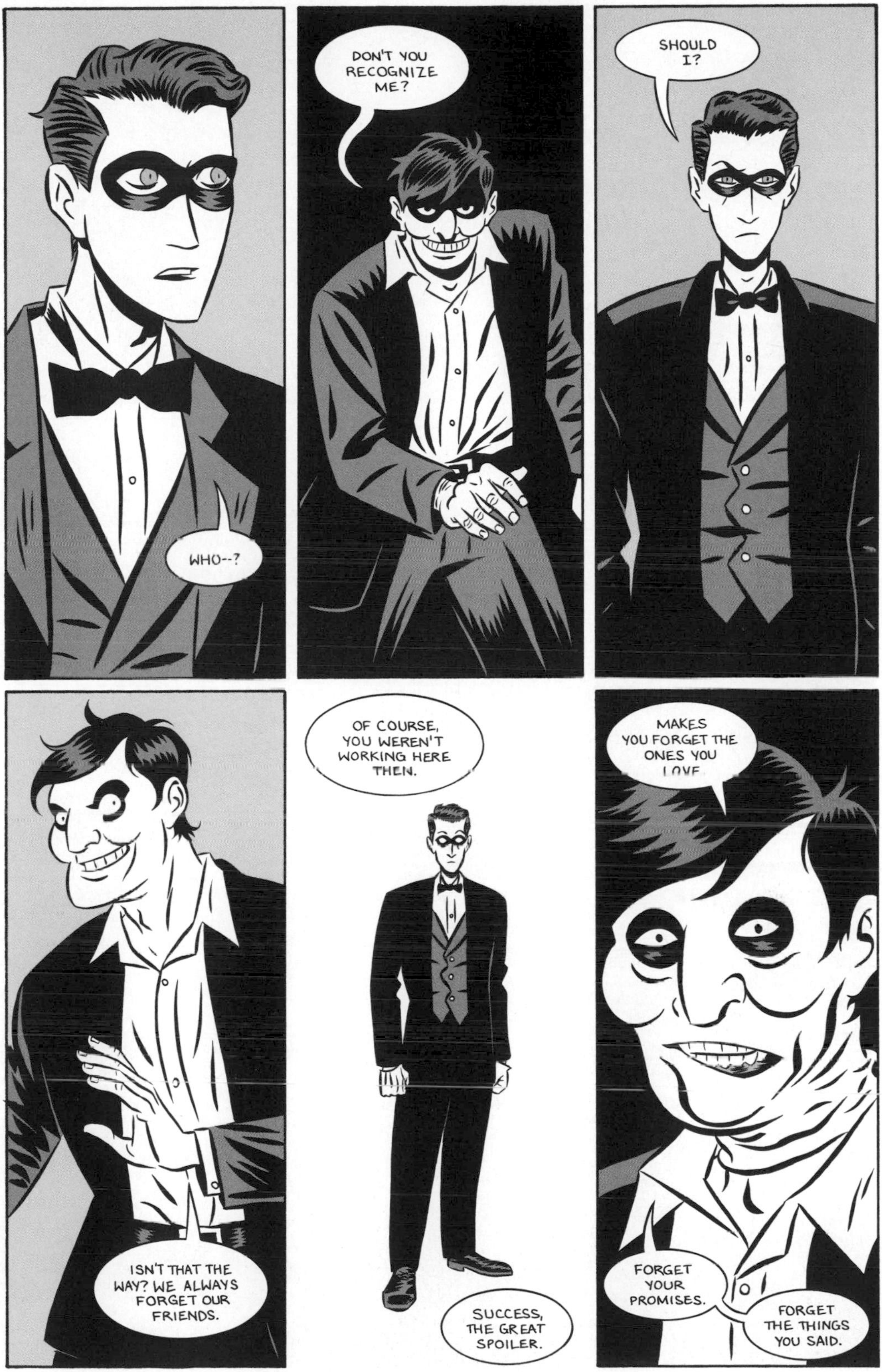
WHO--?
DON'T YOU RECOGNIZE ME?
SHOULD I?
ISN'T THAT THE WAY? WE ALWAYS FORGET OUR FRIENDS.
OF COURSE, YOU WEREN'T WORKING HERE THEN.
SUCCESS, THE GREAT SPOILER.
MAKES YOU FORGET THE ONES YOU LOVE.
FORGET YOUR PROMISES.
FORGET THE THINGS YOU SAID.

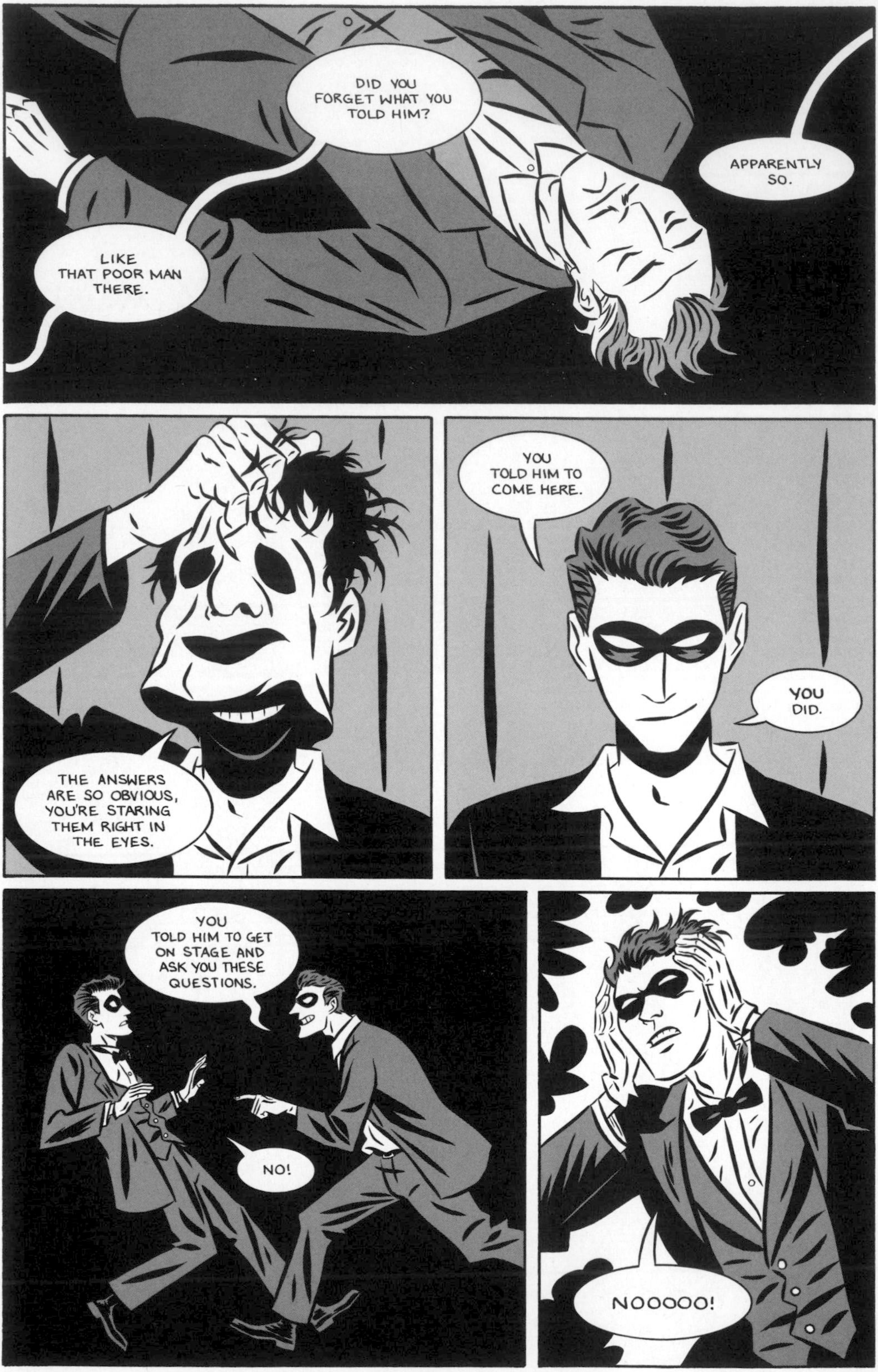
DID YOU FORGET WHAT YOU TOLD HIM?
APPARENTLY SO.
LIKE THAT POOR MAN THERE.
THE ANSWERS ARE SO OBVIOUS, YOU'RE STARING THEM RIGHT IN THE EYES.
YOU TOLD HIM TO COME HERE.
YOU DID.
YOU TOLD HIM TO GET ON STAGE AND ASK YOU THESE QUESTIONS.
NO!
NOOOOO!

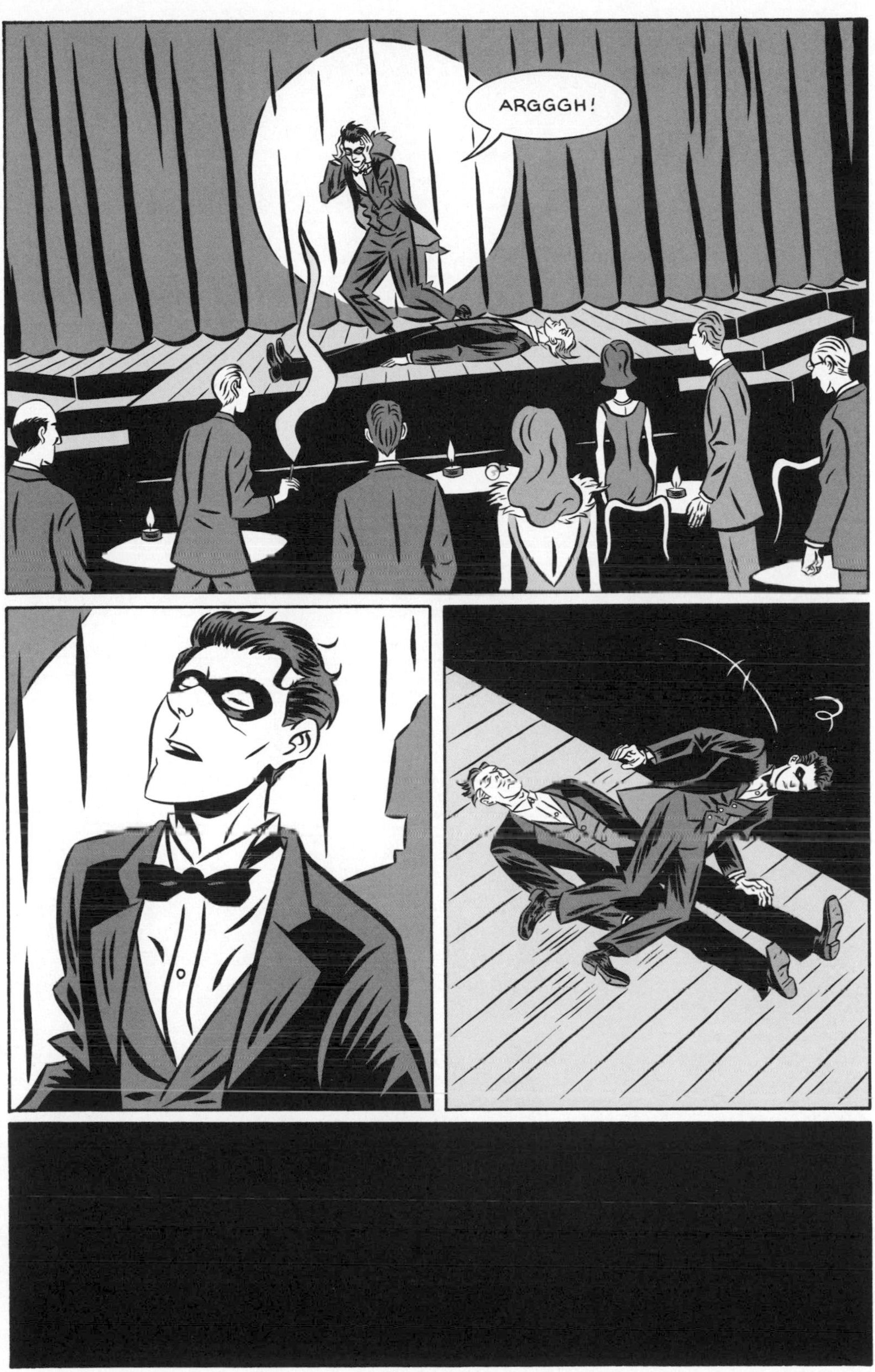
ARGGGH!

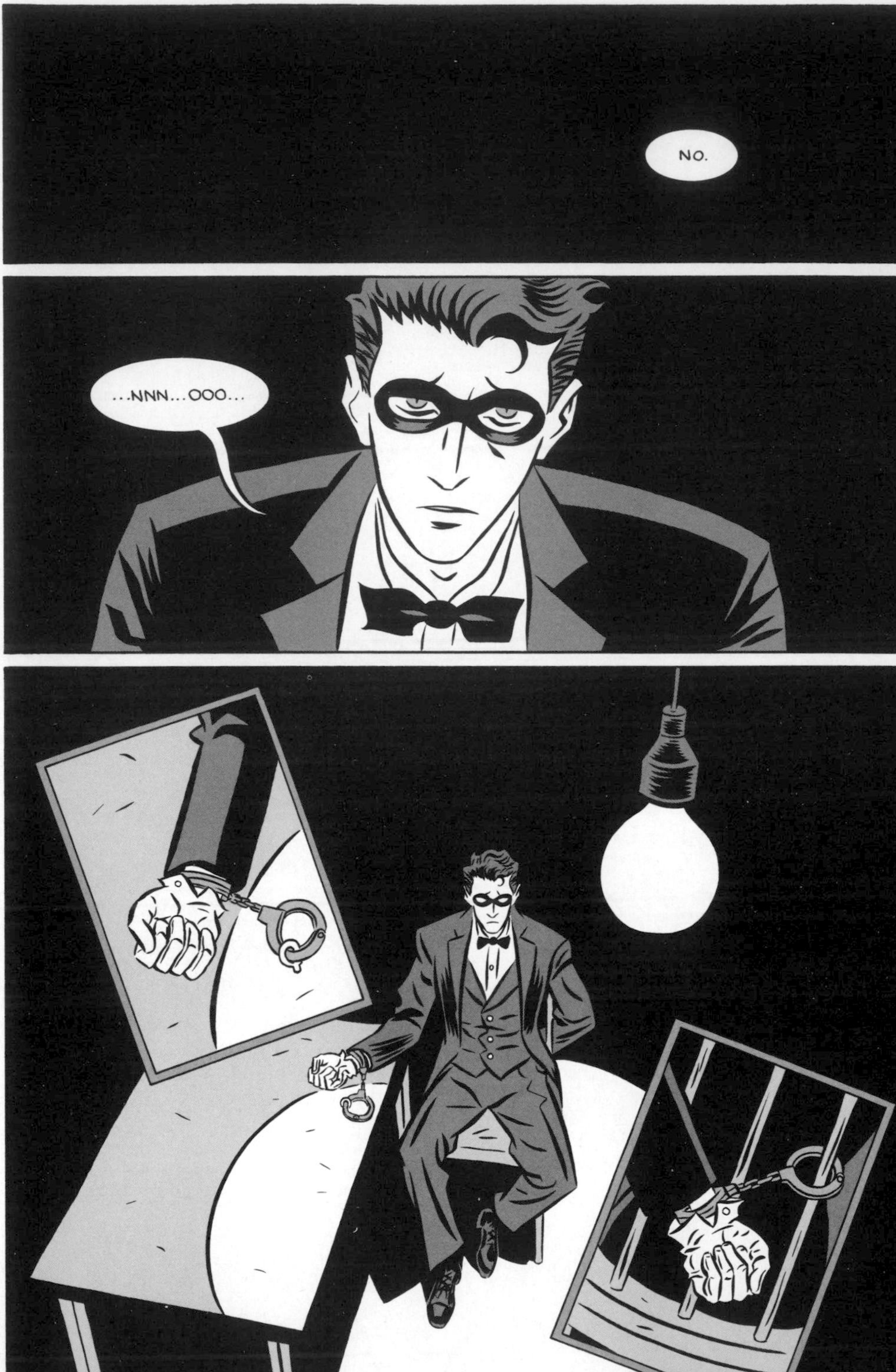
NO.
...NNN...OOO...

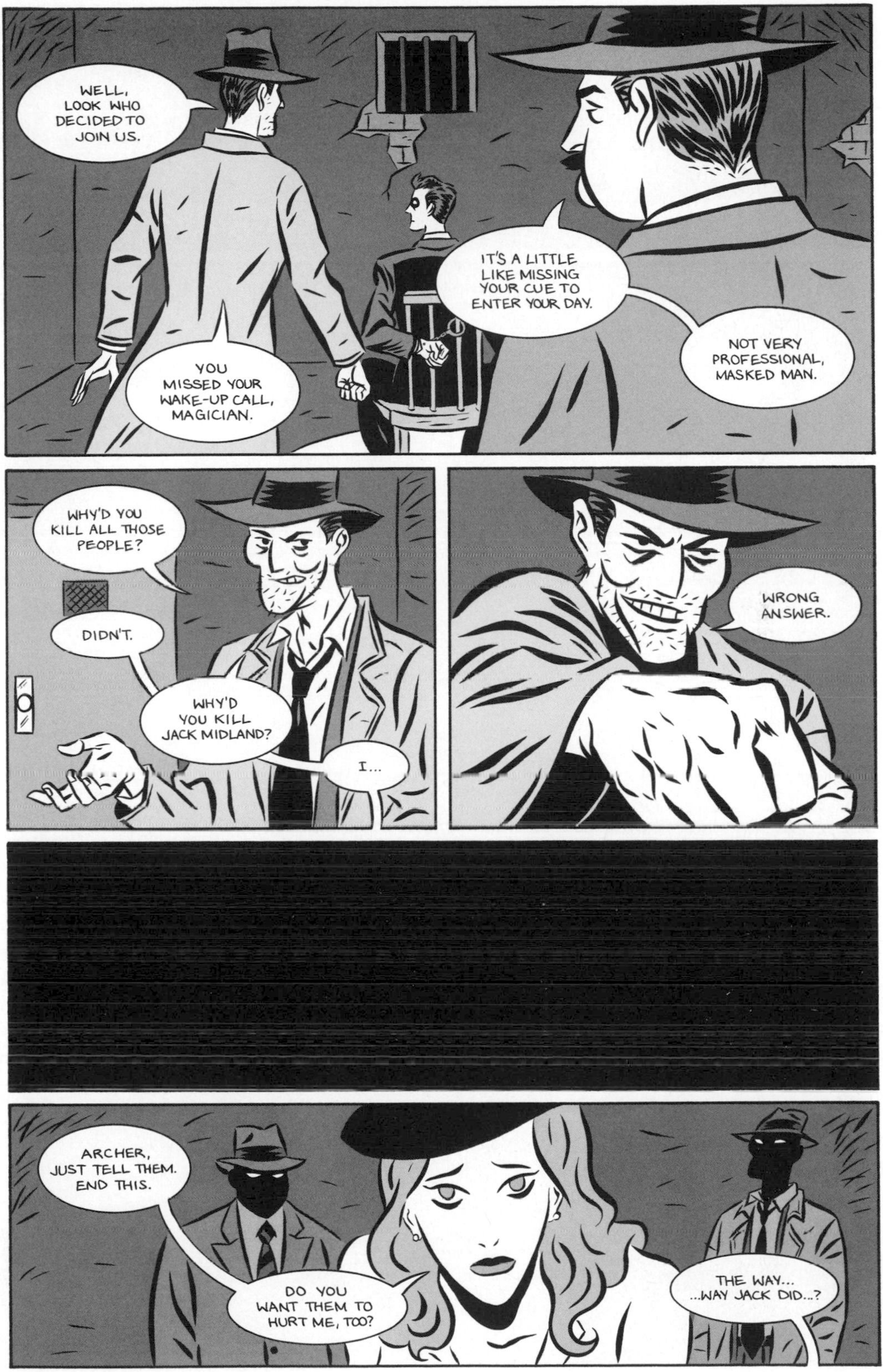
WELL, LOOK WHO DECIDED TO JOIN US.
YOU MISSED YOUR WAKE-UP CALL, MAGICIAN.
IT'S A LITTLE LIKE MISSING YOUR CUE TO ENTER YOUR DAY.
NOT VERY PROFESSIONAL, MASKED MAN.
WHY'D YOU KILL ALL THOSE PEOPLE?
DIDN'T.
WHY'D YOU KILL JACK MIDLAND?
I...
WRONG ANSWER.
ARCHER, JUST TELL THEM. END THIS.
DO YOU WANT THEM TO HURT ME, TOO?
THE WAY... ...WAY JACK DID...?

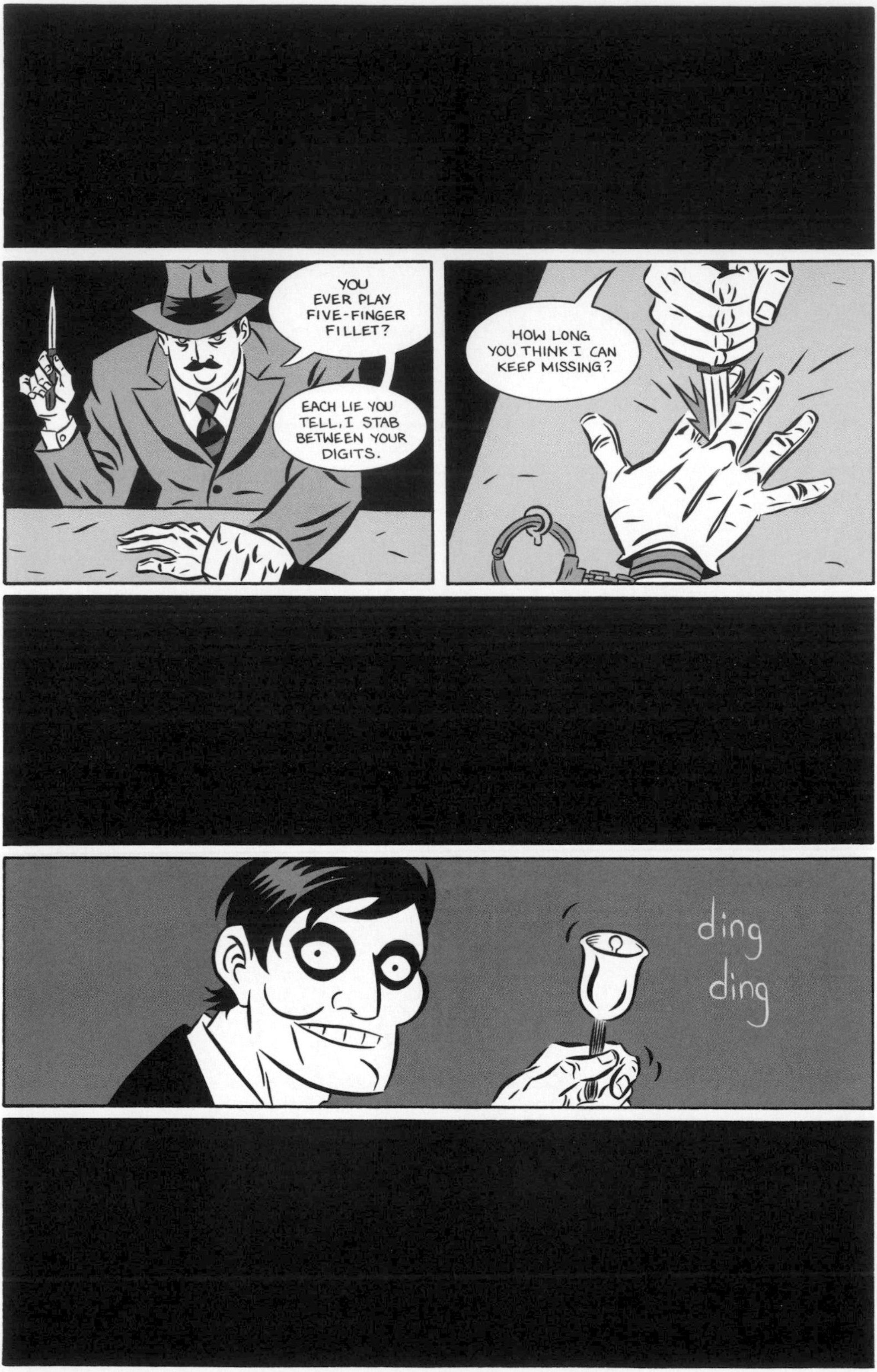
YOU EVER PLAY FIVE-FINGER FILLET?
EACH LIE YOU TELL, I STAB BETWEEN YOUR DIGITS.
HOW LONG YOU THINK I CAN KEEP MISSING?
ding ding

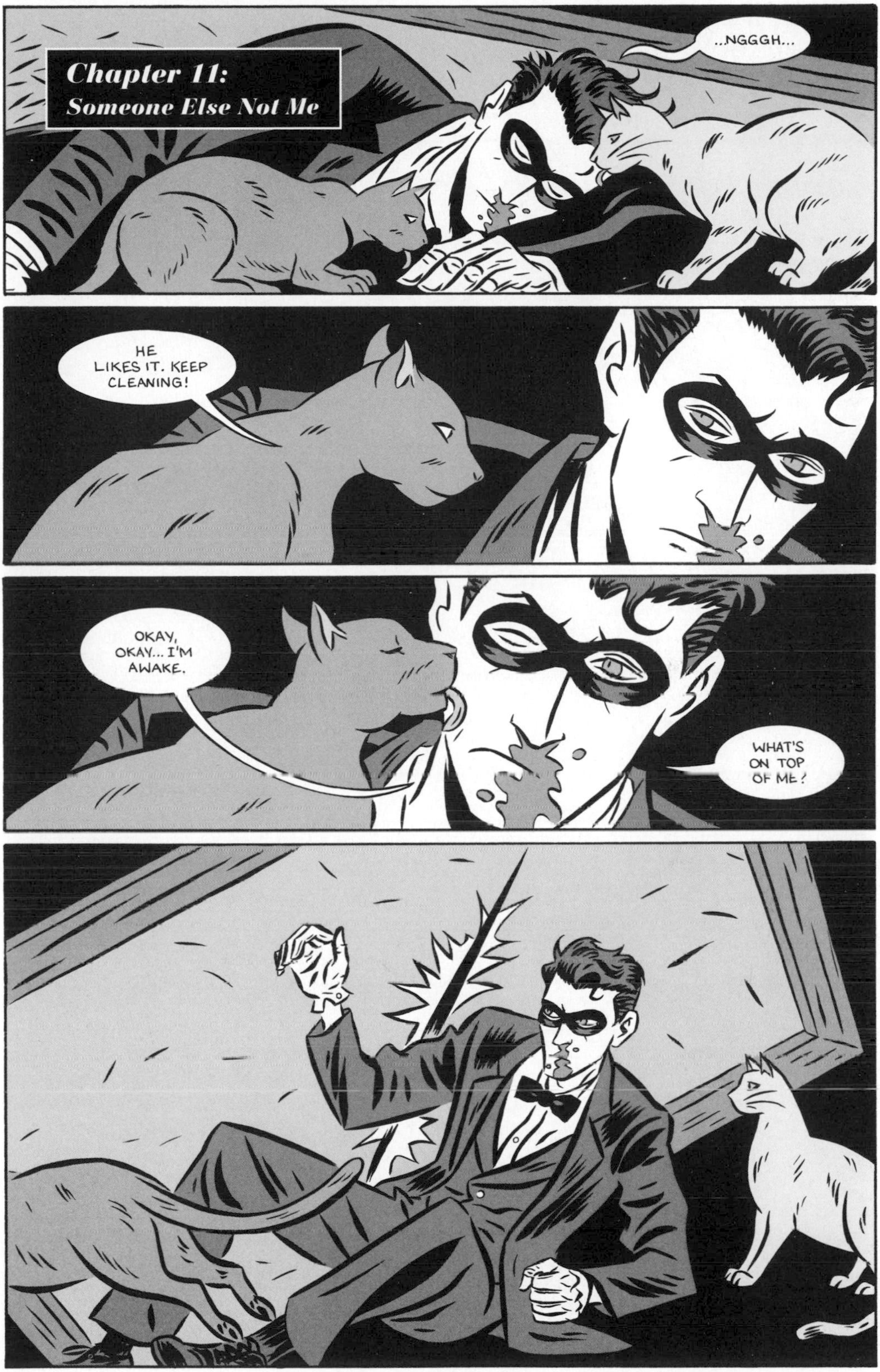
Chapter 11:
Someone Else Not Me
...NGGGH...
HE LIKES IT. KEEP CLEANING!
OKAY, OKAY... I'M AWAKE.
WHAT'S ON TOP OF ME?

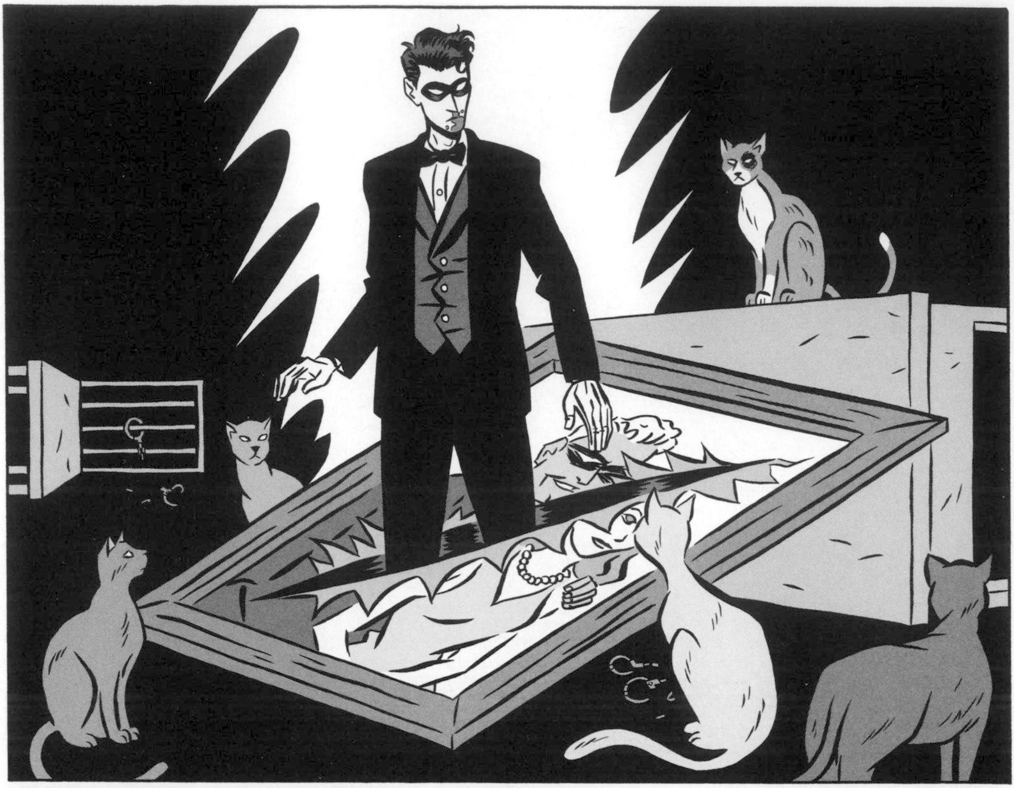

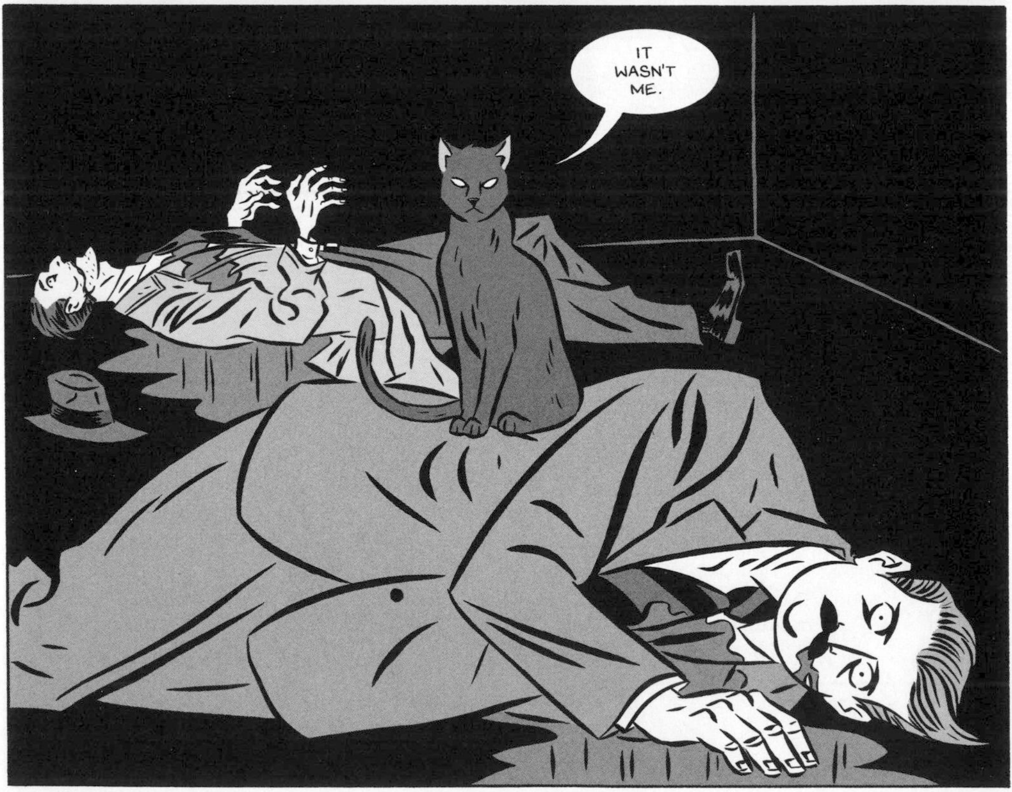
IT WASN'T ME.

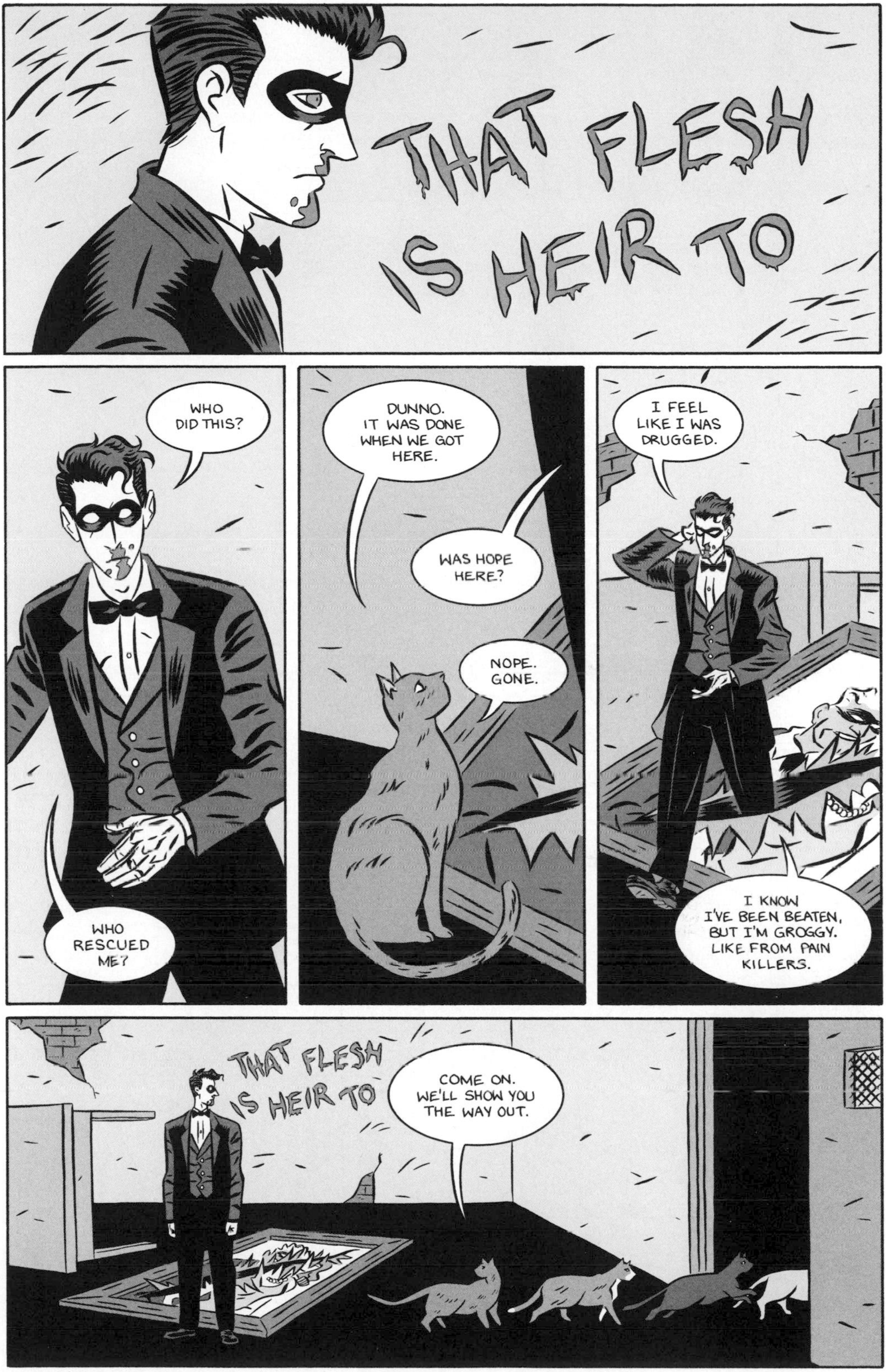
THAT FLESH IS HEIR TO
WHO DID THIS?
WHO RESCUED ME?
DUNNO. IT WAS DONE WHEN WE GOT HERE.
WAS HOPE HERE?
NOPE. GONE.
I FEEL LIKE I WAS DRUGGED.
I KNOW I'VE BEEN BEATEN, BUT I'M GROGGY. LIKE FROM PAIN KILLERS.
THAT FLESH IS HEIR TO
COME ON. WE'LL SHOW YOU THE WAY OUT.

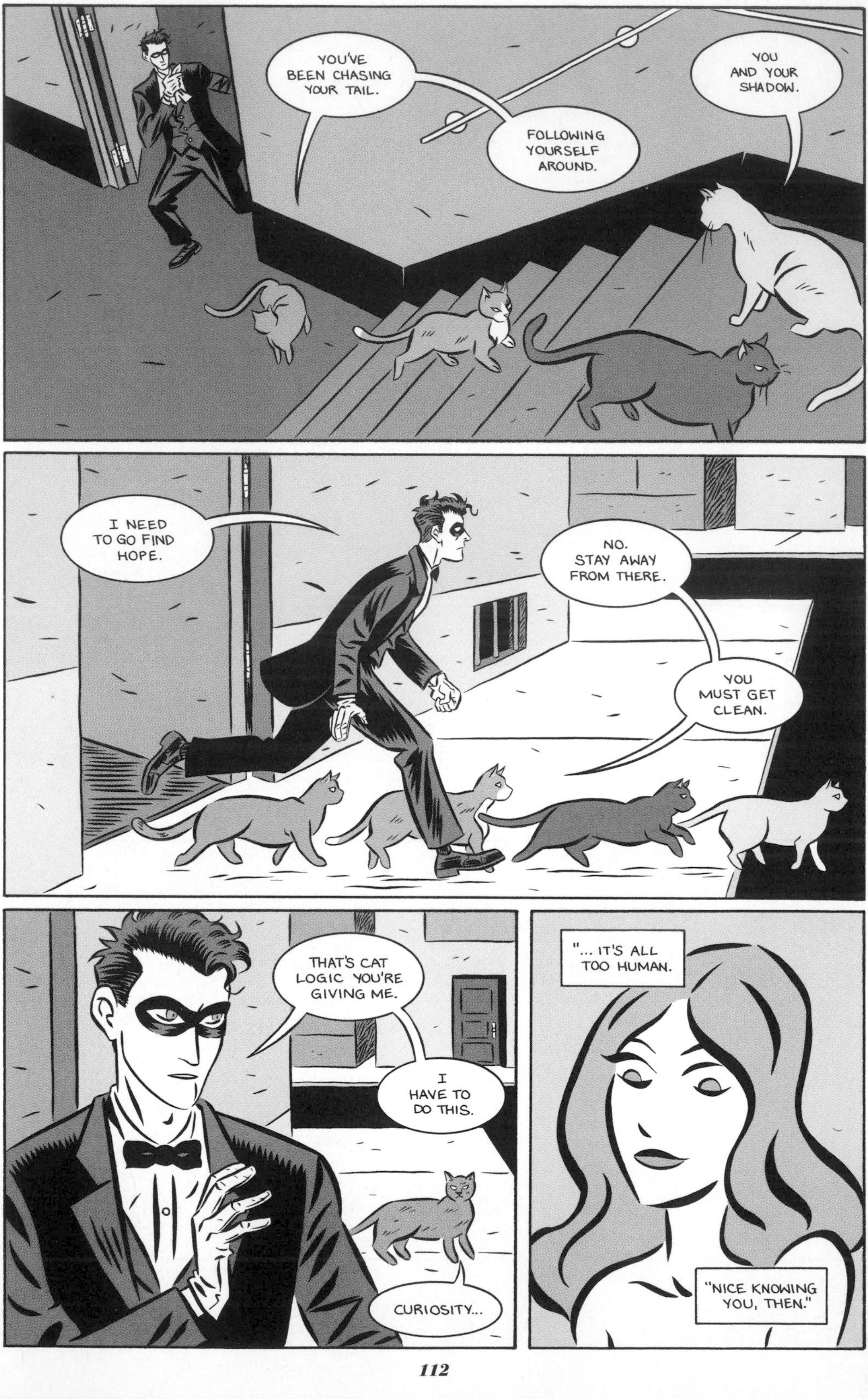
YOU'VE BEEN CHASING YOUR TAIL.
FOLLOWING YOURSELF AROUND.
YOU AND YOUR SHADOW.
I NEED TO GO FIND HOPE.
NO. STAY AWAY FROM THERE.
YOU MUST GET CLEAN.
THAT'S CAT LOGIC YOU'RE GIVING ME.
I HAVE TO DO THIS.
CURIOSITY...
"... IT'S ALL TOO HUMAN.
"NICE KNOWING YOU, THEN."

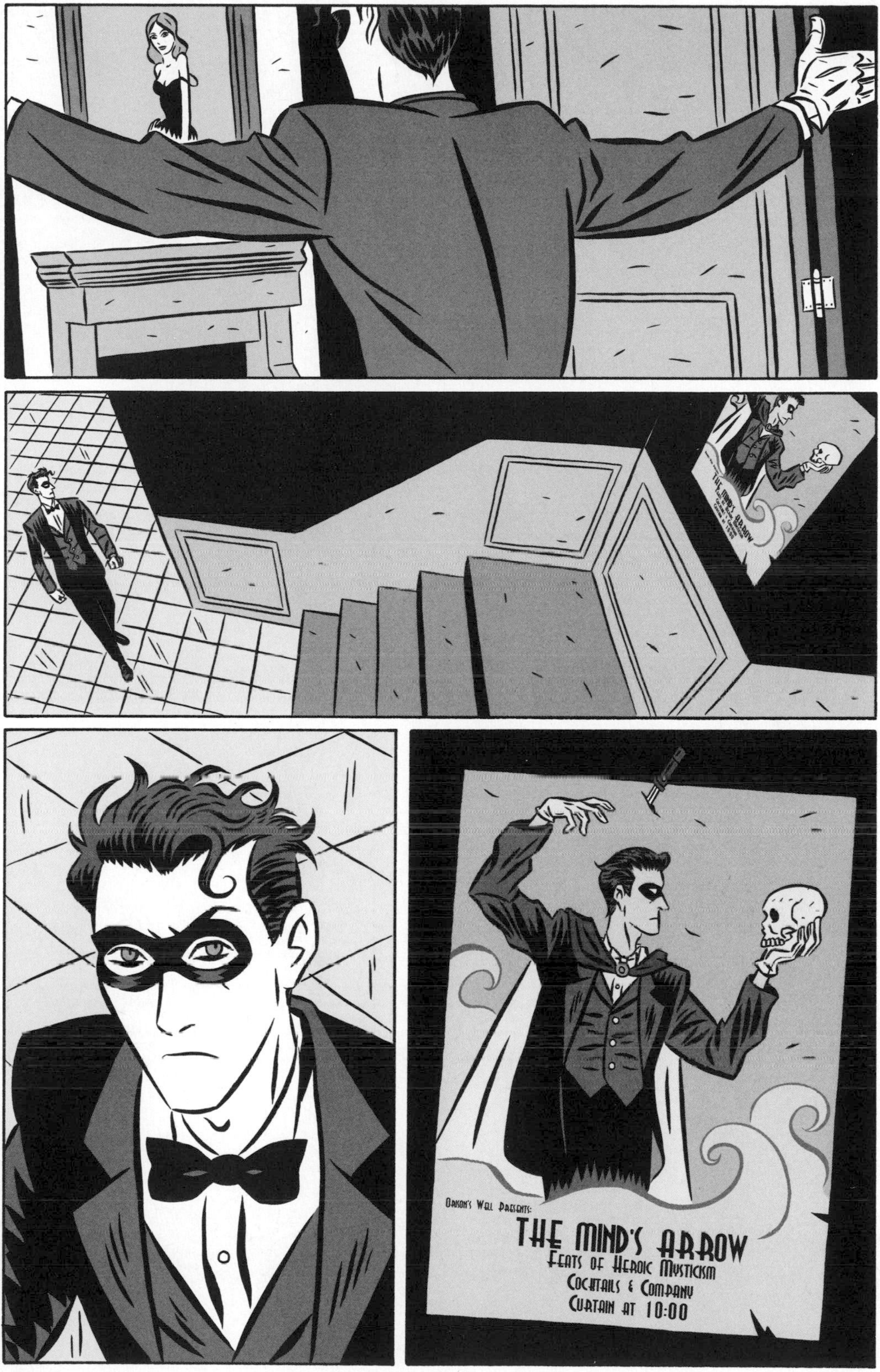
Orison's Well Presents:
THE MIND'S ARROW
Feats of Heroic Mysticism
Cocktails & Company
Curtain at 10:00

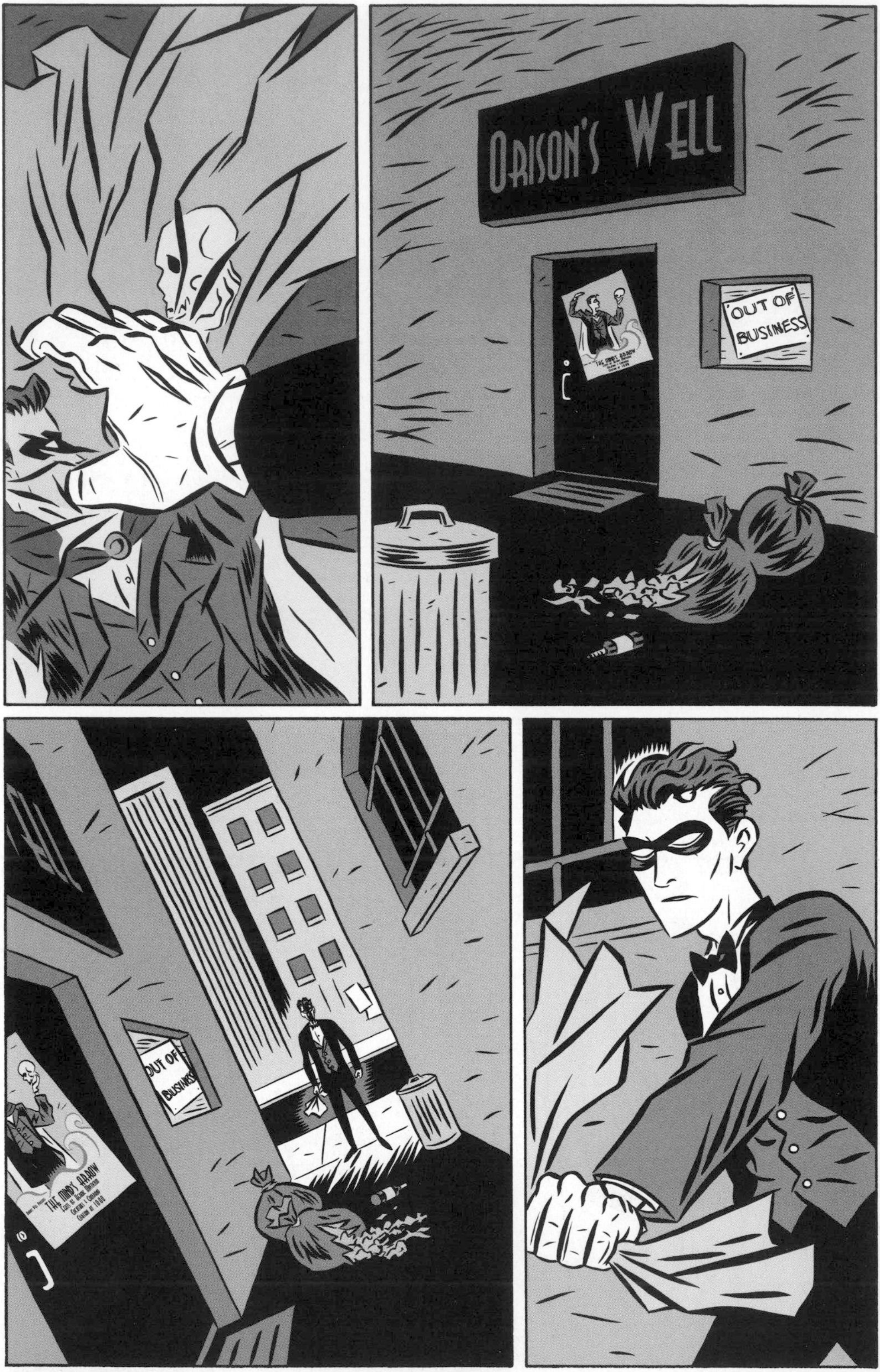
ORISON'S WELL
OUT OF BUSINESS
OUT OF BUSINESS

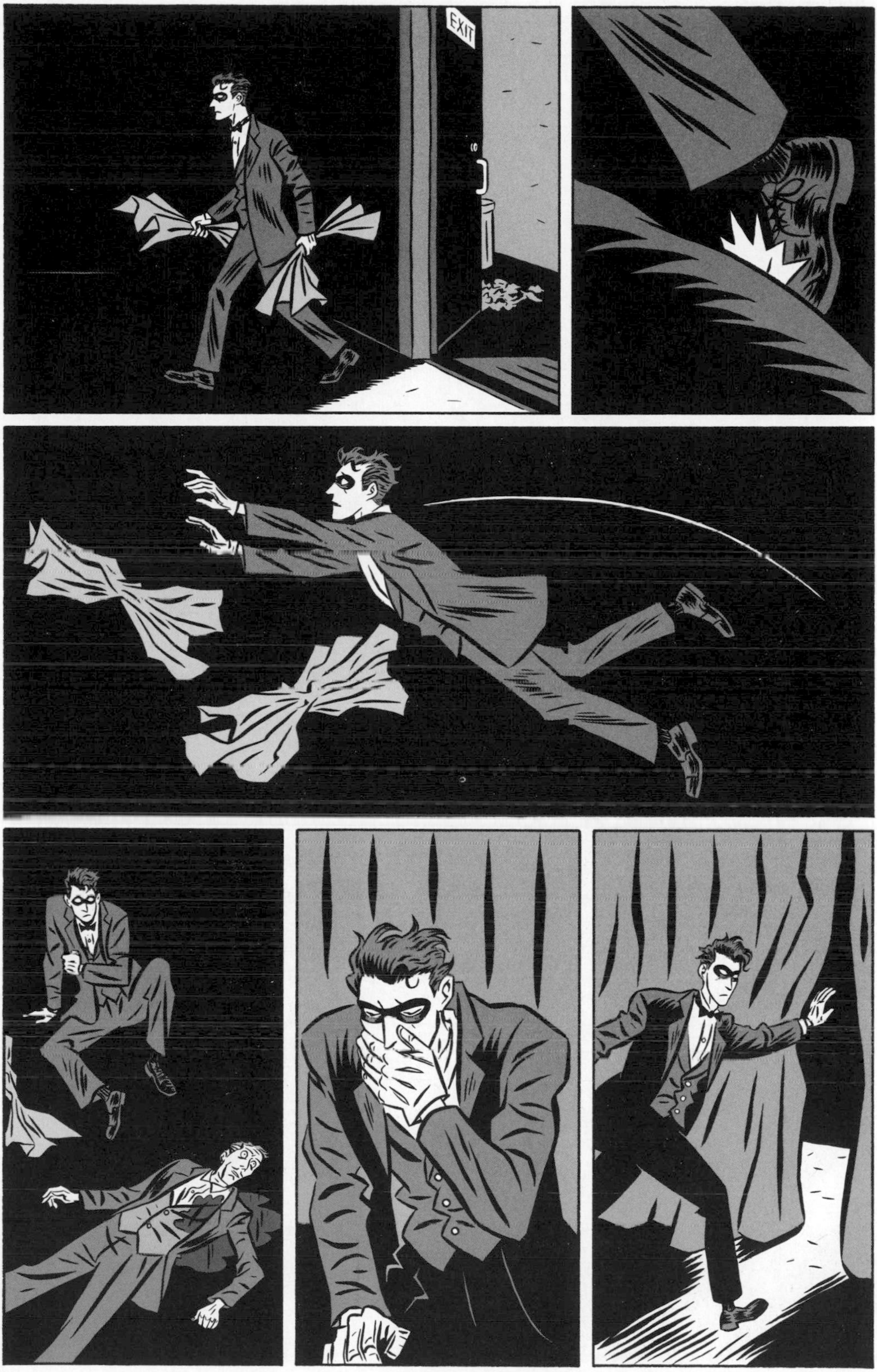
EXIT

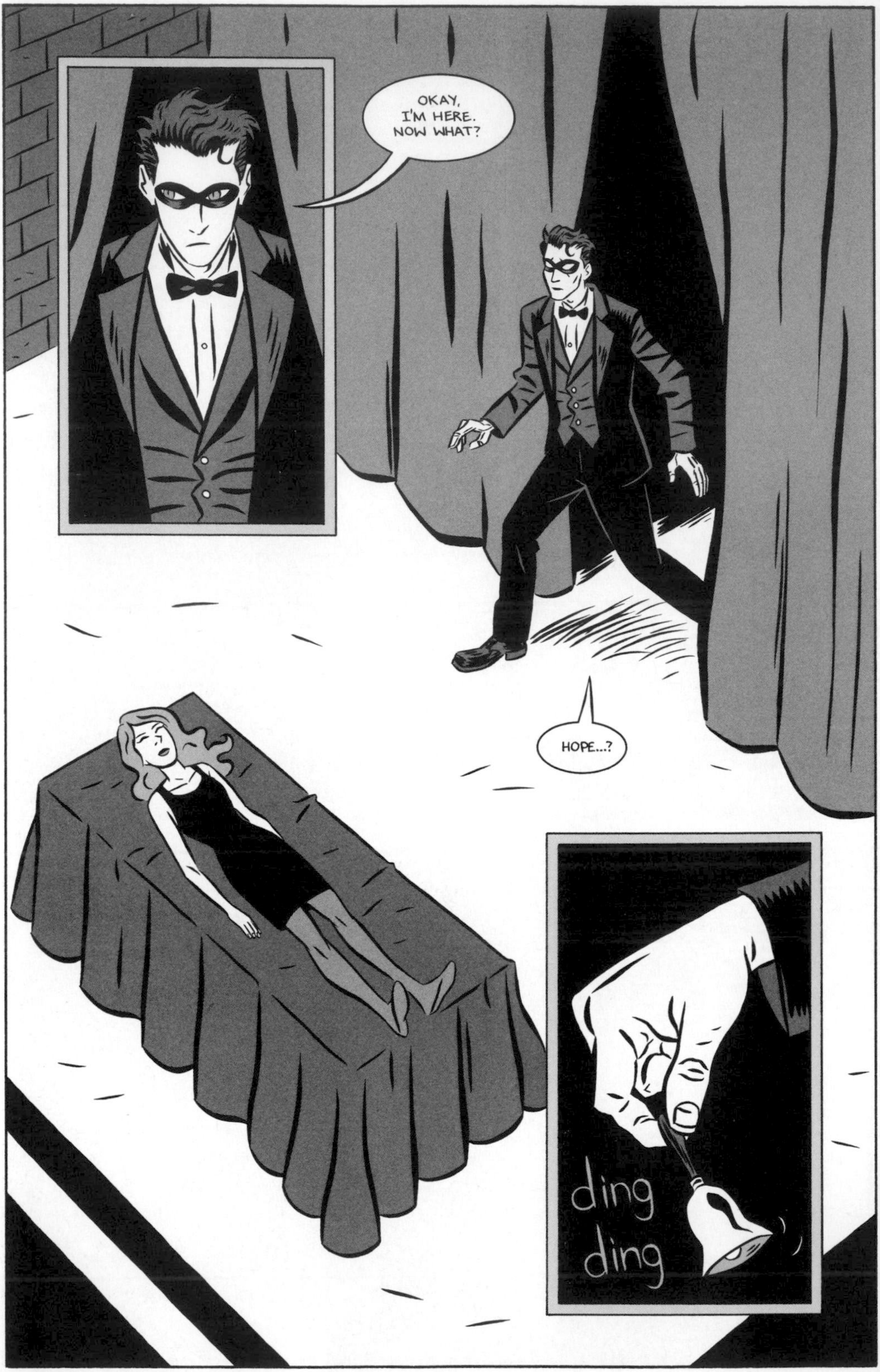
OKAY, I'M HERE. NOW WHAT?
HOPE...?
ding ding

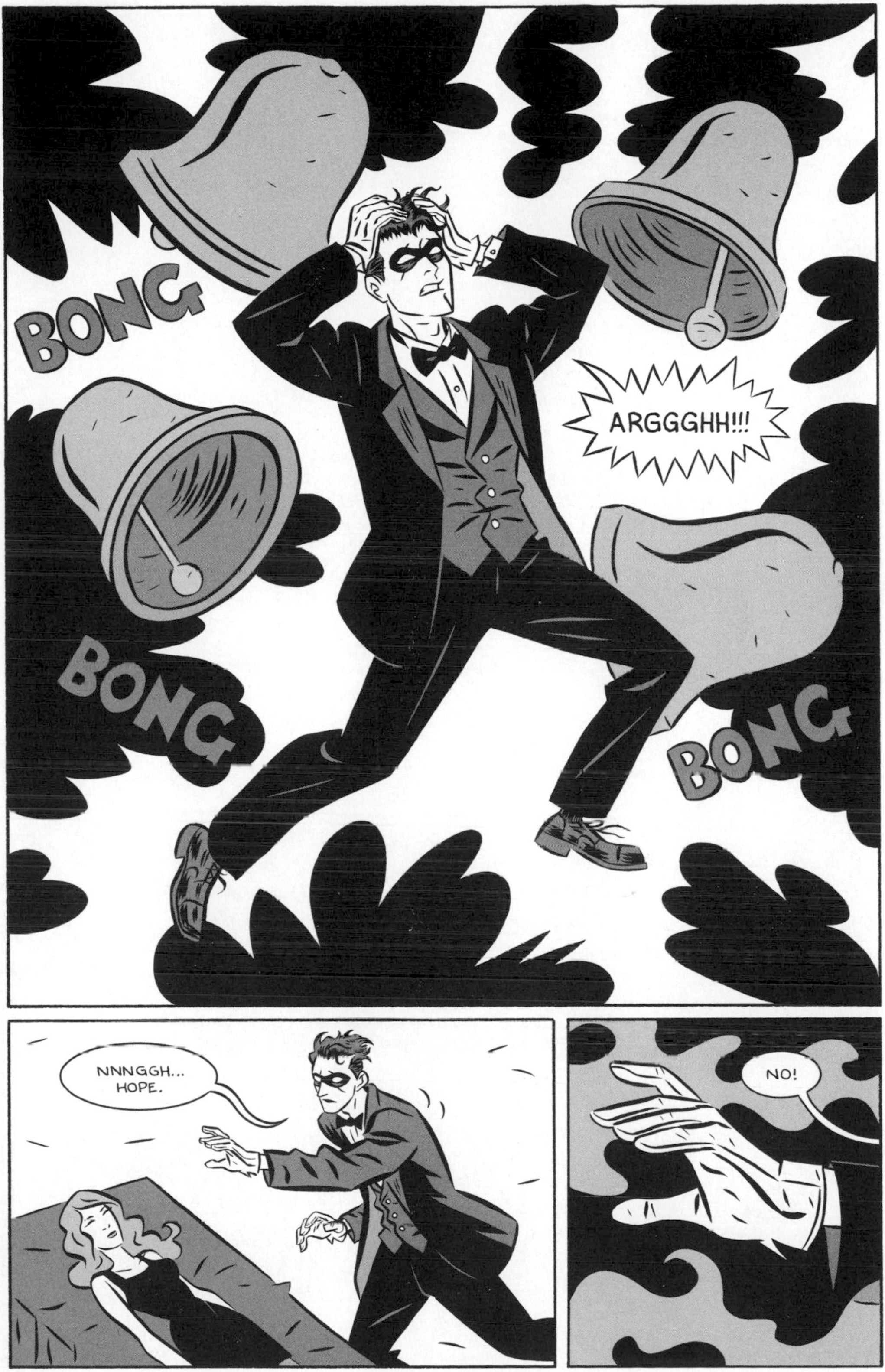
BONG
ARGGGHH!!!
BONG
BONG
BONG
NNNGGH...
HOPE.
NO!

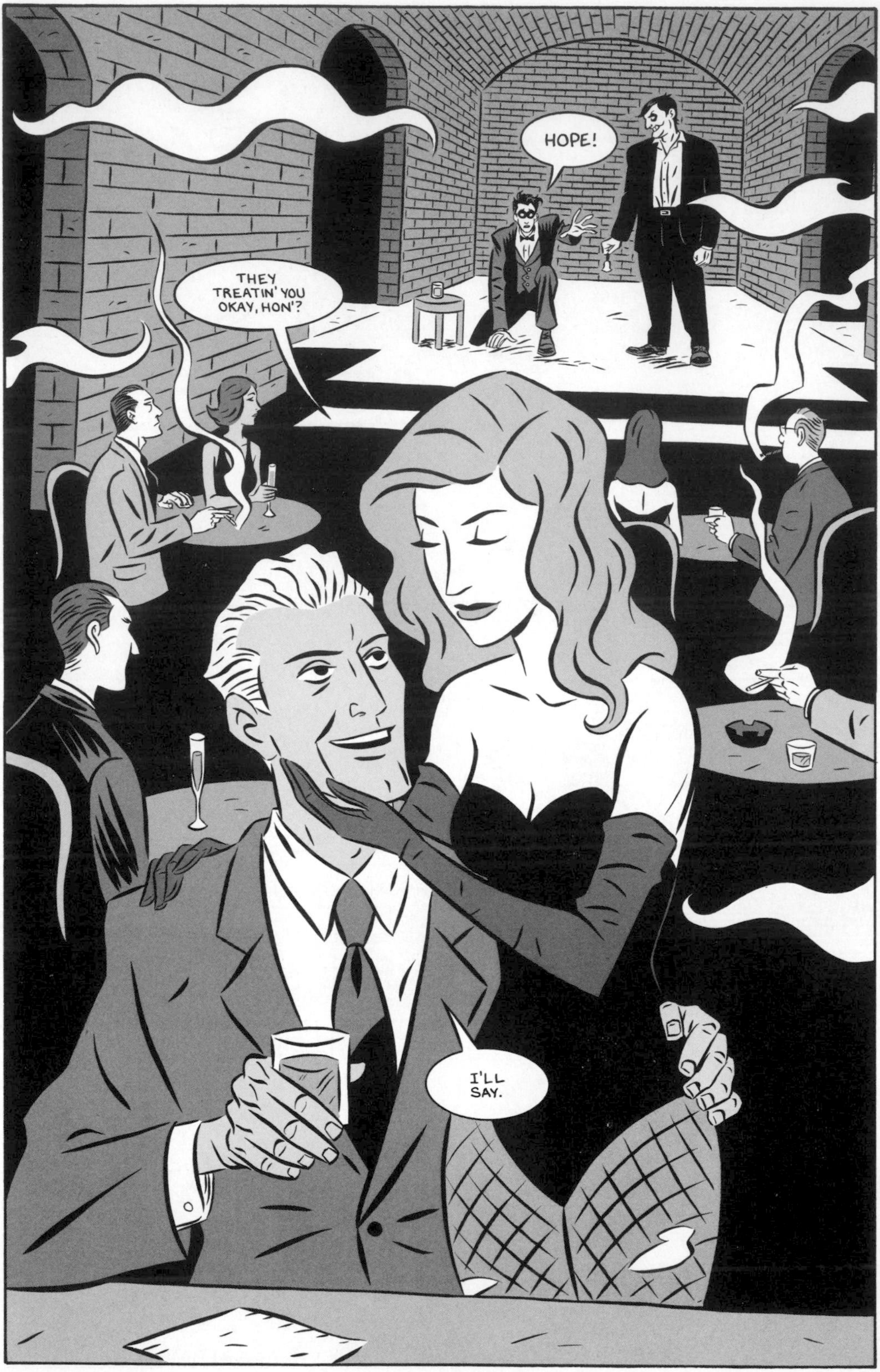
HOPE!
THEY TREATIN' YOU OKAY, HON'?
I'LL SAY.

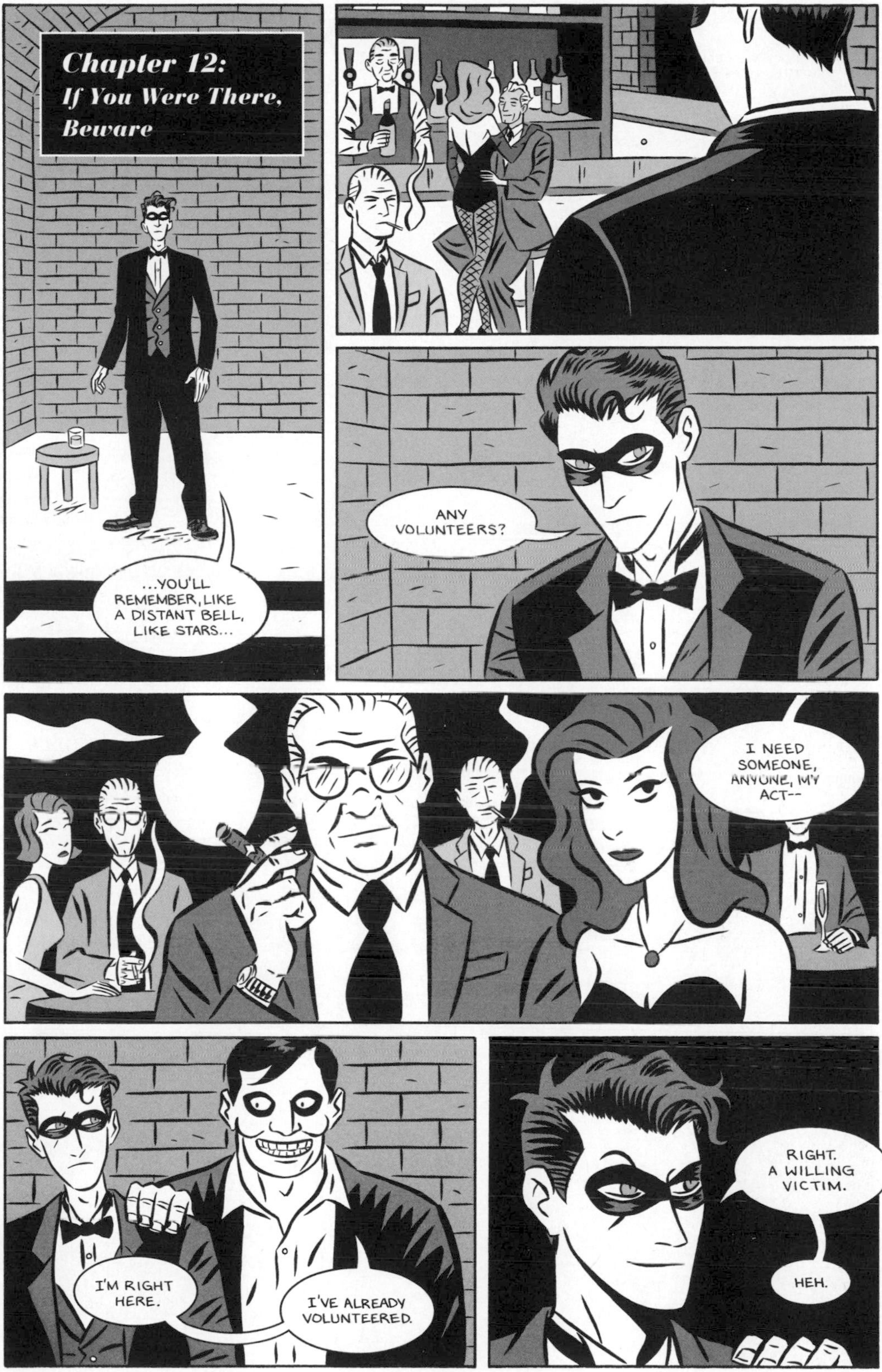
Chapter 12:
If You Were There, Beware
...YOU'LL REMEMBER, LIKE A DISTANT BELL, LIKE STARS...
ANY VOLUNTEERS?
I NEED SOMEONE, ANYONE, MY ACT--
I'M RIGHT HERE.
I'VE ALREADY VOLUNTEERED.
RIGHT. A WILLING VICTIM.
HEH.

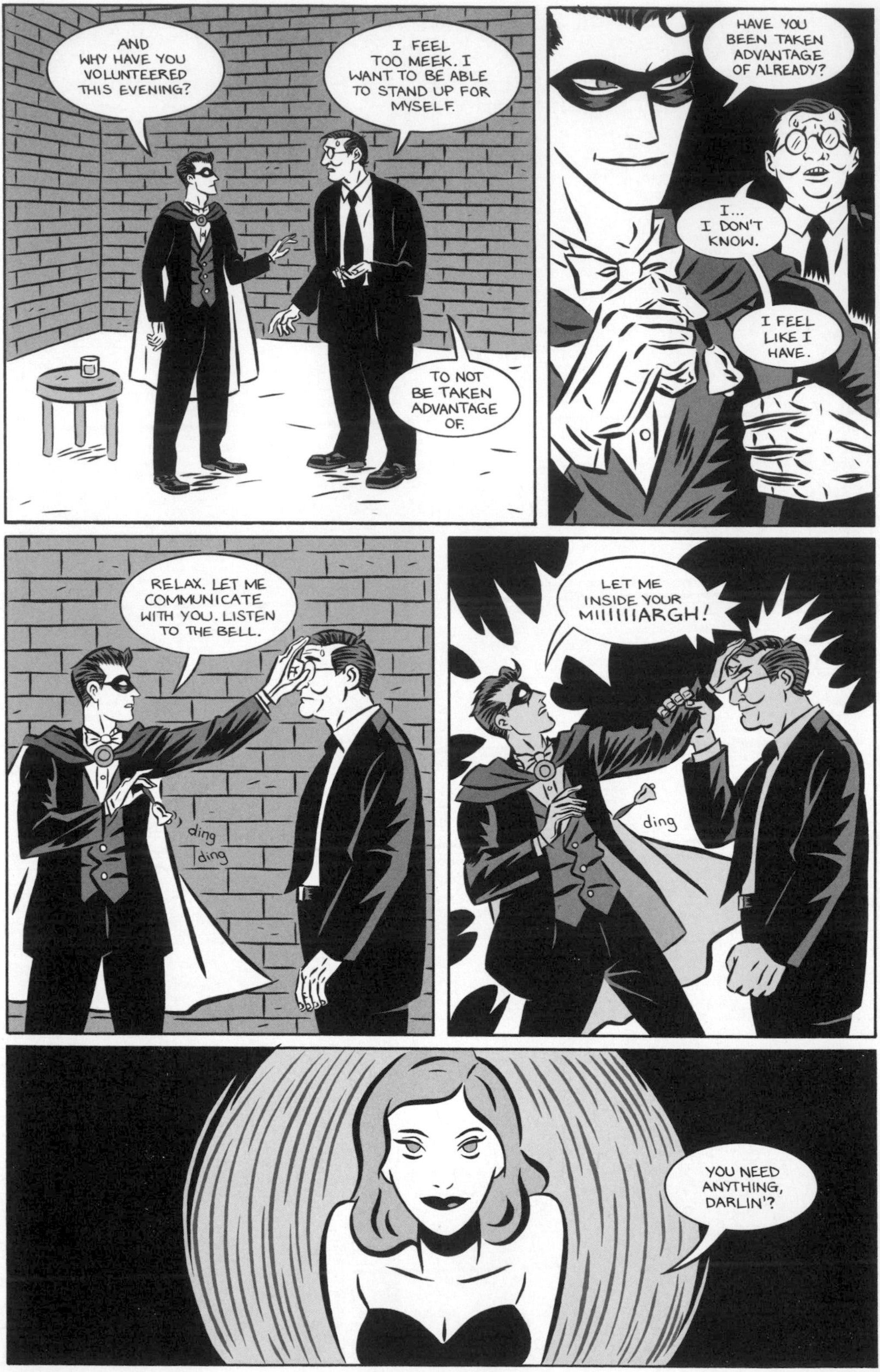
AND WHY HAVE YOU VOLUNTEERED THIS EVENING?
I FEEL TOO MEEK. I WANT TO BE ABLE TO STAND UP FOR MYSELF.
TO NOT BE TAKEN ADVANTAGE OF.
HAVE YOU BEEN TAKEN ADVANTAGE OF ALREADY?
I... I DON'T KNOW.
I FEEL LIKE I HAVE.
RELAX. LET ME COMMUNICATE WITH YOU. LISTEN TO THE BELL.
ding
ding
LET ME INSIDE YOUR MIIIIIIARGH!
ding
YOU NEED ANYTHING, DARLIN'?

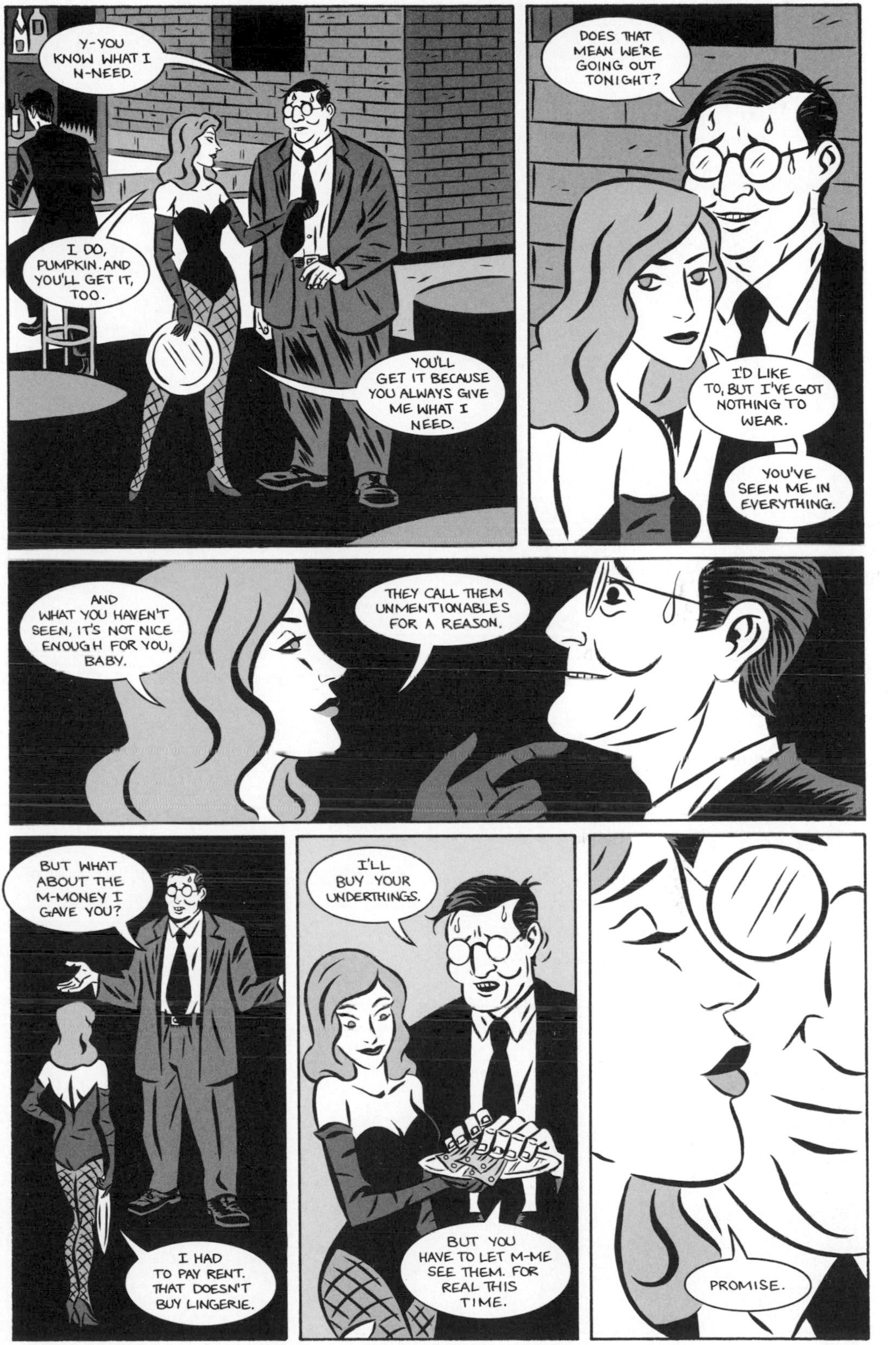
Y-YOU KNOW WHAT I N-NEED.
I DO, PUMPKIN. AND YOU'LL GET IT, TOO.
YOU'LL GET IT BECAUSE YOU ALWAYS GIVE ME WHAT I NEED.
DOES THAT MEAN WE'RE GOING OUT TONIGHT?
I'D LIKE TO, BUT I'VE GOT NOTHING TO WEAR.
YOU'VE SEEN ME IN EVERYTHING.
AND WHAT YOU HAVEN'T SEEN, IT'S NOT NICE ENOUGH FOR YOU, BABY.
THEY CALL THEM UNMENTIONABLES FOR A REASON.
BUT WHAT ABOUT THE M-MONEY I GAVE YOU?
I HAD TO PAY RENT. THAT DOESN'T BUY LINGERIE.
I'LL BUY YOUR UNDERTHINGS.
BUT YOU HAVE TO LET M-ME SEE THEM. FOR REAL THIS TIME.
PROMISE.

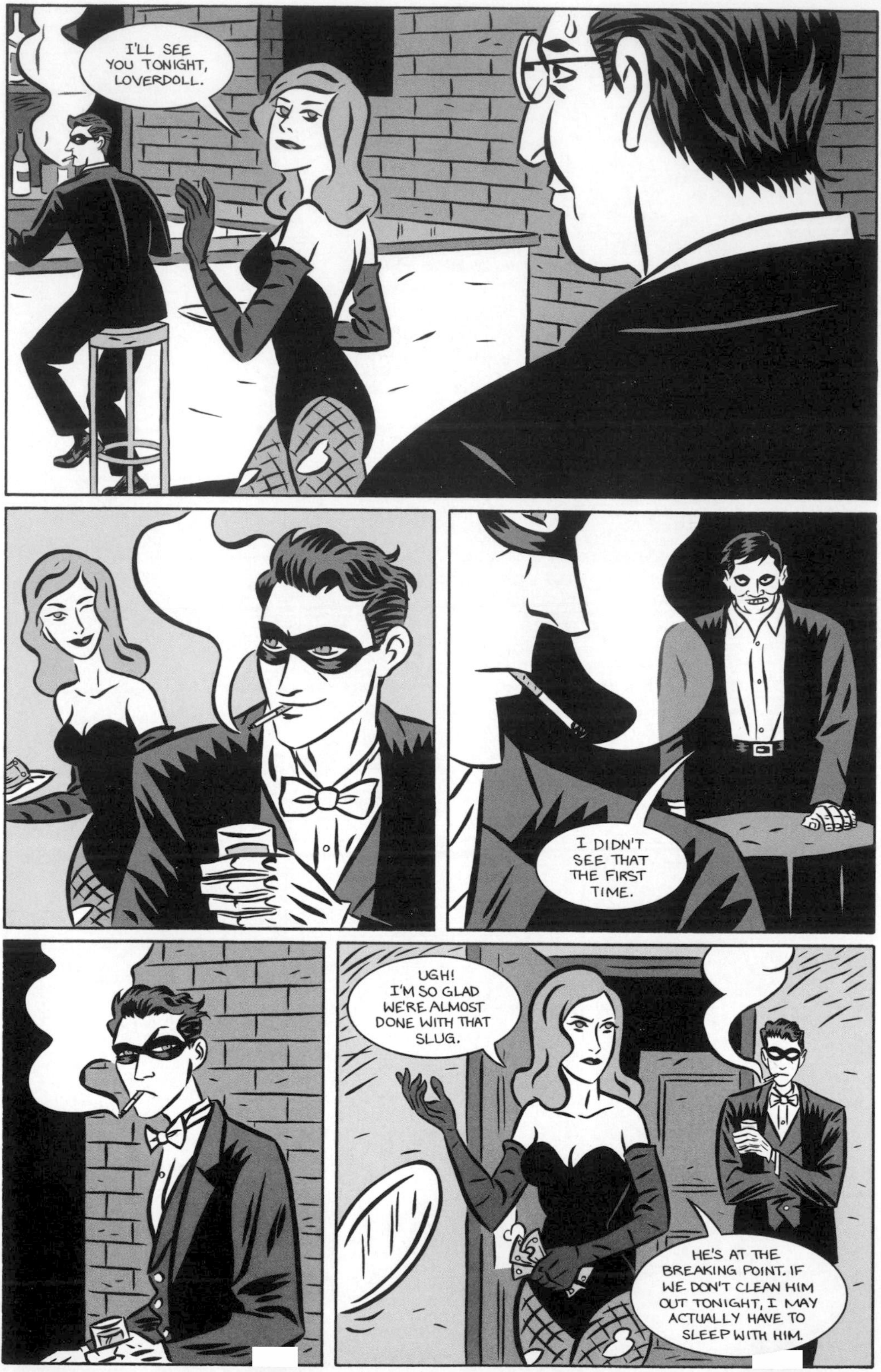
I'LL SEE YOU TONIGHT, LOVERDOLL.
I DIDN'T SEE THAT THE FIRST TIME.
UGH! I'M SO GLAD WE'RE ALMOST DONE WITH THAT SLUG.
HE'S AT THE BREAKING POINT. IF WE DON'T CLEAN HIM OUT TONIGHT, I MAY ACTUALLY HAVE TO SLEEP WITH HIM.

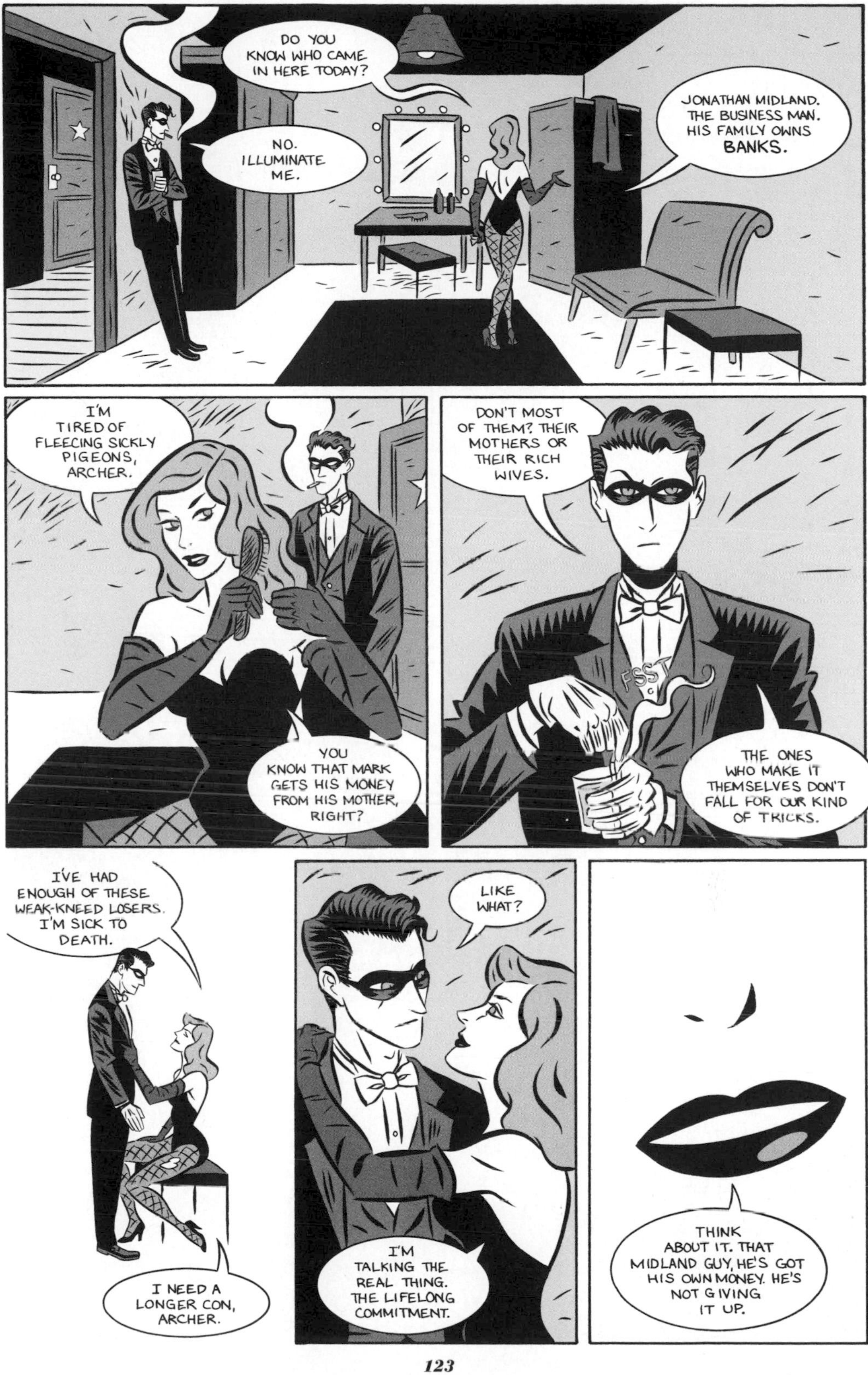
DO YOU KNOW WHO CAME IN HERE TODAY?
NO. ILLUMINATE ME.
JONATHAN MIDLAND. THE BUSINESS MAN. HIS FAMILY OWNS BANKS.
I'M TIRED OF FLEECING SICKLY PIGEONS, ARCHER.
YOU KNOW THAT MARK GETS HIS MONEY FROM HIS MOTHER, RIGHT?
DON'T MOST OF THEM? THEIR MOTHERS OR THEIR RICH WIVES.
FSST
THE ONES WHO MAKE IT THEMSELVES DON'T FALL FOR OUR KIND OF TRICKS.
I'VE HAD ENOUGH OF THESE WEAK-KNEED LOSERS. I'M SICK TO DEATH.
I NEED A LONGER CON, ARCHER.
LIKE WHAT?
I'M TALKING THE REAL THING. THE LIFELONG COMMITMENT.
THINK ABOUT IT. THAT MIDLAND GUY, HE'S GOT HIS OWN MONEY. HE'S NOT GIVING IT UP.

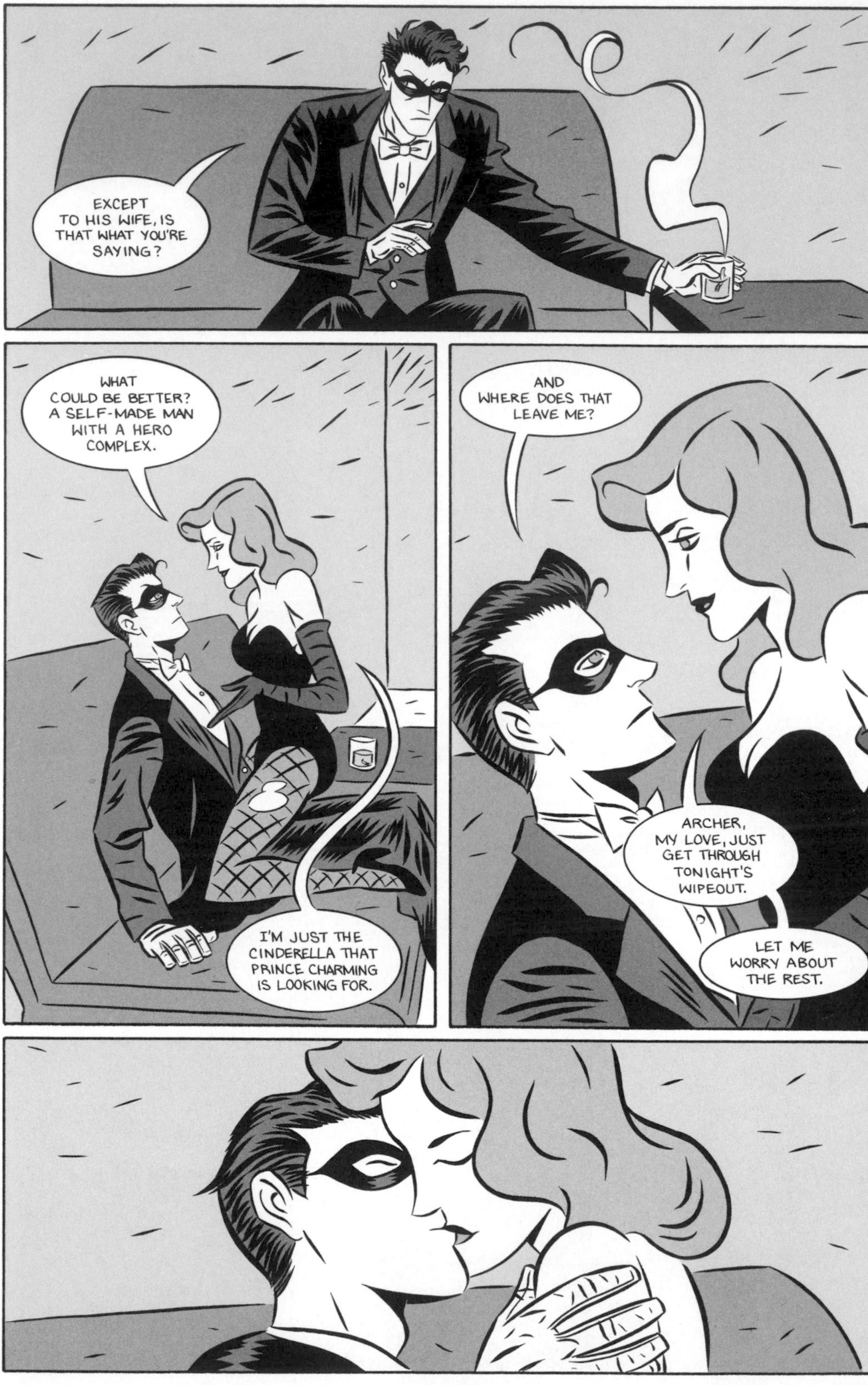
EXCEPT TO HIS WIFE, IS THAT WHAT YOU'RE SAYING?
WHAT COULD BE BETTER? A SELF-MADE MAN WITH A HERO COMPLEX.
I'M JUST THE CINDERELLA THAT PRINCE CHARMING IS LOOKING FOR.
AND WHERE DOES THAT LEAVE ME?
ARCHER, MY LOVE, JUST GET THROUGH TONIGHT'S WIPEOUT.
LET ME WORRY ABOUT THE REST.

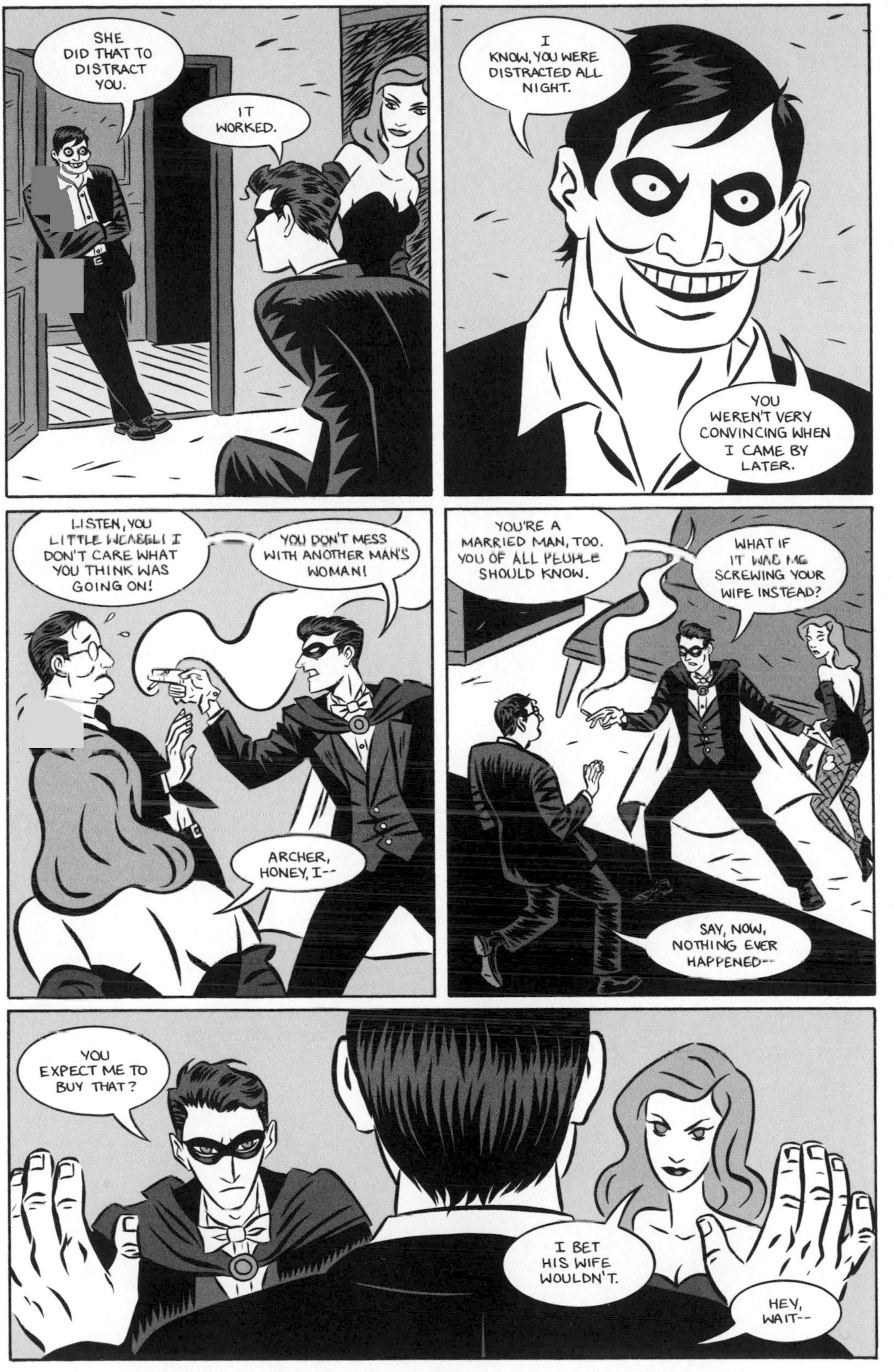
SHE DID THAT TO DISTRACT YOU.
IT WORKED.
I KNOW, YOU WERE DISTRACTED ALL NIGHT.
YOU WEREN'T VERY CONVINCING WHEN I CAME BY LATER.
LISTEN, YOU LITTLE WEASEL! I DON'T CARE WHAT YOU THINK WAS GOING ON!
YOU DON'T MESS WITH ANOTHER MAN'S WOMAN!
ARCHER, HONEY, I--
YOU'RE A MARRIED MAN, TOO. YOU OF ALL PEOPLE SHOULD KNOW.
WHAT IF IT WAS ME SCREWING YOUR WIFE INSTEAD?
SAY, NOW, NOTHING EVER HAPPENED--
YOU EXPECT ME TO BUY THAT?
I BET HIS WIFE WOULDN'T.
HEY, WAIT--

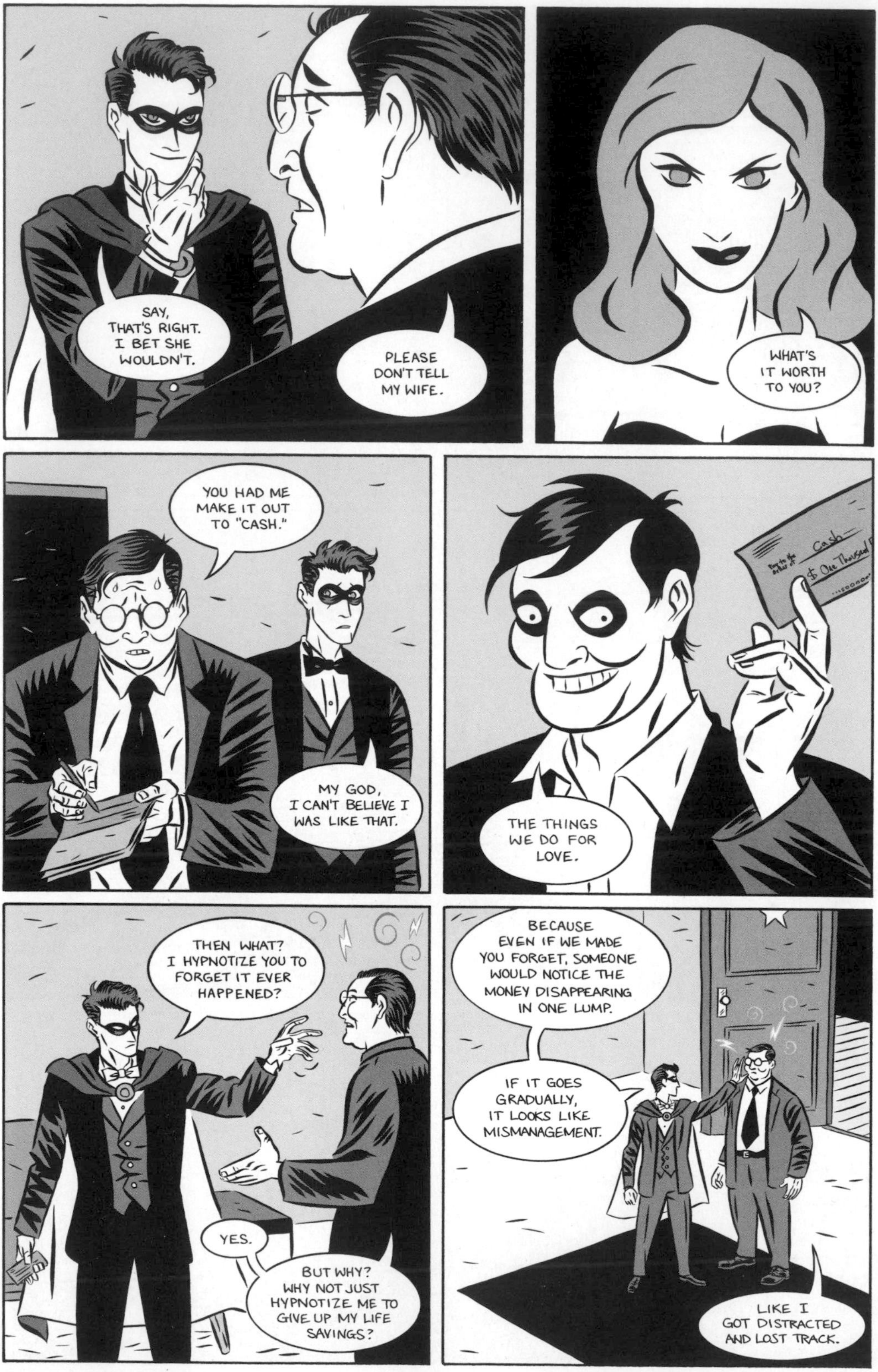
SAY, THAT'S RIGHT. I BET SHE WOULDN'T.
PLEASE DON'T TELL MY WIFE.
WHAT'S IT WORTH TO YOU?
YOU HAD ME MAKE IT OUT TO "CASH."
MY GOD, I CAN'T BELIEVE I WAS LIKE THAT.
Cash
One Thousand
THE THINGS WE DO FOR LOVE.
THEN WHAT? I HYPNOTIZE YOU TO FORGET IT EVER HAPPENED?
YES.
BUT WHY? WHY NOT JUST HYPNOTIZE ME TO GIVE UP MY LIFE SAVINGS?
BECAUSE EVEN IF WE MADE YOU FORGET, SOMEONE WOULD NOTICE THE MONEY DISAPPEARING IN ONE LUMP.
IF IT GOES GRADUALLY, IT LOOKS LIKE MISMANAGEMENT.
LIKE I GOT DISTRACTED AND LOST TRACK.

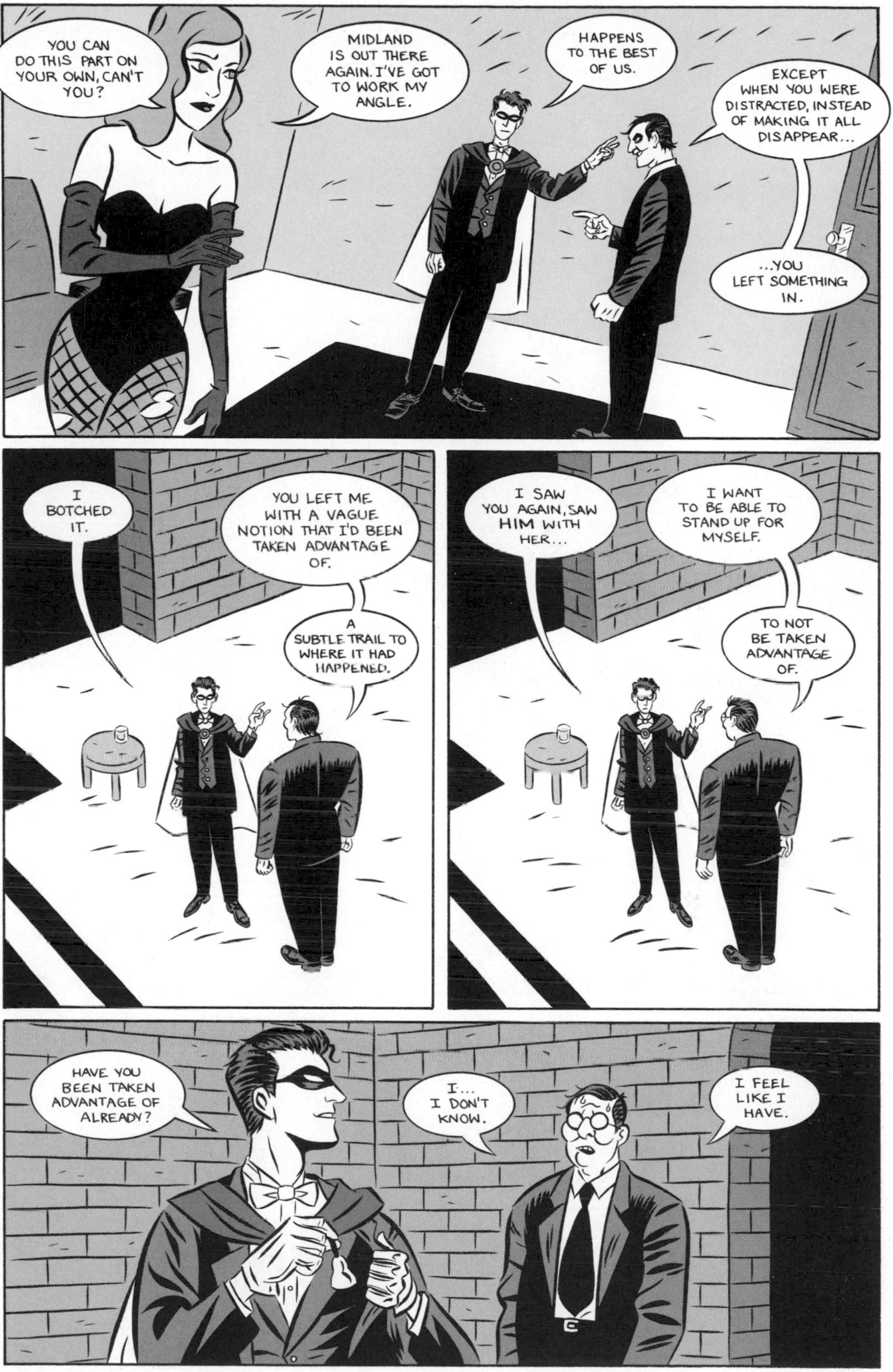
YOU CAN DO THIS PART ON YOUR OWN, CAN'T YOU?
MIDLAND IS OUT THERE AGAIN. I'VE GOT TO WORK MY ANGLE.
HAPPENS TO THE BEST OF US.
EXCEPT WHEN YOU WERE DISTRACTED, INSTEAD OF MAKING IT ALL DISAPPEAR...
...YOU LEFT SOMETHING IN.
I BOTCHED IT.
YOU LEFT ME WITH A VAGUE NOTION THAT I'D BEEN TAKEN ADVANTAGE OF.
A SUBTLE TRAIL TO WHERE IT HAD HAPPENED.
I SAW YOU AGAIN, SAW HIM WITH HER...
I WANT TO BE ABLE TO STAND UP FOR MYSELF.
TO NOT BE TAKEN ADVANTAGE OF.
HAVE YOU BEEN TAKEN ADVANTAGE OF ALREADY?
I... I DON'T KNOW.
I FEEL LIKE I HAVE.

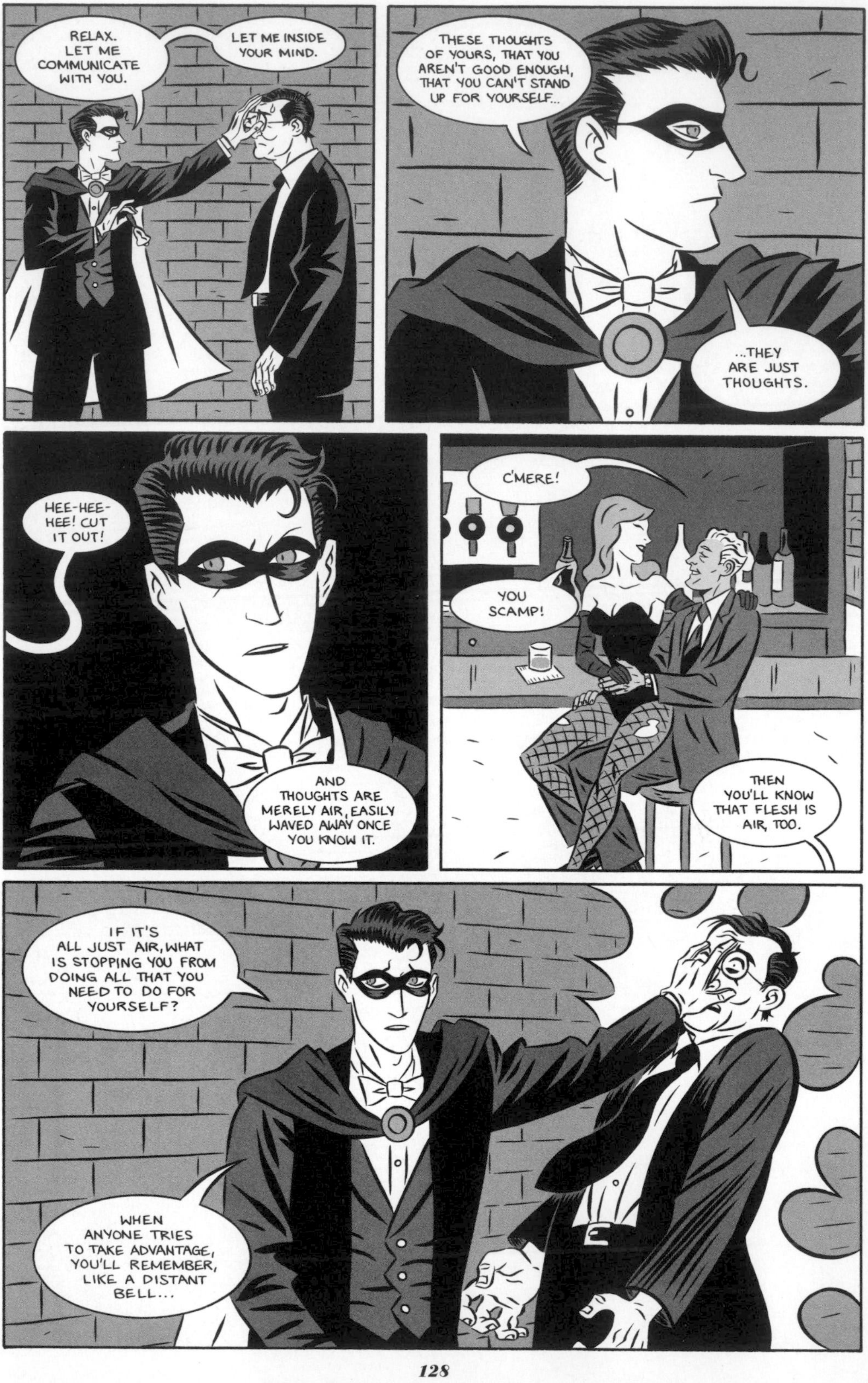
RELAX. LET ME COMMUNICATE WITH YOU.
LET ME INSIDE YOUR MIND.
THESE THOUGHTS OF YOURS, THAT YOU AREN'T GOOD ENOUGH, THAT YOU CAN'T STAND UP FOR YOURSELF...
...THEY ARE JUST THOUGHTS.
HEE-HEE-HEE! CUT IT OUT!
AND THOUGHTS ARE MERELY AIR, EASILY WAVED AWAY ONCE YOU KNOW IT.
C'MERE!
YOU SCAMP!
THEN YOU'LL KNOW THAT FLESH IS AIR, TOO.
IF IT'S ALL JUST AIR, WHAT IS STOPPING YOU FROM DOING ALL THAT YOU NEED TO DO FOR YOURSELF?
WHEN ANYONE TRIES TO TAKE ADVANTAGE, YOU'LL REMEMBER, LIKE A DISTANT BELL...

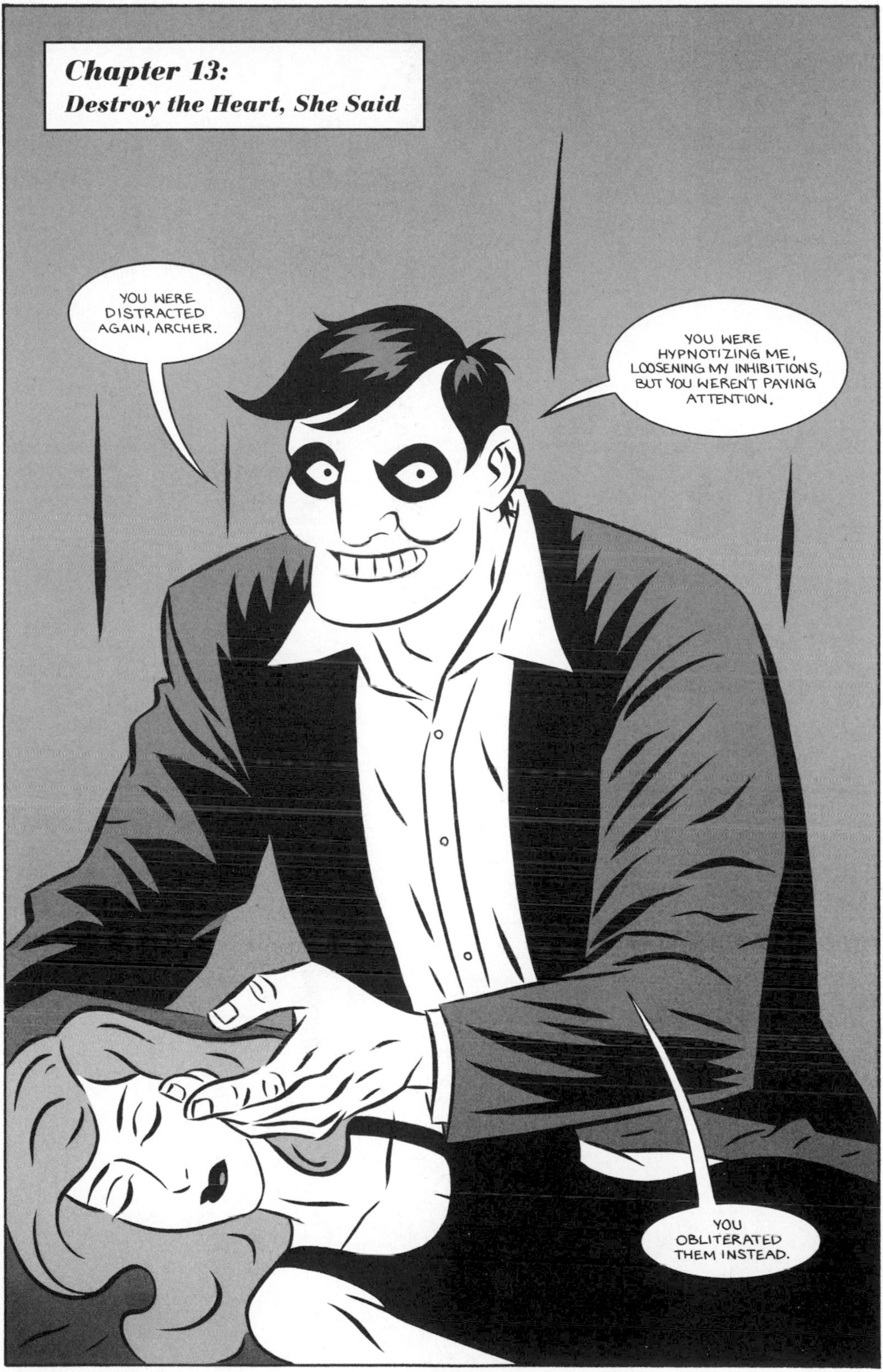
Chapter 13:
Destroy the Heart, She Said
YOU WERE DISTRACTED AGAIN, ARCHER.
YOU WERE HYPNOTIZING ME, LOOSENING MY INHIBITIONS, BUT YOU WEREN'T PAYING ATTENTION.
YOU OBLITERATED THEM INSTEAD.

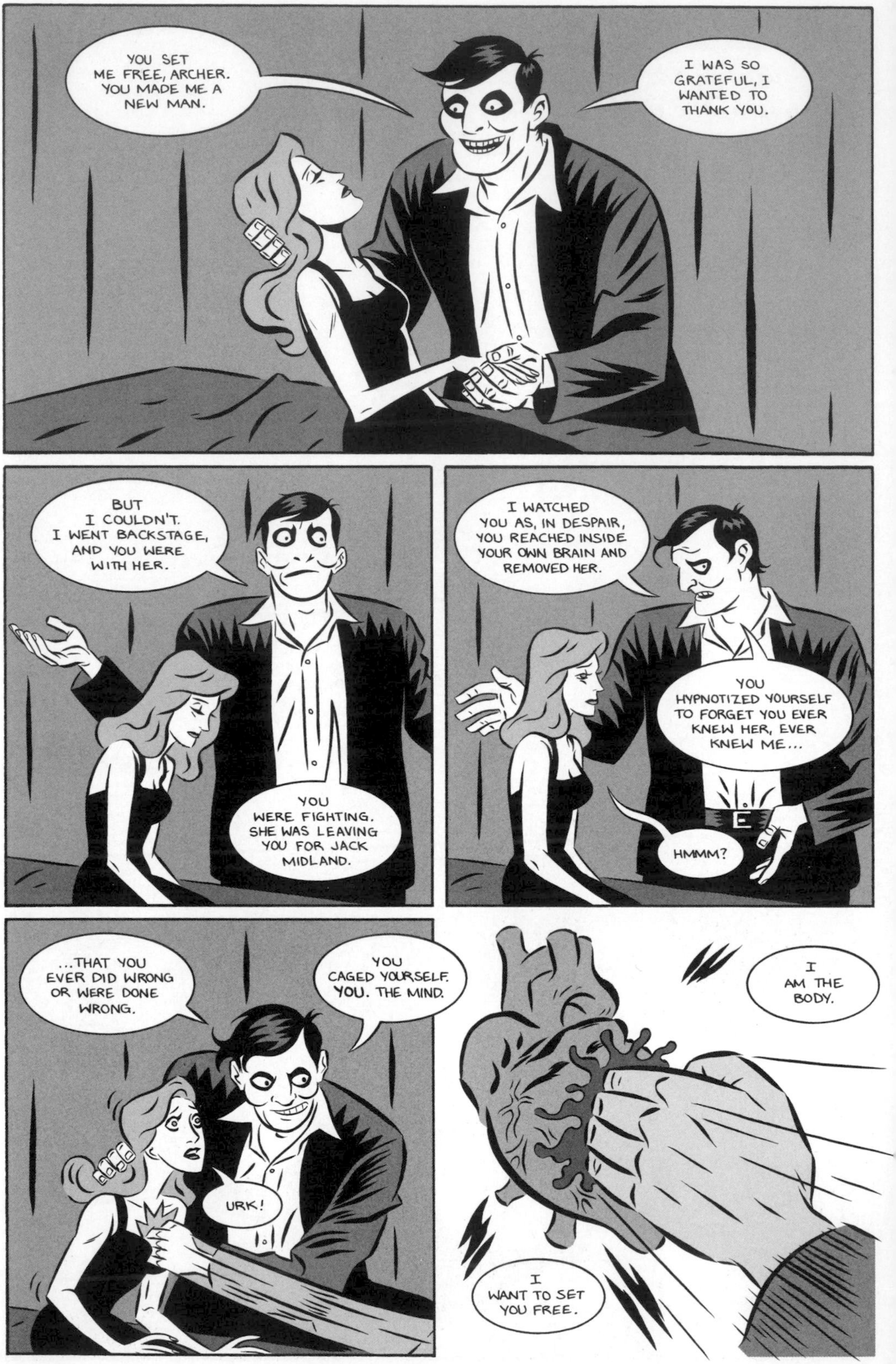
YOU SET ME FREE, ARCHER. YOU MADE ME A NEW MAN.
I WAS SO GRATEFUL, I WANTED TO THANK YOU.
BUT I COULDN'T. I WENT BACKSTAGE, AND YOU WERE WITH HER.
YOU WERE FIGHTING. SHE WAS LEAVING YOU FOR JACK MIDLAND.
I WATCHED YOU AS, IN DESPAIR, YOU REACHED INSIDE YOUR OWN BRAIN AND REMOVED HER.
YOU HYPNOTIZED YOURSELF TO FORGET YOU EVER KNEW HER, EVER KNEW ME...
HMMM?
...THAT YOU EVER DID WRONG OR WERE DONE WRONG.
YOU CAGED YOURSELF. YOU. THE MIND.
URK!
I AM THE BODY.
I WANT TO SET YOU FREE.

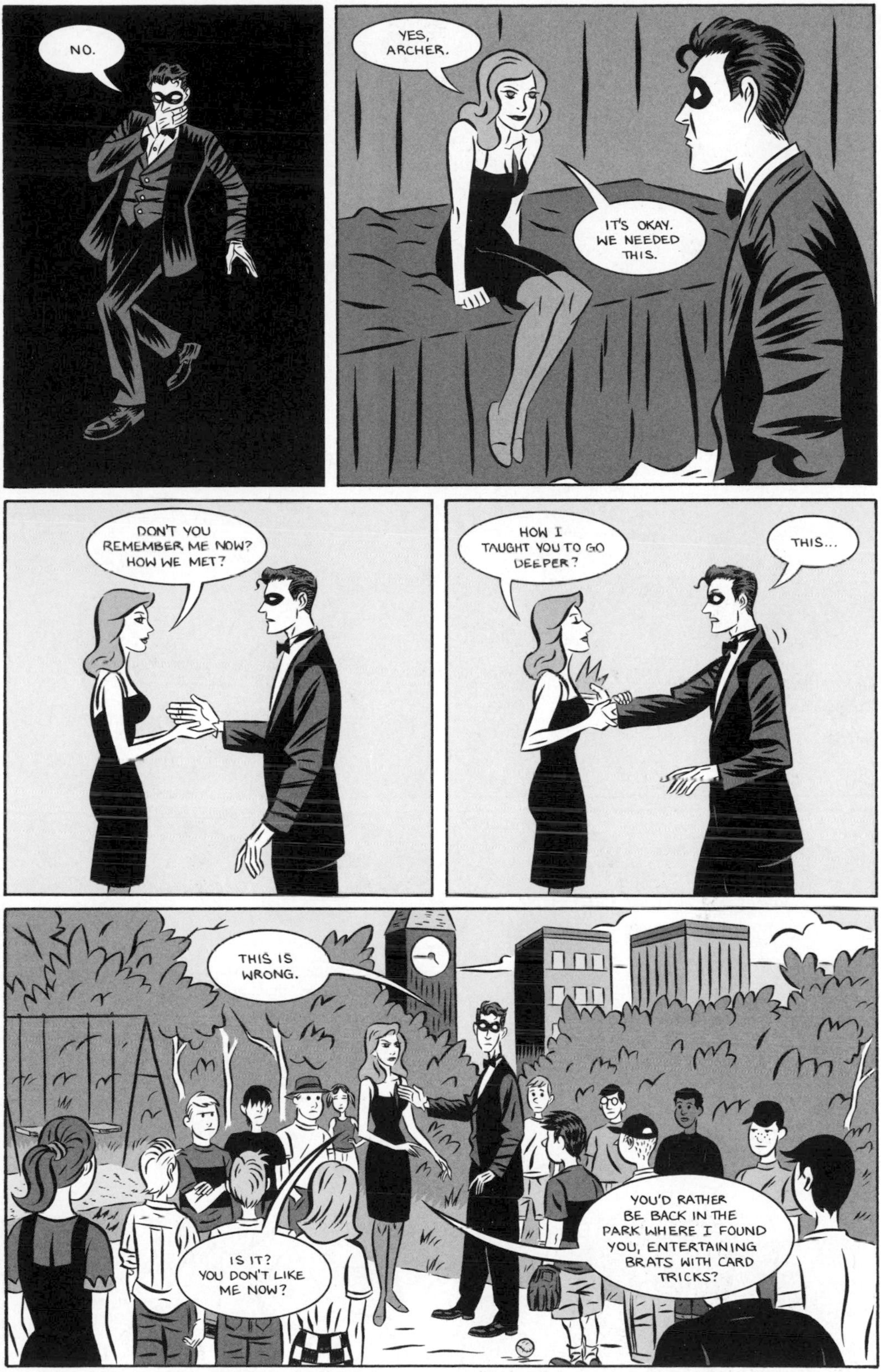
NO.
YES, ARCHER.
IT'S OKAY. WE NEEDED THIS.
DON'T YOU REMEMBER ME NOW? HOW WE MET?
HOW I TAUGHT YOU TO GO DEEPER?
THIS...
THIS IS WRONG.
IS IT? YOU DON'T LIKE ME NOW?
YOU'D RATHER BE BACK IN THE PARK WHERE I FOUND YOU, ENTERTAINING BRATS WITH CARD TRICKS?

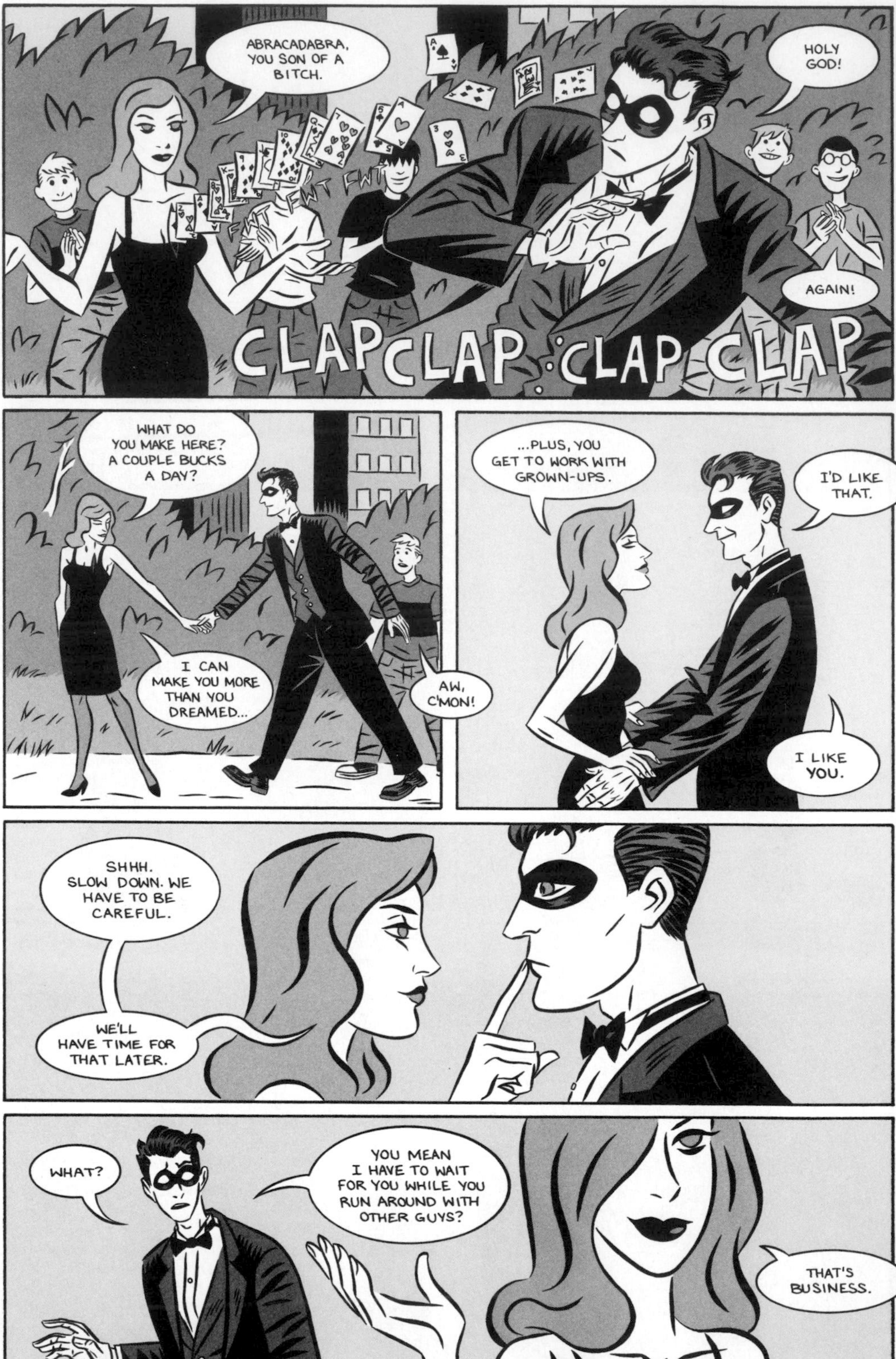
ABRACADABRA, YOU SON OF A BITCH.
FWT FWT FWT
HOLY GOD!
AGAIN!
CLAP CLAP CLAP CLAP
WHAT DO YOU MAKE HERE? A COUPLE BUCKS A DAY?
I CAN MAKE YOU MORE THAN YOU DREAMED...
AW, C'MON!
...PLUS, YOU GET TO WORK WITH GROWN-UPS.
I'D LIKE THAT.
I LIKE YOU.
SHHH. SLOW DOWN. WE HAVE TO BE CAREFUL.
WE'LL HAVE TIME FOR THAT LATER.
WHAT?
YOU MEAN I HAVE TO WAIT FOR YOU WHILE YOU RUN AROUND WITH OTHER GUYS?
THAT'S BUSINESS.

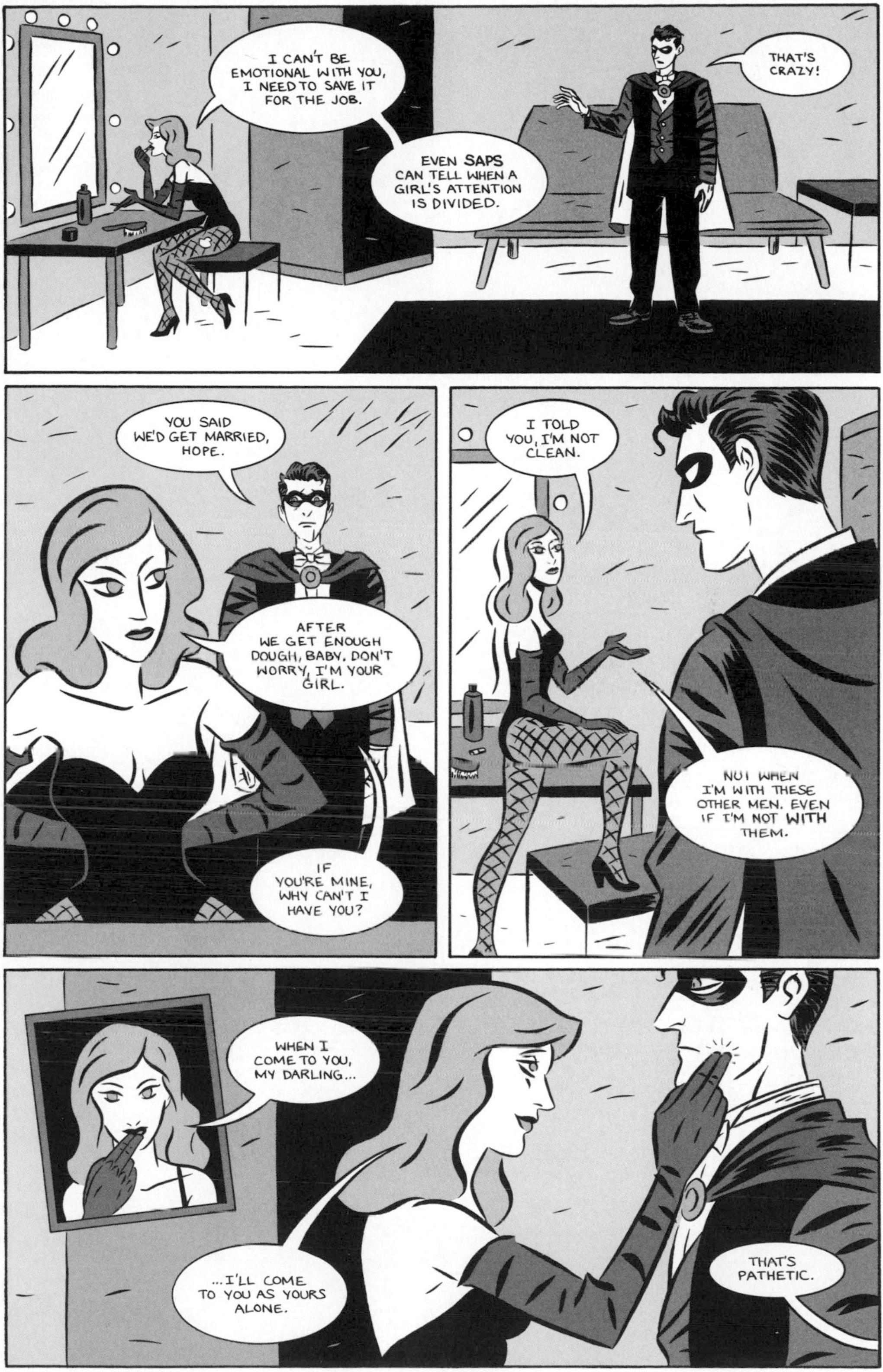
I CAN'T BE EMOTIONAL WITH YOU, I NEED TO SAVE IT FOR THE JOB.
EVEN SAPS CAN TELL WHEN A GIRL'S ATTENTION IS DIVIDED.
THAT'S CRAZY!
YOU SAID WE'D GET MARRIED, HOPE.
AFTER WE GET ENOUGH DOUGH, BABY. DON'T WORRY, I'M YOUR GIRL.
IF YOU'RE MINE, WHY CAN'T I HAVE YOU?
I TOLD YOU, I'M NOT CLEAN.
NOT WHEN I'M WITH THESE OTHER MEN. EVEN IF I'M NOT WITH THEM.
WHEN I COME TO YOU, MY DARLING...
...I'LL COME TO YOU AS YOURS ALONE.
THAT'S PATHETIC.

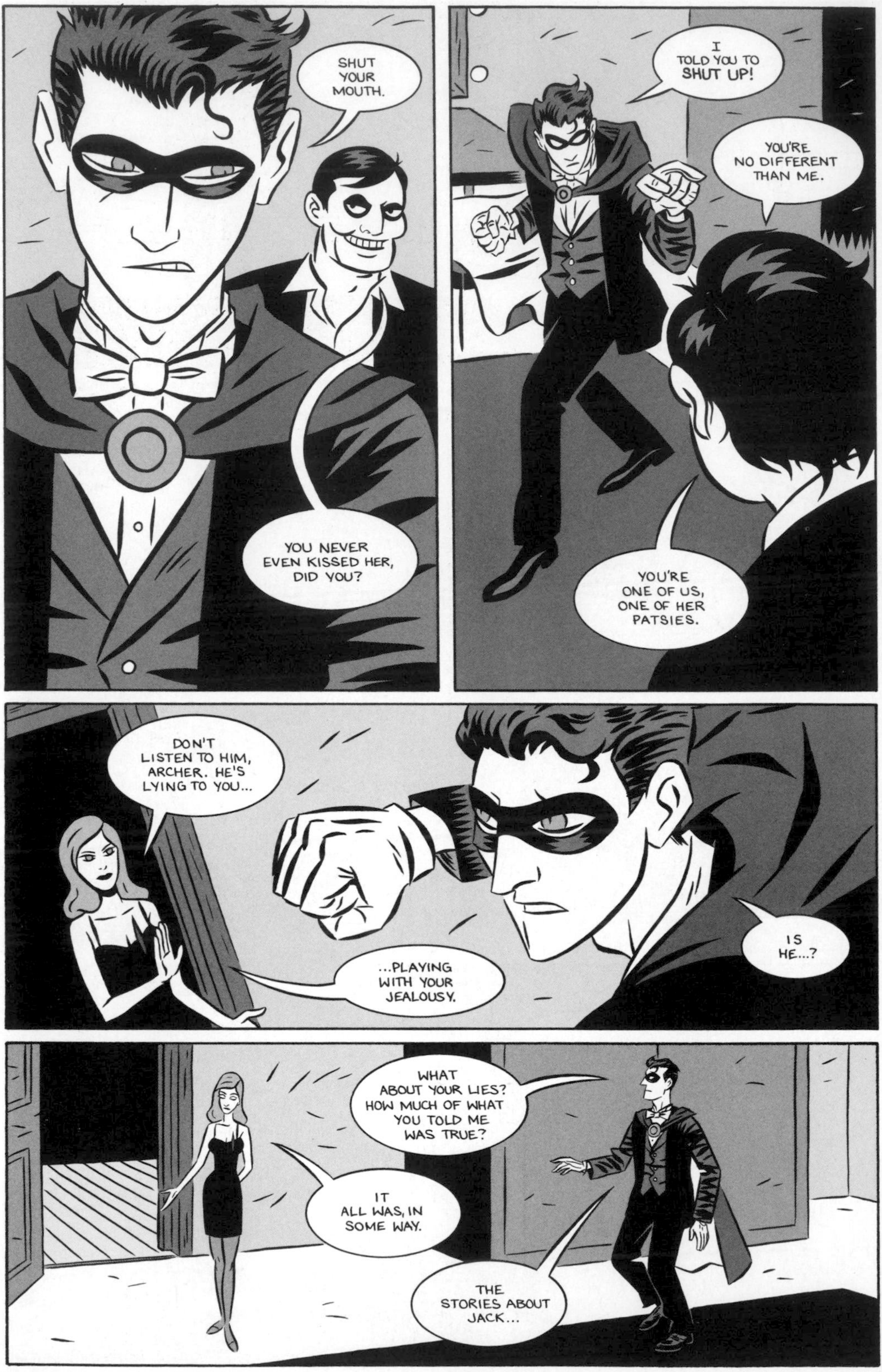
SHUT YOUR MOUTH.
YOU NEVER EVEN KISSED HER, DID YOU?
I TOLD YOU TO SHUT UP!
YOU'RE NO DIFFERENT THAN ME.
YOU'RE ONE OF US, ONE OF HER PATSIES.
DON'T LISTEN TO HIM, ARCHER. HE'S LYING TO YOU...
...PLAYING WITH YOUR JEALOUSY.
IS HE...?
WHAT ABOUT YOUR LIES? HOW MUCH OF WHAT YOU TOLD ME WAS TRUE?
IT ALL WAS, IN SOME WAY.
THE STORIES ABOUT JACK...

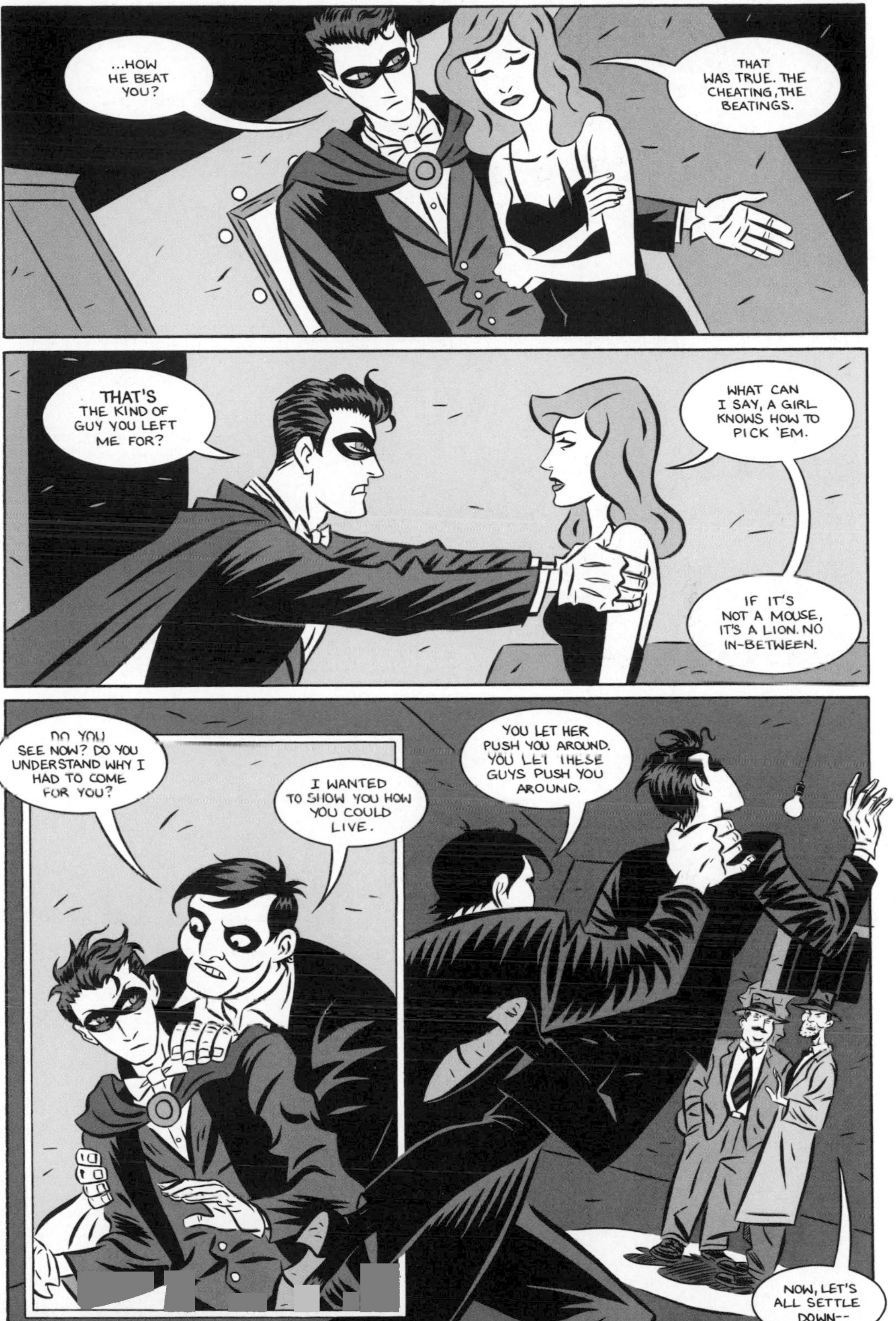
...HOW HE BEAT YOU?
THAT WAS TRUE. THE CHEATING, THE BEATINGS.
THAT'S THE KIND OF GUY YOU LEFT ME FOR?
WHAT CAN I SAY, A GIRL KNOWS HOW TO PICK 'EM.
IF IT'S NOT A MOUSE, IT'S A LION. NO IN-BETWEEN.
DO YOU SEE NOW? DO YOU UNDERSTAND WHY I HAD TO COME FOR YOU?
I WANTED TO SHOW YOU HOW YOU COULD LIVE.
YOU LET HER PUSH YOU AROUND. YOU LET THESE GUYS PUSH YOU AROUND.
NOW, LET'S ALL SETTLE DOWN--

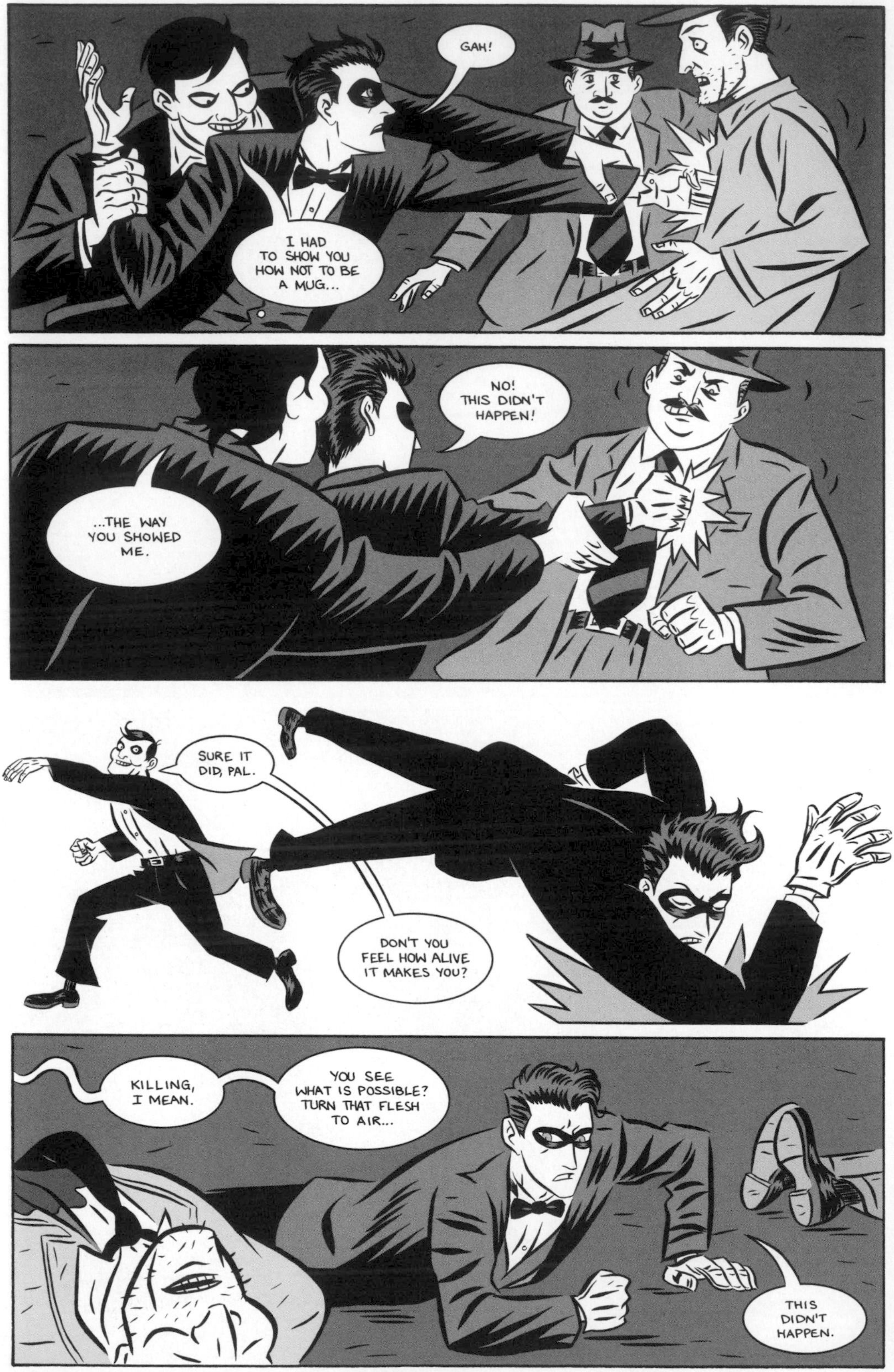
GAH!
I HAD TO SHOW YOU HOW NOT TO BE A MUG...
NO! THIS DIDN'T HAPPEN!
...THE WAY YOU SHOWED ME.
SURE IT DID, PAL.
DON'T YOU FEEL HOW ALIVE IT MAKES YOU?
KILLING, I MEAN.
YOU SEE WHAT IS POSSIBLE? TURN THAT FLESH TO AIR...
THIS DIDN'T HAPPEN.

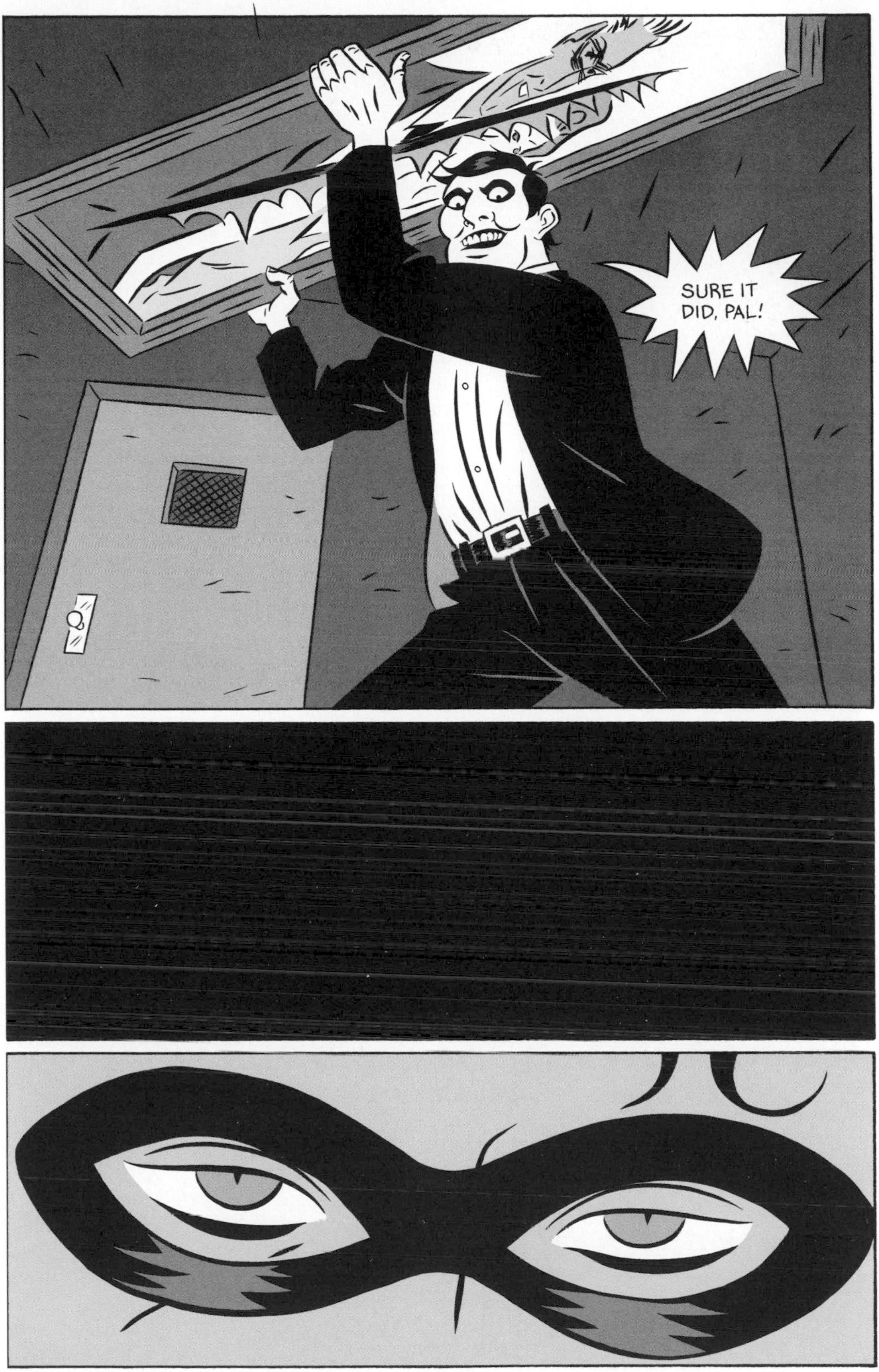
SURE IT DID, PAL!

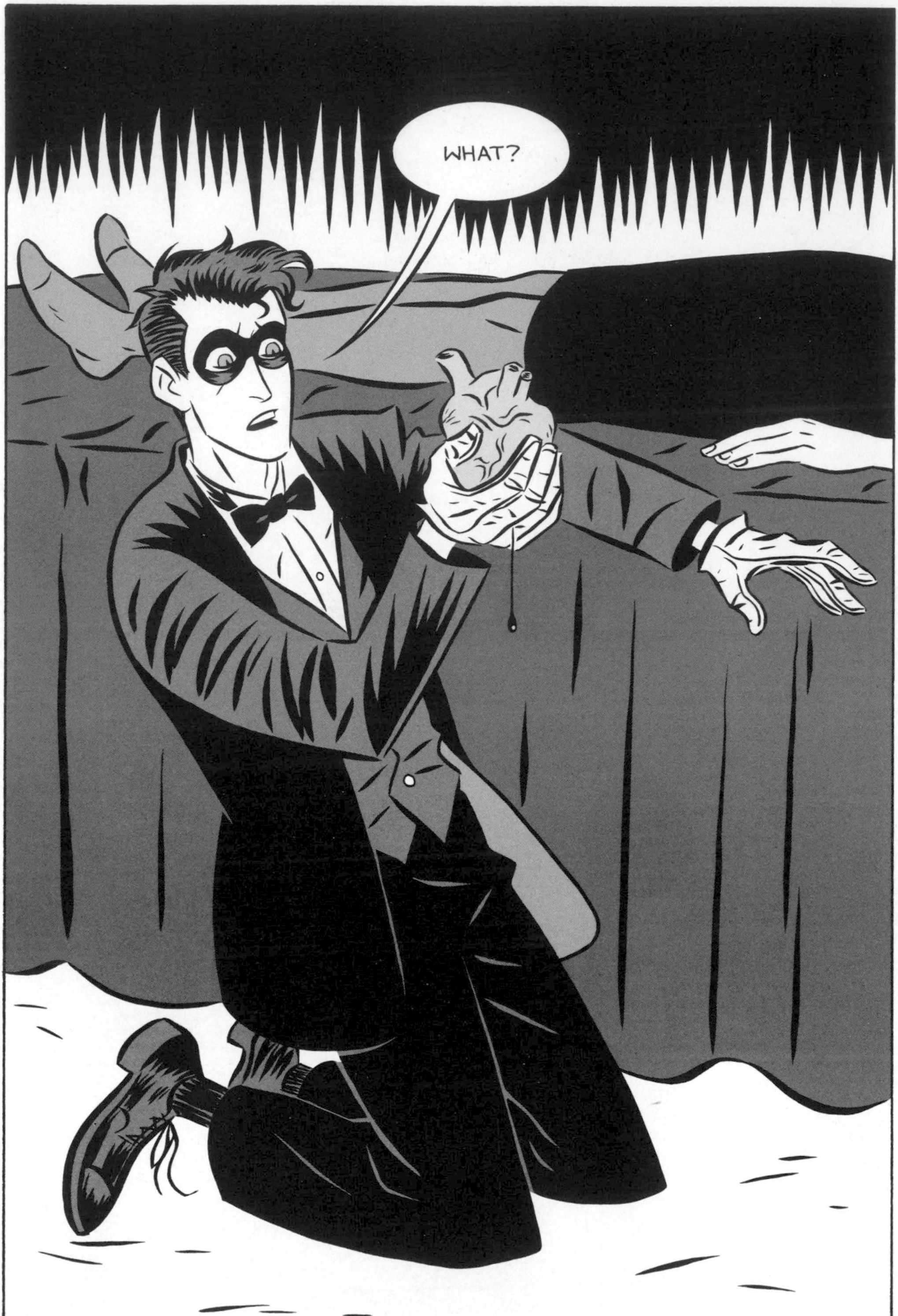
WHAT?

Chapter 14:
Blue on Blue

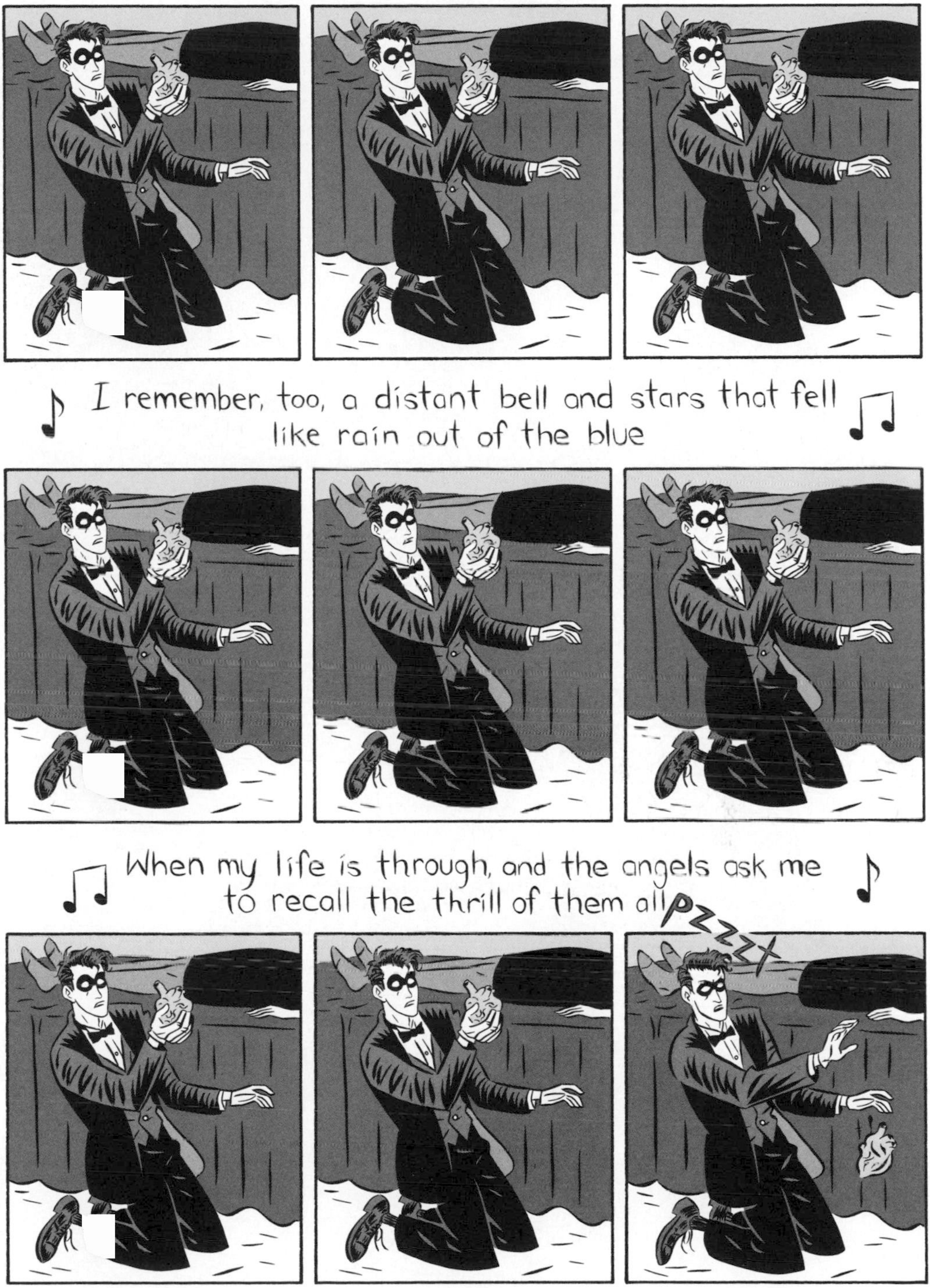
I remember, too, a distant bell and stars that fell like rain out of the blue
When my life is through, and the angels ask me to recall the thrill of them all
PZZZX

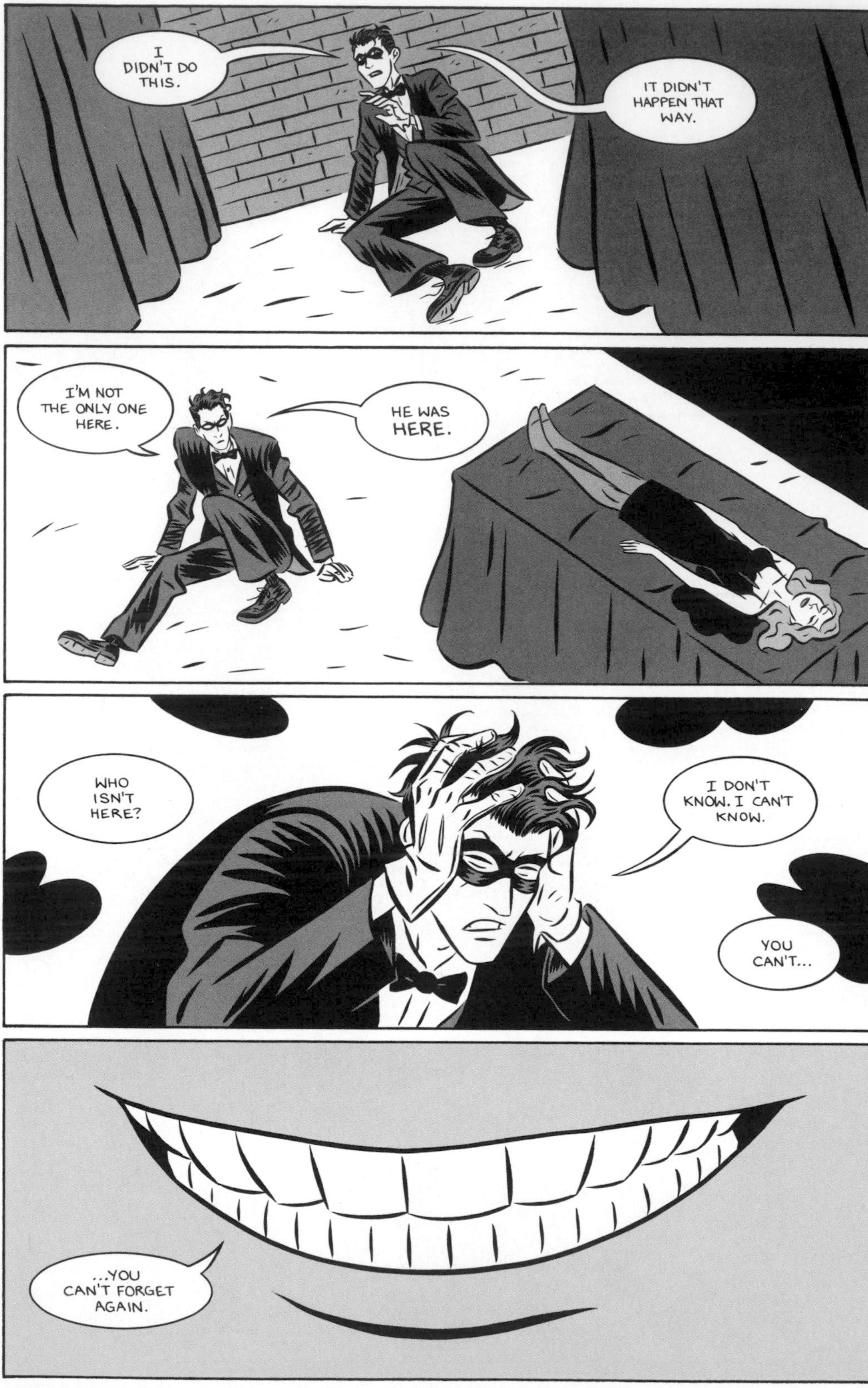
I DIDN'T DO THIS.
IT DIDN'T HAPPEN THAT WAY.
I'M NOT THE ONLY ONE HERE.
HE WAS HERE.
WHO ISN'T HERE?
I DON'T KNOW. I CAN'T KNOW.
YOU CAN'T...
...YOU CAN'T FORGET AGAIN.

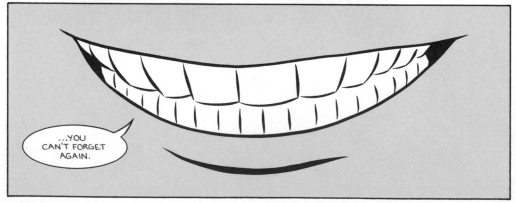

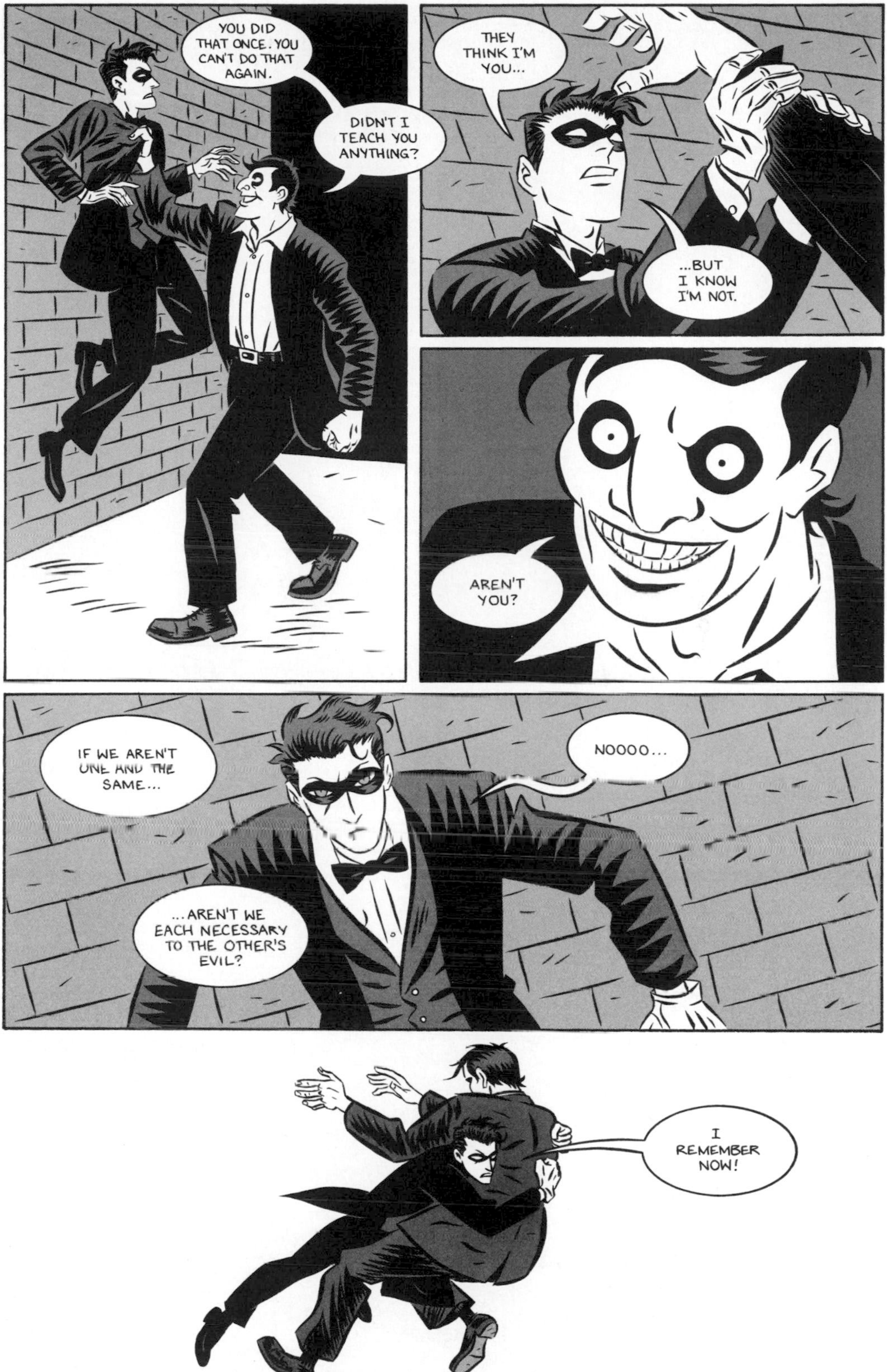
YOU DID THAT ONCE. YOU CAN'T DO THAT AGAIN.
DIDN'T I TEACH YOU ANYTHING?
THEY THINK I'M YOU...
...BUT I KNOW I'M NOT.
AREN'T YOU?
IF WE AREN'T ONE AND THE SAME...
NOOOO...
...AREN'T WE EACH NECESSARY TO THE OTHER'S EVIL?
I REMEMBER NOW!

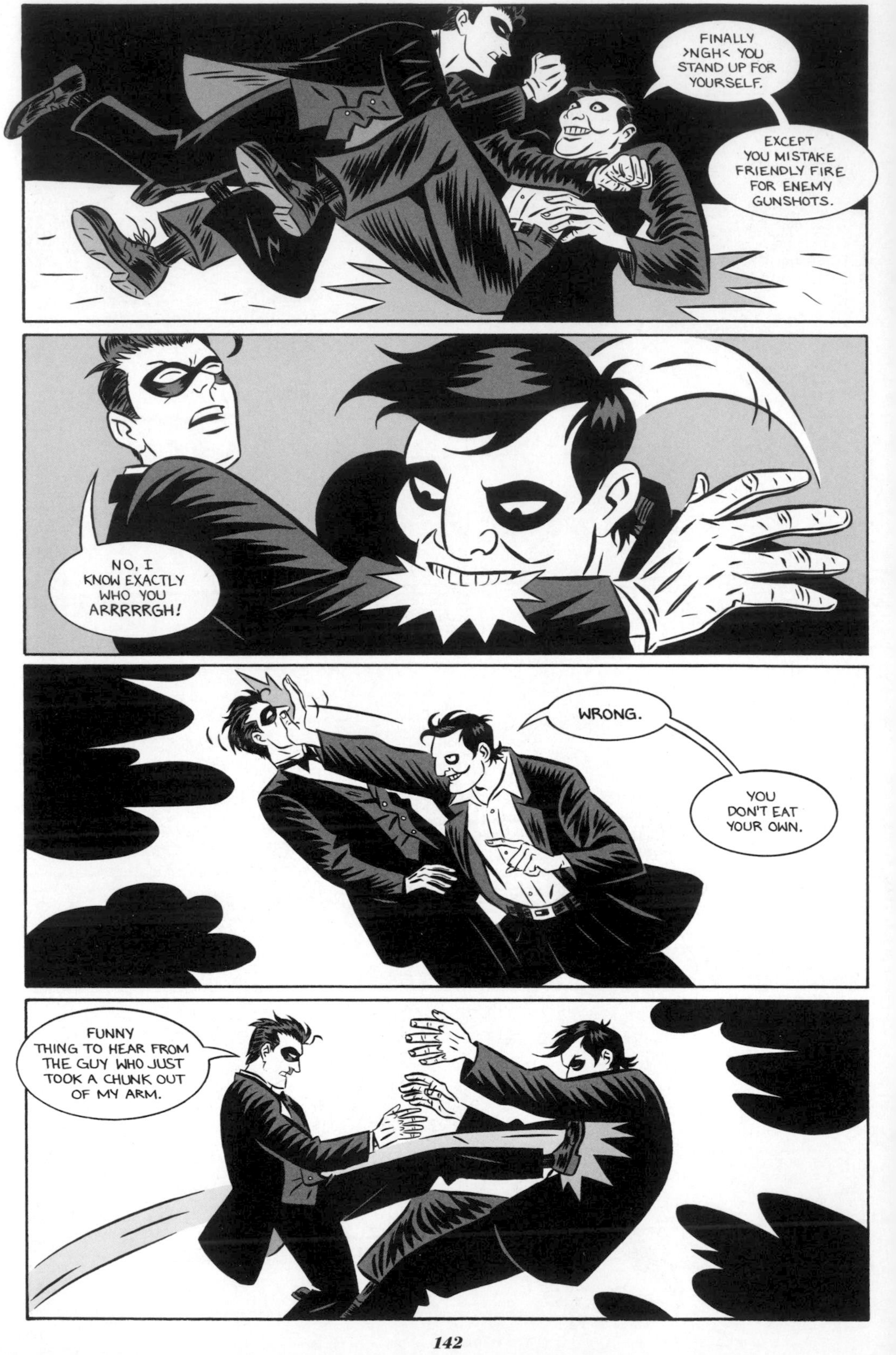
FINALLY >NGH< YOU STAND UP FOR YOURSELF.
EXCEPT YOU MISTAKE FRIENDLY FIRE FOR ENEMY GUNSHOTS.
NO, I KNOW EXACTLY WHO YOU ARRRRRGH!
WRONG.
YOU DON'T EAT YOUR OWN.
FUNNY THING TO HEAR FROM THE GUY WHO JUST TOOK A CHUNK OUT OF MY ARM.

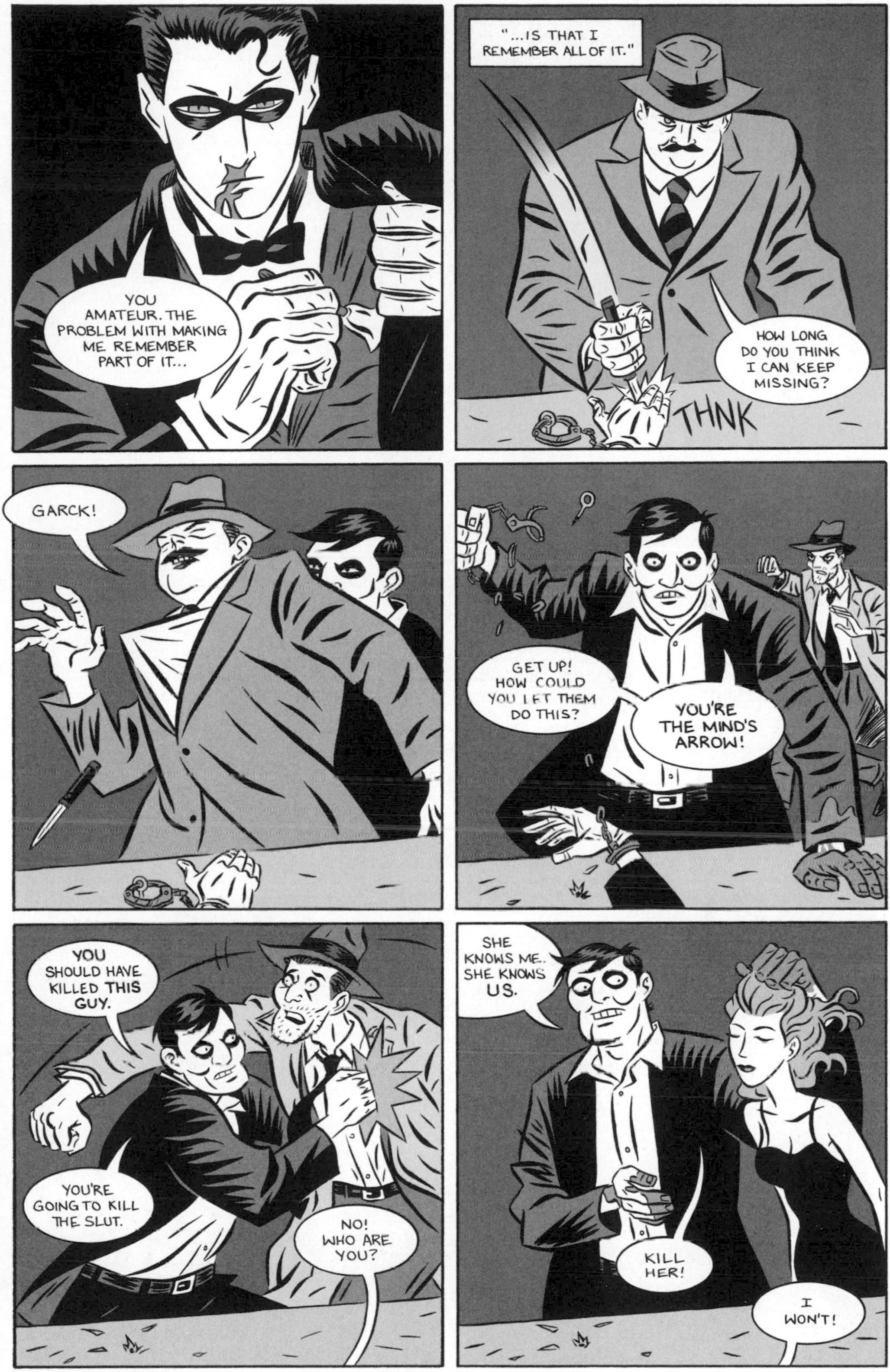
YOU AMATEUR. THE PROBLEM WITH MAKING ME REMEMBER PART OF IT...
"...IS THAT I REMEMBER ALL OF IT."
HOW LONG DO YOU THINK I CAN KEEP MISSING?
THNK
GARCK!
GET UP! HOW COULD YOU LET THEM DO THIS?
YOU'RE THE MIND'S ARROW!
YOU SHOULD HAVE KILLED THIS GUY.
YOU'RE GOING TO KILL THE SLUT.
NO! WHO ARE YOU?
SHE KNOWS ME. SHE KNOWS US.
KILL HER!
I WON'T!

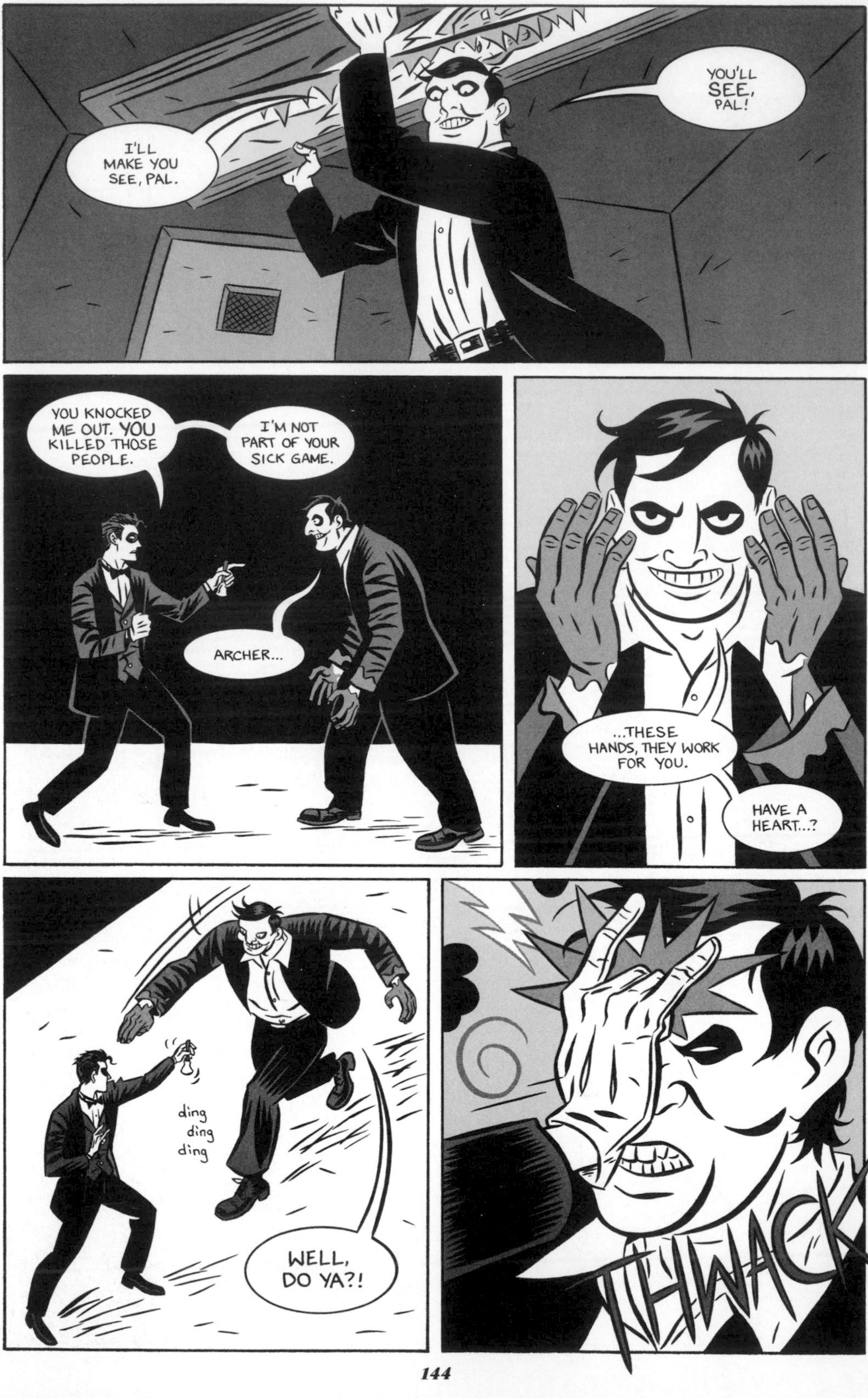
I'LL MAKE YOU SEE, PAL.
YOU'LL SEE, PAL!
YOU KNOCKED ME OUT. YOU KILLED THOSE PEOPLE.
I'M NOT PART OF YOUR SICK GAME.
ARCHER...
...THESE HANDS, THEY WORK FOR YOU.
HAVE A HEART...?
ding ding ding
WELL, DO YA?!
THWACK

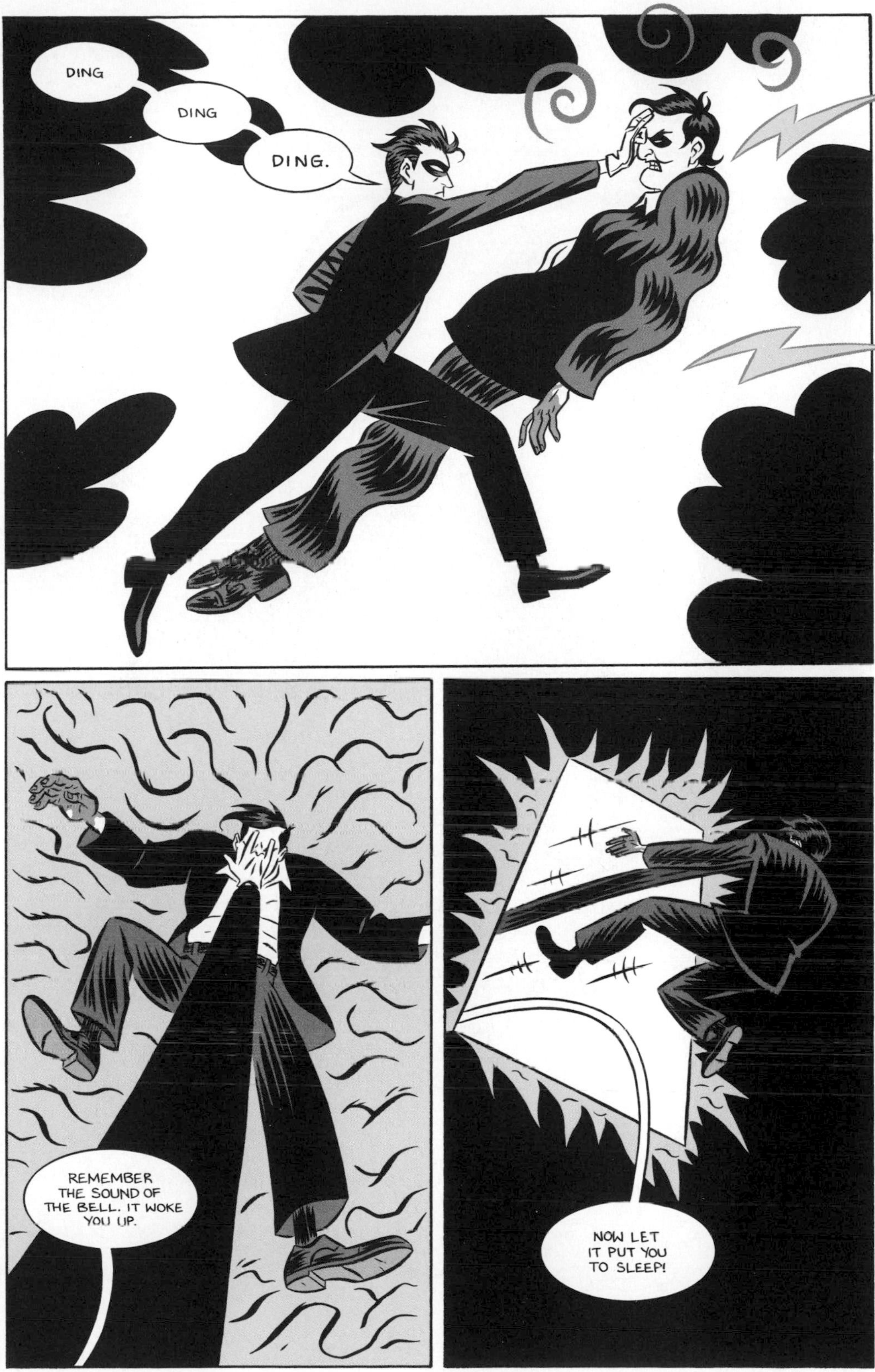
DING
DING
DING.
REMEMBER THE SOUND OF THE BELL. IT WOKE YOU UP.
NOW LET IT PUT YOU TO SLEEP!

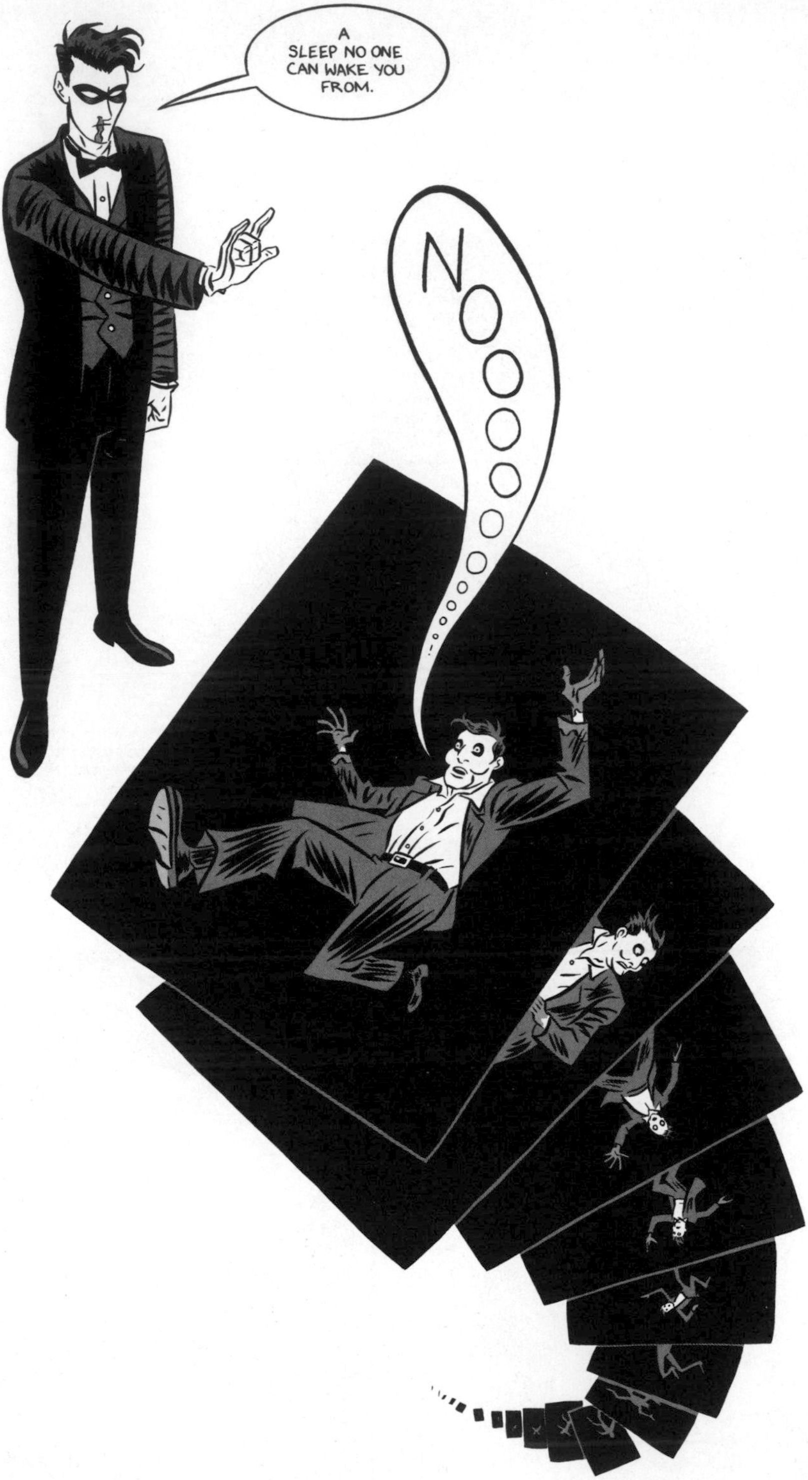
A SLEEP NO ONE CAN WAKE YOU FROM.
NOOOOOOOO...!

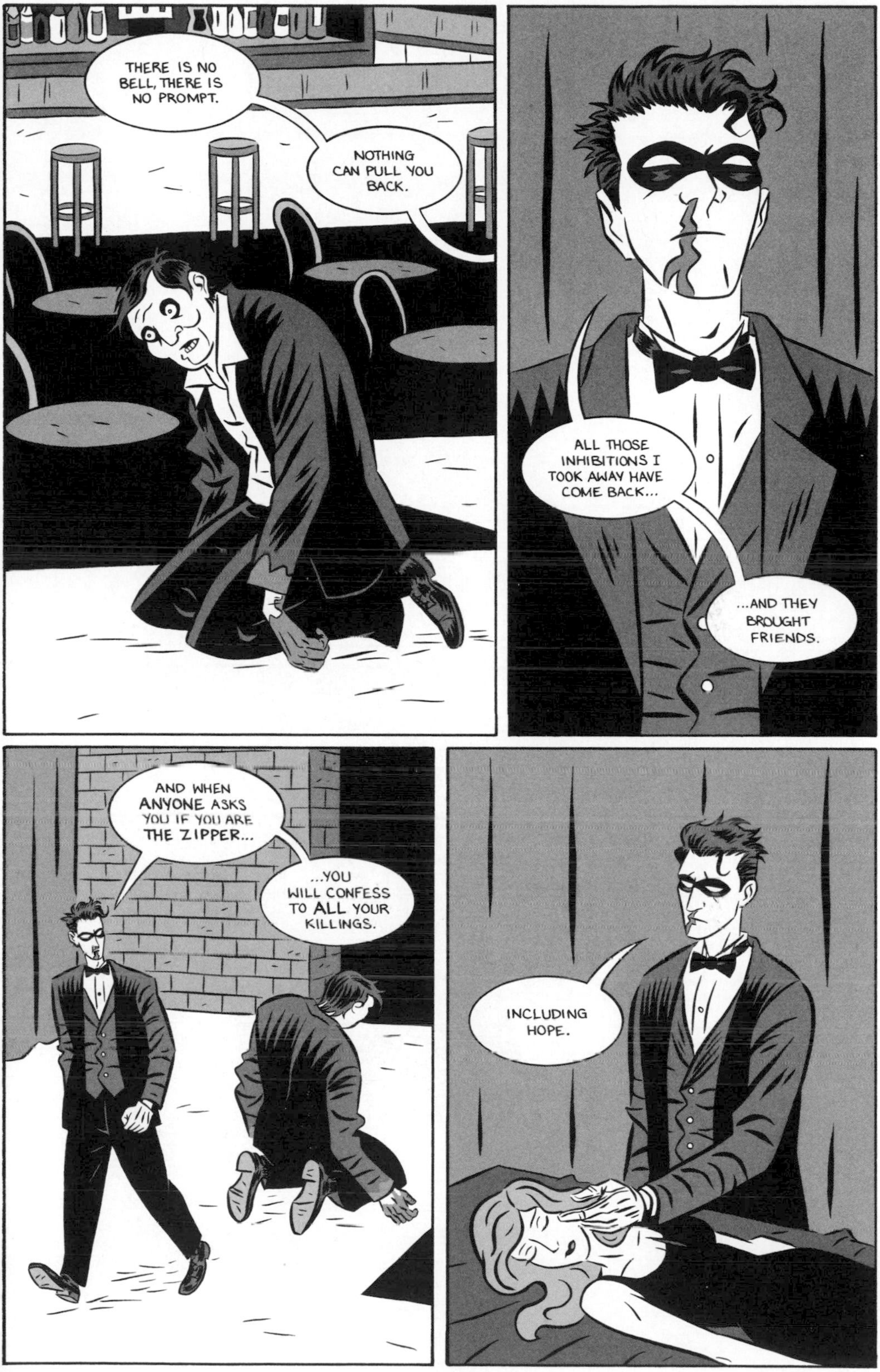
THERE IS NO BELL, THERE IS NO PROMPT.
NOTHING CAN PULL YOU BACK.
ALL THOSE INHIBITIONS I TOOK AWAY HAVE COME BACK...
...AND THEY BROUGHT FRIENDS.
AND WHEN ANYONE ASKS YOU IF YOU ARE THE ZIPPER...
...YOU WILL CONFESS TO ALL YOUR KILLINGS.
INCLUDING HOPE.

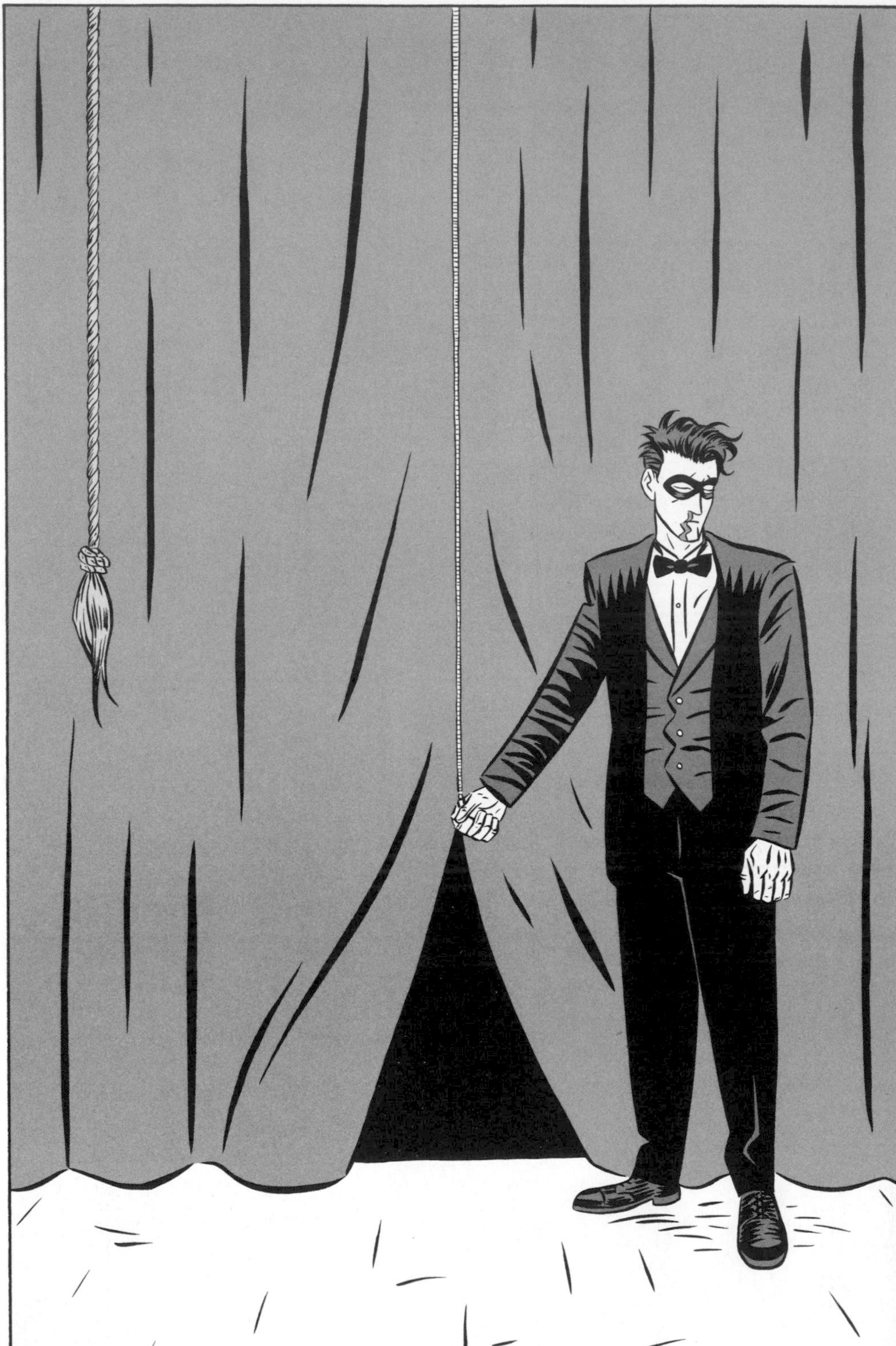

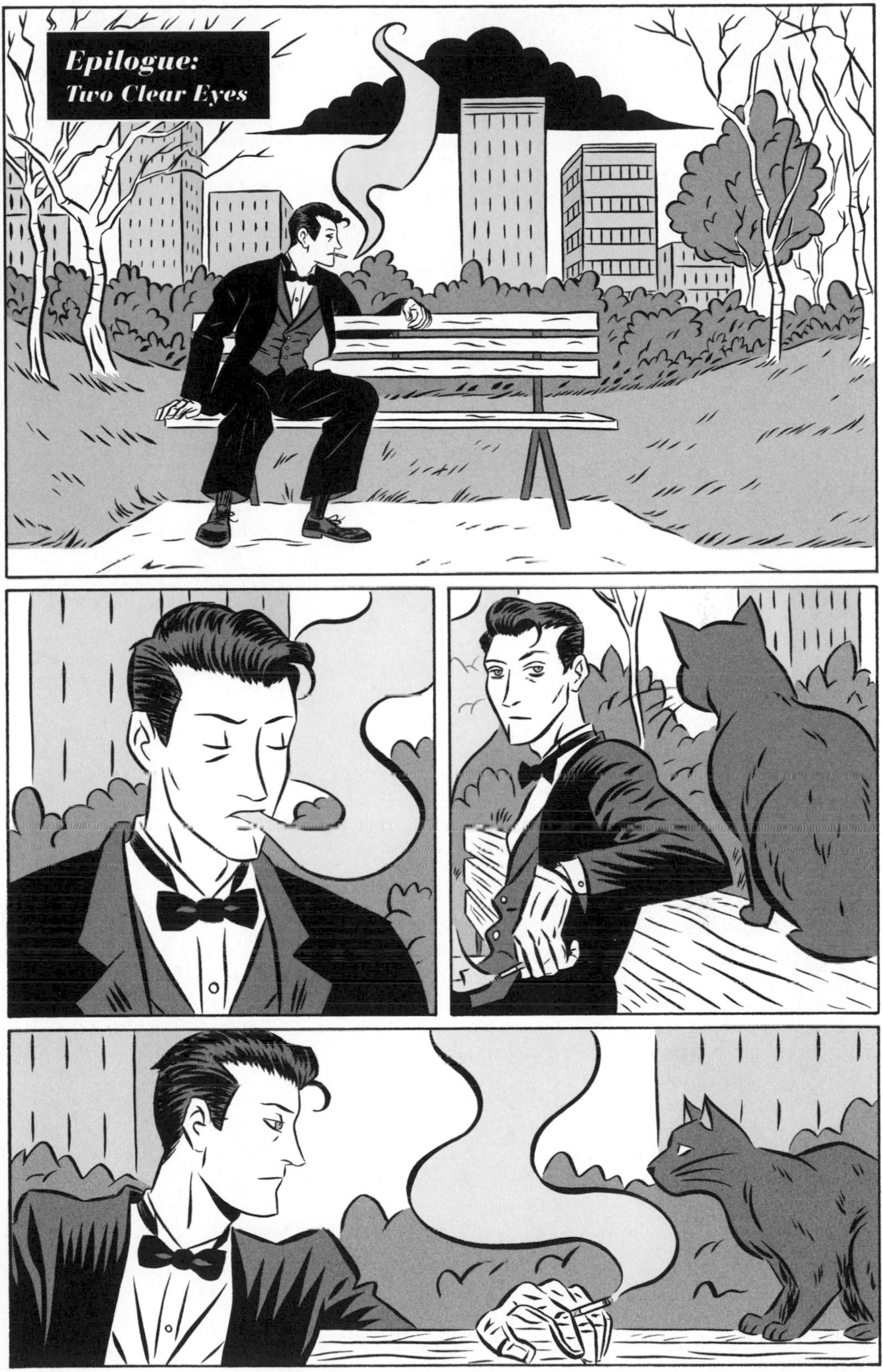
Epilogue:
Two Clear Eyes

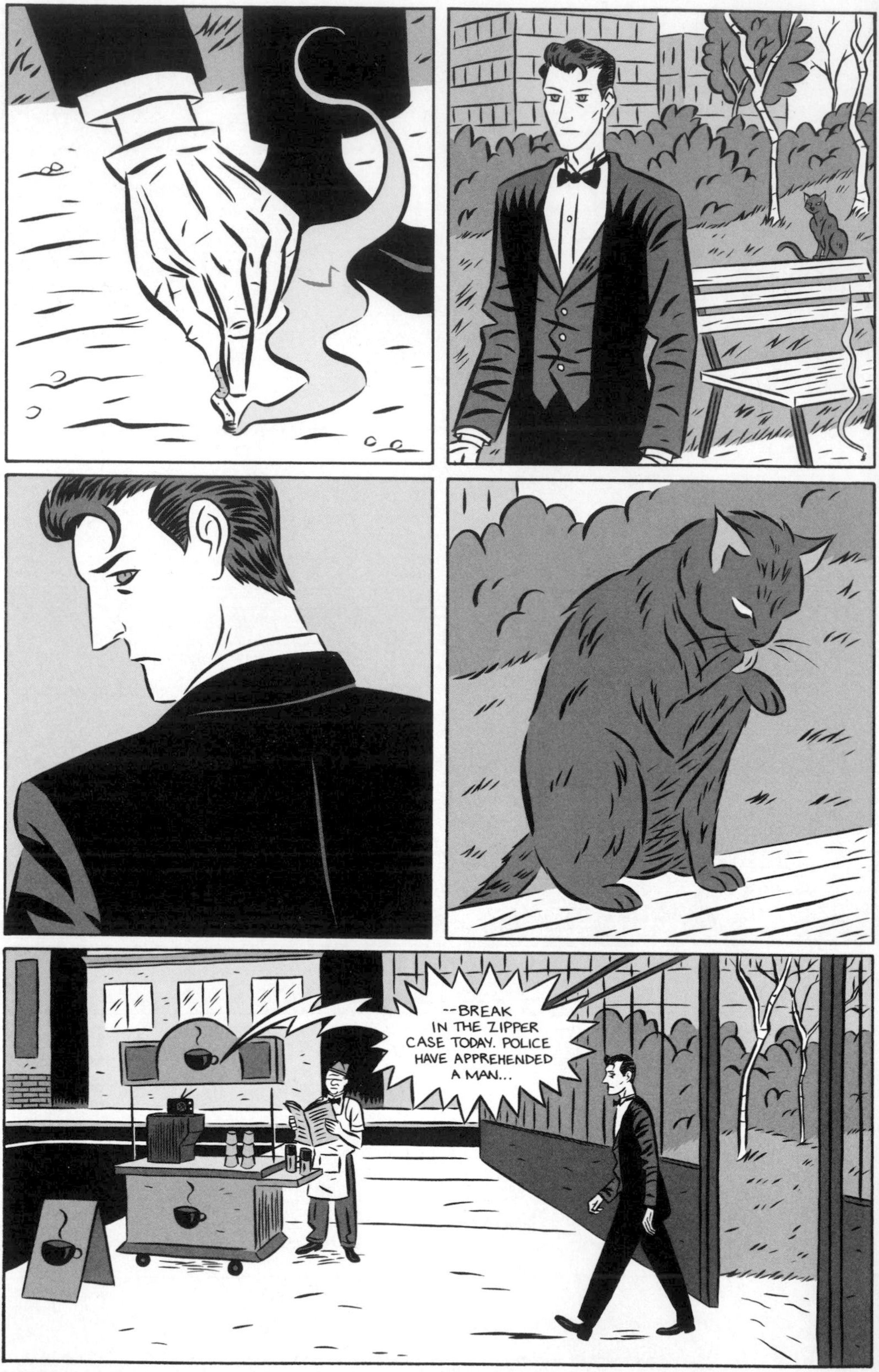
--BREAK
IN THE ZIPPER
CASE TODAY. POLICE
HAVE APPREHENDED
A MAN...

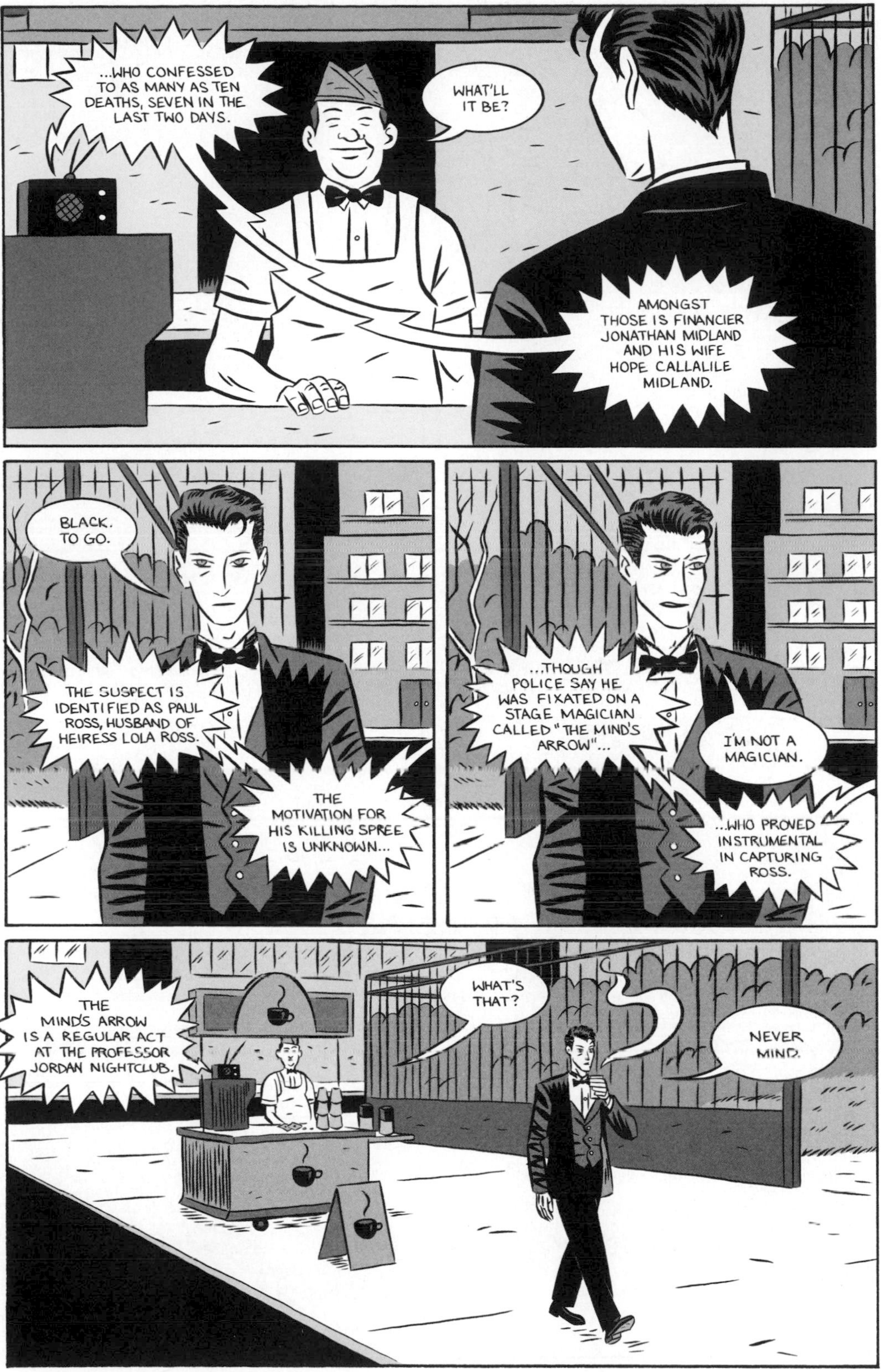
...WHO CONFESSED TO AS MANY AS TEN DEATHS, SEVEN IN THE LAST TWO DAYS.
WHAT'LL IT BE?
AMONGST THOSE IS FINANCIER JONATHAN MIDLAND AND HIS WIFE HOPE CALLALILE MIDLAND.
BLACK. TO GO.
THE SUSPECT IS IDENTIFIED AS PAUL ROSS, HUSBAND OF HEIRESS LOLA ROSS.
THE MOTIVATION FOR HIS KILLING SPREE IS UNKNOWN...
...THOUGH POLICE SAY HE WAS FIXATED ON A STAGE MAGICIAN CALLED "THE MIND'S ARROW"...
I'M NOT A MAGICIAN.
...WHO PROVED INSTRUMENTAL IN CAPTURING ROSS.
THE MIND'S ARROW IS A REGULAR ACT AT THE PROFESSOR JORDAN NIGHTCLUB.
WHAT'S THAT?
NEVER MIND.

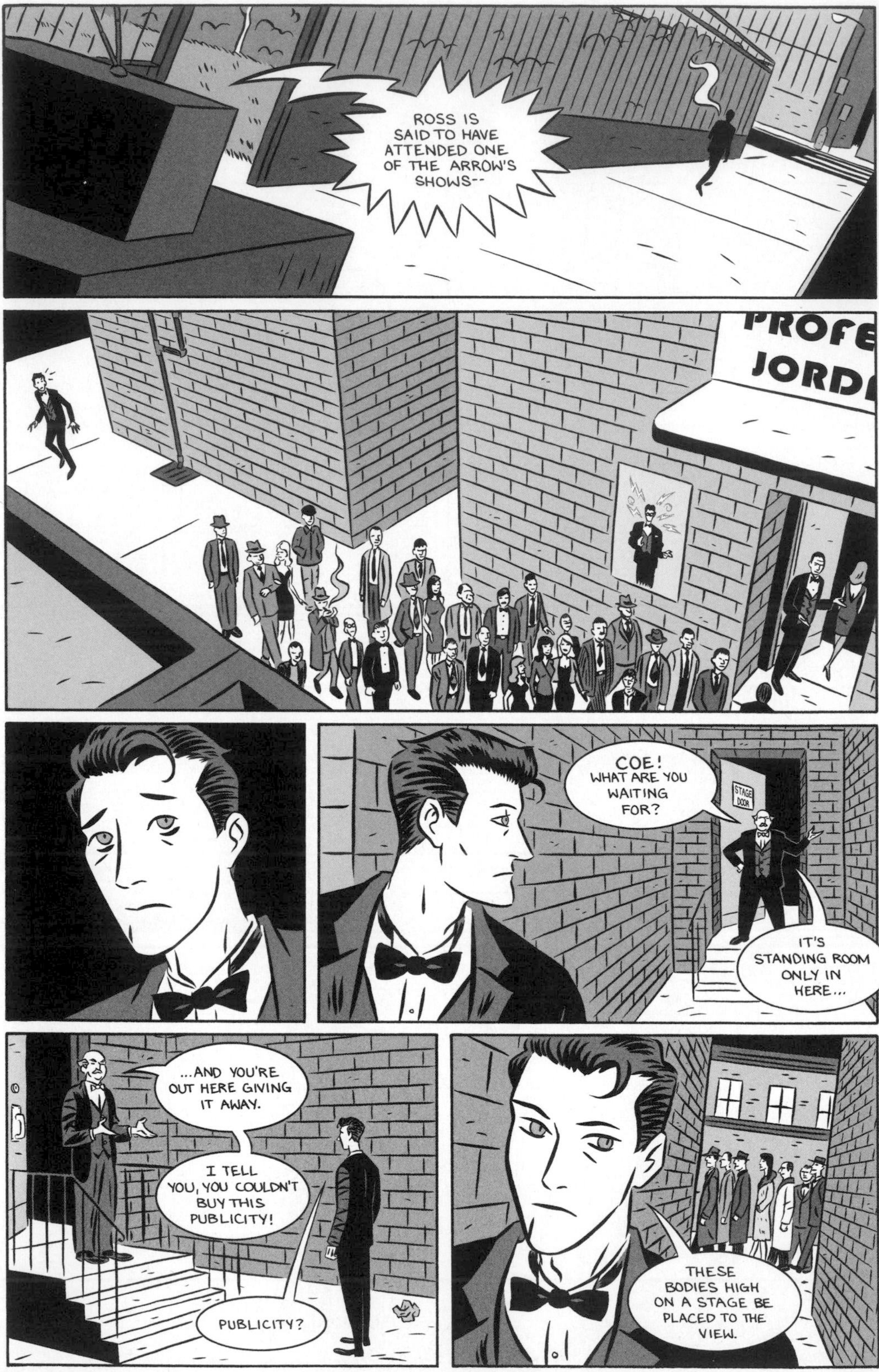
ROSS IS SAID TO HAVE ATTENDED ONE OF THE ARROW'S SHOWS--
PROFE
JORD
COE! WHAT ARE YOU WAITING FOR?
STAGE DOOR
IT'S STANDING ROOM ONLY IN HERE...
...AND YOU'RE OUT HERE GIVING IT AWAY.
I TELL YOU, YOU COULDN'T BUY THIS PUBLICITY!
PUBLICITY?
THESE BODIES HIGH ON A STAGE BE PLACED TO THE VIEW.

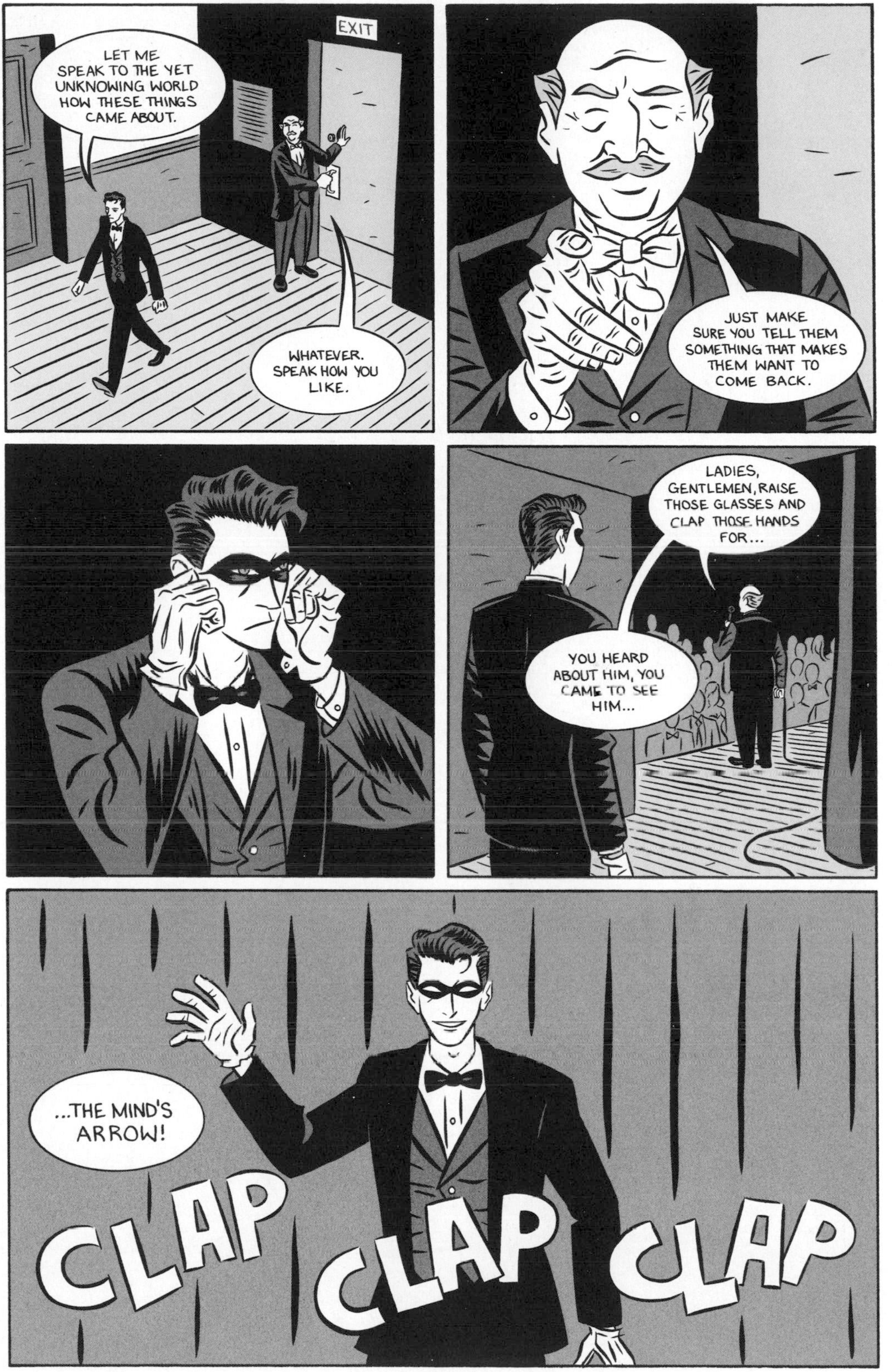
EXIT
LET ME SPEAK TO THE YET UNKNOWING WORLD HOW THESE THINGS CAME ABOUT.
WHATEVER. SPEAK HOW YOU LIKE.
JUST MAKE SURE YOU TELL THEM SOMETHING THAT MAKES THEM WANT TO COME BACK.
LADIES, GENTLEMEN, RAISE THOSE GLASSES AND CLAP THOSE HANDS FOR...
YOU HEARD ABOUT HIM, YOU CAME TO SEE HIM...
...THE MIND'S ARROW!
CLAP
CLAP
CLAP

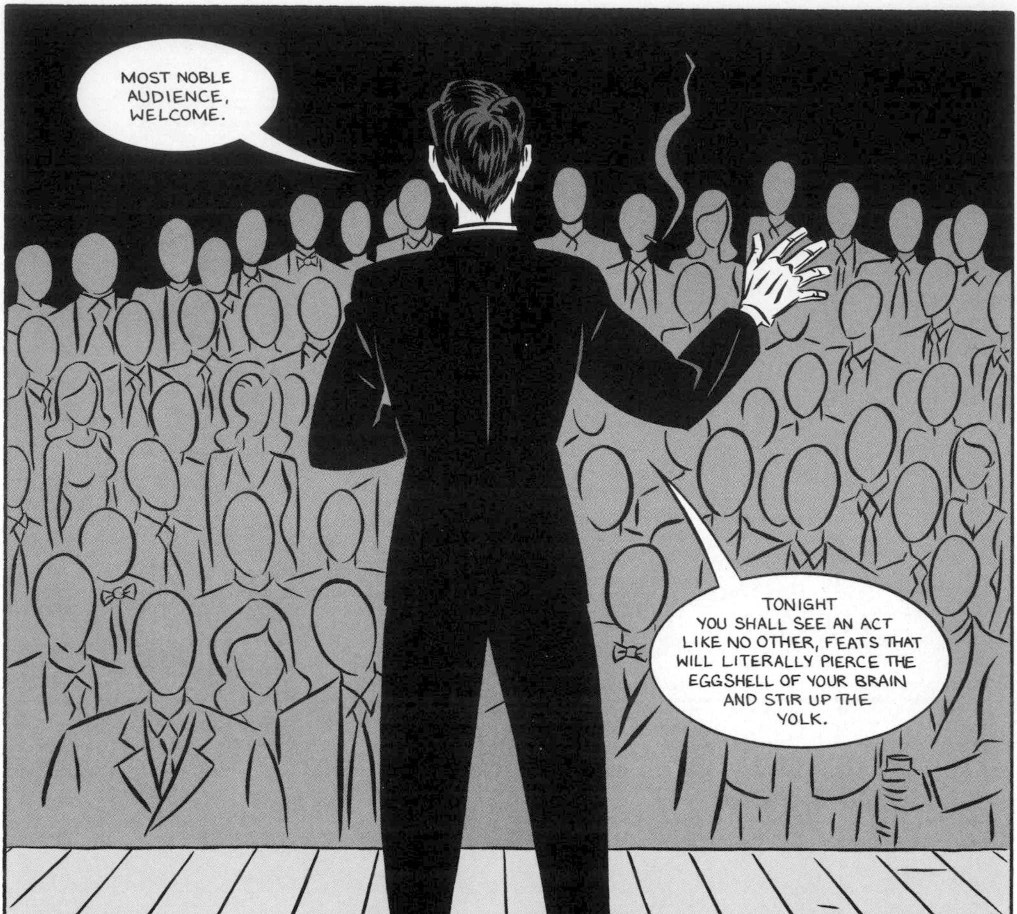
MOST NOBLE AUDIENCE, WELCOME.
TONIGHT YOU SHALL SEE AN ACT LIKE NO OTHER, FEATS THAT WILL LITERALLY PIERCE THE EGGSHELL OF YOUR BRAIN AND STIR UP THE YOLK.

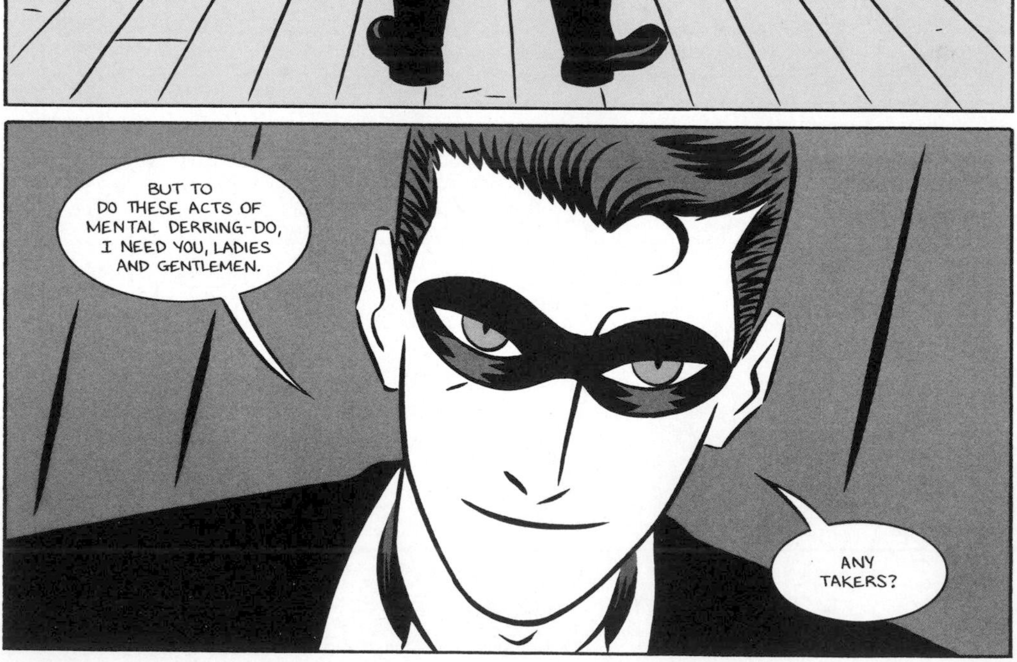
BUT TO DO THESE ACTS OF MENTAL DERRING-DO, I NEED YOU, LADIES AND GENTLEMEN.
ANY TAKERS?

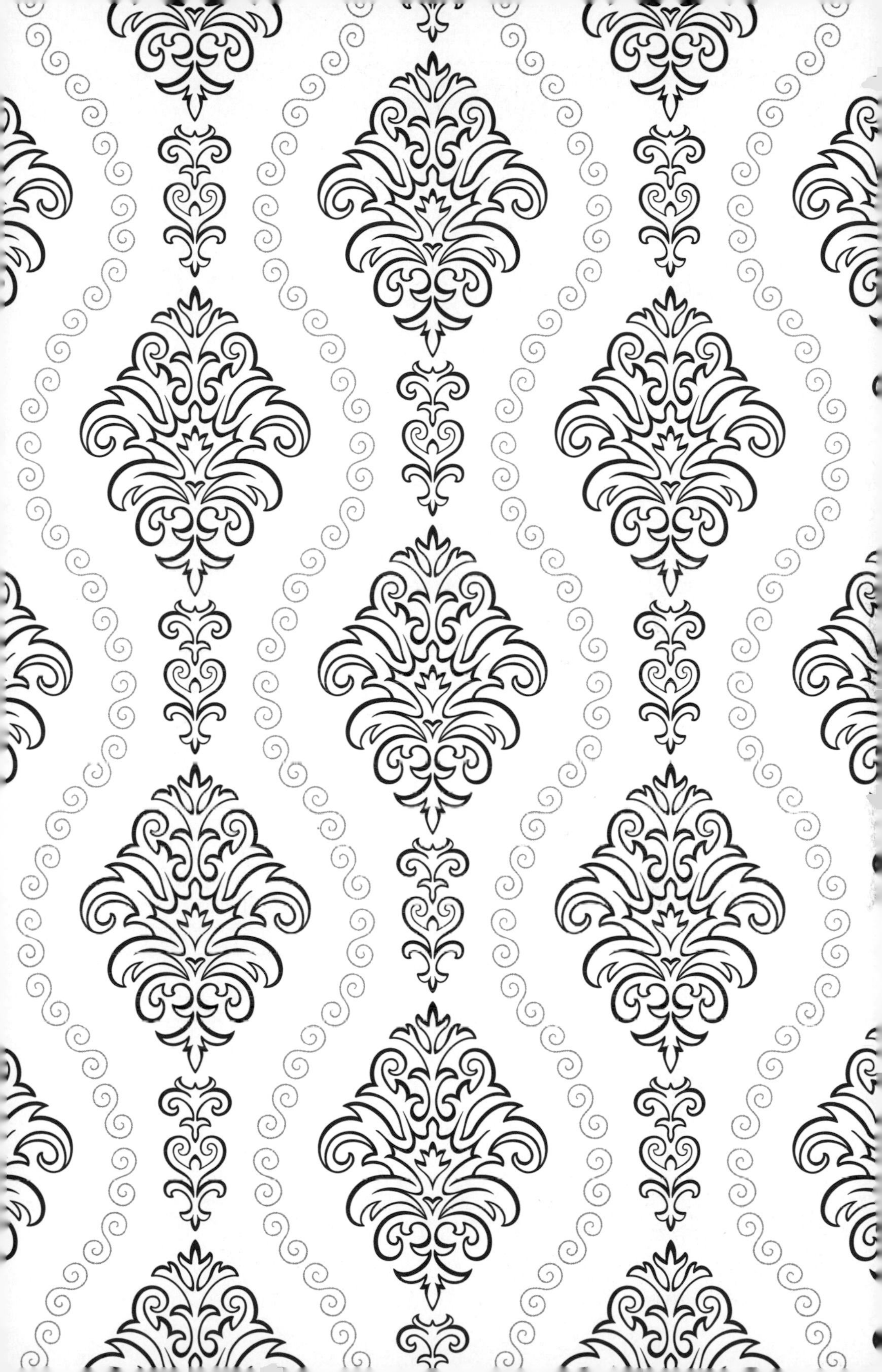

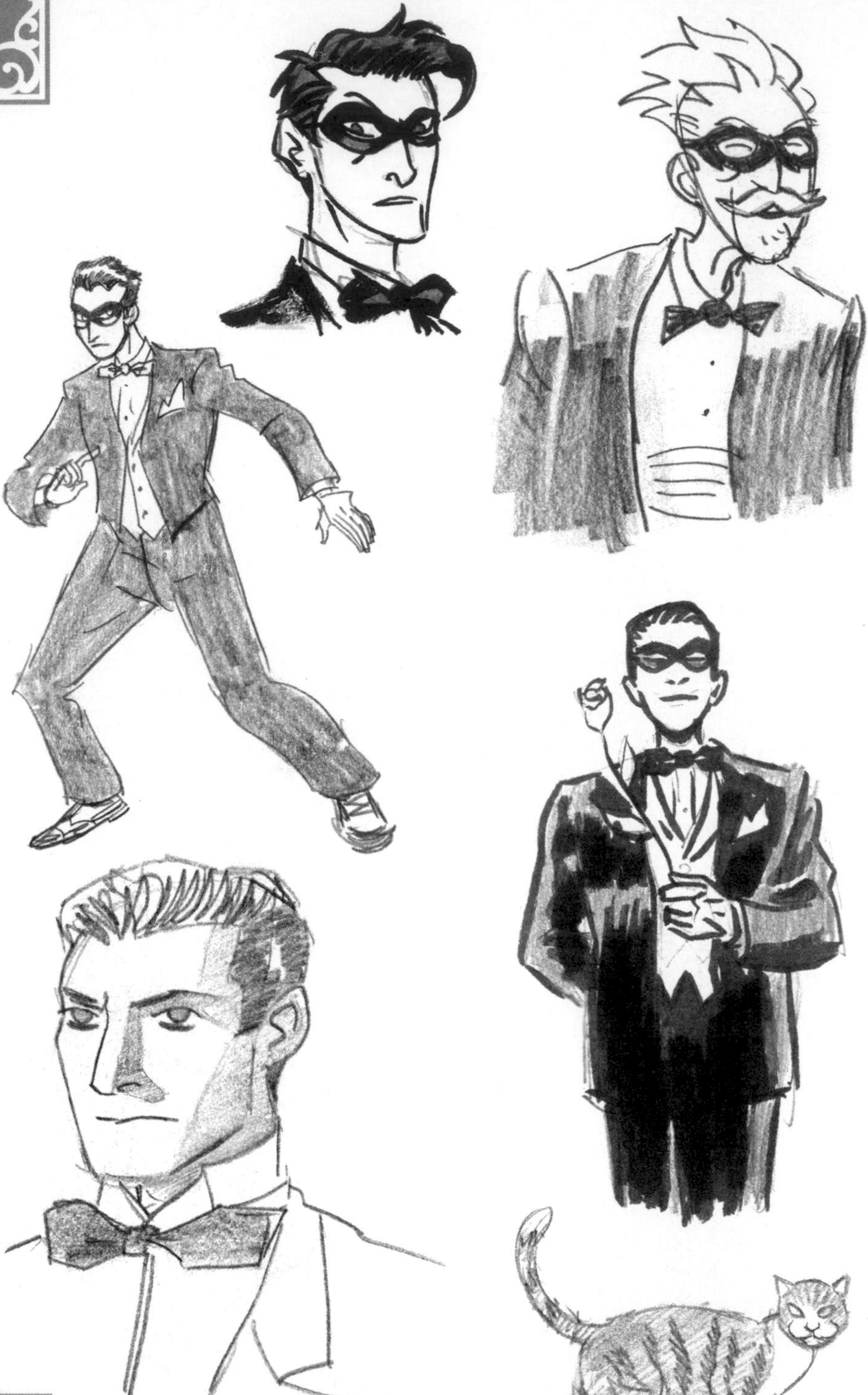

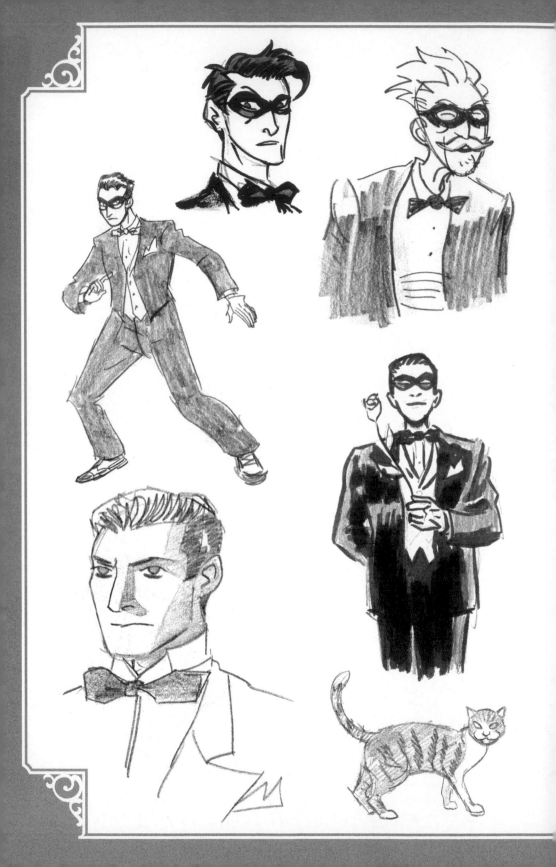

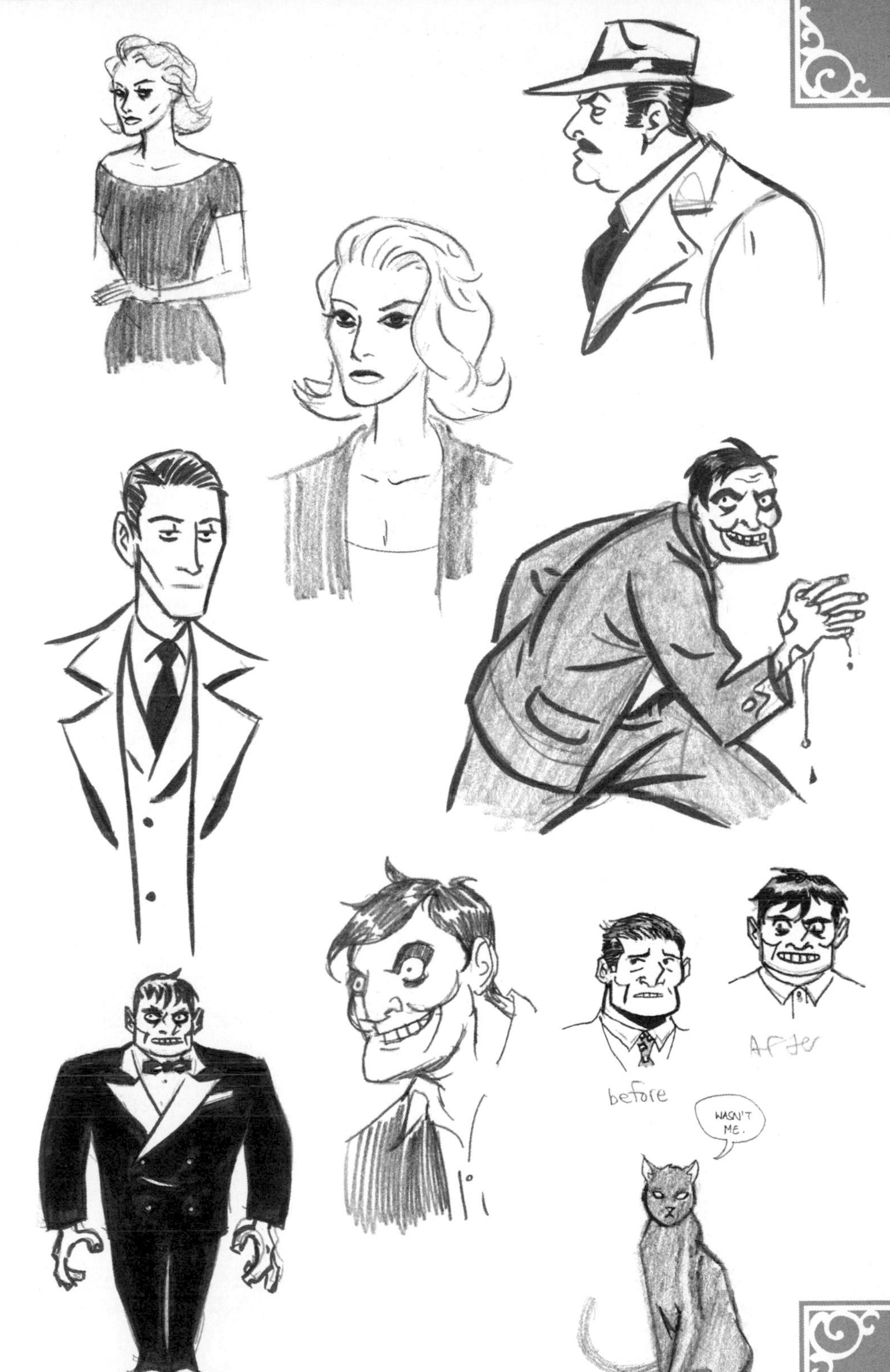
before
After
WASN'T ME.

More Books from

Jamie S. Rich

Jamie S. Rich
& Joëlle Jones
12 Reasons Why I Love Her

12 REASONS WHY I LOVE HER
Jamie S. Rich & Joëlle Jones
152 Pages • Softcover
Black & White Interiors
ISBN 978-1-932664-51-5

MICHAEL ALLRED'S
iT giRL!
& THE ATOMICS
ROUND 1
"DARK STREETS, SNAP CITY"
RICH
NORTON
PASSALAQUA
CLUGSTON FLORES
CRANK!

IT GIRL & THE ATOMICS, VOL. 1
Jamie S. Rich, Mike Norton, & Chynna Clugston Flores
168 Pages • Softcover
Full Color Interiors
ISBN 978-1-607067-25-5

A BOY
& A GIRL

A BOY AND A GIRL
Jamie S. Rich & Natalie Nourigat
176 Pages • Softcover
Two Color Interiors
ISBN 978-1-62010-089-9

YOU HAVE KILLED ME
by
JAMIE S. RICH
&
JOËLLE JONES

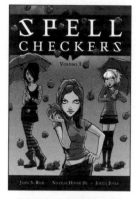

YOU HAVE KILLED ME
Jamie S. Rich & Joëlle Jones
192 Pages • Hardcover
Black & White Interiors
ISBN 978-1-932664-88-1

MICHAEL ALLRED'S
iT giRL!
& THE ATOMICS
"THE WORLD IS FLAT"
RICH
NORTON
NOURIGAT
CLUGSTON FLORES
PASSALAQUA
CRANK!

IT GIRL & THE ATOMICS, VOL. 2
Jamie S. Rich, Mike Norton, Natalie Nourigat, & Chynna Clugston Flores
168 Pages • Softcover
Full Color Interiors
ISBN 978-1-607067-91-7

SPELL CHECKERS
VOLUME 1

SPELL CHECKERS, VOL. 1
Jamie S. Rich, Joëlle Jones, & Nicolas Hitori De
152 Pages • Softcover
Black & White Interiors
ISBN 978-1-934964-32-3

For more information on these and other fine Oni Press comic books and graphic novels, visit www.onipress.com.

To find a comic specialty store in your area, call 1-888-COMICBOOK or visit www.comicshops.us.

More Books from

Oni Press

CAPOTE
IN KANSAS
ANDE PARKS CHRIS SAMNEE

CAPOTE IN KANSAS
Ande Parks & Chris Samnee
160 Pages • Hardcover
Black & White Interiors
ISBN 978-1-934964-87-3

PAST LIES
CHRISTINA WEIR / NUNZIO DEFILIPPIS / CHRISTOPHER MITTEN

PAST LIES: AN AMY DEVLIN MYSTERY, VOL. 1
Christina Weir, Nunzio Defilippis, & Christoper Mitten
176 Pages • Hardcover
Black & White Interiors
ISBN 978-1-934964-39-2

ANTONY JOHNSTON
THE
COLDEST
CITY
ILLUSTRATED BY
SAM HART

THE COLDEST CITY
Antony Johnston & Sam Hart
176 Pages • Hardcover
Black & White Interiors
ISBN 978-1-934964-53-8

"STUMPTOWN IS, FOR MY MONEY, THE PERFECT RUCKA BOOK."
STUMPTOWN
GREG RUCKA • MATTHEW SOUTHWORTH

STUMPTOWN, VOL. 1
Greg Rucka & Matthew Southworth
160 Pages • Hardcover
Full Color Interiors
ISBN 978-1-934964-37-8

UNION
STATION
ANDE PARKS
EDUARDO BARRETO

UNION STATION
Ande Parks & Eduardo Barreto
176 Pages • Hardcover
Black & White Interiors
ISBN 978-1-934964-27-9

PETROGRAD
PHILIP GELATT • TYLER CROOK

PETROGRAD
Philip Gelatt & Tyler Crook
264 Pages • Hardcover
Two Color Interiors
ISBN 978-1-934964-44-6

ONI PRESS
REVOLUTIONIZE COMICS
www.onipress.com

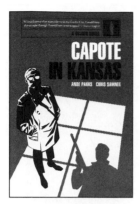

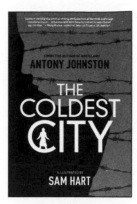

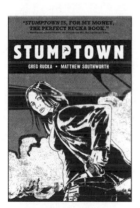

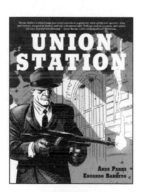

Jamie S. Rich is an author whose venues include Oni Press, Image Comics, DVDTalk.com, and various dive bars around Portland, OR. He is best known for his collaborations with artist Joëlle Jones on the graphic novels *12 Reasons Why I Love Her* and *You Have Killed Me*. He published his first prose novel, *Cut My Hair*, in 2000, and his first superhero comic book, *It Girl and the Atomics*, in 2012. In between, he has worked on multiple projects in both mediums, including his most recent graphic novel, *A Boy and a Girl*, drawn by Natalie Nourigat, and *The Double Life of Miranda Turner* with George Kambadais. He currently reviews film for the *Oregonian*, hosts the online comics-related chat show *From the Gutters*, and blogs at confessions123.com.

Dan Christensen was born in California, grew up in Arizona, then moved to France. He attended art school in Angoulême, and has since written and drawn several graphic novels, including *Red Hands* and *Paranormal*. In addition to drawing comics, Dan works as a freelance translator for French comic book publishers Ankama, Dargaud and Futuropolis, and has illustrated books for role-playing game publisher Hero Games.

He currently lives and works on the west coast of France with his wife and two boys.